Financial Modelling

market editions

Mastering Financial Modelling

A practitioner's guide to applied corporate finance

ALASTAIR L. DAY

FINANCIAL TIMES
Prentice Hall

An imprint of Pearson Education

London · New York · San Francisco · Toronto · Sydney
Tokyo · Singapore · Hong Kong · Cape Town · Madrid
Paris · Milan · Munich · Amsterdam

PEARSON EDUCATION LIMITED

Head Office:
Edinburgh Gate
Harlow CM20 2JE
Tel: +44 (0)1279 623623
Fax: +44 (0)1279 431059

London Office:
128 Long Acre
London WC2E 9AN
Tel: +44 (0)20 7447 2000
Fax: +44 (0)20 7240 5771
Website: www.financialminds.com

First published in Great Britain in 2001

ISBN 0 273 64310 X

British Library Cataloguing in Publication Data
A CIP catalogue record for this book can be obtained from the British Library.

10 9 8 7 6 5

Typeset by Pantek Arts Ltd, Maidstone, Kent
Printed and bound in Great Britain by Bell & Bain Ltd, Glasgow

The Publishers' policy is to use paper manufactured from sustainable forests.

ABOUT THE AUTHOR

Alastair Day has worked in the finance industry for twenty years in treasury and marketing functions. He worked originally for the NFC, negotiating funding and administering leases, and switched to marketing finance upon the privatization of NFC in 1980. During the 1980s he was a director of a leasing company whose rapid growth was based on programmes in the IT, print and machine tool industries. The directors sold the company to a PLC at the end of the decade. In 1990 Alastair established Systematic Finance plc as a consultancy and financial lessor concentra-ting on the computer and communications industries.

Alastair has a degree in Economics and German from London University, an MBA from the Open University Business School, and is an associate lecturer in corporate finance with the OUBS. Other publications include books such as *The Finance Director's Guide to Purchasing Leasing* published by Financial Times Prentice Hall, and a range of software products. In addition, he develops and presents public and in-house courses on a range of topics including financial modelling, leasing, credit and cash flow analysis and other corporate finance topics.

CONTENTS

Introduction – who needs this book ? ix

Acknowledgements xi

Conventions xiii

Executive summary xv

Part A DEVELOPING FINANCIAL MODELS

1 Overview 3

2 Design introduction 9

3 Features and techniques 18

4 Sample model 58

5 Example model 78

Part B APPLICATIONS

6 Analysing performance 101

7 Cash flow 116

8 Forecasting models 122

9 Forecasting financials 131

10 Variance analysis 145

11 Breakeven analysis 153
12 Portfolio analysis 163
13 Cost of capital 172
14 Bonds 186
15 Investment analysis 199
16 Risk analysis 218
17 Depreciation 242
18 Leasing 255
19 Company valuation 279
20 Optimization 296
21 Decision trees 312
22 Risk management 323
23 Modelling checklist 351
Appendices 355

Bibliography 363
Index 365

INTRODUCTION – WHO NEEDS THIS BOOK?

I was introduced to Microsoft® Excel about 15 years ago when a client asked me to prepare a lease versus purchase analysis to prove that leasing was indeed more beneficial than purchasing. I spent much of the following weekend developing a Basic program to provide an after-tax net present value for both options. The client produced his own Lotus 1-2-3® model and while we both derived similar answers, the development time for the spreadsheet was only a couple of hours.

After this experience, I began to use Lotus 1-2-3 to review funding alternatives, lease pricing and portfolio cash flows. As spreadsheets have become more powerful, I have increased the scope of models and improved my own approach and design, which has had benefits in development time and accuracy. It is this personal approach which is outlined in this book and disk combination.

The success of spreadsheets, especially since the introduction of Office 95, means that most managers have Microsoft Excel as part of their desktop. Yet few receive specific training in modelling procedures just as few business schools teach Excel as a core part of their curriculum. Managers achieve a certain standard, but this means that many spreadsheet models are:

- incomprehensible except to the author;
- contain serious structural errors;
- not able to be audited without a great deal of effort;
- not maintainable or flexible enough to be developed further;
- failing in their key objectives.

The simplicity of Excel means that models can be written 'on the fly' with no thought to any of the above problems. Excel is a sophisticated tool and I would argue that it should be a core skill for managers to produce clear maintainable applications and be proficient in spreadsheet design. There is much management writing about 'empowering individuals' and providing them with 'decision tools' and Excel can assist in providing solutions.

This is what I call 'Applied Financial Excel', which brings together:

- financial skills;
- modelling;
- design methodology.

This book will provide managers with an approach not covered in corporate finance textbooks or Excel manuals. The objective here is to write a practical book to help users, rather than yet another book on financial mathematics or Excel functions. The first part of the book discusses a design methodology and features for improving model design. The second part of the book provides templates for solving particular corporate finance problems and includes briefly the underlying theory. As an added bonus, the book contains a CD containing all the software introduced in the book.

The book is aimed at groups with differing levels of responsibility:

- CFOs and finance directors
- financial controllers
- analysts
- accountants
- corporate finance personnel
- treasury managers
- risk managers
- middle office staff
- general managers
- personnel in banks, corporates and government who make complex decisions and who could benefit from a modelling approach
- academics, business and MBA students.

HOW TO USE THIS BOOK

- Install the Excel application templates using the simple SETUP command. The files are named by subject and referenced in each chapter.
- Work through each of the chapters and the examples.
- Use the book, spreadsheets and templates as a reference guide. There is a complete list of titles together with their relevant chapters in Appendix Three.
- Apply the design methodology to all your models and applications.
- Practise and improve your efficiency and competence with Excel.

Alastair L. Day
www.financial-models.com

ACKNOWLEDGEMENTS

I would like to thank my wife, Angela Miles, for her support and assistance in editing and proofreading the book. In addition, Laurie Donaldson and Richard Stagg of Financial Times Prentice Hall have provided valuable support and backing for this project.

CONVENTIONS

The main part of the text is set in Times Roman, whereas entries are set in Courier. For example:

Enter the Scenario Name as `Base Case`

Items on the menu bars also shown in Courier.

Select `Tools, Goalseek`

The names of functions are in capitals. This is the payment function, which requires inputs for the interest rate, number of periods, present value and future value:

`=PMT(INT,NPER,PV,FV,TYPE)`

Equations are formed with the equation editor and shown in normal notation. For example, net present value:

$$NPV = \frac{(CashFlow)^N}{(1 + r)^N}$$

Genders: the use of 'he' or 'him' refers to masculine or feminine and this is used for simplicity to avoid repetition.

EXECUTIVE SUMMARY

This is a summary of the book by chapter presented in a tabular form.

PART A – MODEL DESIGN

1. Overview	History of spreadsheets Power of spreadsheets Common faults Objectives of the book – good design method and templates for further use Example poor 'flat' spreadsheet
2. Design introduction	Follow design process and method for all models Set aims and objectives Examine user needs and required user interface Set out key variables and rules Break down the calculations into manageable groups Produce the individual modules Menu structure Management reports and summaries Development e.g. sensitivity Testing and auditing Protection as an application Documentation Ask for peer group comments
3. Features and techniques	Formats Number formats Lines and borders Colour and patterns Specific colour for inputs and results Data validation Controls – combo boxes and buttons

	Conditional formatting Use of functions and types of functions Add-ins for more functions Text and updated labels Record a version number, author etc. Use names to make formulas easier Paste a names table as part of documentation Comment cells Graphics Dynamic graphs to plot individual lines Data tables Scenarios Goalseek Solver Use of templates
4. Sample model planning	Objectives Set aims and objectives Examine user needs and required user interface Key variables and rules – Flowchart/ mind map/information flow Break down the calculations into manageable groups Setting up individual modules Menu structure Program sheets and macros User assistance Management reports and summaries Risk and multiple answers Testing and trouble shooting Protecting and securing Help and documentation Show to peers – take their advice Control loop – listen, learn and modify
5. Example model	Case design layout Calculation Formatting, functions, comments, validation and printing Menus, combo boxes, macros and buttons Scenarios, data tables and risk Documentation, testing and protecting User comment and areas for improvement

PART B – APPLICATIONS

6. Analysing performance	Profit and loss Balance sheet Key ratios – Du Pont ratios (core ratios) Profitability Operating efficiency Leverage, liquidity and capital structure Coverage on interest Trend analysis Sustainability
7. Cash flow	Deriving cash flow – NOCF, free cash flow Cover ratios Strained cash flow and over trading
8. Forecasting models	Linear regression Trend lines Trend lines for analysis Data smoothing Cyclicality and seasonality
9. Forecast financials	Key drivers Deriving financial statements Analysis
10. Variance analysis	Budget variances Cash flow budgets Monthly cash model Flash report and graphics
11. Break-even analysis	Break-even Operating and financial leverage
12. Portfolio analysis	Determining risk and return Expected portfolio return
13. Cost of capital	Cost of Capital – CAPM, Growth model, WACC WACC step cost of capital model
14. Bonds	Pricing Yield measures Duration and modified duration

	Convexity and sensitivity Portfolio duration
15. Investment analysis	Investment model revisited Payback and discounted payback Net present value Management tests – cash flow etc. Sensitivity analysis and graphs Capital rationing
16. Risk	Risk assessment process and analysis Risk adjusted rate Variation Standard deviation Coefficient of variation Real options Simulation
17. Depreciation	Straight-line Sum of digits Declining balance US MACRS
18. Leasing	Rental calculations Lease versus purchase Classification Accounting Settlements
19. Company valuation	Assets Adjusted assets Gordon's growth model Market-based Simple free cash Methodology – leveraging betas etc.
20. Optimisation	Linear programming Profit maximisation Pensions
21. Decision trees	Probability concepts Decision tree model

22.	Risk management	Forward rate agreements SWAPS Foreign exchange forwards Futures Options Black–Scholes options pricing
23.	Modelling checklist	Summary of design features Pointers for the future
24.	Bibliography	

Part

A

Developing Financial Models

Part A concentrates on model design and practice and outlines a methodology for planning, designing and developing financial models. The emphasis is on simplicity, modularity and ease of use, while making use of Excel features to speed up development and reduce errors.

The chapters in Part A are:

1 Overview

2 Design introduction

3 Features and techniques

4 Sample model

5 Example model

1

Overview

This book seeks to provide you with tools to help you develop, write and maintain Excel models. Modelling is often seen as an add-on or a method of adding accounting numbers. However, this book seeks to show good practice and provide tips with examples of different techniques and a selection of model templates. It is not an Excel manual since there are already many comprehensive handbooks, but rather a compendium of techniques to save you time and help you to become more productive.

1. WHAT IS FINANCIAL MODELLING?

Financial modelling covers a wide area from simple sheets to add up expenses to sophisticated risk modelling for projects. While there are aspects of design to be considered, the financial aspects could cover:

- developing specialist programs which answer specific business problems, e.g. cash flow cover and variability;
- analysing and processing data;
- modelling the future or a considered view of the future;
- processing data quickly and accurately into management information;
- testing assumptions in a 'safe' environment, e.g. project scenarios;
- supporting management decision making through a structured approach;
- understanding more precisely the variables or rules in a problem;
- learning more about processes and behaviour of variables;
- discovering the key variables and their sensitivity.

2. HISTORY OF SPREADSHEETS

Spreadsheets have been available for personal computers since VisiCalc® for Apple machines in the late 1970s was launched. The rise of Lotus 1-2-3® parallels the rise of the IBM PC since the spreadsheet represented vast increases in productivity and accuracy over earlier methods (such as comptometers). In addition, finance managers could analyse for the first time their own data without recourse to a data or systems manager. Accounting models such as budgets and cash flows could be produced at the user level leading to:

- more detailed information for decision making;
- potential for decision making at a lower level;
- flexibility for examining scenarios and alternatives.

Microsoft introduced Excel® for the Apple Macintosh in 1985 and extended it to the PC in the late 1980s. With the introduction of Windows 3.0 sales increased rapidly and on Excel's inclusion in Office 95, Excel became the leading spreadsheet package and available to the majority of PC users. Microsoft's domination of this market has increased with the introduction of Office 97 and Office 2000.

3. POWER OF SPREADSHEETS

The inclusion of Excel in the Microsoft packages means that it is now the *de facto* standard in the same way as Word is for text processing. The power of spreadsheets has progressively increased with the inclusion of:

- specialist functions;
- macros for automating spreadsheets or producing functions in code;
- workbook technology to save linking individual spreadsheets;
- Visual Basic to provide a common language with other Microsoft applications;
- data exchange with other applications;
- add-ins such as Solver for targeting and optimization;
- third-party analysis packages such as FinancialCAD, @RISK or Crystal Ball.

The result is today's sophisticated analysis package, which allows non-programmers to design and develop specialist applications for solving business problems.

Excel is also a simple package to use and most people are introduced to it when they need to solve a business problem. The author once needed to analyse lease profitability and wrote a model to review different portfolio funding strategies. After great time and effort, the model worked and provided an answer, but was unclear and difficult for others to understand. There was no design methodology and indeed the model 'just happened'.

This is common for most managers, where many companies or academic institutions provide little guidance in applying Excel to finance problems. The result is that many produce models with little or no regard to design and future maintenance.

Furthermore, it has been estimated that many commercial models contain serious errors. Visual Basic or C++ applications are written to design standards within IT departments. However, Excel is usually not subject to the same constraints. This may not always be a problem; however, a budget model may be the 'pet project' of the finance manager, who either leaves the company or is promoted to Singapore. There are of course no notes in the file and nobody knows how the model works. It is often said that information constitutes power and therefore managers often fail to document their work sufficiently. The net result is that organizations spend large amounts of money in auditing models or tracing errors.

Thus, the simplicity and power of Excel may also constitute a weakness. The author argues that Excel users should follow simple design strategies and should be aware of the need to provide background information on applications. Following a specific methodology and spending time on planning applications should pay dividends in the long term:

- usability and ease of use;
- maintainability;
- confidence in the answers or outcomes.

The following chapters outline features that you can incorporate in Excel models to make more powerful and robust spreadsheets.

4. OBJECTIVES FOR THE BOOK

The objective is to demonstrate applied financial Excel by a non-programmer who has worked for ten years in applying corporate finance theory to spreadsheets. Modelling requires an understanding of modelling, finance and design together with Excel, and in particular:

- design methodology and process;
- how to develop ideas into application;

- useful techniques for improving existing models;
- making simple models more useful and reliable;
- adding risk techniques;
- using optimization and targeting;
- putting all the techniques together as integrated standards and templates.

Managers need to understand spreadsheet techniques as a core skill. Organizations now hold more and more data and need simple analysis tools at lower levels. By constructing models, managers should understand better:

- how individual variables 'flex';
- how to discover new variables which should be included in the calculations;
- how to isolate key variables for further testing;
- how to avoid costly mistakes by testing scenarios and potential cases.

For example, a simple outsourcing model could show a positive net present value by producing a spreadsheet in the place of some accounting model. A correctly produced application would not only find the answer but also:

- outline all the rules and inputs;
- provide a series of answers based on different parameters;
- provide graphs of key variables demonstrating how they flex with changes;
- demonstrate levels of risk and uncertainty;
- show how likely you are to be close to the forecasted answer.

Thus, the objective of this book is to apply Excel and finance combined and to assist you in building more powerful and robust spreadsheet applications.

5. EXAMPLE SPREADSHEET

Figure 1.1 is an example of a poorly designed spreadsheet which you could produce to show the net present value of a project. It is typical of many of the spreadsheets used in organizations and exhibits a number of problems which are listed below. This model is on the disk as Simple_Model.xls.

Fig 1.1

	A	B	C	D	E	F	G	H	I
1		**Project Appraisal Model**							
2									
3					Year 0	Year 1	Year 2	Year 3	Year 4
4									
5		Cost of equipment			-750,000				
6		Maintenance			0	-10,000	-10,000	-10,000	-10,000
7		Installation			-50,000				
8		Reduction in overheads			75,000	125,000	0	0	0
9		Saving in production time			0	130,000	130,000	125,000	125,000
10		Tax @ 30%			0	82500	-6000	14600	3468.75
11		Net cash flows			-725,000	327,500	114,000	129,600	118,469
12									
13		Factor			1.0000	0.9434	0.8900	0.8396	0.7921
14									
15		Cash Flow			-725,000	308,962	101,460	108,815	93,838
16									
17		NPV @ 6%			5,411.99				
18									
19									
20				WDV		Cashflow	Year		
21				1,200,000					
22		CA	0	-300000		90000	1		
23				900,000					
24		CA	1	-225000		67500	2		
25				675,000					
26		CA	2	-168750		50625	3		
27				506,250					
28		CA	3	-126563		37968.75	4		
29				379,688					
30		CA	4	-94922		28476.56	5		
31				284,766					
32		BA	5	-284,766		85429.8	6		
33		Sales proceeds		0					
34						360000			
35									

The main problems can be summarized as:

- No form of layout with inputs, calculations and outputs clearly marked.
- No inputs section – indeed what are the individual variables in this model?
- No specific colour for inputs.
- No borders or shading to improve appearance of report.
- No data validation of inputs, e.g. to ensure that the inputs contain the correct type or length of data.
- Mixture of number formats with differing numbers of decimal places. Use of brackets and the colour red can improve the model since brackets are easier to read on a printed report and red is a usual colour for negative numbers.
- Mixture of numbers and formulas. Line 10 contains tax calculations and the tax rate is 'hard-coded' into every cell. What happens if the tax rate changes?

- G10 contains an arithmetic error where the cell formula has been overwritten with a number.
- The test labels in B10 and B17 have been typed in and they will not change if the discount or tax rate changes.
- No management reporting on the answer. Is 5,411 enough and above a management threshold?
- Conditional formatting would help to highlight the answer. For example, the cell could be colour-coded according to the answer.
- No use of functions since the net present value is built up using a factor for each period. Use of the function NPV would help to reduce the number of possible errors by reducing the individual cell codes.
- No sensitivity analysis. What happens if you change the discount rate or fail to generate the benefits on schedule?
- Graphics normally help to show to management cash flows or the sensitivity analysis. For example, a graph of the cumulative cash flow to demonstrate the payback would assist.
- No use of names for key variables.
- Workings are not shown separately. The table at the bottom calculates the tax depreciation on the equipment, but it is not clear if this is part of the cash flow.
- No commenting of individual cells and overall no documentation on how the model works.
- There is no information on the version number or the author.
- The model is not set up for printing. There is no header or footer to denote, for example, the file name and date. Printing will output everything including the tax workings.

The list above demonstrates the weakness in this model, in terms of structure, design and method. If management were taking key decisions based on these workings, then there is a good chance that a wrong decision could be made. Even as quick workings, this sheet fails due to the arithmetic errors. If provided to management then there are serious failings, which could be rectified through a complete redesign of the model. Setting up the model correctly would eradicate many of the issues above.

6. SUMMARY

The use of Excel is a core skill for managers. Excel is a powerful tool, however, few users receive formal training in modelling techniques. This chapter has demonstrated a simple spreadsheet and the inherent errors in design and construction. The next chapters outline methods for you to apply to models and develop robust and maintainable applications.

2

Design introduction

The last chapter exposed weaknesses in traditional layouts, which essentially use Excel as a large piece of automated accounting paper. To base decisions on Excel or to have confidence in the answers, a different approach is required. This requires a more disciplined approach, which centres much more on the objectives, user reports and the process of producing an answer. Figure 2.1 outlines some of the stages in design.

Fig 2.1

Model Design

1. Follow design process and method for all models
2. Set aims and objectives
3. Examine user needs and required user interface
4. Set out key variables and rules
5. Break down the calculations into manageable groups
6. Produce the individual modules
7. Menu structure
8. Management reports and summaries
9. Development e.g. sensitivity
10. Testing and auditing
11. Protection as an application
12. Documentation
13. Ask for peer group comments

1. BASICS OF DESIGN

Design is personal and you develop a style that you approve of, like and can repeat easily. This may sound simplistic, but a sound methodology cuts development time and error correction. While there are degrees of planning needed depending on the complexity of the application, you have to have a plan and a method for different sorts of spreadsheets. How many times do you insert and delete columns or rows or at a later stage wonder how a particular cell formula works? It is easy to start keying formulas without thinking too carefully. The objective is to set out a tick list of considerations for superior design.

Follow a design process and method on all models and make the sheets follow a pattern. The examples with this book unashamedly follow exactly the same layout and design. While simple spreadsheets may be sufficient for one person, models should conform to simple rules, especially when used by others or are incorporated into decision making. In its basic form, this means splitting the functions in the model between inputs, calculations and outputs.

2. OBJECTIVES

Many people do not think through the aims and objectives. Although it sounds simplistic, it is a good idea to write them down somewhere in the documentation and refer to them during development to make sure that you do not deviate from the original aims.

In many examples, it is difficult to work out where the answer is as it is hidden in the calculations. Models are often capable of providing more information. For example, a simple cash flow budget could also use further sheets for recording the actual profit and loss and balance sheet. With both budget and actual figures, variance reports based on absolute and percentage differences are possible together with management reports and graphs for divisional reporting.

3. USER INTERFACE

This needs to be reviewed critically since this is what you and your users will work with. There may be a number of different audiences for the same model with different requirements for inputs, detail and information. Older models sometimes put the variables on the left between the label and the figures, for example the tax rate could be placed here. However, users may like to see all the inputs in one place and be directed as to what and where to input data. It is very frustrating for somebody who has received a copy of a new application to have to spend time understanding how it works and where to enter data. Visual Basic programming works by designing the interface of forms first and then attaching code to buttons and controls to make it work. This is not a bad analogy for Excel, since many authors have not placed themselves in the user's shoes and critically examined the user's perceptions.

The interface should be:

- intuitive
- clear
- guide the user through a logical flow of information.

The use of borders, colours and formats assists this process as in the calculator shown in Figure 2.2 (Calculator.xls). The user is directed to enter variables and press buttons to calculate an answer as with a hand-held financial calculator such as an HP17BII. The answer is updated at the bottom based on the button the user pushes so that the flow of information is from top to bottom.

Fig 2.2

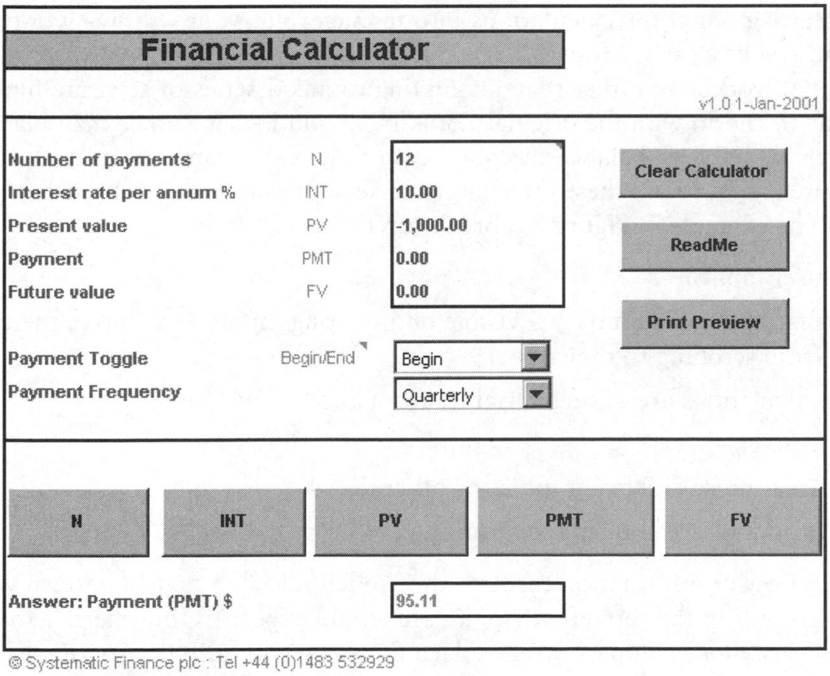

4. KEY VARIABLES AND RULES

Variables and rules should be broken down and variables must be placed together as in the calculator above. It is essential that variables are not hard coded. For example, the frequency must be a user input. Otherwise what would the user change if the payments were monthly as opposed to quarterly? Distilling out the rules means that the author becomes better organized and may understand the process of solving the business problem more succinctly. The process may also uncover new variables which need to be modelled.

Rules are also important: corporate taxes are complex in most jurisdictions and models need to reflect exactly tax shields and tax settlement dates. The corporate tax payment method is changing in the UK to a four-quarter payment system from once a year and this presents the modeller with a fresh set of challenges to understand both the transitional and final arrangements. Using names for the main variables and a modular approach assists with simplifying the maintenance of existing models.

5. LAYOUT

Breaking down the calculations into manageable groups shows workings and results clearly. Modern Excel allows separate sheets in one two-dimensional workbook rather than attempting to link a series of separate files as was the norm with the original Lotus 1-2-3 and Excel. Rather than placing a profit and loss, balance sheet and cash flow on the same sheet, it is surely more logical to put these three facets on separate sheets in a single file.

The example in Figure 2.3 breaks up the layout into:

- user inputs;
- management summary – visible on updating inputs. This saves the user from scrolling to the answer;
- calculations area using variables from above inputs area;
- answer;
- area for sensitivity, graphics or other detail;
- workings area outside the printing area.

The flow of information through the model follows a logical pattern with the inputs in the top left where a user would expect to find them. Models that are more complex would place these areas on different worksheets, but again inputs and calculations should not be mixed and development should be split into logical sections.

As in Figure 2.3, the use of colours, typefaces, patterns and borders for different data and information in a consistent manner can assist to show the logical framework. The models in this book follow this format.

Fig 2.3

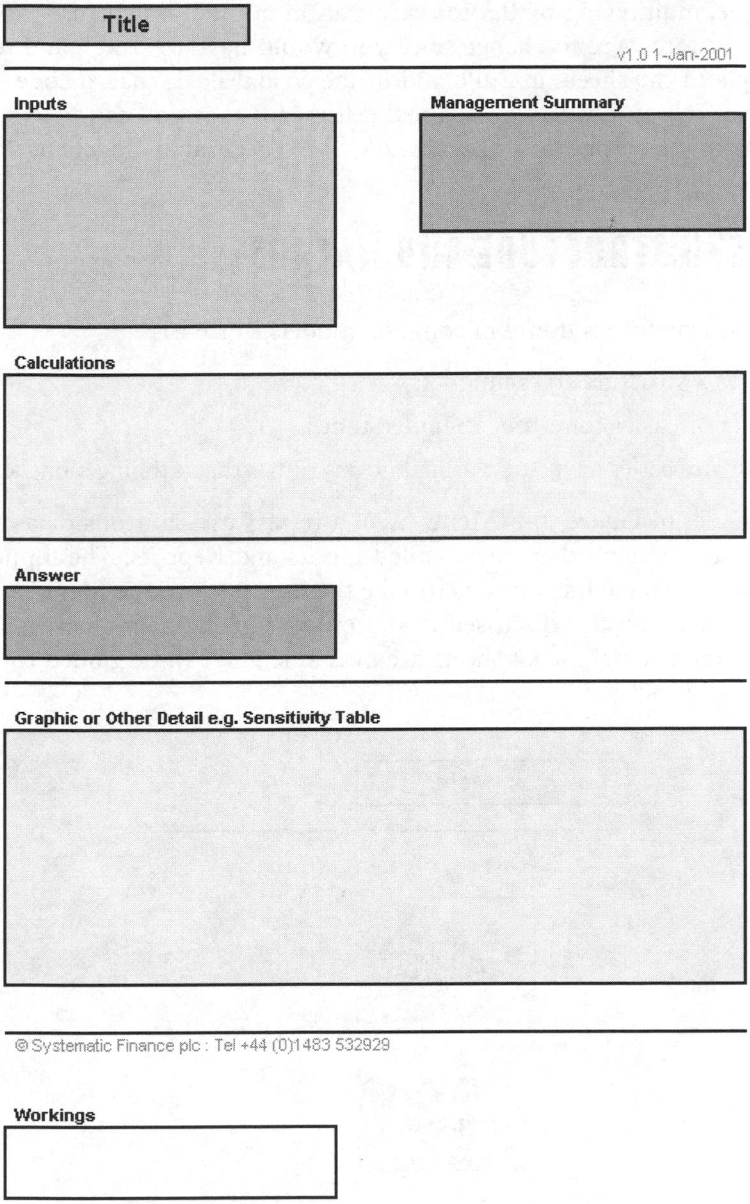

6. INDIVIDUAL MODULES

Individual modules can then be produced within a planned framework and calculations broken up into separate areas or sheets. The layout is important for user and author understanding and it is critical for ease of further development.

Calculation areas must contain only formulas and they must not be mixed with numbers. This is to ensure the integrity of the calculations. For example, multiplying by 0.3 for corporation tax will only cause problems if the tax rate were to change since you would have to search and replace through all the sheets in a file and in the Visual Basic macro code. Using an input cell as a range or a named cell means that you can be confident of only changing one cell for the whole file to accurately update itself.

7. MENU STRUCTURE AND MACROS

A menu structure is useful in complex models, since it:

- forces a structure to the model;
- makes it easier for a user to understand;
- facilitates easier navigation using buttons rather than tabbing along sheets.

The model in Figure 2.4 (Menu_Structure.xls) uses buttons or a combo box to access two other sheets called Inputs and Reports. The Inputs and Reports sheets include buttons to take the user back to the Menu.

These features are discussed in more detail in the next chapter. A user can see immediately what sheets are available and can be guided to where data is required.

Fig 2.4

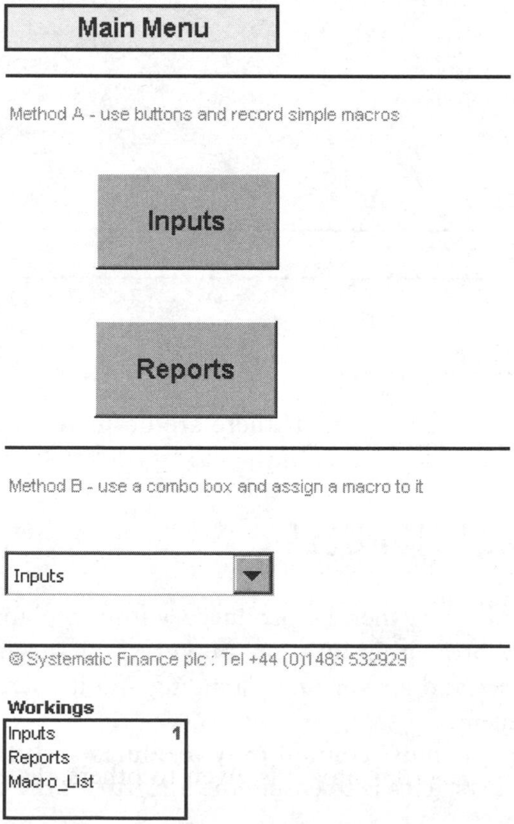

8. MANAGEMENT REPORTING

Management reports and summaries are normally required for larger models as they would be in a full management report. Not everybody needs all the detail and calculations, and summaries assist the user in understanding the results and the important outcomes. For example, a project management application could demonstrate the coverage ratios and the degree of security in the model.

9. FUTURE DEVELOPMENT

Development within a model is important: a budget model may need further variables in the next year and a structured model aids future development. The test is: see how new variables could be added and check the disruption in the design.

Alternatively sensitivity tables and scenarios allow a user to produce multiple answers within the same model and test the variance based on changing inputs. A single net present value is not enough for informed decision making and development should include some further testing of how variables 'flex' the eventual results.

Risk may also be a decisive factor and therefore the design of a model may need to allow for risk or simulation techniques. Simulation involves developing models to allow for a range of inputs rather than single point figures, which produce a range of outputs.

Similarly, graphs can be useful in demonstrating the answer to management or other audiences. People often grasp complex ideas more easily through pictures. For example, a cash flow model could include a coverage graph of the cash coverage above a minimum limit.

10. TESTING

Testing is required to ensure that there are no mathematical errors and that the information flow through the model is correct. The calculator in Figure 2.2 can be tested against discount rate tables or the output from another financial calculator. Test data is required, which makes uses of all the buttons, inputs, frequencies and payment types. A later chapter outlines a number of techniques for reviewing the accuracy of model output.

11. PROTECTION

Protection is beneficial if a model is given to others. This is simple if the author clusters all the inputs together and colour codes them. Entire sheets can be protected and then the input cells can be unprotected in blocks. Protecting sheets and workbooks preserves the author's work and ensures that the application is used as intended. For example, if a budget model were given out to a user who then overwrote cell formulas with numbers, then the integrity of the model is threatened and one would have to begin by checking every cell for possible changes.

12. DOCUMENTATION

Many authors do not bother to write notes about a spreadsheet and its construction. This is risky since either they or their colleagues may have difficulty at some point in the future in maintaining the code. Many models may start as 'pet projects' and, as with any other computer program need background information. Ideally, notes should be in the model rather than on scraps of paper in a file and show:

- reasons for adopting a particular design or template;
- outline key formulas and calculations;
- rules and methodology.

13. PEER GROUP COMMENTS

Users or colleagues can often make constructive suggestions and although this process is often painful after you have spent time on producing a masterpiece, potential users need to attempt to enter data and be comfortable with how a model operates. Users involved in the design process and asked for their opinions may be more enthusiastic users. The main factors are:

- ease of use with a clear interface;
- user guidance from inputs through calculation to answers and reports;
- complexity reduced to a minimum for audit and checking purposes;
- answers shown clearly.

The above 13 points will help you produce more organized work. Review some of your own models and see how many of these points you include regularly in your applications. Obviously, the degree of complexity affects how much you need to do. However, this represents good practice which the author has developed over a number of years.

The next chapter discusses a number of features to make your models more powerful and the following chapter applies the design methodology to the original example in Chapter 1. The objective is to show how applied Excel leads to more powerful and error-free models.

14. SUMMARY

Design is personal and you develop a style over time. It is important to be consistent and follow a clear methodology. The stages discussed in this chapter are not exhaustive and include the following:

- Follow the design process and method for all models.
- Set aims and objectives.
- Examine user needs and required user interface.
- Set out key variables and rules.
- Break down the calculations into manageable groups.
- Produce the individual modules.
- Menu structure.
- Management reports and summaries.
- Development, e.g. sensitivity.
- Testing and auditing.
- Protection as an application.
- Documentation.
- Ask for peer group comments.

3

Features and techniques

The basics of design revolve around planning and logic whereas this chapter concentrates on a list of features that can be included to make models more user-friendly. This is not an exhaustive list, but aims to show the difference between the original and the finished model. The features in this chapter are:

- formats;
- number formats;
- lines and borders;
- colour and patterns;
- specific colour for inputs and results;
- data validation to control inputs;
- controls – combo boxes and buttons;
- conditional formatting to illustrate changes in data;
- use of functions and types of function;
- add-ins for more financial functions;
- text and updated labels;
- recording a version number, author, development date and other information;
- using names to make formulas easier to understand;
- pasting a names table as part of documentation;
- comment cells;
- graphics and charts;
- dynamic graphs to plot individual lines;
- data tables for sensitivity;
- scenarios for 'what-if' analysis;
- goalseek for simple targeting;

- solver for optimization and targeting;
- use of templates to speed up development.

The model is Features.xls as shown in Figure 3.1. Each of the sections in this chapter is covered by a sheet in the model. Open the file and click along the bottom to see the progression of sheets.

Fig 3.1

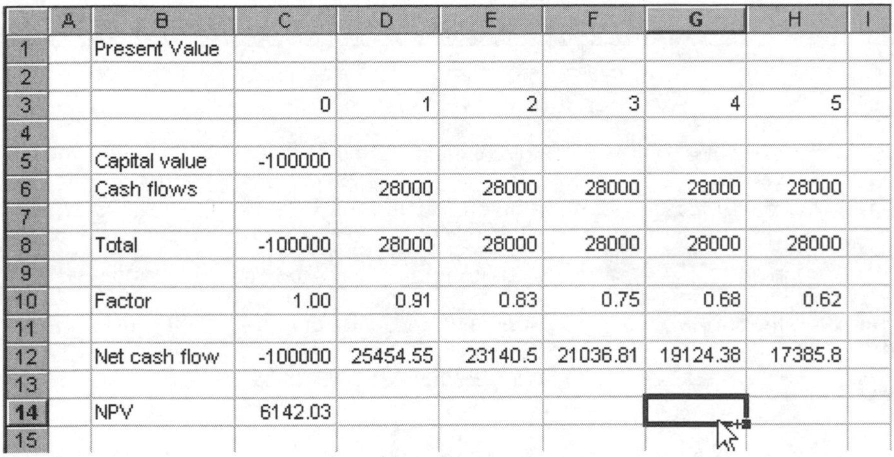

	A	B	C	D	E	F	G	H	I
1		Present Value							
2									
3			0	1	2	3	4	5	
4									
5		Capital value	-100000						
6		Cash flows		28000	28000	28000	28000	28000	
7									
8		Total	-100000	28000	28000	28000	28000	28000	
9									
10		Factor	1.00	0.91	0.83	0.75	0.68	0.62	
11									
12		Net cash flow	-100000	25454.55	23140.5	21036.81	19124.38	17385.8	
13									
14		NPV	6142.03						
15									

Figure 3.1 is a simple net present value model which adds up the cash flows for a period and multiples them by a 10% discount factor. The net present value in cell C14 is gained by adding up the discounted cash flows.

If you go to `Tools Options View`, you can select `View Formulas`, which allows you to see the formulas (see Figure 3.2). Alternatively you can press `Ctrl + `` together and this toggles between formulas and

Fig 3.2

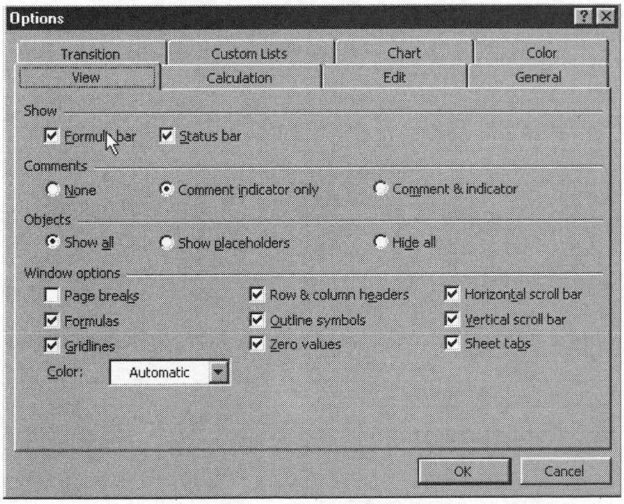

normal view. As you can see this is only producing a net present value based on the cash flows using the formula:

$$Period\_Factor = \frac{(1)}{(1 + 10\%)^{\ Period\_Number}}$$

Figure 3.3 is the formulas view showing all the cell references.

Fig 3.3

	A	B	C	D	E
1		Present Value			
2					
3			0	1	2
4					
5		Capital value	-100000		
6		Cash flows		28000	28000
7					
8		Total	=SUM(C5:C7)	=SUM(D5:D7)	=SUM(E5:E7)
9					
10		Factor	=1/(1+10%)^(C3)	=1/(1+10%)^(D3)	=1/(1+10%)^(E3)
11					
12		Net cash flow	=C8*C10	=D8*D10	=E8*E10
13					
14		NPV	=SUM(C12:H12)		
15					

1. FORMATS

The model shown in Figure 3.4 is presently mixed up with inputs and calculations together and the first job is to organize the layout. This involves:

Fig 3.4

	A	B	C	D	E	F	G	H	I
1		**Present Value**							
2									
3		**Capital value**	**100000**		**Management Summary**				
4		**Periodic cash flow**	**28000**		**NPV**	**6142.03**			
5		**Discount rate**	**10%**						
6									
7			**0**	**1**	**2**	**3**	**4**	**5**	
8									
9		Capital value	-100000						
10		Periodic cash flow		28000	28000	28000	28000	28000	
11									
12		Total	-100000	28000	28000	28000	28000	28000	
13									
14		Factor	1.00	0.91	0.83	0.75	0.68	0.62	
15									
16		Net cash flow	-100000	25454.55	23140.5	21036.81	19124.38	17385.8	
17									
18		**NPV**	**6142.03**						
19									

- inserting lines and moving the inputs;
- referring to the inputs in the cash flows and calculations;
- labels where possible lookup the values in inputs. For example B9 is now =C3;
- correcting the factors with an input;
- using different fonts and typefaces to break up the monotony.

The title, inputs, summary and answer are now clear in a bold typeface and the model follows a defined layout as shown in Figure 3.5.

Fig 3.5

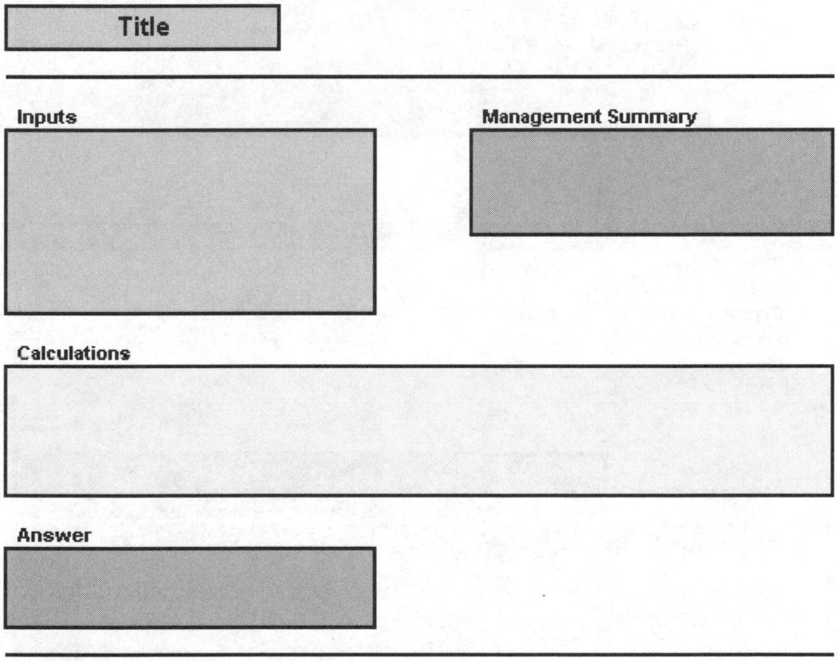

2. NUMBER FORMATS

The number formats are inconsistent with no separators and two different sets of decimal places. Go to `Format`, `Format Cells`, `Number` to change the default settings (see Figure 3.6).

You can experiment with different custom formats where positive, negative and zero are separated by semi-colons. Colours are in square brackets. Text is enclosed in inverted commas, e.g. Format so that 'years' is added to the number: `0 "years"`. You insert your custom format in the Type box or amend an existing format (see Figure 3.7).

Fig 3.6

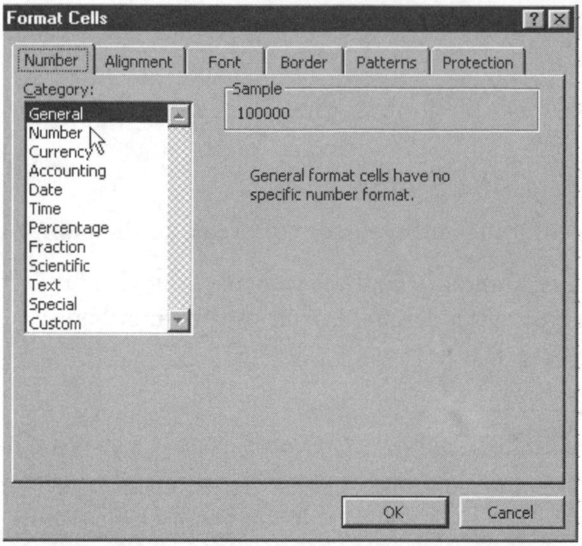
Format Cells
Number
Alignment
Font
Border
Patterns
Protection
Category:
General
Number
Currency
Accounting
Date
Time
Percentage
Fraction
Scientific
Text
Special
Custom
Sample
100000
General format cells have no specific number format.
OK
Cancel

Fig 3.7

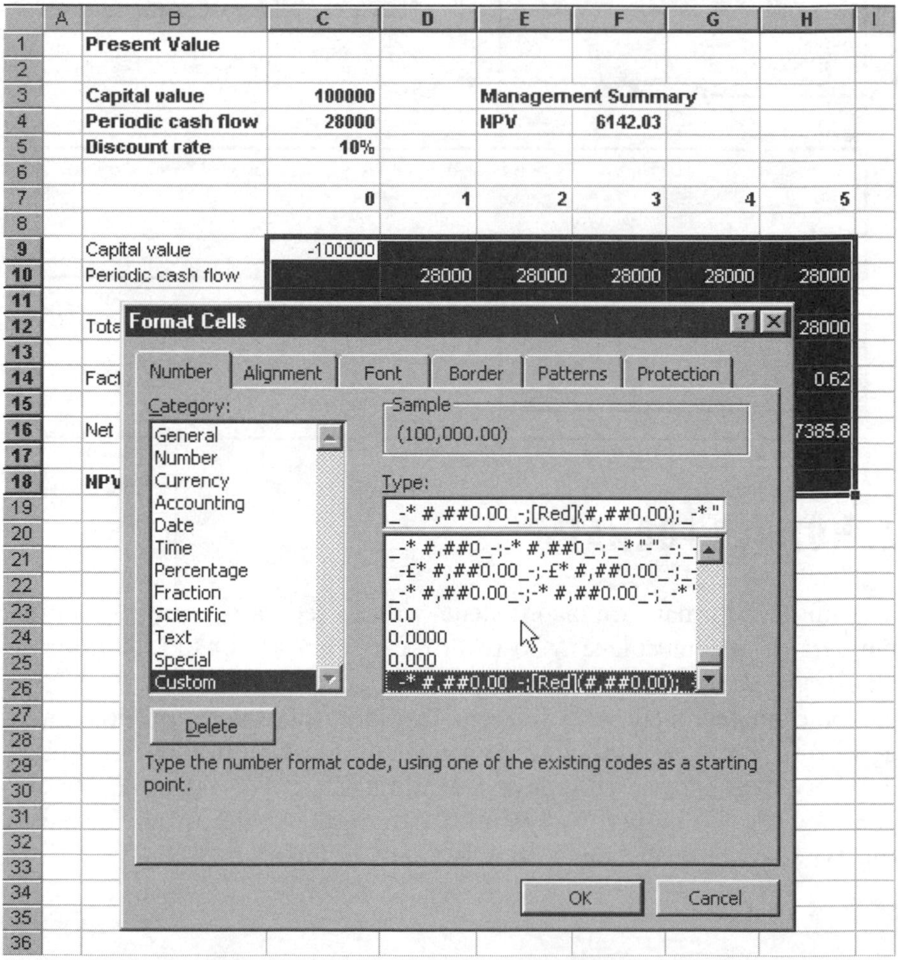
Present Value
Capital value
100000
Periodic cash flow
28000
Discount rate
10%
Management Summary
NPV
6142.03
0
1
2
3
4
5
Capital value
-100000
Periodic cash flow
28000
28000
28000
28000
28000
Format Cells
Number
Alignment
Font
Border
Patterns
Protection
Category:
General
Number
Currency
Accounting
Date
Time
Percentage
Fraction
Scientific
Text
Special
Custom
Sample
(100,000.00)
Type:
_-* #,##0.00_-;[Red](#,##0.00);_-* "
0.0
0.0000
0.000
Delete
Type the number format code, using one of the existing codes as a starting point.
OK
Cancel

This extract shows the accounting format with positive numbers slightly set to the left and negative numbers in red with brackets around them. Zero is a dash. This type of format is easy to read on laser printers whereas a minus is often hard to read on negative numbers.

Accounting style format: `_-* #,##0.00_-;[Red](#,##0.00);_-* "-"_-`

The effect is to control the view of the numbers to a maximum of two decimal places.

3. LINES AND BORDERS

Lines and borders assist in breaking up the cell code and make the model look more interesting for the audience both on the screen and in printed output. It is best to keep the Formatting toolbar visible. Go to `View`, `Toolbars`, `Formatting` to show this toolbar (see Figure 3.8). This saves always going to `Format`, `Cells`, `Borders` etc. to add lines.

Fig 3.8

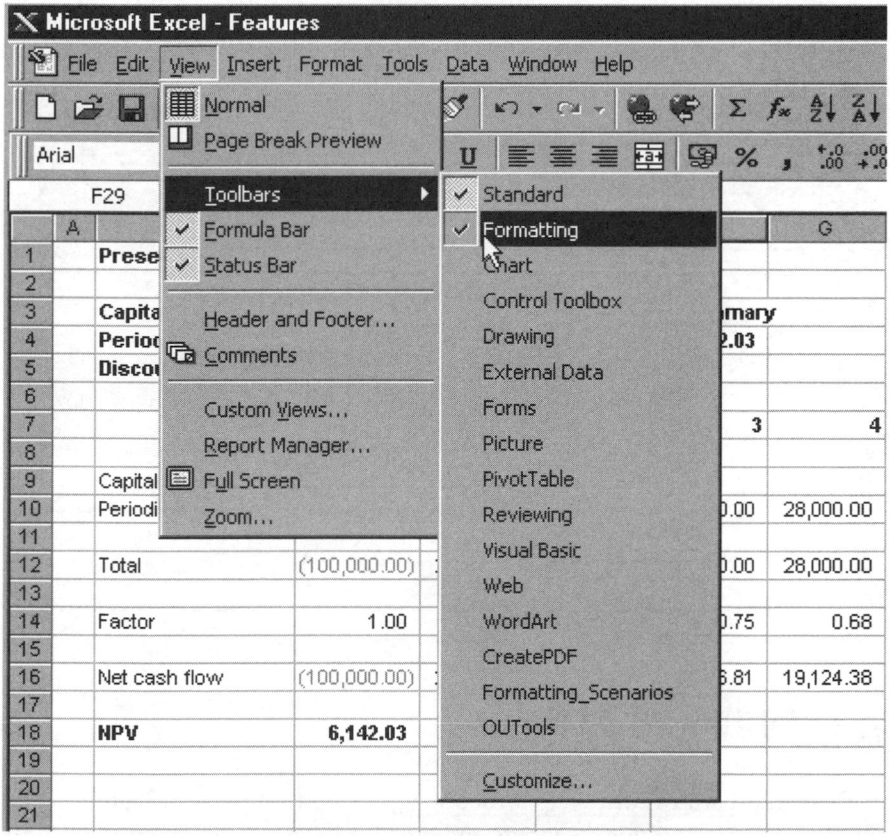

Figures 3.9 and 3.10 show highlighting cells and then applying a border from the toolbox. Thick lines are placed around the main sections and double lines to indicate a total.

Fig 3.9

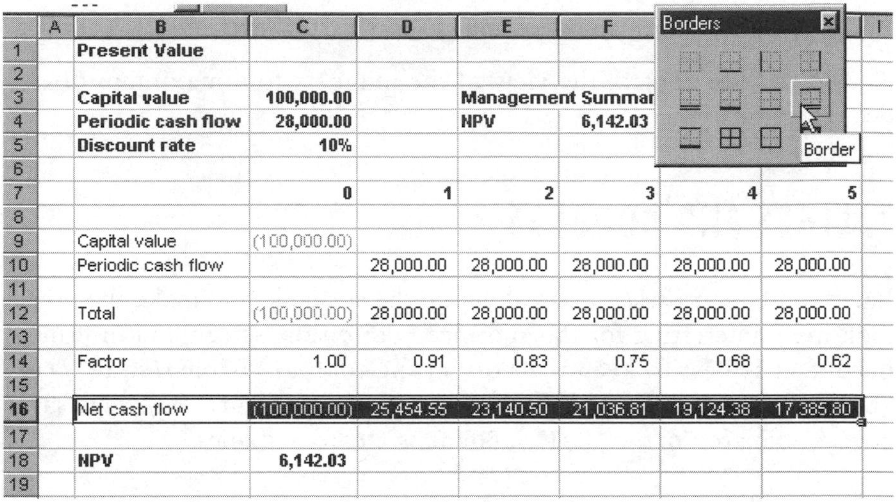

	A	B	C	D	E	F	G	H
1		Present Value						
3		Capital value	100,000.00		Management Summar			
4		Periodic cash flow	28,000.00		NPV	6,142.03		
5		Discount rate	10%					
7			0	1	2	3	4	5
9		Capital value	(100,000.00)					
10		Periodic cash flow		28,000.00	28,000.00	28,000.00	28,000.00	28,000.00
12		Total	(100,000.00)	28,000.00	28,000.00	28,000.00	28,000.00	28,000.00
14		Factor	1.00	0.91	0.83	0.75	0.68	0.62
16		Net cash flow	(100,000.00)	25,454.55	23,140.50	21,036.81	19,124.38	17,385.80
18		NPV	6,142.03					

Fig 3.10

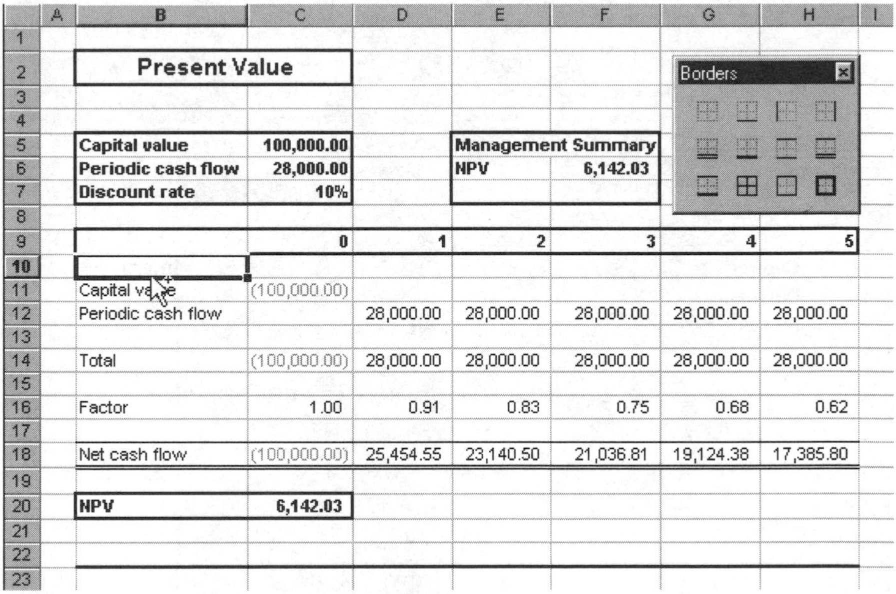

	A	B	C	D	E	F	G	H
2		Present Value						
5		Capital value	100,000.00		Management Summary			
6		Periodic cash flow	28,000.00		NPV	6,142.03		
7		Discount rate	10%					
9			0	1	2	3	4	5
11		Capital value	(100,000.00)					
12		Periodic cash flow		28,000.00	28,000.00	28,000.00	28,000.00	28,000.00
14		Total	(100,000.00)	28,000.00	28,000.00	28,000.00	28,000.00	28,000.00
16		Factor	1.00	0.91	0.83	0.75	0.68	0.62
18		Net cash flow	(100,000.00)	25,454.55	23,140.50	21,036.81	19,124.38	17,385.80
20		NPV	6,142.03					

4. COLOUR AND PATTERNS

Colours and patterns also help to define inputs and outputs. In Figure 3.11 a neutral colour is used for the inputs and grey for the answers. These colours are personal, but it is important to be consistent in the use of colours and formats.

Fig 3.11

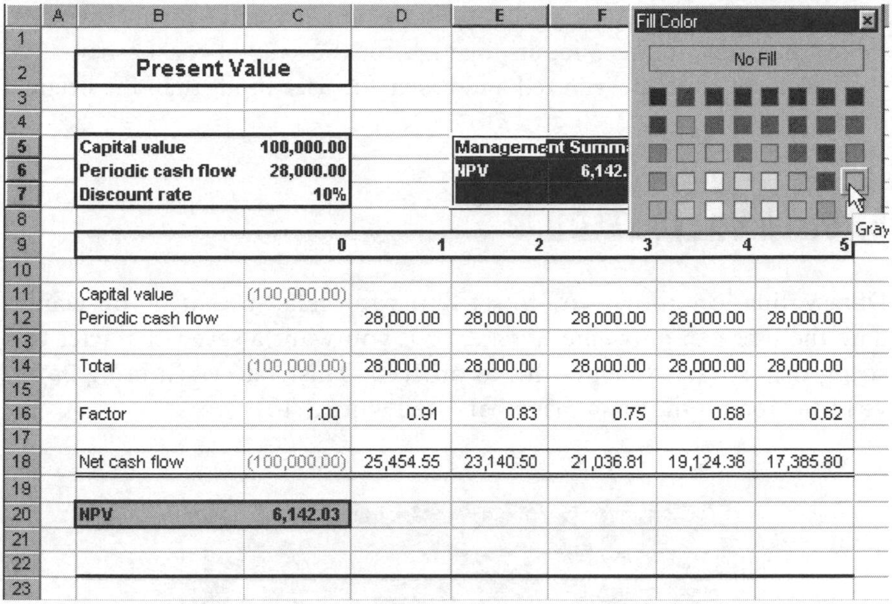

5. SPECIFIC COLOUR FOR INPUTS AND RESULTS

Specific colours for inputs show where data is required. The author always uses blue for inputs, green or black for totals and red or black for calculated results (see Figure 3.12). Colour should be used sparingly as the effect can be too garish for most tastes.

Fig 3.12

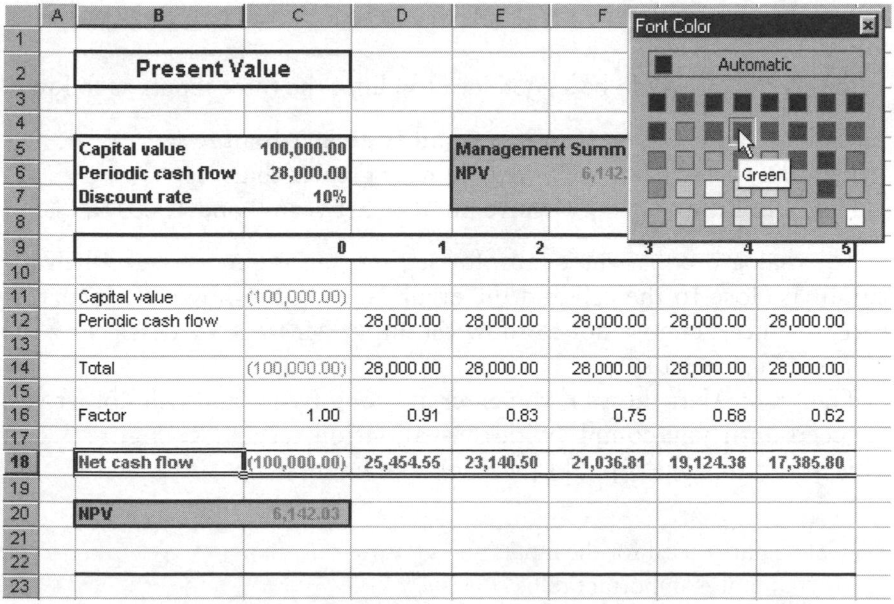

With limited colour, the model becomes much clearer for the user and forces the author to keep inputs together for the sake of consistency.

The model is now organized and easier for user input than the original model.

6. DATA VALIDATION

Data validation allows you to set limits for cells so that if you want a date the user can only enter a date, or if you want a seven-character text string the user has to enter this to proceed. This is accessed using `Data`, `Validation` on the main menu bar (see Figure 3.13).

Fig 3.13

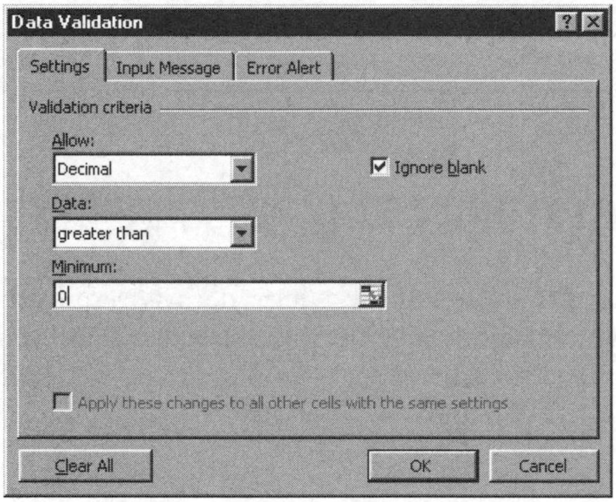

In this case, it would be a good idea top limit the three inputs as follows:

Capital Value	Positive number greater than zero
Periodic Cash Flow	Positive number greater than zero
Discount Rate	Positive number between 0 and 1, i.e. 100%

The dialog box has three tabs, for settings, an input message when the cursor is close to the cell and the error alert to be shown on incorrect entry. You can choose not to show the Input Message by deselecting the box (see Figure 3.14).

The Error Alert shows if you enter a wrong figure and will not let you proceed until you comply with the validation terms (see Figure 3.15). This means that the capital value should always be a positive figure.

Fig 3.14

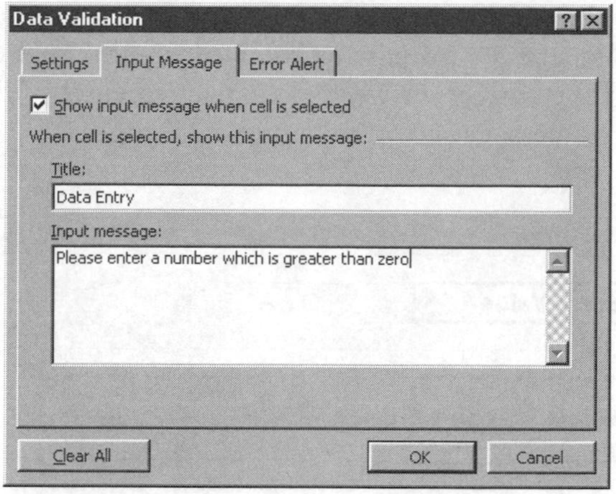

Fig 3.15

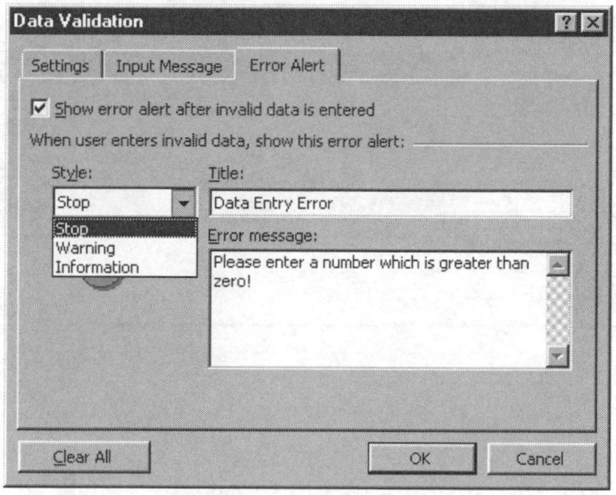

Since the periodic cash flows share the same validation, you can `Copy` and then `Edit`, `Paste Special`, `Validation` rather than typing in all the parameters again (see Figure 3.16).

Fig 3.16

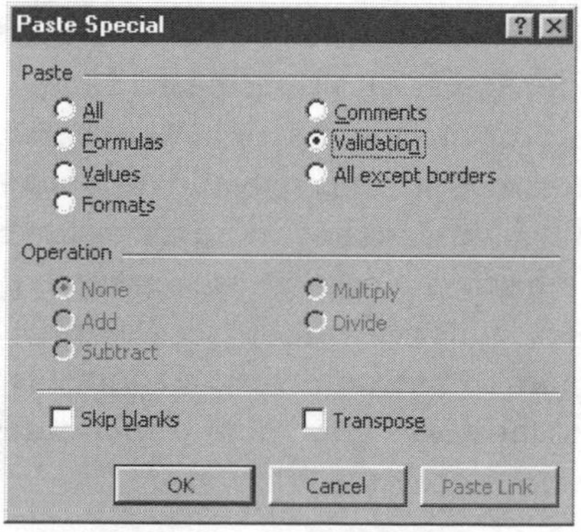

The final validation is simply to ensure that the discount rate is less than 100%. The effect is to narrow the inputs and hopefully ensure that a user will get the correct answers. If he tries to enter a discount rate of 120%, the error message shown in Figure 3.17 appears.

Fig 3.17

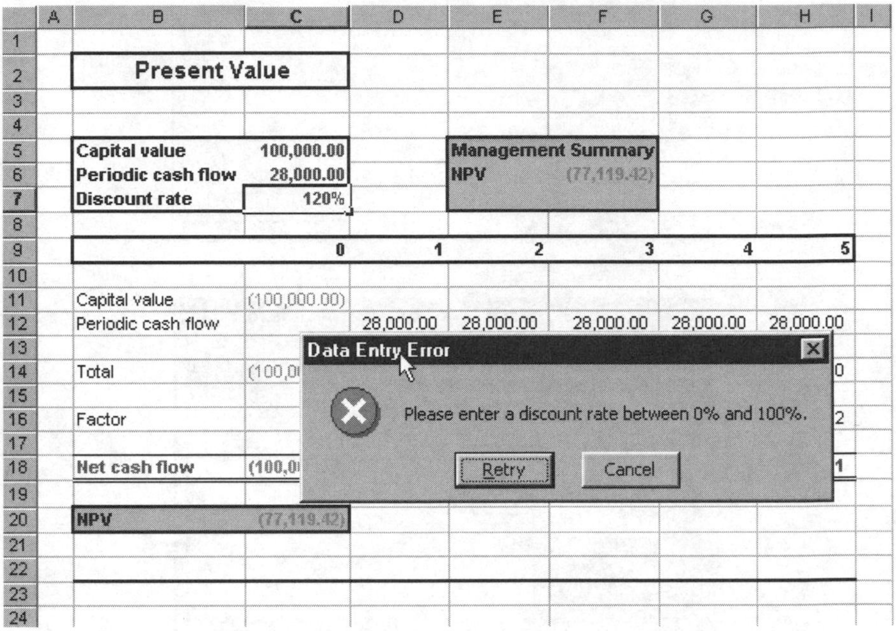

Again this is simply looking at the model from a user standpoint and trying to coach the user on what he is required to do.

7. CONTROLS – COMBO BOXES AND BUTTONS

Further assistance in speeding up inputs and assisting users can be found on the Forms toolbar under `View`, `Toolbars`. These are the same controls, which you also find in Access or Visual Basic. In this example, you might wish to allow the user to input a discount rate between 8% and 12% at 0.5% intervals. This cannot be done by validation and a different approach is needed. Validation will only permit an upper or lower value.

The first stage is to insert a workings area at the bottom of the sheet and to cut and paste the discount rate into it (see Figure 3.18). This is to ensure that the model continues to function when a control is placed at cell C7.

The Workings box shows an interval and then rates starting at 8% and incrementing by the amount of the interval.

Fig 3.18

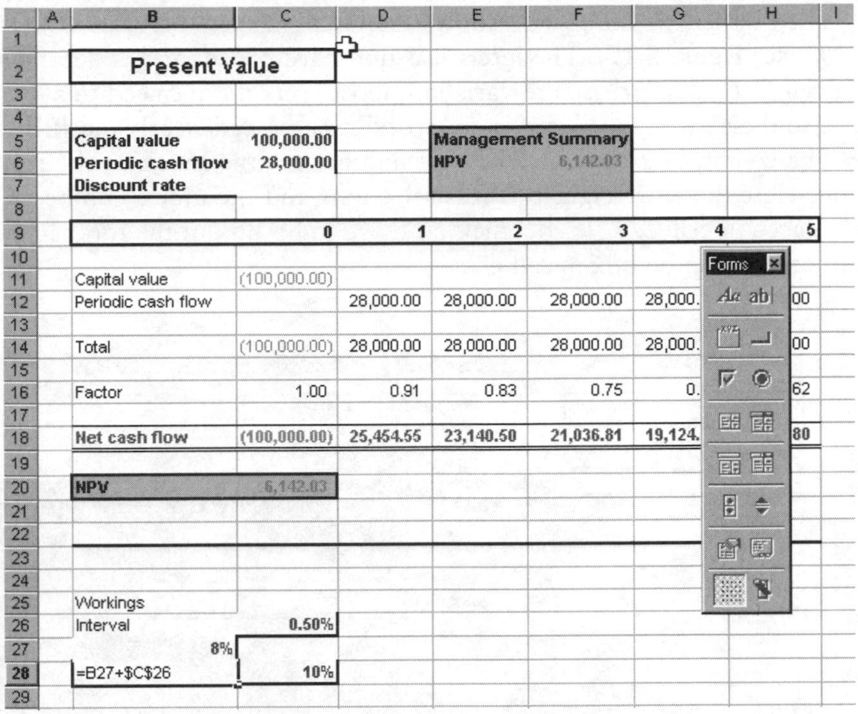

	A	B	C	D	E	F	G	H
2		Present Value						
5		Capital value	100,000.00		Management Summary			
6		Periodic cash flow	28,000.00		NPV	6,142.03		
7		Discount rate						
9			0	1	2	3	4	5
11		Capital value	(100,000.00)					
12		Periodic cash flow		28,000.00	28,000.00	28,000.00	28,000.	00
14		Total	(100,000.00)	28,000.00	28,000.00	28,000.00	28,000.	00
16		Factor	1.00	0.91	0.83	0.75	0.	62
18		Net cash flow	(100,000.00)	25,454.55	23,140.50	21,036.81	19,124.	80
20		NPV	6,142.03					
25		Workings						
26		Interval	0.50%					
27		8%						
28		=B27+$C$26	10%					

Fig 3.19

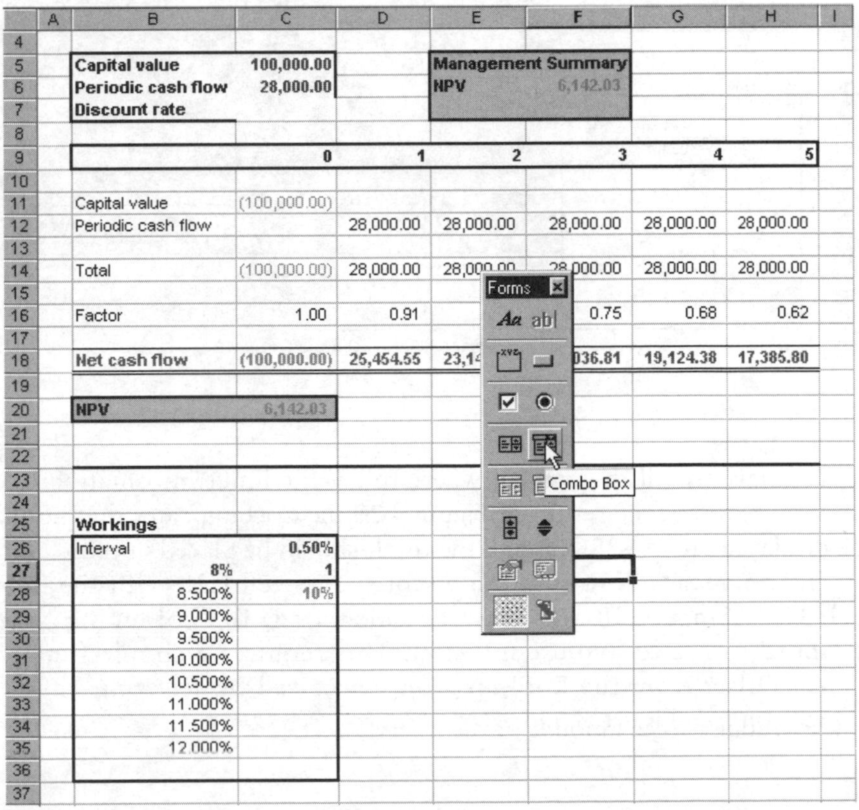

	A	B	C	D	E	F	G	H
5		Capital value	100,000.00		Management Summary			
6		Periodic cash flow	28,000.00		NPV	6,142.03		
7		Discount rate						
9			0	1	2	3	4	5
11		Capital value	(100,000.00)					
12		Periodic cash flow		28,000.00	28,000.00	28,000.00	28,000.00	28,000.00
14		Total	(100,000.00)	28,000.00	28,00	28,000.00	28,000.00	28,000.00
16		Factor	1.00	0.91		0.75	0.68	0.62
18		Net cash flow	(100,000.00)	25,454.55	23,1	036.81	19,124.38	17,385.80
20		NPV	6,142.03					
25		Workings						
26		Interval	0.50%					
27		8%	1					
28		8.500%	10%					
29		9.000%						
30		9.500%						
31		10.000%						
32		10.500%						
33		11.000%						
34		11.500%						
35		12.000%						

The finished workings box shows the discount rates between 8% and 12% (see Figure 3.19). The interval is not 'hard coded' and is dependent on cell C26. While these are variables, most users do not need this detail and so these items are placed in the workings area and clearly marked.

The combo box control returns a number for the index of the selection. Here there are eight possible selections and the index number will be placed in cell C27. If you click on the Combo Box in the toolbar, you can draw a combo box in cell C7.

Fig 3.20

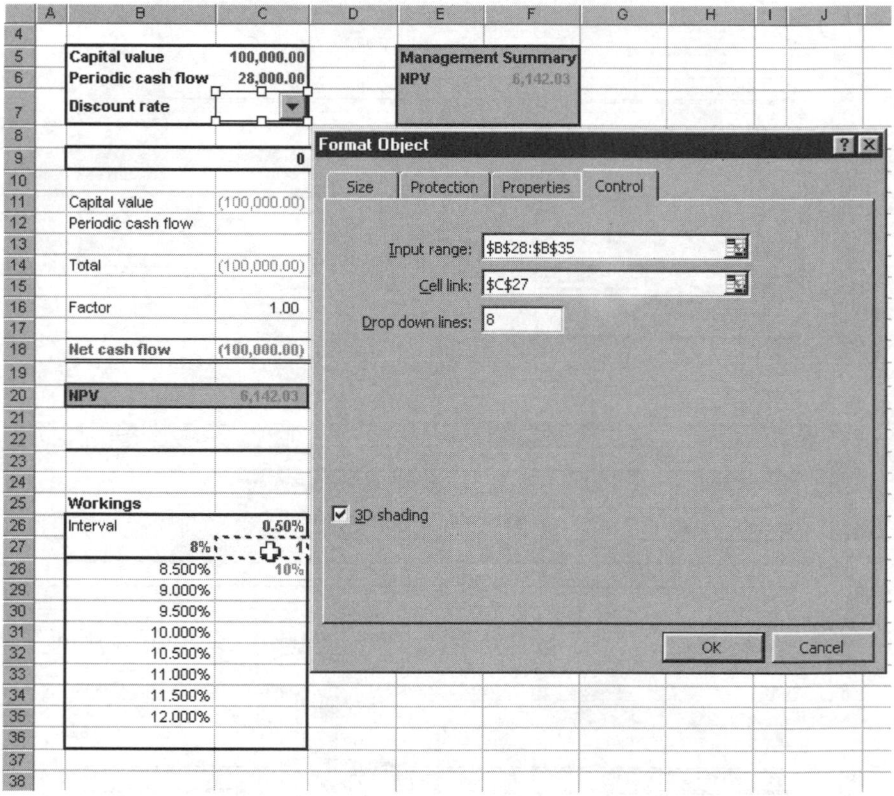

You have to tell the control where to get the input information from and where to put the result. In Figure 3.20 the discount rates that need to be displayed are in B28:B35 and the result should be placed in cell C27.

The final stage is to link the discount rate cell C28 with the index cell C27. Since C28 will now be calculated, the colour has been changed to red to avoid confusion. This requires a simple function called Offset from the Lookup group, accessed by selecting `Insert, Function` (see Figure 3.21).

Fig 3.21

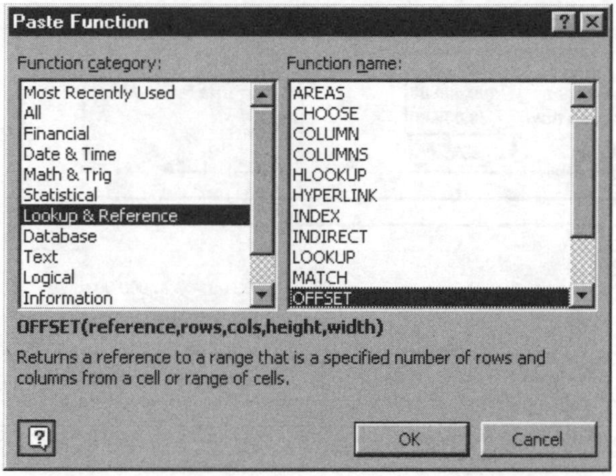

This function allows you to nominate a starting call and then go down by X rows and across by Y columns and return the value. Here the example should start at cell B27 and go down by the number of rows returned by the control. You start at B27 and go down by C27 and no columns (see Figure 3.22). This should return the discount rate to be used in the present value calculations.

Fig 3.22

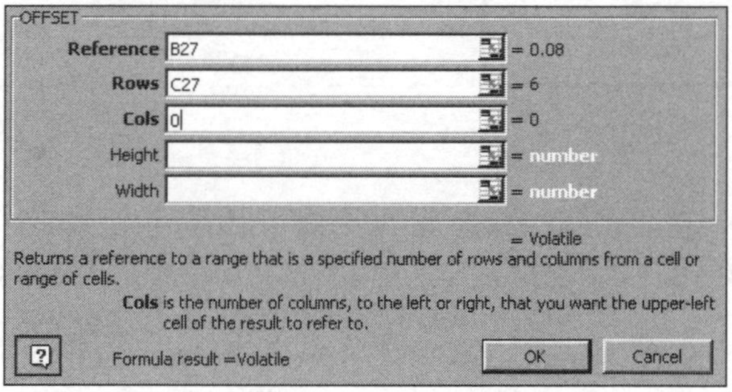

The combo box controls the user input and makes it faster to select the individual discount rates (see Figure 3.23). Note that a user could still send data to cells B27, C26 and C27. The combo box runs a macro or routine to update the cell, but does not protect it.

There are other controls in the toolbox that you could use to make the inputs more intuitive. For example, spinners and scroll bars allow you to increment a value by one click and provide an input variable for specifying the click value.

Fig 3.23

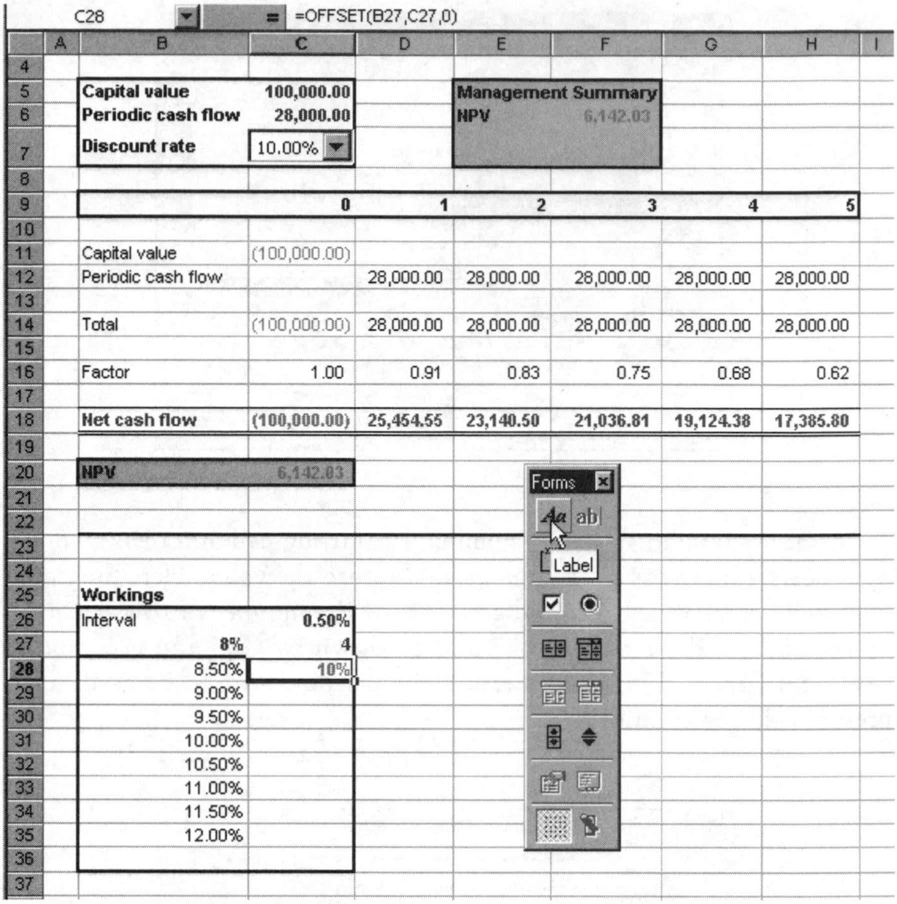

The Spinner_ScrollBar sheet shows the inclusion of these two controls as an alternative. Here you select an upper and lower value and an incremental value. The solution is slightly more complex since the control does not accept fractions. You therefore have to calculate the eventual discount rate from the position of the scroll bar.

The scroll bar in Figure 3.24 is set to accept values from 1 to 8 and to increment by one. The cell link is cell C26 and the Offset function in cell C27 uses this index number.

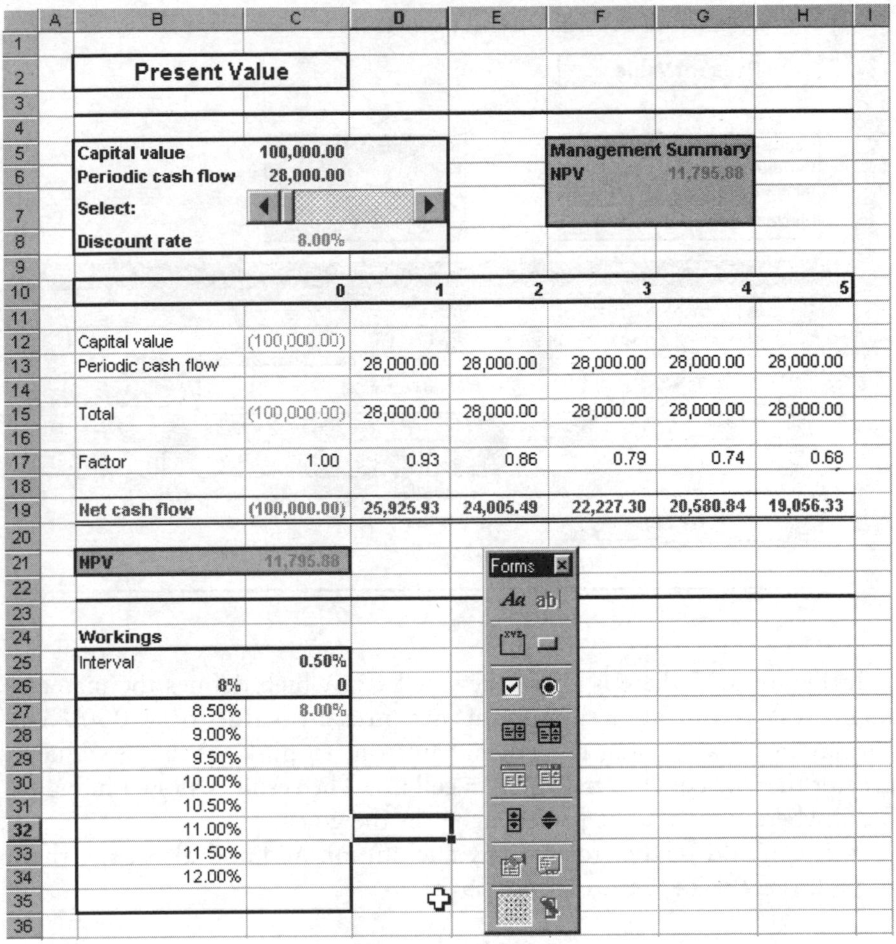

Fig 3.24

8. CONDITIONAL FORMATTING

Conditional formatting allows you to display cells differently depending on the value in the cell. This means fonts, borders and patterns. In this example, it could be useful to introduce a management test to show if the project succeeds or fails and then display the result accordingly.

Fig 3.25

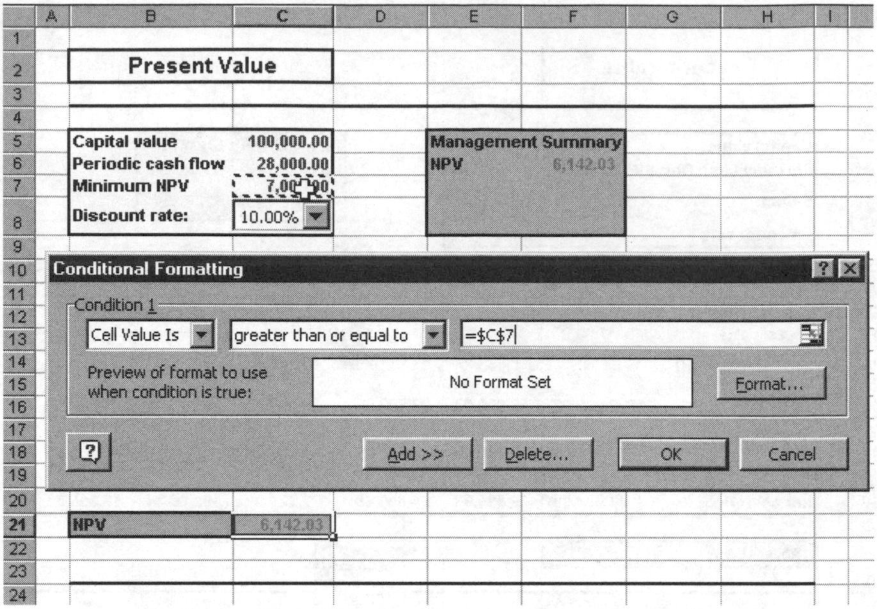

In Figure 3.25 there is now a new cell C7, which defines the management test requiring a minimum net present value of 7,000. The formatting is set, using the Format button, to pink when the value is greater than or equal to the value in cell C7. The result is shown in Figure 3.26, where, at 9.5% the project achieves the goal.

You can add further formats by clicking on Add and also copy them using `Edit, Paste Special, Formats`.

Fig 3.26

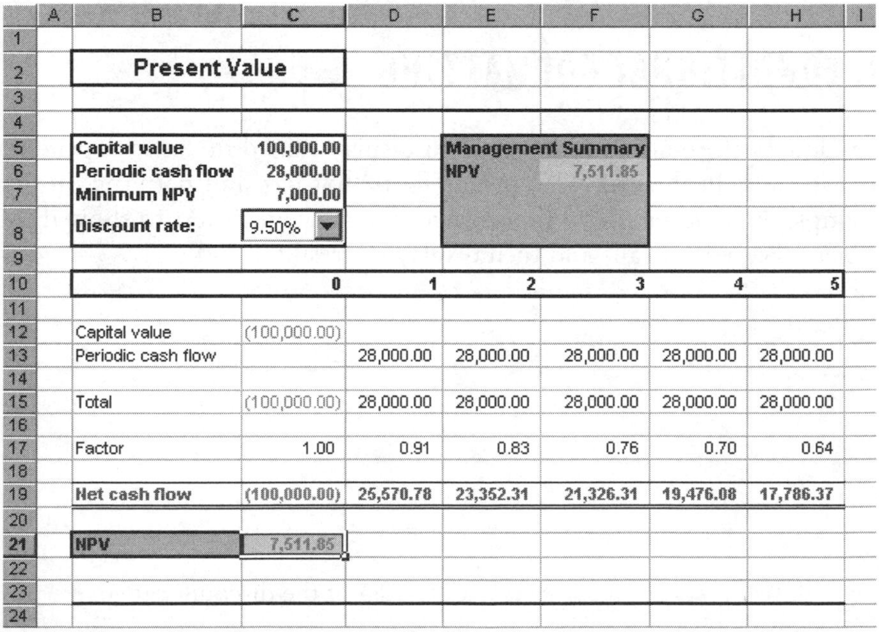

Present Value

Capital value	100,000.00
Periodic cash flow	28,000.00
Minimum NPV	7,000.00
Discount rate:	9.50%

Management Summary
NPV 7,511.85

	0	1	2	3	4	5
Capital value	(100,000.00)					
Periodic cash flow		28,000.00	28,000.00	28,000.00	28,000.00	28,000.00
Total	(100,000.00)	28,000.00	28,000.00	28,000.00	28,000.00	28,000.00
Factor	1.00	0.91	0.83	0.76	0.70	0.64
Net cash flow	(100,000.00)	25,570.78	23,352.31	21,326.31	19,476.08	17,786.37

NPV 7,511.85

9. USE OF FUNCTIONS AND TYPES OF FUNCTION

The model already includes the function OFFSET; however, the net present values could more easily by calculated using the NPV function. At present, there is code in cells C17 to H19, which means there are potentially twelve mistakes. The goal should be to reduce code in order to reduce the potential for errors. The solution at present is equivalent to using Excel instead of a set of discount tables.

You can use `Insert, Function` from the Menu Bar or the Standard toolbar and functions are divided into sections for easy reference. Select Financial Functions and scroll down to NPV (see Figure 3.27).

Fig 3.27

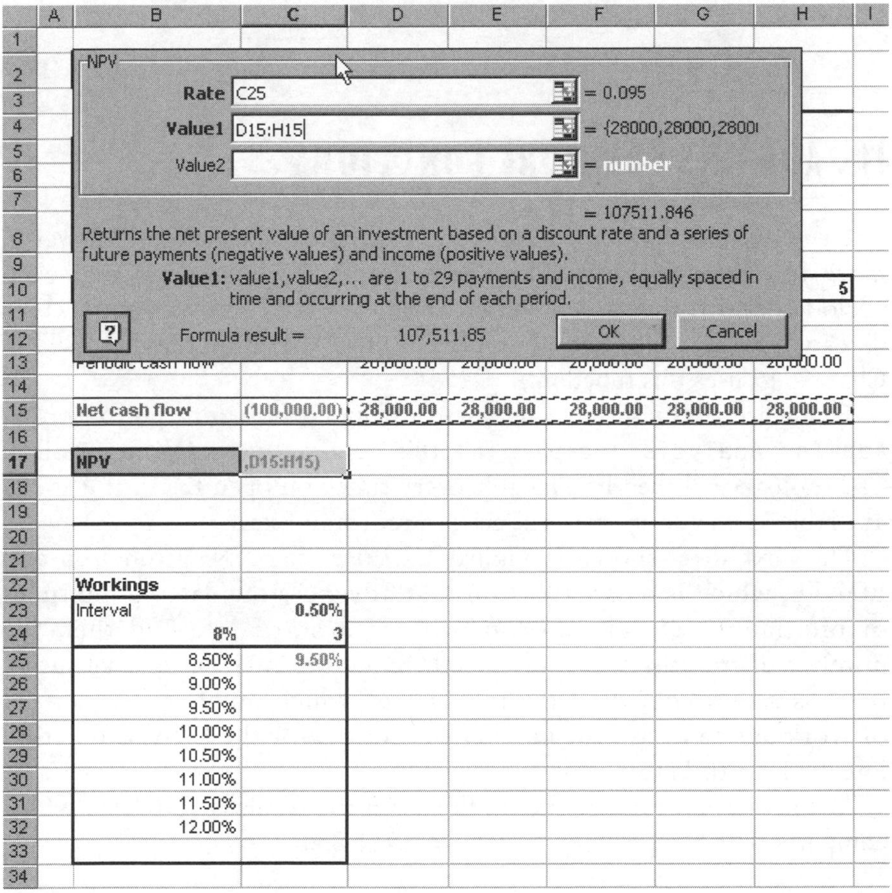

The net present value function discounts outstanding cash flows and so the years one to five are selected. You then add the cash flow at period 0.

```
=NPV(C25,D15:H15)+C15
```

This results in the correct answer of 7,511.85 at the discount rate of 9.5%.

Notice the spreadsheet is now much simpler with a reduction in the necessary rows. You can always obtain help on the functions by pressing the Question Mark as in Figure 3.28. Within the Help for the selected function, you can view a listing of alternative functions by selecting See Also.

Fig 3.28

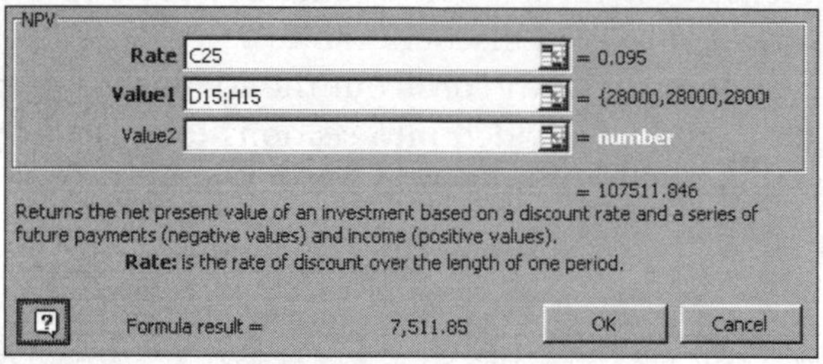

10. ADD-INS FOR MORE FUNCTIONS

The typical installation of Excel contains the basic functions. However, more functions are available. For example, NPV assumes that each period contains the same number of days. XNPV allows you to enter dates when the cash flows are received. (The Valuation file discussed in Chapter 19 uses this function.)

To ensure that you have access to extended functions go to `Tools`, `Add-Ins`, `Analysis Toolpak`. Tick this item and press OK to install it. The toolpak will then be available every time you open Excel. If it is not available as an add-in, you will need to re-install Excel.

The next sheet shown in Figure 3.29 uses the XNPV function and EDATE, which is a date function that advances the date by multiples of one month at a time. You provide a start date and then the number of months to be advanced. Since the interval is a variable, there is a new control in the inputs area which points towards a set of workings to derive the number of months for the EDATE function in cells D13 to H13.

Again you add the initial cash flow and the result is 7,502.58, which compares with the previous answer of 7,511.85.

Fig 3.29

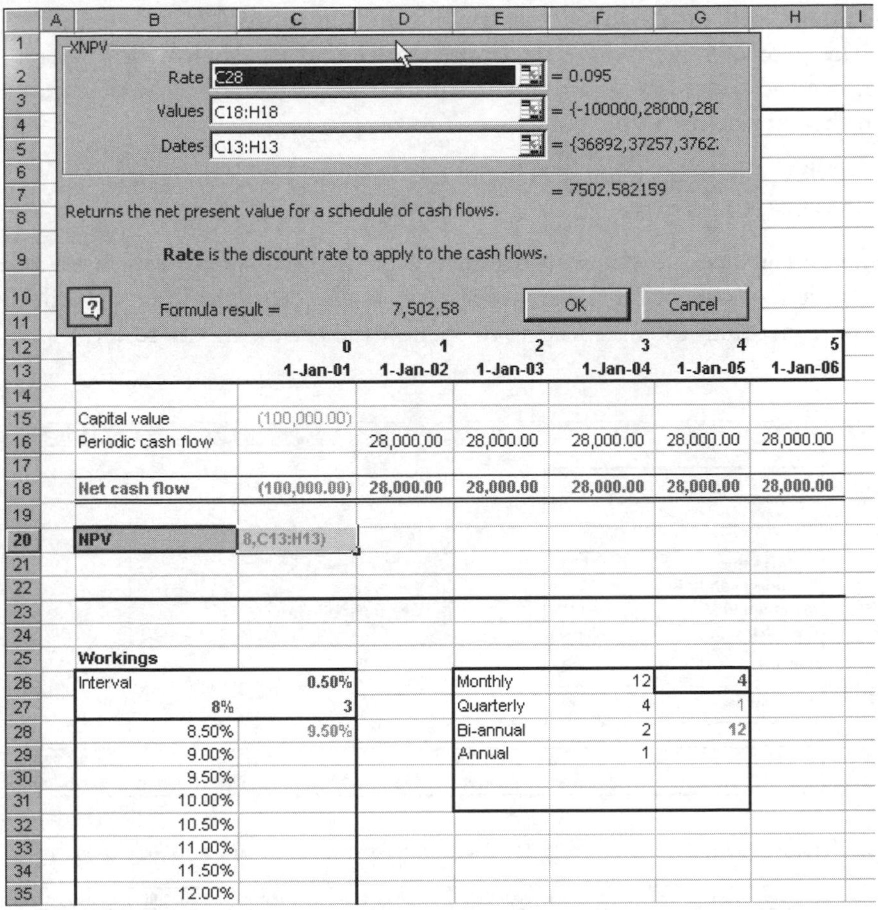

11. TEXT AND UPDATED LABELS

You could improve the clarity of the model by allowing the labels to update and providing some text on the result. If the net present value is above the limit, then you could have a label informing the user. The Text sheet in Features.xls provides these two improvements:

- showing the discount rate in the label;
- feedback on the calculated net present value.

Cell B20 is now an updated label. The Text function converts numbers to text following the number formats. This will display the percentage to two decimal places. The ampersand is used to join or concatenate the text strings:

```
="NPV at "&TEXT(C31,"0.00%")
```

The management feedback uses an IF function to display one text string if the project is above the limit and another if it is below. In order to reduce the code, the IF statement substitutes above or below depending on the net present value.

```
="NPV is "&IF(C20>=C7,"above","below")&" the limit of
"&TEXT(C7,"#,##0")
```

The spreadsheet now will inform the user of the discount rate used and provide a comment on the answer (see Figure 3.30). Excel takes the decision rather than the user having to spend time reviewing the result.

Fig 3.30

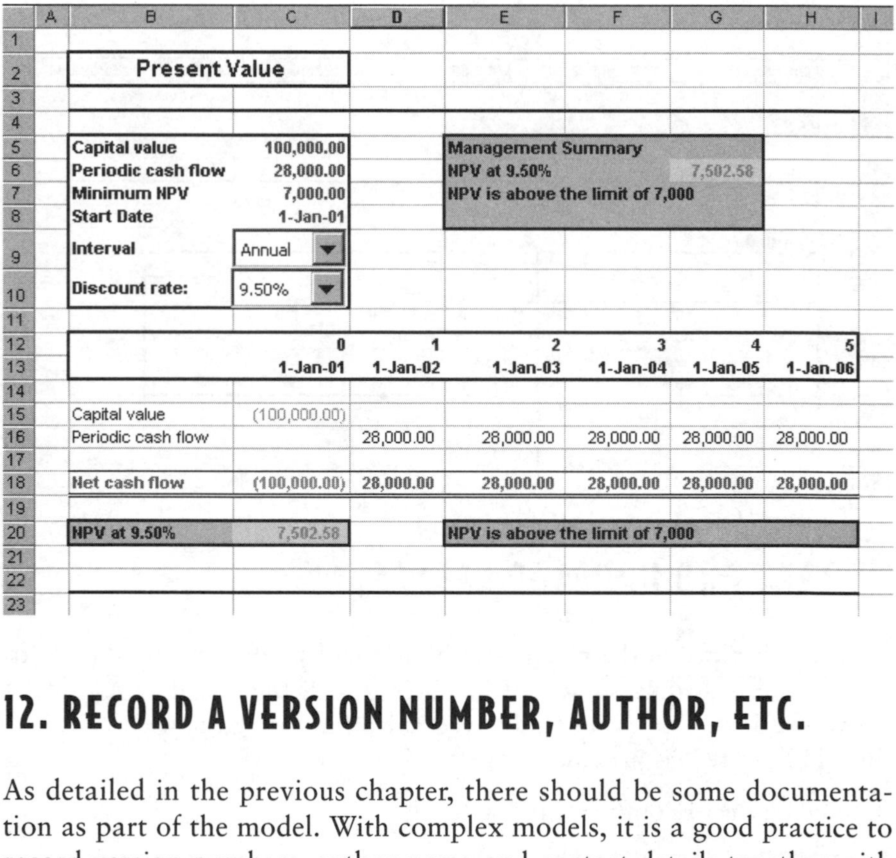

12. RECORD A VERSION NUMBER, AUTHOR, ETC.

As detailed in the previous chapter, there should be some documentation as part of the model. With complex models, it is a good practice to record version numbers, author name and contact details together with notes on how the model works. As a model develops over time, you can record the changes between one version and another. This is particularly important if you find a major error. In addition, it means that a version reference is at the top of every sheet that you print out (see Figure 3.31).

Fig 3.31

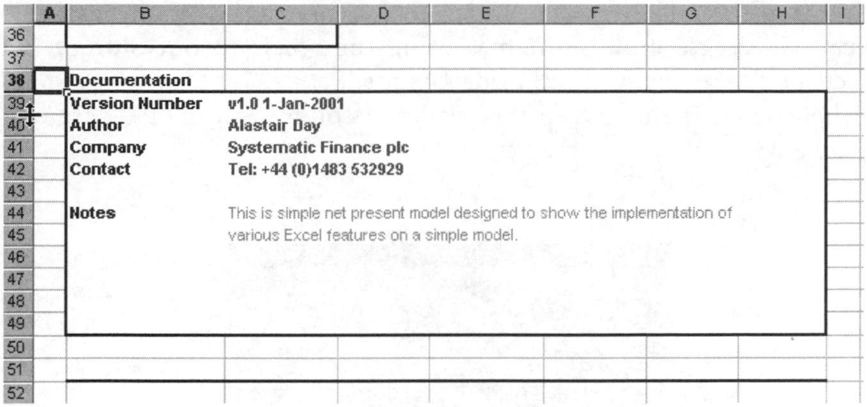

This section could of course run to several pages with diagrams and notes. It is of course better to put the notes in the model and you can always hide a sheet by selecting `Format`, `Sheet`, `Hide`.

13. USE NAMES TO MAKE FORMULAS EASIER TO UNDERSTAND

Names can make formulas easier to understand: for example, rather than using cell C28, you can have PeriodInterestRate. The standard cells above such as Version, Author, etc. would also be better standardized across all your models such that `=Version` will always insert the version number. The files with this book use several standard names such as Author, Company, Version and Product.

Fig 3.32

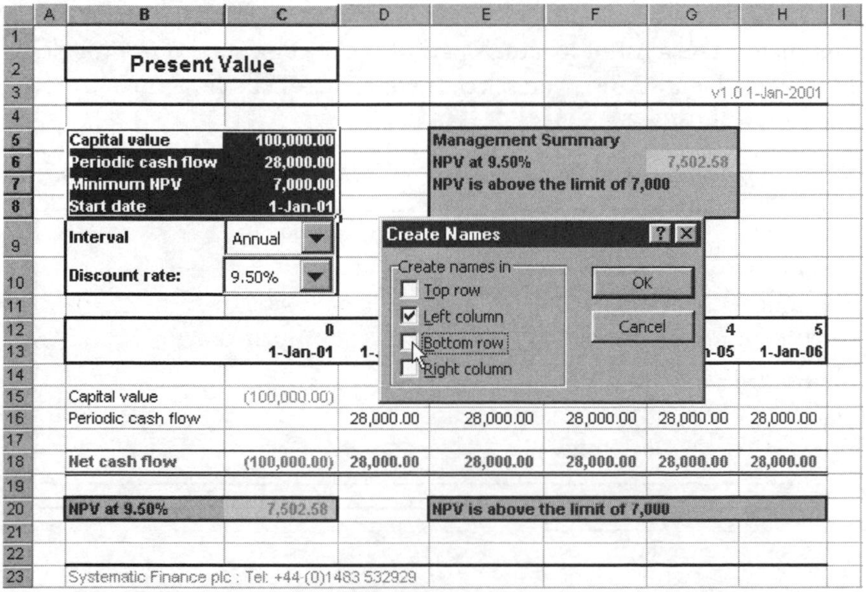

You can use `Insert, Name, Define` to define names or, alternatively, Excel will create multiple names using the labels to one side of the selected cells (see Figure 3.32) using `Insert, Names, Create`.

This creates the names in the left-hand column, e.g. Start_date (see Figure 3.33).

Fig 3.33

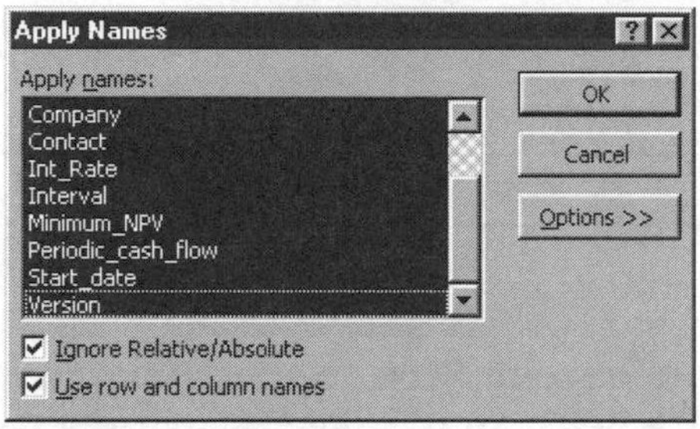

The function is now easier to understand since it refers to the periodic interest rate in cell C20.

```
=XNPV(Int_Rate,C18:H18,C13:H13)
```

If you copy a sheet containing names, then the new sheet will continue to refer to the original sheet. Similarly, if you copy a sheet to a new workbook, Excel creates a link between the two workbooks. You can always check for links by selecting `Edit, Links`. If this is the case, you have to remove them manually and reinsert the cell formulas.

14. PASTE A NAMES TABLE AS PART OF DOCUMENTATION

It is useful to paste a list of names as part of the documentation to provide an audit trail (see Figure 3.34). You select `Insert, Name, Paste, Paste List`.

Fig 3.34

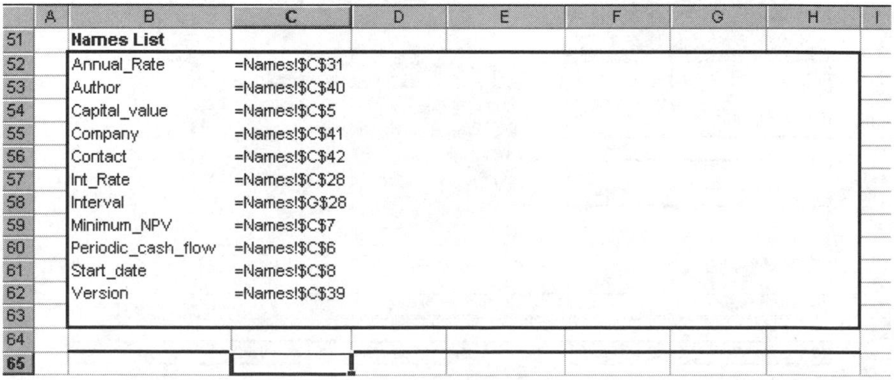

	A	B	C	D	E	F	G	H	I
51		**Names List**							
52		Annual_Rate	=Names!$C$31						
53		Author	=Names!$C$40						
54		Capital_value	=Names!$C$5						
55		Company	=Names!$C$41						
56		Contact	=Names!$C$42						
57		Int_Rate	=Names!$C$28						
58		Interval	=Names!$G$28						
59		Minimum_NPV	=Names!$C$7						
60		Periodic_cash_flow	=Names!$C$6						
61		Start_date	=Names!$C$8						
62		Version	=Names!$C$39						
63									
64									
65									

15. COMMENT CELLS

Commenting cells allow notes to be placed against cells to provide background or to help the user. Go to `Insert Comment` or right mouse click on a cell. Enter a text message and then format the font size and colours (see Figure 3.35).

Fig 3.35

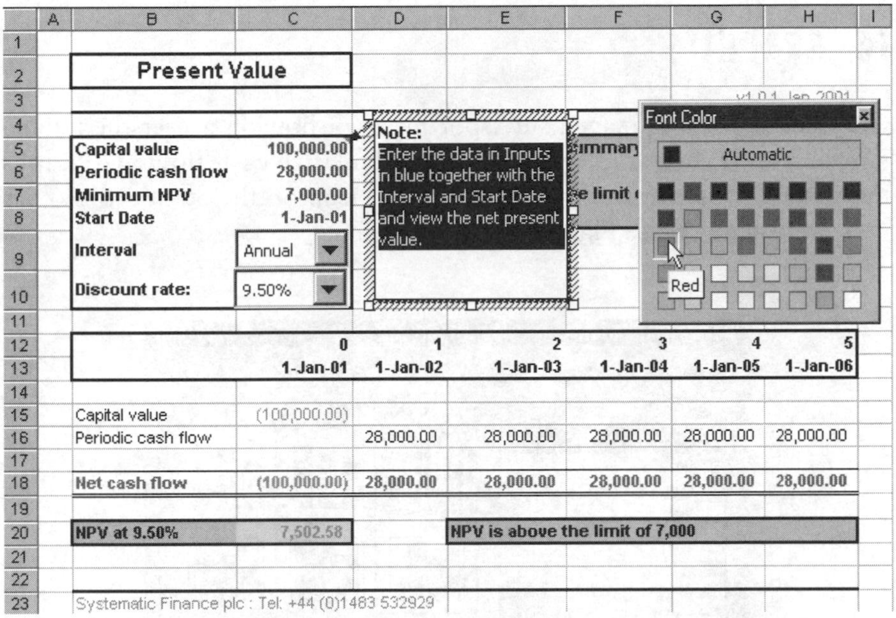

Fig 3.36

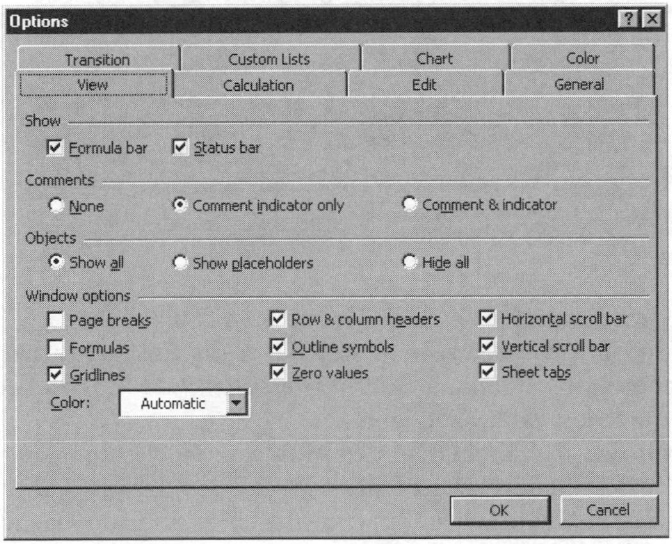

You can control how Comments are viewed using `Tools`, `Options`, `View` (see Figure 3.36). You can turn them off, show the indicator or have the comment permanently visible. In the second case, the cell displays a red triangle at its top right-hand corner. Again, comments can assist in explaining important formulas or telling the user what to do. For example, some people use numbers for percentages and then divide by 100 in code. A comment could inform a user to insert a number rather than a percentage.

16. GRAPHICS

Graphics assist in management reporting and showing a user the important answer. The example now adds a cumulative cash flow and graphs the pattern. You can use the Chart Wizard icon on the Standard toolbar or `Insert Chart` (see Figure 3.37).

Fig 3.37

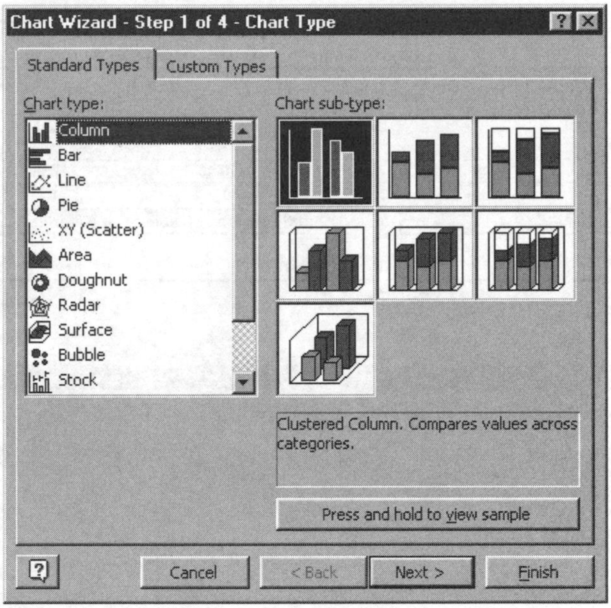

This is just charting a single series and so a column graph will produce a clear print-out. On the second step, click the `Series` rather than the `Data Range` tab (see Figure 3.38). Then click `Add Series` to add the name of the series, values and labels.

This will plot the cumulative cash flow values with the dates as the X labels across the chart (see Figure 3.39). The name is also in code as Graphics!$B$20. If you click on Next, the chart title and legend titles are displayed. Excel will not allow you to enter a cell reference against the name, but you can do this when you have finished the Wizard.

Fig 3.38

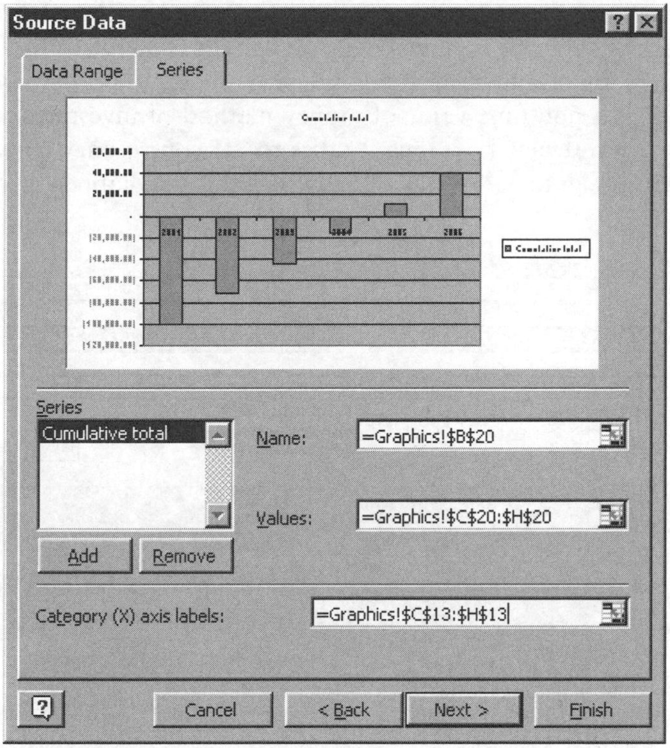

Fig 3.39

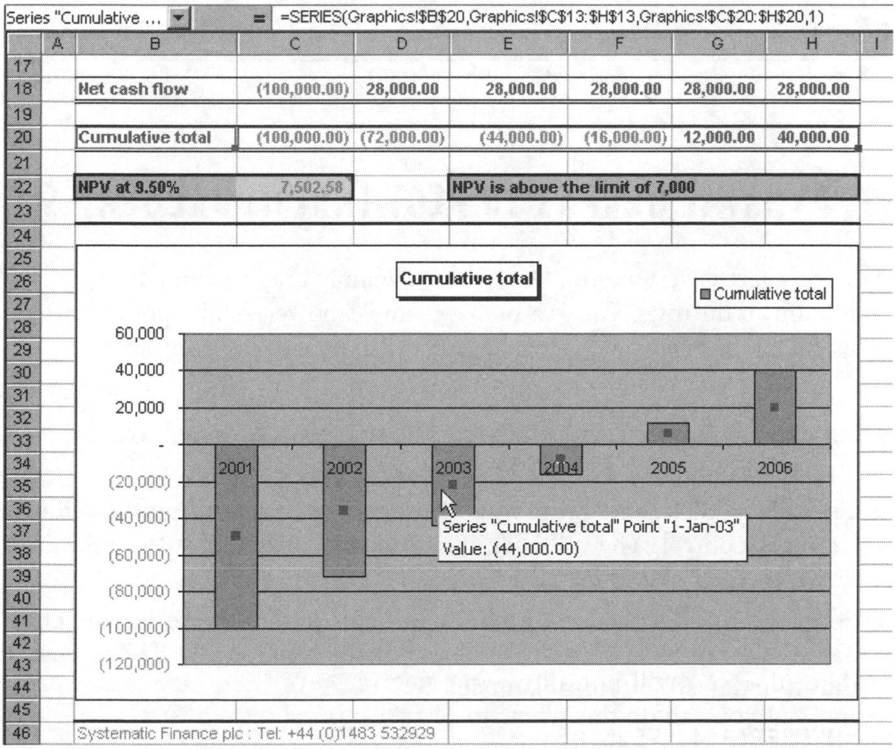

If you right click the X axis, it can be formatted so that the tick marks are low. The chart title is entered as `=Graphics!$B$20` so that it updates itself. This is important since you do not want labels to be 'hard wired'.

Payback is a non time value of money method of investment appraisal. Essentially, you review how long it takes to get your money back. The finished chart in Figure 3.40 shows clearly that this will happen in year four.

Fig 3.40

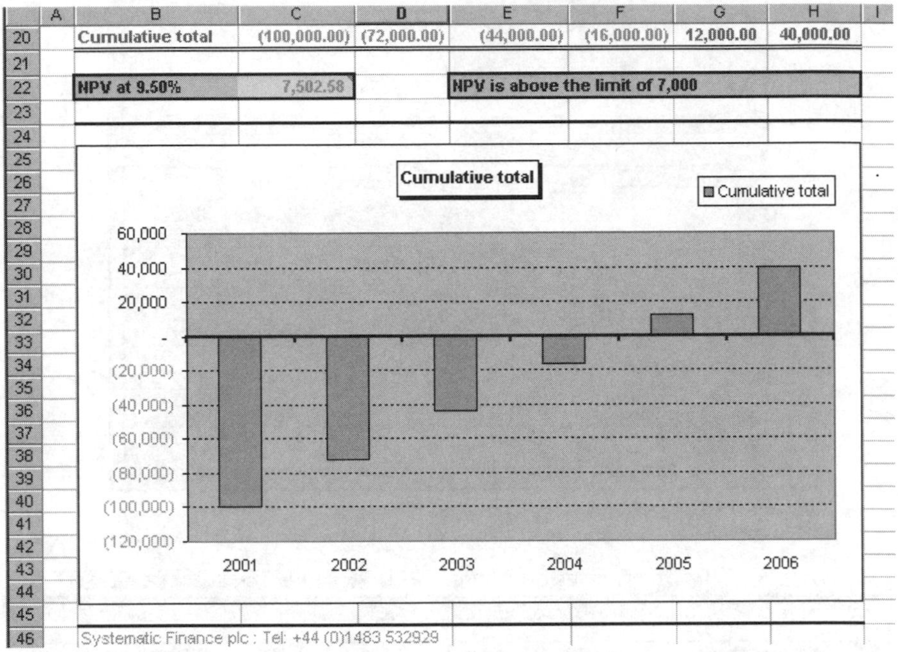

17. DYNAMIC GRAPHS TO PLOT INDIVIDUAL SERIES

A single chart is very useful; however, a dynamic graph would allow you to review any of the rows. This is a simple example, however, this approach would be useful for examining individual lines in a cash flow or company analysis.

The steps are as follows:

- Set up a combo box with the inputs as the labels to the individual lines and a cell link to update (F25).
- Use an OFFSET function to look up the relevant line using the cell link from the control. The OFFSET function starts from row 14 and moves down by the number in cell F25.
- Point the chart at the look-up lines and ensure that the series and chart names are not hard-coded. The name of the series is cell B27 to ensure that it updates. The formula in cell B27 is:

```
=OFFSET(B14,$F$25,0)
```

Fig 3.41

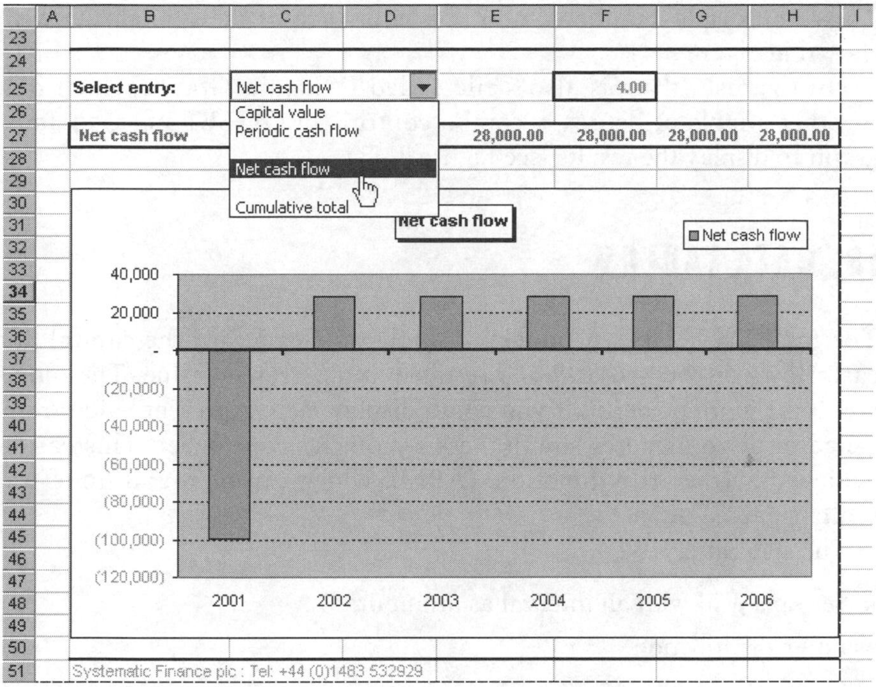

Fig 3.42

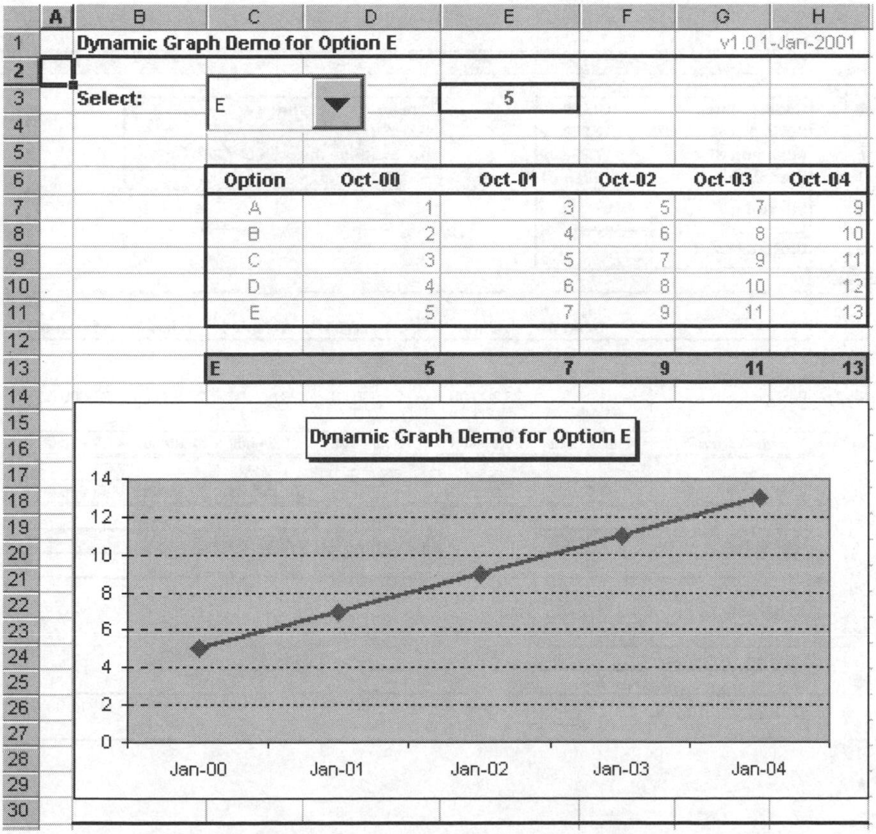

The result displaying the combo box with each of the available rows is shown in Figure 3.41.

On the disk, there is also a file called Dynamic_Graph, which puts together a table of figures, a combo control, an OFFSET function and a graph to display the results (see Figure 3.42).

18. DATA TABLES

The model so far has produced a single point answer: the capital and cash flows discounted at 9.5% result in a net present value. The model would be more powerful if you could display the net present values for a range of discount rates simultaneously on the same sheet. This can be achieved by the array function TABLE, which can be found under the toolbar `Data, Table`.

The steps are:

- Set up a grid with an interval as an input.
- Enter the function.
- Graph the results.

Fig 3.43

B30 = =C22

	A	B	C	D	E	F	G	H	I
4									
5		**Capital value**	**100,000.00**		**Management Summary**				
6		**Periodic cash flow**	**28,000.00**		**NPV at 9.50%**		**7,502.58**		
7		**Minimum NPV**	**7,000.00**		**NPV is above the limit of 7,000**				
8		**Start Date**	**1-Jan-01**						
9		**Interval**							
10		**Discount rate:**							
11									
12			**0**	**1**	**2**	**3**	**4**	**5**	
13			**1-Jan-01**	**1-Jan-02**	**1-Jan-03**	**1-Jan-04**	**1-Jan-05**	**1-Jan-06**	
14									
15		Capital value	(100,000.00)						
16		Periodic cash flow		28,000.00	28,000.00	28,000.00	28,000.00	28,000.00	
17									
18		**Net cash flow**	**(100,000.00)**	**28,000.00**	**28,000.00**	**28,000.00**	**28,000.00**	**28,000.00**	
19									
20		**Cumulative total**	**(100,000.00)**	**(72,000.00)**	**(44,000.00)**	**(16,000.00)**	**12,000.00**	**40,000.00**	
21									
22		**NPV at 9.50%**	**7,502.58**		**NPV is above the limit of 7,000**				
23									
24									
25		**Sensitivity Table for the Discount Rate**							
26									
27		**Interval**	**0.50%**						
28									
29			8.50%	9.00%	**9.50%**	10.00%	10.50%	11.00%	
30		7,502.58							
31									

The dynamic graph has been moved down on the Data_Tables sheet to make room for the data or sensitivity table (see Figure 3.43). The grid consists of an interval and then a row of discount rates in line 29. The 9.5% is an absolute and is marked in blue as an input. The cells on either side are plus or minus the interval. Cell B30 looks up the answer in cell C22. When complete the data table will show the net present value at each of these interest rates.

The next stage is to highlight the grid area and enter the data table (see Figure 3.44).

Fig 3.44

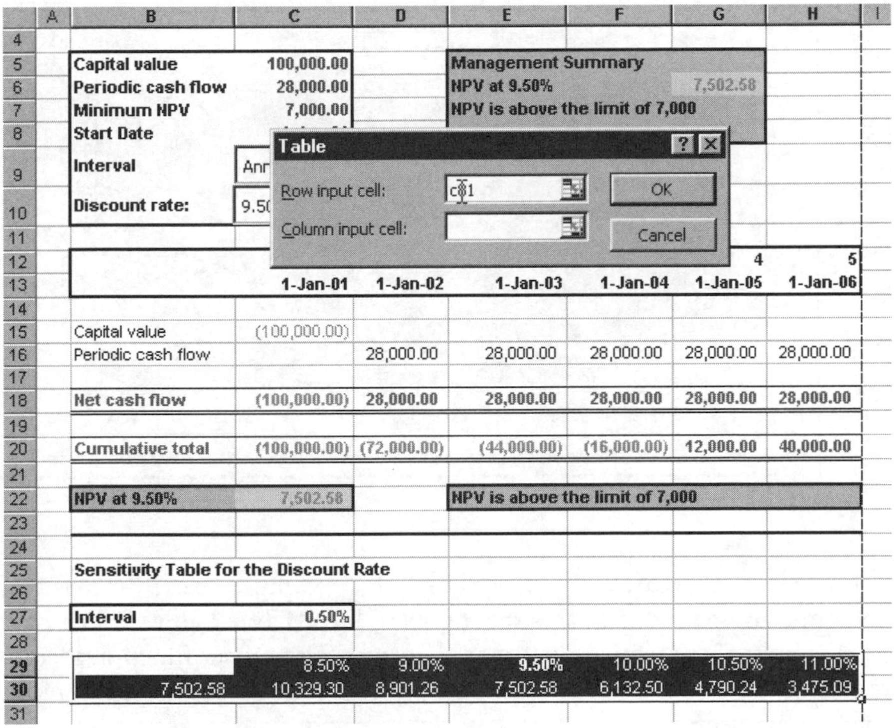

Cell C81 in this interim version is the periodic discount rate derived from the combo box. Excel inserts the figures in the grid and the answer of 7,502.58 at 9.5% is visible. This shows the sensitivity of the final answer to changes in the discount rate.

Table is an array function, which means that you cannot alter individual cells within the group. If you try to alter any of cells C31 to H31, you will get an error message. Similarly, if you copy a data table from one sheet to another, only the values will be pasted. You have to highlight the grid and re-input the table on the new sheet.

Fig 3.45

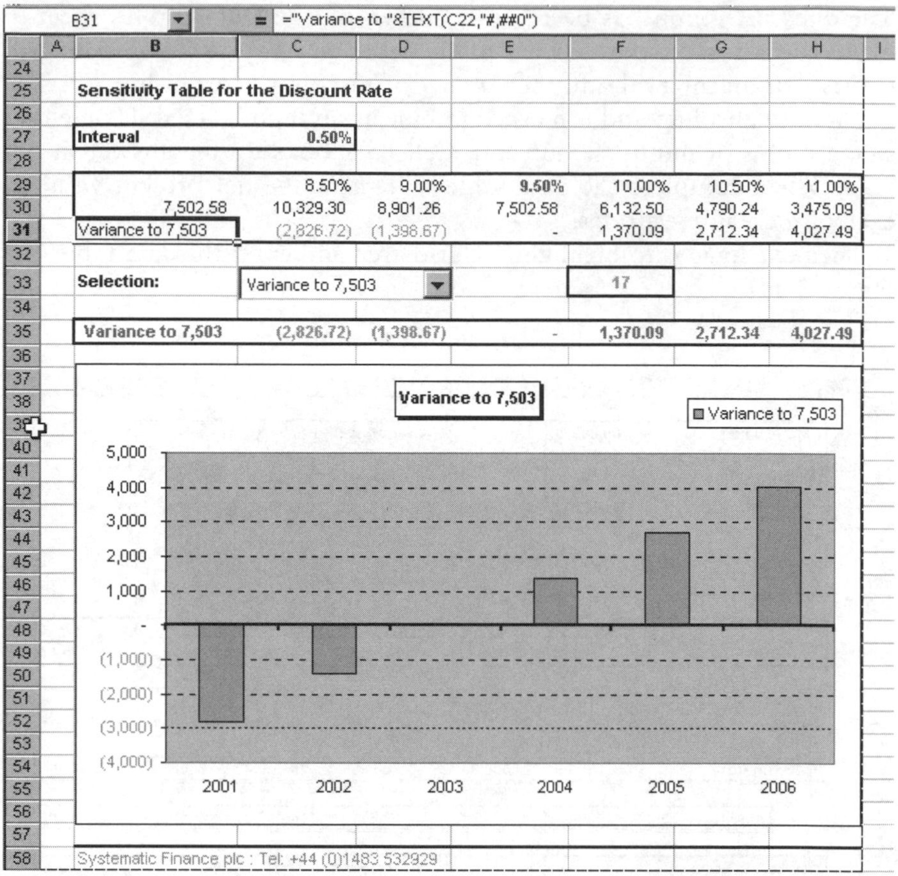

Rather than create a further chart, this example uses the existing 'dynamic graph' and increases the inputs to line 31 (see Figure 3.45). Line 31 is simply a variance to the original answer. The Offset function merely requires the rows to index down by and so no other programming changes are necessary.

Data tables can be single dimensional as above or two dimensional. There are often two dominant variables in a model and this approach allows you to 'flex' the variables. It is important to use a grid to set out the table and best not to hard code the interval. This means that you can always change the interval quickly and see on any printouts the interval used. In addition, it is best practice to input the current value for the variable in the middle so you can see the values on either side. Some applications with the book then use a macro to update the input values on the table by copying down the values from the inputs area.

19. SCENARIOS

If there were several versions of this simple example project, producing multiple spreadsheets would be wasteful and potentially could introduce errors. Similar spreadsheets tend to diverge over time and be more difficult to maintain. Scenarios provide the facility to 'remember' inputs so that you can load them at any time. As an added bonus, Excel will produce a management report based on the scenarios.

Scenarios are accessed using `Tools`, `Scenarios`, `Add` (see Figure 3.46). There are saved cases on the Scenarios sheet.

Fig 3.46

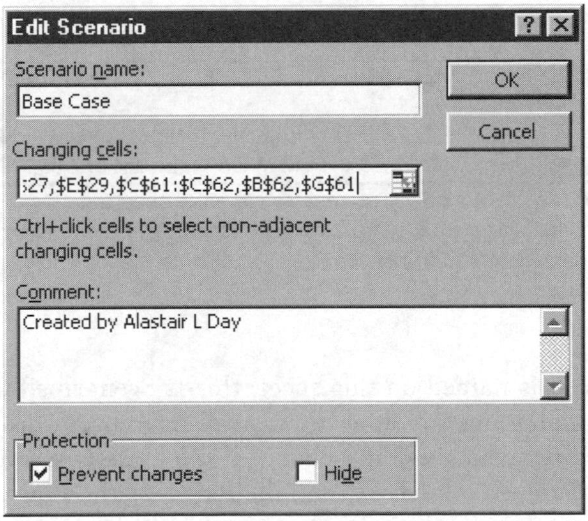

You can select multiple cells by separating them with a comma. When you have selected them, Excel allows you to review the values in each of the cells before saving them. Press `Show` to display the scenario.

There are further examples on the sheet, named best and worst case. These vary only the capital value and periodic cash flow. If you press `Tools`, `Scenarios`, `Summary` and select cells C22 and E22 as the result cells, Excel produces the management report shown in Figure 3.47.

It is always best to start from a Base Case and vary these inputs rather than developing further scenarios. Here Worst and Best Case vary only two cells from the original scenario. It is therefore clearer what changes from the initial estimate.

Fig 3.47

	A	B	C	D	E	F	G
1							
2		Scenario Summary					
3				Current Values:	Base Case	Worst Case	Best Case
5		Changing Cells:					
6			$C$5	100,000.00	100,000.00	103,000.00	99,000.00
7			$C$6	28,000.00	28,000.00	27,000.00	28,500.00
8			$C$7	7,000.00	7,000.00	7,000.00	7,000.00
9			$C$8	1-Jan-01	1-Jan-01	1-Jan-01	1-Jan-01
10			$C$27	0.50%	0.50%	0.50%	0.50%
11			$E$29	9.50%	9.50%	9.50%	9.50%
12			$C$61	0.50%	0.50%	0.50%	0.50%
13			$C$62	3	3	3	3
14			$B$62	8%	8%	8%	8%
15			$G$61	4	4	4	4
16		Result Cells:					
17			NPV	7,502.58	7,502.58	663.20	10,422.27
18			$E$22	NPV is above the limit of 7,000	NPV is above the limit of 7,000	NPV is below the limit of 7,000	NPV is above the limit of 7,000
19		Notes: Current Values column represents values of changing cells at					
20		time Scenario Summary Report was created. Changing cells for each					
21		scenario are highlighted in gray.					
22							

Only one cell is named on this sheet: this is Scenarios!$C$22, which shows as a name in line 17 rather than a cell reference. This is a static or values only report which will not change if the underlying values change. If the model changes, you have to run the report again. It also acts like an audit trail since you could print this out and keep it in a file to show what inputs produce the range of results.

20. GOALSEEK

Data Tables and Scenarios produce management information and make the model more powerful while reducing the amount of necessary code to derive the results. Goalseek assists with 'what-if' by working back from an answer and changing one variable. Suppose you wanted to know what periodic cash flow produces a net present value of 8,000. Rather than entering numbers into cell C6, you could go to `Tools`, `Goalseek` (see Figure 3.48).

The parameters are set cell X to Y by changing Z. This is changing only one parameter at a time by working backward from the answer and converging on the correct input. In this example on the Goalseek sheet, Excel will set the answer to 8,000 by varying the periodic cash flow. The answer is 28129.5568837666. Note that there are no constraints to the calculation and Excel will display an error if it does not find an answer within a specified time or number of attempts. There is no possibility also of using constraints such as forcing a positive answer in the variable. For problems with rules and constraints, you need Solver.

Fig 3.48

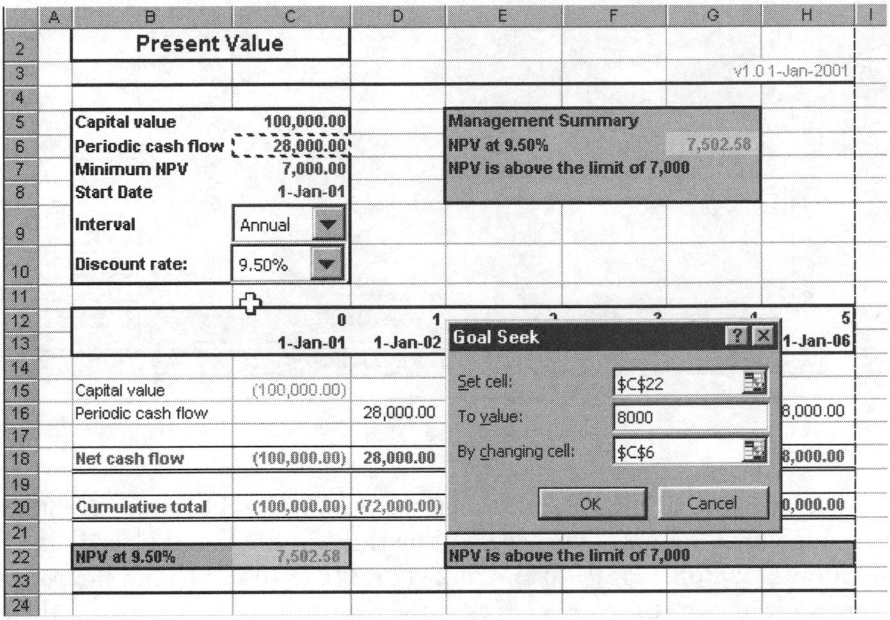

21. SOLVER

Solver is a more advanced form of Goalseek since you can optimize or find values by changing multiple cells subject to constraints. Solver is an add-in to Excel, which has to be installed at the time of installation. Go to `Tools`, `Solver` and if Solver is not there, check that Solver is ticked at `Tools Add-Ins`. If you still cannot find Solver, re-install Excel with this option.

Solver makes it possible to work back from an answer, which can be:

- minimum;
- maximum;
- particular value.

In this example, management wants to know if a net present value of 8,000 is possible if:

- capital value is greater than or equal to 98,500;
- periodic cash flow is less than or equal to 28,500.

Select the Solver sheet and the example can be accessed through `Tools`, `Solver` (see Figure 3.49).

Fig 3.49

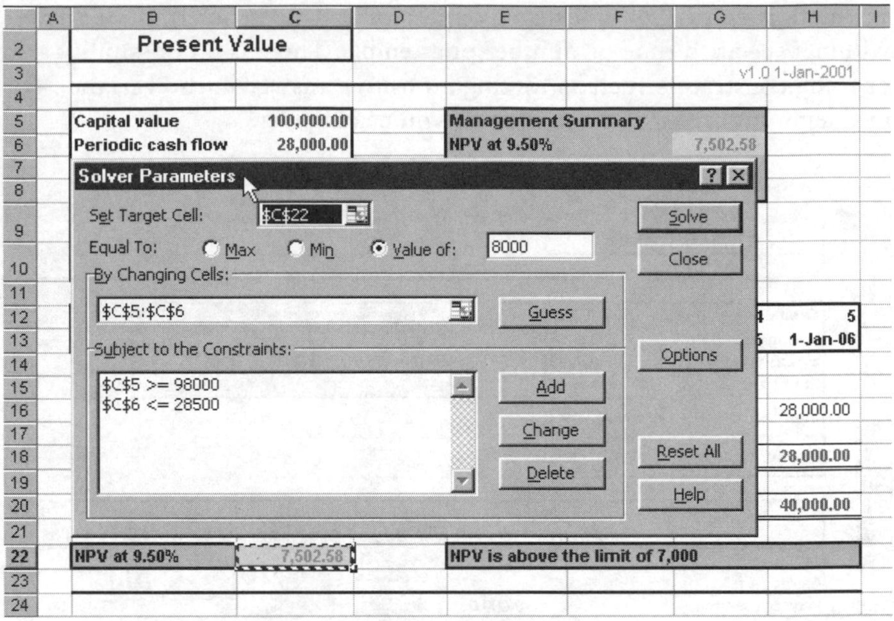

When you press Solve, Excel sets up the problem and tries to solve it. If it cannot, then an error message will be displayed. Here, Solver finds a solution as 99968.3995017415 and 28121.3262540137 within the parameters set above. Usually it is best to get a problem to work and then tighten the parameters. This allows you to see which of your constraints are not allowing Solver to converge on a solution. Solver also produces a management report as shown in Figure 3.50 when you select the option on the Answer dialog.

Fig 3.50

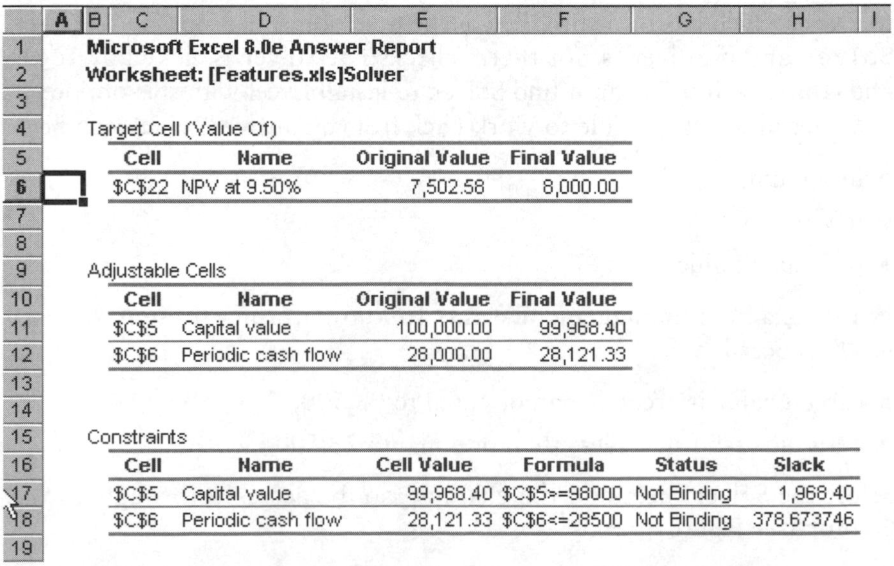
Microsoft Excel 8.0e Answer Report
Worksheet: [Features.xls]Solver

Target Cell (Value Of)

Cell	Name	Original Value	Final Value
$C$22	NPV at 9.50%	7,502.58	8,000.00

Adjustable Cells

Cell	Name	Original Value	Final Value
$C$5	Capital value	100,000.00	99,968.40
$C$6	Periodic cash flow	28,000.00	28,121.33

Constraints

Cell	Name	Cell Value	Formula	Status	Slack
$C$5	Capital value	99,968.40	$C$5>=98000	Not Binding	1,968.40
$C$6	Periodic cash flow	28,121.33	$C$6<=28500	Not Binding	378.673746

The management report shows the amount of 'slack' in the solution. 1,968.40 of 98,000 is not needed as the model stopped at 99,968.40. It is also beneficial to save each of the answers as a scenario since there are now five answers with differing inputs. You can show all the scenarios on the Solver sheet (see Figure 3.51).

Fig 3.51

Scenario Summary	Current Values:	Base Case	Worst Case	Best Case	Goalseek	Solver
Changing Cells:						
$C$5	99,968.40	100,000.00	103,000.00	99,000.00	99,968.40	99,968.40
$C$6	28,121.33	28,000.00	27,000.00	28,500.00	28,129.56	28,121.33
$C$7	7,000.00	7,000.00	7,000.00	7,000.00	7,000.00	7,000.00
$C$8	1-Jan-01	1-Jan-01	1-Jan-01	1-Jan-01	1-Jan-01	1-Jan-01
$C$27	0.50%	0.50%	0.50%	0.50%	0.50%	0.50%
$C$61	0.50%	0.50%	0.50%	0.50%	0.50%	0.50%
$C$62	3	3	3	3	3	3
$B$62	8%	8%	8%	8%	8%	8%
$G$61	4	4	4	4	4	4
Result Cells:						
NPV	8,000.00	7,502.58	663.20	10,422.27	8,031.60	8,000.00
Test	NPV is above the limit of 7,000	NPV is above the limit of 7,000	NPV is below the limit of 7,000	NPV is above the limit of 7,000	NPV is above the limit of 7,000	NPV is above the limit of 7,000

Notes: Current Values column represents values of changing cells at time Scenario Summary Report was created. Changing cells for each scenario are highlighted in gray.

22. USE OF TEMPLATES

Many of the features and formatting in this chapter could be incorporated on a template. It is a waste of time to 'start from scratch' with every new project, when it is advantageous to build up a library of different templates. There is a template on the disk called App_Template, which contains a menu structure and a number of basic macros to automate tasks such as setting up a sheet for printing and basic formatting. It consists of the following sheets:

- a menu with a combo box for selecting sheets – as you add and delete sheets, the macro attached to the combo box updates itself (GetSheetNames);
- a model set out with specific areas together with an area for Scenarios and Goalseek;
- a schedule;
- an explanation sheet ready for documentation on the model;
- a spare.

There is also a series of built-in macros; examples are listed in Table 3.1.

Table 3.1 **Built-in macro**

Macro name	Description
Auto_Open	Sets each sheet to cell A2 and selects Menu sheet.
GetSheetNames	Lists the names of the sheets on the Menu at cell B51.
GetScenarioNames	Lists names of current scenarios on the Model sheet.
Goalseek	Specimen Goalseek program on the Model sheet.
OpenExportForm	Open the Export form where you select a sheet. It exports values only as a copy.
NoticeShow	Displays Notice form.
FormShow	Displays Export form.
CopytoNewBook	Copies sheet values to a new workbook.
CopySheet	Utility routine to copy values.
SetupMenu	Sets up a Menu sheet.
FullScreen	Displays full screen.
AutoCalculation	Sets calculation to automatic.
ManualCalculation	Sets calculation to manual.
SetUpColumns_Sheet	Sets up sheet with title, borders, number formats, etc. as per standard model. This also prepares a sheet for printing together with custom headers and footers.
SetUpSheet	Utility routine to SetUpColumn_Sheet.
Protect_NoPassword	Removes gridlines, row and column headers and protects sheets and workbook with no password.
Unprotect_NoPassword	Reverses the above macro.

Using templates speeds up the development process and reduces the prospect of errors by using a standardized design. The applications in this book have been built using this template and, as one example, the model Features_Application constitutes the completed version. It contains all the features discussed in this chapter.

Similarly, if you have broken down your calculations into segments, you will have generated batches of code that could be used. For example, you produce a grid for calculating UK or US tax allowances. The next time you need this, you can copy and paste the code rather than starting from scratch. You need only update the references and test it with known data. Over time, you can build up code and formulas that can be used in new applications.

The completed Features_Application model shown in Figure 3.52 consists of:

- menu for selecting other schedules;
- model with cash flows and scenario analysis;
- Scenario summary;
- Solver report;
- explanation;
- spare.

Fig 3.52

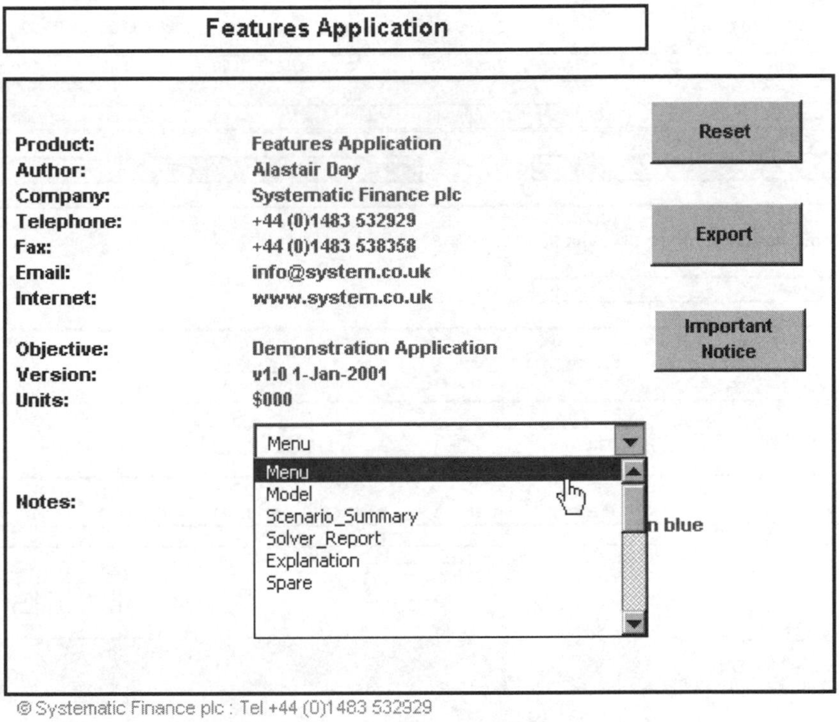

The grid lines, row and column headers have been removed using `Tools`, `Options`, `View`. The schedule is now much more comprehensive than the original spreadsheet shown in Figure 3.53.

The model has been protected using the Protect_NoPassword macro in order to stop accidental overwriting of the cells. This can easily be reversed using Unprotect_NoPassword. For distribution, a password could be added to the macro using this syntax.

```
strPassword = "AAAA"
ActiveSheet.Protect Password:=strPassword
ActiveWorkbook.Protect Password:= strPassword
```

Fig 3.53

Features Application

Menu

v1.0 1-Jan-2001

Capital value	**100,000.00**
Periodic cash flow	**28,000.00**
Minimum NPV	**7,000.00**
Start Date	**1-Jan-01**
Interval	Annual
Discount rate:	9.50%

Management Summary
NPV at 9.50% 7,502.58
NPV is above the limit of 7,000

	0 1-Jan-01	1 1-Jan-02	2 1-Jan-03	3 1-Jan-04	4 1-Jan-05	5 1-Jan-06
Capital value	(100,000.00)					
Periodic cash flow		28,000.00	28,000.00	28,000.00	28,000.00	28,000.00
Net cash flow	**(100,000.00)**	**28,000.00**	**28,000.00**	**28,000.00**	**28,000.00**	**28,000.00**
Cumulative total	**(100,000.00)**	**(72,000.00)**	**(44,000.00)**	**(16,000.00)**	**12,000.00**	**40,000.00**

NPV at 9.50% 7,502.58

NPV is above the limit of 7,000

Sensitivity Table for the Discount Rate

Interval **0.50%**

	8.50%	9.00%	**9.50%**	10.00%	10.50%	11.00%
7,502.58	10,329.30	8,901.26	7,502.58	6,132.50	4,790.24	3,475.09
Variance to 7,503	(2,826.72)	(1,398.67)	-	1,370.09	2,712.34	4,027.49

Selection: 7,502.58 **16**

	8.50%	9.00%	9.50%	10.00%	10.50%	11.00%
NPV: 7,503	**10,329.30**	**8,901.26**	**7,502.58**	**6,132.50**	**4,790.24**	**3,475.09**

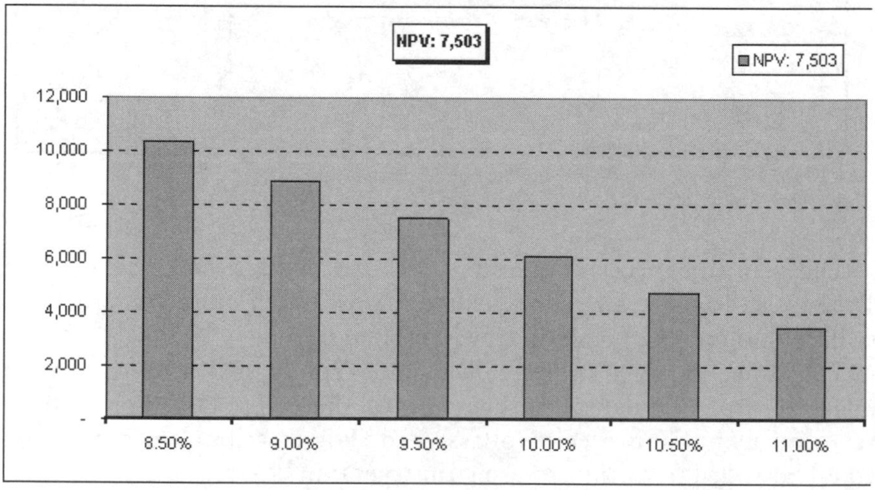

23. SUMMARY

This chapter has concentrated on features within Excel to make financial models clearer and more maintainable and the ways in which different features can be used together. While the NPV example is simplistic, it acts as a vehicle to show the layering and development of this type of model. The features discussed were:

- formats;
- number formats;
- lines and borders;
- colour and patterns;
- specific colour for inputs and results;
- data validation;
- controls – combo boxes and buttons;
- conditional formatting;
- use of functions and types of function;
- add-ins for more functions;
- text and updated labels;
- recording a version number, author, etc.;
- using names to make formulas easier;
- pasting a names table as part of documentation;
- comment cells;
- graphics;
- dynamic graphs to plot individual lines;
- data tables;
- Scenarios;
- Goalseek;
- Solver;
- use of templates and reusable code.

4

Sample model

The first chapter reviewed a simple model and listed a number of shortcomings with the design methodology. This section reintroduces the model (Simple_Model.xls) and progresses through the design using the methods in Chapters 2 and 3. As already stated, it is imperative to use a consistent approach to reduce uncertainty and errors and make your work more accessible to others. The revised model is called Investment_Model.xls. The original model is shown in Figure 4.1.

Fig 4.1

	A	B	C	D	E	F	G	H	I	J	K
1		**Project Appraisal Model**									
2											
3					Year 0	Year 1	Year 2	Year 3	Year 4	Year 5	Year 6
4											
5		Cost of equipment			-750,000						
6		Maintenance			0	-10,000	-10,000	-10,000	-10,000	-10,000	
7		Installation			-50,000						
8		Reduction in overheads			75,000	125,000	0	0	0	0	
9		Saving in production time			0	130,000	130,000	125,000	125,000	125,000	
10		Tax @ 30%			0	82500	-6000	14600	3468.75	-6023.44	50929.8
11		Net cash flows			-725,000	327,500	114,000	129,600	118,469	108,977	50,930
12											
13		Factor			1.0000	0.9434	0.8900	0.8396	0.7921	0.7473	0.7050
14											
15		Cash Flow			-725,000	308,962	101,460	108,815	93,838	81,434	35,903
16											
17		NPV @ 6%			5,411.99						
18											
19											
20				WDV		Cashflow	Year				
21				1,200,000							
22		CA	0	-300000		90000	1				
23				900,000							
24		CA	1	-225000		67500	2				
25				675,000							
26		CA	2	-168750		50625	3				
27				506,250							
28		CA	3	-126563		37968.75	4				
29				379,688							
30		CA	4	-94922		28476.56	5				
31				284,766							
32		BA	5	-284,766		85429.8	6				
33		Sales proceeds		0							
34						360000					
35											

1. AIMS AND OBJECTIVES

The main objective is to produce a spreadsheet model that clearly shows the variables for the net present value calculation and calculates the correct answer. The aims are:

- simplicity;
- easy to use;
- easy to maintain and modify;
- reduction in code as far as possible;
- precise management reporting.

The file Investment_Model was started using the template file, App_Template.xlt with the basic layout, formats, macros and other utilities. This was to save time and ensure the adoption of a structure.

2. USER NEEDS AND USER INTERFACE

The user needs to understand what to do. As he opens the file, the Auto_Open macro runs. If you call a macro Auto_Open, the macro runs every time you open the file. Similarly, a macro called Auto_Close will run when the file is closed. This macro:

- counts the number of sheets in the workbook and for each sheet sets it to cell A2 at the top of the page;
- selects the first sheet, which is the Menu (see Figure 4.2).

There is room on the Menu to write notes about the application. The user can then select a sheet using the control and a macro is attached to it to display the selected sheet. The workings for the control are at row 50 out of sight.

Selecting the Model sheet presents the standard layout of inputs, calculations, answer, management summary and workings. This is consistent with other models and the user knows what to expect. The inputs are in the top left as the most logical place. As the inputs change, the summary updates and this saves scrolling to the bottom of the page.

The interface uses a selection of the features such as borders, colours, etc. to make it more attractive. The input cells are in bold blue to inform the user where data is required and go down the page. This is more logical than scrolling across to enter data.

Fig 4.2

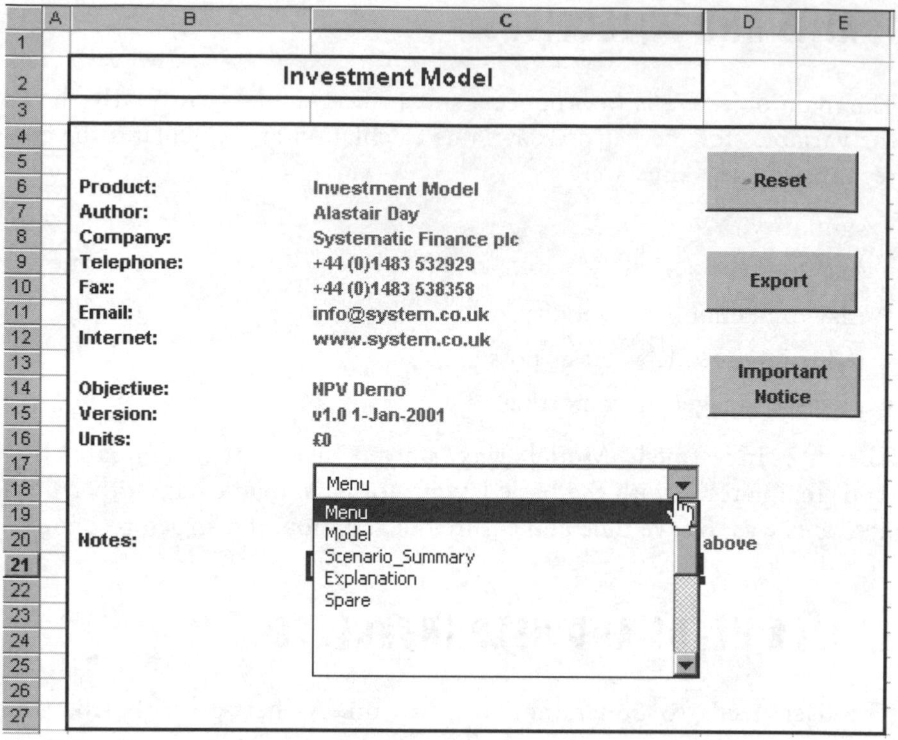

3. KEY VARIABLES AND RULES

The original sheet entered the data on the sheet, whereas the revised version lists all the possible variables (see Figure 4.3).

Fig 4.3

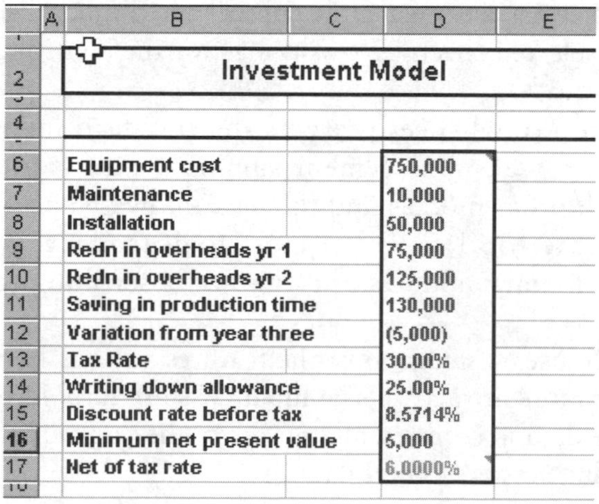

Lines 8 and 9 of the original model show changes to the overheads, which need to be modelled here on rows 9 and 10. Similarly the saving in production time reduces in year 3 and this is hard coded on the original model. These items are placed together so that the user knows that a change in this area will ripple through the model.

For simplicity, the tax delay is assumed as one year, but strictly this is also a variable. The tax depreciation for equipment cost of 750,000 starts in year 2. This is calculated as per UK methodology in the workings at the bottom (see Figure 4.4). The depreciation is 25% of the balance such that year one is 25% of 750,000. (Depreciation methods are discussed in more detail in Chapter 17.)

Fig 4.4

	A	B	C	D	E	F	G
67							
68		**Workings**					
69				**WDV**		**Cashflow**	**Year**
70				750,000			
71		CA	0	(187,500)		56,250	1
72				562,500			
73		CA	1	(140,625)		42,188	2
74				421,875			
75		CA	2	(105,469)		31,641	3
76				316,406			
77		CA	3	(79,102)		23,730	4
78				237,305			
79		CA	4	(59,326)		17,798	5
80				177,979			
81		BA	5	(177,979)		53,394	6
82		Sales proceeds		-			
83						225,000	
84		Calculation Check: No tax depreciation errors					
85							

This is the corrected table: 25% of 750,000 is 187,500 and the tax cash flow at 30% is 56,250. In the next year the depreciation is 25% of the balance brought forward of 562,500. At the bottom, there is a calculation check to ensure that the cumulative total is 30% of the capital value, i.e. 225,000. The formula in cell B84 is:

```
=IF(F83<>D6*D13,"ERROR: Tax does not add up to capital
*tax", "Calculation Check: No tax depreciation errors")
```

This is an IF statement to ensure that the model is self-checking and Excel takes as many decisions as possible (see Figure 4.5).

Another feature is the sign for the cash flows. You make fewer errors if you consider money out to be negative and money in to be positive. In this example, the depreciation is negative in the workings; however, the expenditure saves tax so this is positive.

Fig 4.5

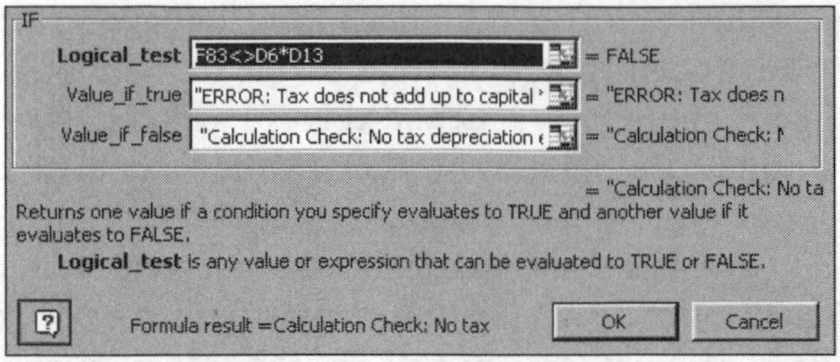

Looking at the problem in detail and checking that all the possible variables are isolated can assist in understanding the problem and the processes. In this example, why do the savings and overheads reduction fall in the later years and are there any other factors that are not included? The initial example simply coded the numbers without explanation. With this group of inputs, there is more scope for examining the sensitivity of the model or running a series of scenarios.

4. BREAK DOWN THE CALCULATIONS INTO MANAGEABLE GROUPS

The model uses areas on the sheet to delineate

- inputs
- calculations
- output answer
- sensitivity table
- management summary
- workings.

The calculations area gains its data from the input cells and the information flows logically through the model to the answers at the bottom. Colours, formats and borders are used sparingly to ensure that the printout will be readable on a black and white laser printer.

5. SETTING UP INDIVIDUAL MODULES

The programming of the calculations area is kept as simple as possible and the tax calculation is separate in the workings shown in Figure 4.6. Here they can be audited and checked with a calculator for mathematical errors. Similarly, the author does not try to calculate the complete tax calculation on one line. The equipment is on line 29 and the tax payment on the maintenance and cost savings on line 30.

Fig 4.6

Investment Model

Menu | Update Tab

6	Equipment cost	750,000	Results Summary	
7	Maintenance	10,000	Net Present Value @ 6.00%:	
8	Installation	50,000	NPV greater than 5,000:	
9	Reduction in overheads year 1	75,000	NPV % of initial investment:	
10	Reduction in overheads year 2	125,000	Internal Rate of Return:	
11	Saving in production time	130,000	Margin above net of tax rate:	
12	Variation from year three	(5,000)		
13	Tax Rate	30.00%		
14	Writing down allowance	25.00%		
15	Discount rate before tax	8.5714%		
16	Minimum net present value	5,000		
17	Net of tax rate	6.0000%		

20	Year	0	1	2	3	4
22	Equipment cost	(750,000)				
23	Maintenance		(10,000)	(10,000)	(10,000)	(10,000)
24	Installation	(50,000)				
25	Reduction in overheads	75,000	125,000			
26	Saving in production time		130,000	130,000	125,000	125,000
27	**Pre-tax cash flows**	**(725,000)**	**245,000**	**120,000**	**115,000**	**115,000**
29	Tax depreciation		56,250	42,188	31,641	23,730
30	Tax @ 30.00%		(7,500)	(73,500)	(36,000)	(34,500)
31	**Net after-tax cash flows**	**(725,000)**	**293,750**	**88,688**	**110,641**	**104,230**
33	**Net Present Value @ 6.00%:**	(106,716.14)				
34	**NPV greater than 5,000:**	No				
35	**Internal Rate of Return:**	-0.57%				

There is also a line for pre- and post-tax cash flows, so that you can test the result if the company is not tax paying. Again, this is trying to make the model as flexible as possible and providing a total that can be checked using a calculator.

Cell B33 contains the NPV function, which discounts the cash flows in years 1–6 and adds the initial expenditure.

```
=NPV(D17,E31:J31)+D31
```

There is a management test on the answer against the minimum of 5,000 and for completeness an internal rate of return using the function IRR.

6. MENU STRUCTURE

The model uses a simple menu structure as per the Application Template. A macro is attached to the combo box, which runs a macro called

GetSheetNames. This:

- counts the number of sheets in the workbook;
- obtains the name of each sheet;
- populates a table at row 50, by offsetting down by one row;
- breaks out of the loop when it reaches the total number of sheets;
- selects the sheet index for the control in cell C50.

This is the menu macro assigned to the combo box in the file Menu_Structure, which simplifies the above. The code is provided in the Application Template so that you can use it in your own work. This macro below:

- assigns a value to a variable called IndexNumber;
- selects Worksheet 1 – i.e. the menu;
- selects the sheet number returned by the combo box.

```
Sub SelectSheet()
Dim IndexNumber
IndexNumber = Range("C30") + 1
Worksheets(1).Select
Range("A2").Select
Sheets(IndexNumber).Select
Range("A2").Select
End Sub
```

7. PROGRAM SHEETS AND MACROS

It is useful to automate simple tasks such as Print Preview. This is not intended to be a programming manual for Visual Basic, although you can record simple macros: insert a button from `View`, `Toolbars`, `Forms` and then assign the macro to it.

The steps in recording the PrintPreview macro (see Figure 4.7) were:

- Go to `Tools`, `Macros`, `Record New Macro`.
- Give the macro a name.
- Record the key strokes, in this case simply `Print Preview`.

Fig 4.7

- Press the `Stop Recording` button to turn off the recorder.
- Go to `Tools`, `View`, `Toolbars`, `Forms`.
- Press the button and then draw a button on the sheet.
- When asked for a macro name, select PrintPreview or the name you gave it.
- Update the text while the button is highlighted. You can update the button at any time by right clicking it.

The button should then run the macro every time you press it. While this command is available on the main toolbar, it is usually easier for a user simply to click the button. There are further examples of macros in later chapters.

8. USER ASSISTANCE

User assistance is provided by:

- comments cells;
- data validation.

Comments and instructions are in the inputs area in Figure 4.8 to inform the user what is required.

Fig 4.8

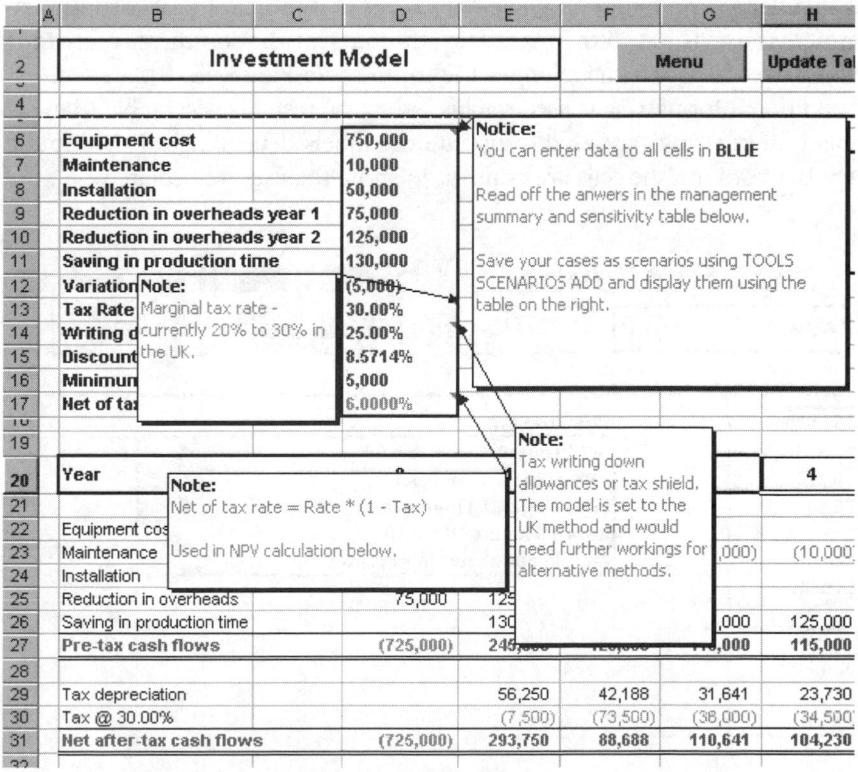

The percentages in cells D13 to D15 are validated to ensure that the value is less than 1 or 100% (see Figure 4.9).

Fig 4.9

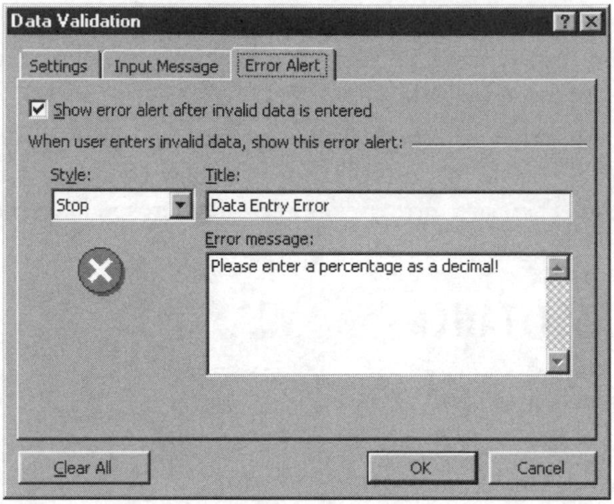

9. MANAGEMENT REPORTS AND SUMMARIES

This is a very simple model. Nevertheless, it is important that a summary is immediately visible to the user. The summary at the top displays instant feedback to the user as he changes the inputs (see Figure 4.10).

Conditional formatting is used to check that the result is acceptable to management. Text strings are used to update the labels depending on the inputs. Where the test fails, the cells are crimson to show the user immediately.

Fig 4.10

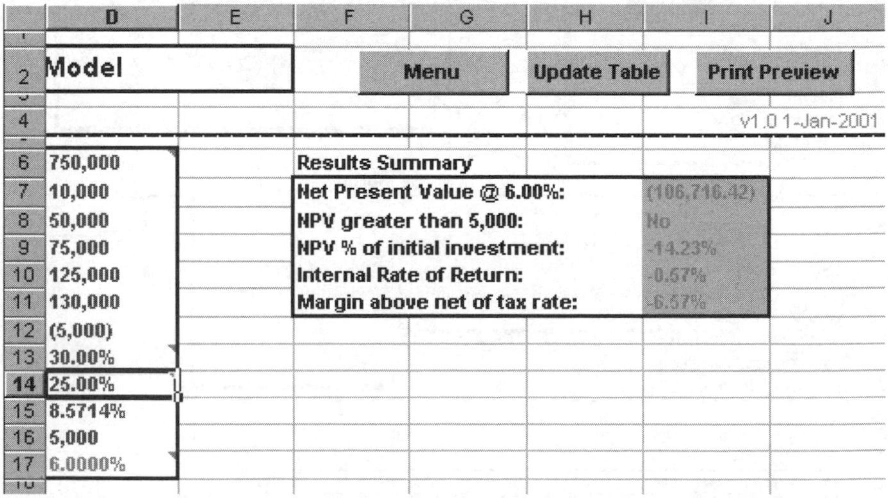

In a larger model, a management summary would normally be placed on a separate sheet. For example, in accounts analysis, the summary would consolidate the profit and loss, balance sheet, cash flow statement and ratio analysis.

10. RISK AND MULTIPLE ANSWERS

The model includes a sensitivity table of the net present value based on a series of discount rates (see Figure 4.11). The printing of the schedule places the detail in the sensitivity tables on page 2, with the title rows on page 1 repeated at the top of page 2.

Fig 4.11

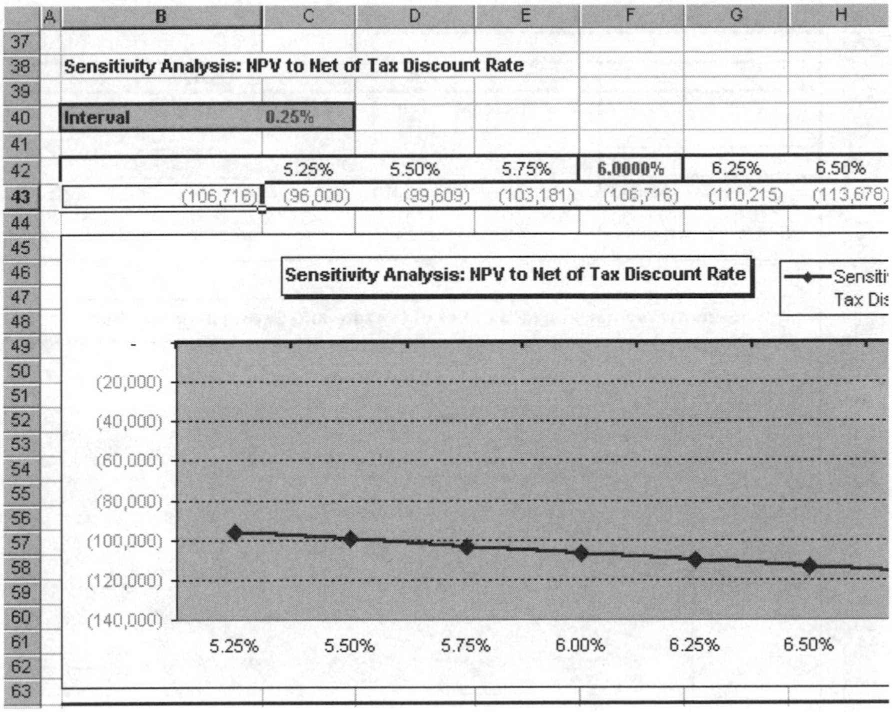

With the correct tax calculations, the net present value is –106,716 as opposed to 5,411. Cell D102 has to be updated from cell D6. As discussed in Chapter 3, it is important to set the grid for the data table correctly:

- Cell B43 points to the NPV cell and the Table array function is found on the toolbar at `Data, Table`.
- The interval is used to update the row of discount values.
- The current discount rate is placed in the middle.

You insert the function by highlighting cells B42:J43. The row input is D17 and since it is a one-dimensional table, there is no column input. Excel inserts the net present value for each of the discount rates. The table shows the sensitivity of the result to changes in the discount rate. A graph assists since the slope of the graph shows the degree of change.

There is also a two-dimensional table with the discount rate across and the saving in production time down. The format is slightly different, as shown in Figure 4.12.

Fig 4.12

	A	B	C	D	E	F	G
65		**Sensitivity Analysis: NPV to Net of tax rate and Saving in production time**					
66							
67		**Discount Rate Interval**		**0.25%**			
68		**Saving in production time**		**25,000**			
69							
70		(106,716)	5.25%	5.50%	5.75%	**6.00%**	6.25%
71		80,000	(249,707)	(252,409)	(255,081)	(257,726)	(260,342)
72		105,000	(172,853)	(176,009)	(179,131)	(182,221)	(185,279)
73		**130,000**	(96,000)	(99,609)	(103,181)	(106,716)	(110,215)
74		155,000	(19,146)	(23,210)	(27,231)	(31,212)	(35,151)
75		180,000	57,708	53,190	48,719	44,293	39,912

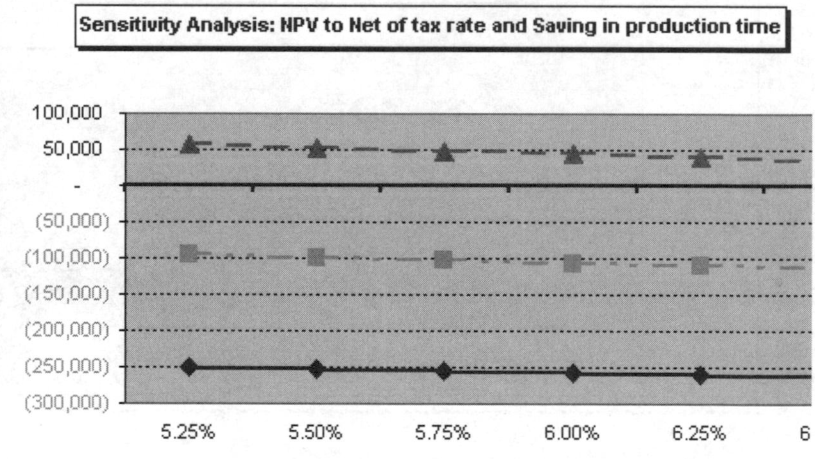

Cell B70 looks up the NPV in the top left-hand corner of the table. Again, the items at the top and left depend on the interval rather than hard coding in the table. Note that one input on each axis has to be an absolute otherwise the table will not function and you will get the same figures either across or down.

You insert the table again by highlighting the whole table from B70 to J75 and going to `Data`, `Table`. The two inputs are cell D17 for the row and cell D11 for the column. Excel fills in the grid of values as above and provides the user with multiple answers of how the model 'flexes'.

Again, a graph helps to show the pattern of the results. In Figure 4.13 the top, bottom and middle lines are added to the chart. The series names are the left-hand labels.

Fig 4.13

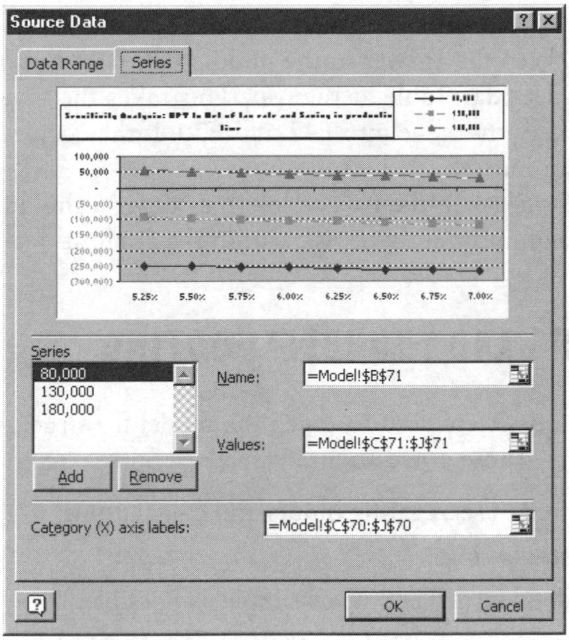

Conditional formatting is used to highlight the answer in the middle. If the answer is visible, one can be more confident that the table is function-

Fig 4.14

ing correctly. This is achieved by highlighting the results (cells C71 to J75) and accessing `Format, Conditional Formatting` (see Figure 4.14).

If the value is equal to the answer in cell B70, then the format changes as above in the table. With the answer in the middle, you could consider the answer to be the cell and those clustered around it. Given that the model is only a considered view of the possible cash flows, sensitivity testing shows in part how likely the end result will be within a range. Here you could consider cells E72 to G74 to be the likely range. Alternatively, you could rephrase it as the risk factors in the model.

In order to keep the answer in the middle there is a button attached to a macro called UpdateTable at the top. This takes the value in cell D17 and paste specials the value into F42 and F70. It then copies cell D11 and paste specials it into B73.

Chapter 16 on risk in the Part B describes other techniques for reviewing the degree of uncertainty or risk within the application.

11. TESTING AND TROUBLESHOOTING

Several techniques were used to check the model for structural and mathematical errors. Those noted so far:

- design method in segregating inputs and calculations;
- splitting out workings;
- keeping individual cell coding as simple as possible;
- self-checking, e.g. cell B116 on the Investment Model calculation displays: 'Check: No tax depreciation errors'. Another example would be making sure a balance sheet adds up on both sides.

Other methods detailed below are possible involving other features in Excel.

Use known data with an entry to every input cell

This was not possible on the model in Chapter 1 (Simple_Model.xls) as the inputs were not defined making it very difficult to check. With the current example, there is data in each of the inputs; however, it would always be a good idea to see what happens if unusual data were entered. Users can always be relied on not to follow instructions. Techniques such as data validation obviously help in avoiding 'rubbish in, rubbish out'.

Graph or data 'looks right'

The graphs on the second sensitivity table in the Investment Model are smooth with no kinks as expected. If the series were curved then this could point to an error in the calculations. People are better in assessing pictures than grids of numbers and can 'see' errors more quickly.

Audit toolbar

The audit toolbar can be displayed by pressing on the menu-bar `Tools`, `Auditing`, `Show Auditing Toolbar` (see Figure 4.15). These examples use Simple_Model.xls which was introduced in Chapter 1. Several errors were noted in the model, which could have been found more easily using simple techniques.

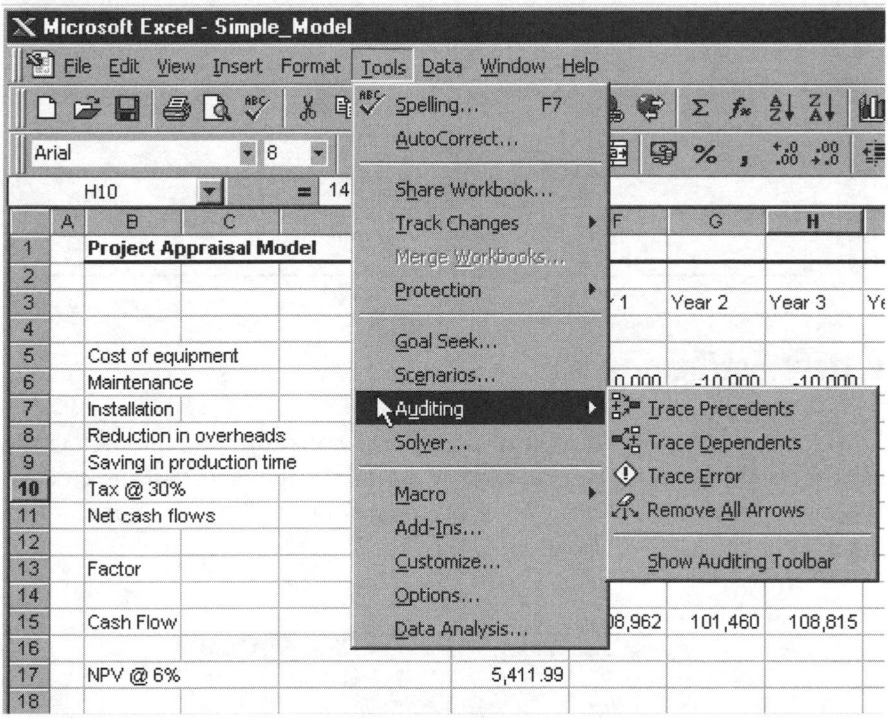

Fig 4.15

You can trace precedents and dependants for a cell (see Figure 4.16). The tax row 10 underlines the errors in cells G10 and H10 since there are no precedents. The cell formulas have been overwritten with numbers. Cell F10 obtains its data from the costs and savings above and the tax depreciation in the lower table.

Fig 4.16

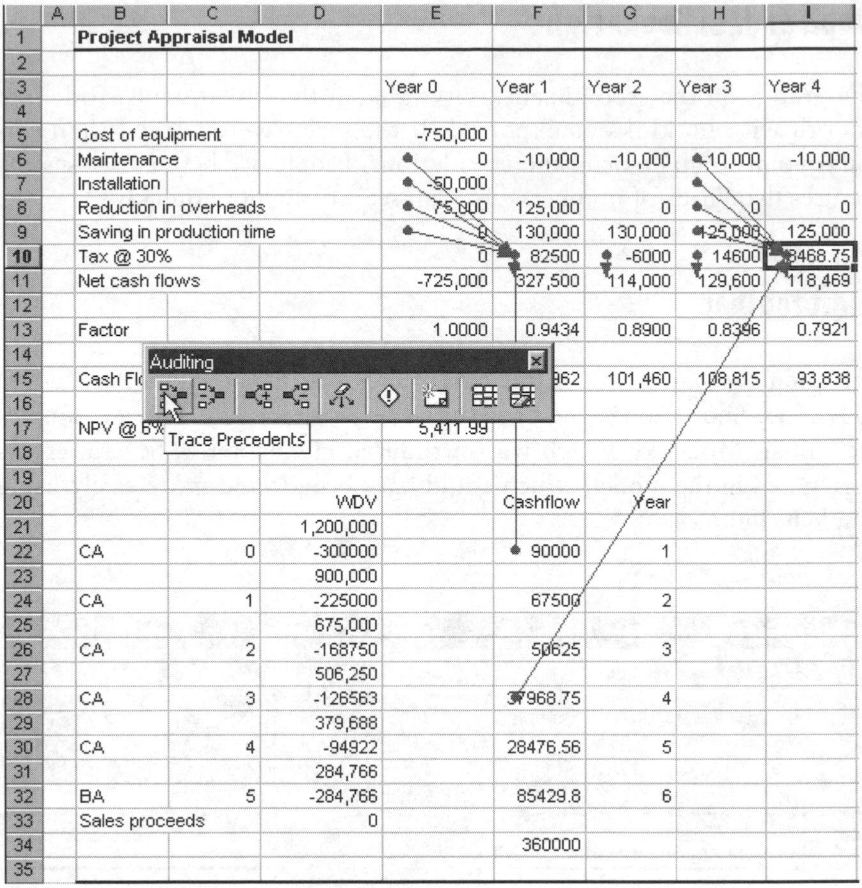

	A	B	C	D	E	F	G	H	I
1		Project Appraisal Model							
2									
3					Year 0	Year 1	Year 2	Year 3	Year 4
4									
5		Cost of equipment			-750,000				
6		Maintenance			0	-10,000	-10,000	-10,000	-10,000
7		Installation			-50,000				
8		Reduction in overheads			75,000	125,000	0	0	0
9		Saving in production time			0	130,000	130,000	125,000	125,000
10		Tax @ 30%			0	82500	-6000	14600	3468.75
11		Net cash flows			-725,000	327,500	114,000	129,600	118,469
12									
13		Factor			1.0000	0.9434	0.8900	0.8396	0.7921
14									
15		Cash Fl				962	101,460	108,815	93,838
16									
17		NPV @ 6%			5,411.99				
18									
19									
20				WDV		Cashflow	Year		
21				1,200,000					
22		CA	0	-300000		90000	1		
23				900,000					
24		CA	1	-225000		67500	2		
25				675,000					
26		CA	2	-168750		50625	3		
27				506,250					
28		CA	3	-126563		37968.75	4		
29				379,688					
30		CA	4	-94922		28476.56	5		
31				284,766					
32		BA	5	-284,766		85429.8	6		
33		Sales proceeds		0					
34						360000			
35									

Pattern matching

Pattern matching allows you to search for constants, formulas, arrays, etc. In the above example, this would highlight the errors in the calculations. Select cells E10 to K15 and access `Edit, Go to Special` to display the dialog box shown in Figure 4.17.

Fig 4.17

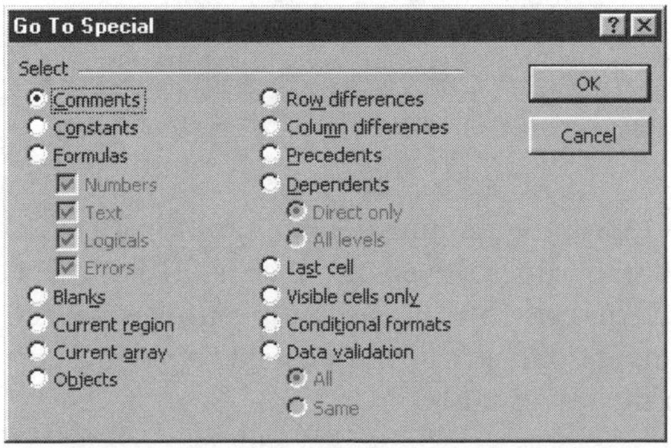

If you highlight formulas, Excel shows the formulas. You would expect to see formulas all across row 10 since it purports to compute the annual tax position (see Figure 4.18).

Fig 4.18

	A	B	C	D	E	F	G	H	I
1		**Project Appraisal Model**							
2									
3					Year 0	Year 1	Year 2	Year 3	Year 4
4									
5		Cost of equipment			-750,000				
6		Maintenance			0	-10,000	-10,000	-10,000	-10,000
7		Installation			-50,000				
8		Reduction in overheads			75,000	125,000	0	0	0
9		Saving in production time			0	130,000	130,000	125,000	125,000
10		Tax @ 30%			0	82500	-6000	14600	3468.75
11		Net cash flows			-725,000	327,500	114,000	129,600	118,469
12									
13		Factor			1.0000	0.9434	0.8900	0.8396	0.7921
14									
15		Cash Flow			-725,000	308,962	101,460	108,815	93,838
16									
17		NPV @ 6%			5,411.99				

View formulas

Viewing formulas shows the formulas, and if there are constant values, these cells will not change. You can select View Formulas at `Tools`, `Options`, `View`. Alternatively you can press `Ctrl` + and ` to toggle between the two views.

Using the above example, the errors again become apparent (see Figure 4.19). The errors in cells G10 and H10 show up against cell F10, which contains the correct code.

Fig 4.19

	E	F	G	H
1				
2				
3	Year 0	Year 1	Year 2	Year 3
4				
5	-750000			
6	0	-10000	-10000	-10000
7	-50000			
8	75000	125000	0	0
9	0	130000	130000	125000
10	0	=+F22-(E6+E7+E8+E9)	-6000	14600
11	=SUM(E5:E10)	=SUM(F5:F10)	=SUM(G5:G10)	=SUM(H5:H10)
12				
13	=1/(1+6%)^0	=1/(1+6%)^1	=1/(1+6%)^2	=1/(1+6%)^3
14				
15	=E11*E13	=F11*F13	=G11*G13	=H11*H13
16				
17	=SUM(E15:K15)			

12. PROTECTING AND SECURING

The Investment Model contains a macro to protect each sheet and the workbook and one to unprotect it. These are attached to buttons on the Explanation sheet. The code also includes passwords with the lines remarked out. Note that passwords are case sensitive. If you lose a password, you will not be able to unprotect them.

Below is the specimen code for protecting the application, which counts the sheets and accesses them in turn on a loop to protect them. Finally, the macro protects the workbook.

```
Sub Protect_NoPassword()
' Keyboard Shortcut: Ctrl+w

Dim Number, Counter
Dim strPassword As String

strPassword = "Systematic"
'On Error GoTo Error:

Application.ScreenUpdating = False
Number = ActiveWorkbook.Sheets.Count
Counter = 1
For Counter = 1 To Number
     Worksheets(Counter).Activate
     ActiveWindow.DisplayHeadings = False
     ActiveWindow.DisplayGridlines = False
     ActiveSheet.Protect
     'ActiveSheet.Protect Password:=strPassword
     ActiveWindow.LargeScroll Up:=100
     ActiveWindow.LargeScroll ToLeft:=100
     Range("A2").Select
Next Counter

Error:
Worksheets(1).Select
Range("A2").Select
ActiveWorkbook.Protect
'ActiveWorkbook.Protect Password:=strPassword
Application.ScreenUpdating = True
End Sub
```

You can also protect your macros. Protecting the workbook does not automatically lock the Visual Basic code.

- Go to `Tools, Macros, Visual Basic Editor`.
- Click on the file name in the VBA project window.
- Select `Tools, VBA Project Properties`.

- Select `Protection`, lock for viewing.
- Enter a password twice to confirm.
- Write down the password or start a separate passwords Excel sheet. If you lose your passwords, you will not be able to access your code.

13. HELP AND DOCUMENTATION

The template framework inserts an Explanation sheet automatically. This sheet contains a listings:

- Notes
- Names List.

There could also be background on the methodology, formulas, reasons for using a particular structure or techniques. It is of course better to place notes in the application as these could assist a user in understanding the methodology. If you do not want others to see your notes, you can always hide the sheet and then protect the workbook only.

Fig 4.20

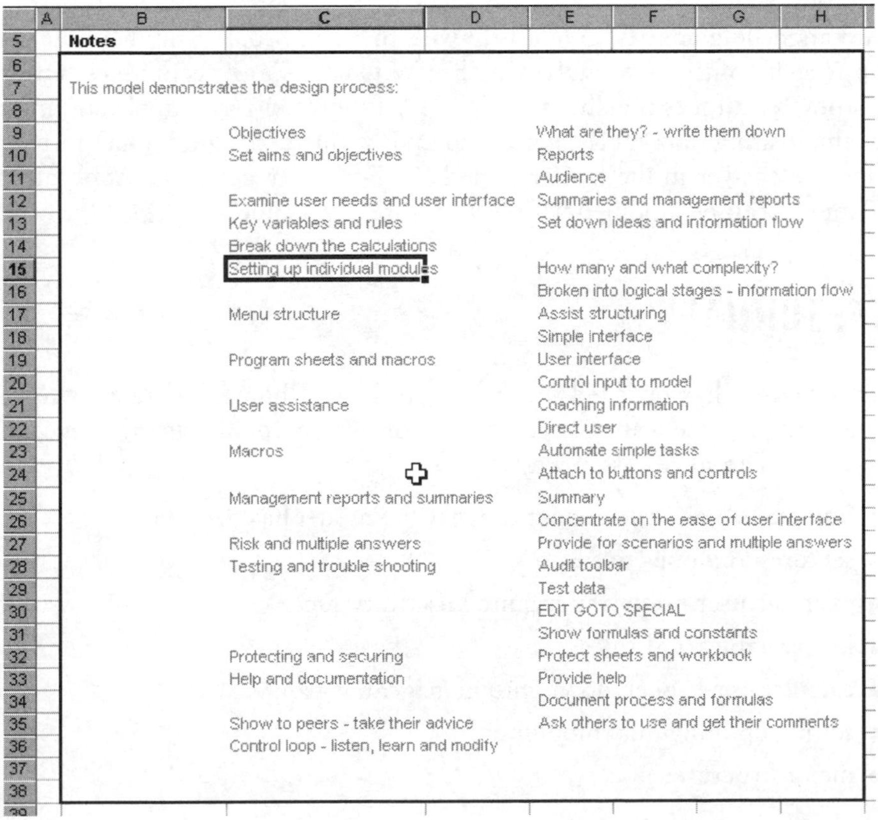

The model may also be more maintainable. If you look at work you did more than a year ago, the reasons for a particular course of action may not always be obvious. The common example is a budget model, which is updated every year. In the interim, you forget how it works and have to spend time understanding the methodology.

14. SHOW TO PEERS – TAKE THEIR ADVICE

The final stage is to expose the model or application to users or others for comments. It is rare that anyone can think of all angles. Particularly with regard to usability, it is important to get a second opinion. Similarly, a user may see an error just by scanning, or alternatively suggest further enhancements to the design. The approach in the previous chapter was to write a simple model and then 'layer' on the features to make the model more powerful. If the design is modular, developments should be possible to the initial design.

15. CONTROL LOOP – LISTEN, LEARN AND MODIFY

Any modelling activity should help with the next project and therefore the approach continually evolves with new features and techniques. Often putting techniques together makes a much more powerful application, for example using data tables, macros to update the table, conditional formatting the answer in the table and a chart. For this reason, the Application Template can be modified with new features over time.

16. SUMMARY

This chapter has revisited the simple model in Chapter 1 and shown the stages to produce a structured application which applies finance concepts to Excel. The stages listed were:

- objectives – clear statement of what the model has to achieve;
- set aims and objectives;
- examine user needs and required user interface;
- key variables and rules;
- calculations broken down into manageable groups;
- setting up individual modules;
- menu structure;

- program sheets and macros;
- user assistance;
- management reports and summaries;
- risk and multiple answers;
- testing and troubleshooting;
- protecting and securing;
- help and documentation;
- show to peers – take their advice;
- control loop – listen, learn and modify.

5

Example model

This chapter builds on the design, features and methodology in previous chapters and demonstrates the development of a further model through six stages. The models are named PPP_1 to PPP_6 and you can either follow the progress using the completed version for that stage or start with the first file and add the features yourself.

The case outlines some of the cash flows in an outsourcing model where government or business can contract with a third party to provide a service. In the UK, this is termed by government Public Private Partnership (PPP) or Private Finance Initiative (PFI), where the government awards a contract in return for private sector investment and commitment and seeks a transfer of risk away from the government. The charges for the service are based on the contractual payment schedules including any penalty charges for non-performance by the contractor.

1. CASE STUDY

The objective is to develop a non-tax investment model, with incremental cash flows, from investing in new equipment on a management contract. The following information is given:

- The client is the Health Authority with 15,000 staff at an average cost of employment of £30,000 per employee.
- It expects 12% savings in steady-state on staff costs from the PFI/PPP.
- Each member of staff has a hardware/software combination costing £2,000 per employee, which the Authority expects to replace over a period of five years.
- Maintenance is based on 10% of the value of the hardware and software.

- These costs would also be saved under PFI/PPP:
  - phasing 50% in year 1 and 100% thereafter;
  - the payments to the contractor are expected to be £60 million a year in steady state, and changes to the tune of £500,000 are budgeted for.
- To simplify the model, inflation is ignored.

The client requires a positive net present value, which is greater than 20% of the annual contractor fee. This is the basic management test to be determined by the model.

2. DESIGN

Table 5.1 summarizes the design methodology followed in this book and is useful as a reminder or tick list of areas to be considered.

Summary of design methodology

Table 5.1

No.	Stage	Comments	Reply
1	Objectives	What are they? Write them down	Management report
2	User needs and interface	Reports	Simple report
		Audience	
		Summaries and management reports	
3	Key variables and rules	Set down ideas and information flow	Inputs/calculations/ reports
		What are the key inputs?	Initial template
4	Calculations	Key calculations	Net present value and management test
5	Write modules and code	How many and what complexity	Menu, model and explanation sheets
		User interface	Menu sheet
		Control input to model	Data validation
6	Menu structure	Direct user	Provide 'coaching'
		Simple interface	Colours, formats, etc.
7	Macros	Automate simple tasks and attach to buttons and controls	Menu macros

		Concentrate on the ease of user interface	Use of controls where possible
8	User assistance	Coaching	Validation, comments
9	Management summary	Single sheet or area	Summary
10	Risk and multiple answers	Provide for scenarios and multiple answers	Data tables and scenarios
11	Testing	Audit toolbar	Check workings of model
		Test data	
		EDIT GOTO SPECIAL	
		Show formulas and constants	
12	Protecting and securing	Protect sheets and workbook to prevent changes	Set up printing and securing ready for distribution
13	Help	Provide help	Comments
		Document process and formulas	Names table
14	Show to peers – take their advice	Ask others to use and get their comments	
15	Control loop	Listen, learn and modify	

3. PPP 1

The first stage on file PPP_1 is to set out a working layout for ease of display and a final management report (see Figure 5.1). This means:

- inputs all in one place and colour coded;
- calculations only in cash flow calculation area;
- some explanation of cash flows;
- summary area for answer and management test.

The rules for each of the cash flows are in cells C23 to C32 to aid understanding. For example, staff costs comprise the number of staff multiplied by the individual cost multiplied by the forecast percentage savings.

Fig 5.1

	A	B	C	D	E	F
1						
2		PPP Case Study 1				
3						
4						
5		Staff Numbers:	15,000		Results	
6		Cost per Head:	30,000		Net Present Value:	
7		Staff Savings:	12.00%		Percentage of Annual Payments:	
8		Equipment per Employee:	2,000			
9		Replacement Period:	5.0 years		Management Tests	
10		Maintenance:	10.00%		Savings	20.00%
11		Annual Payments:	60,000,000			
12		Equipment Changes:	500,000			
13		Discount Rate:	6.00%			
14						
15		Year	Input Reference	-	1	2
16				Jan-01	Jan-02	Jan-03
17						
18		Phasing:			50.00%	100.00%
19		Procurement:			-	-
20		Contract Management:		1,000,000	250,000	500,000
21						
22		(A) Non-adjusted costs and savings				
23		Staff Costs	Nos * Cost * Percent			
24						
25		Hardware and Software	[(Nos * Equipment) / Period]			
26						
27		Maintenance	Nos * Equipment * Saving			
28						
29		Contract Management	Mgt Fee			
30						
31		Contractor and Lease Fees	Annual Pmts			
32		Annual Changes	Equipment Changes			
33						
34		Total				
35						

4. PPP 2

The next stage is to complete the cash flows by multiplying out the variables as shown on file PPP 2 (see Figure 5.2).

The model now exhibits further features.

Names

On the Menu sheet, there are several names assigned for clarity. The author is consistent in the use of names such as Version, Contact, Product, etc. These are common to all models, since it is important that version numbers where possible appear on the printed schedules.

You define Names using `Insert`, `Name` (see Figure 5.3).

It is useful to paste a list of names on a separate sheet as part of the documentation using `Insert Name`, `Paste`, `Paste List` (see Figure 5.4).

Fig 5.2

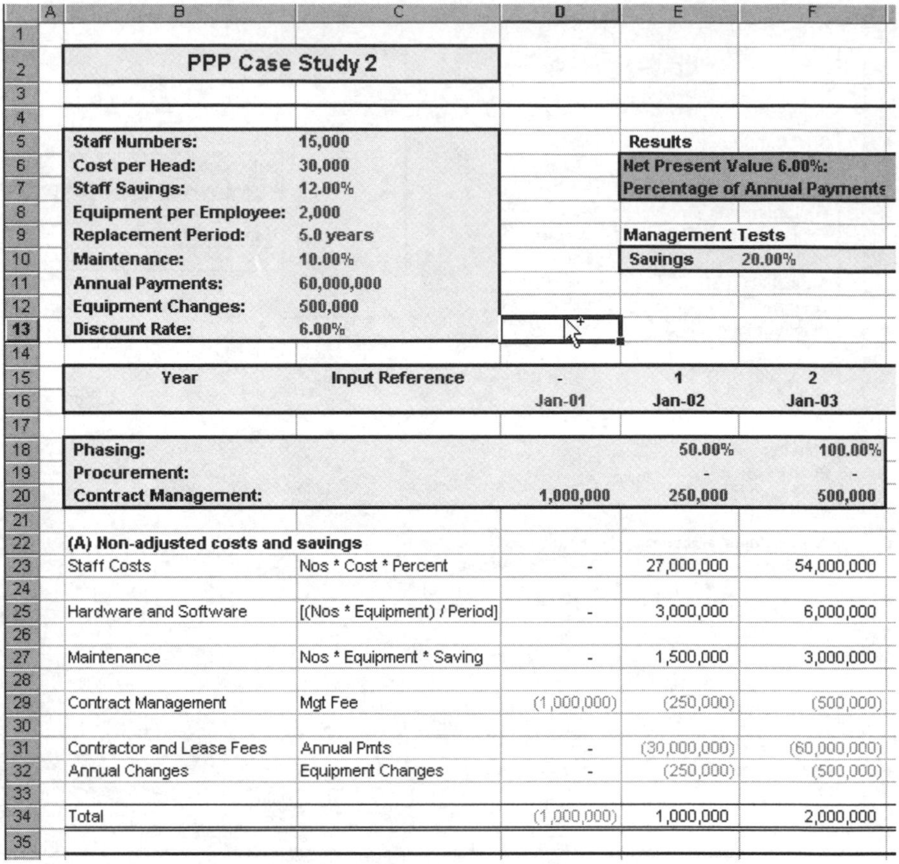

	B	C	D	E	F
2	PPP Case Study 2				
5	**Staff Numbers:**	**15,000**		**Results**	
6	**Cost per Head:**	**30,000**		**Net Present Value 6.00%:**	
7	**Staff Savings:**	**12.00%**		**Percentage of Annual Payments**	
8	**Equipment per Employee:**	**2,000**			
9	**Replacement Period:**	**5.0 years**		**Management Tests**	
10	**Maintenance:**	**10.00%**		**Savings**	**20.00%**
11	**Annual Payments:**	**60,000,000**			
12	**Equipment Changes:**	**500,000**			
13	**Discount Rate:**	**6.00%**			
15	**Year**	**Input Reference**	**-**	**1**	**2**
16			**Jan-01**	**Jan-02**	**Jan-03**
18	**Phasing:**			**50.00%**	**100.00%**
19	**Procurement:**			**-**	**-**
20	**Contract Management:**		**1,000,000**	**250,000**	**500,000**
22	**(A) Non-adjusted costs and savings**				
23	Staff Costs	Nos * Cost * Percent	-	27,000,000	54,000,000
25	Hardware and Software	[(Nos * Equipment) / Period]	-	3,000,000	6,000,000
27	Maintenance	Nos * Equipment * Saving	-	1,500,000	3,000,000
29	Contract Management	Mgt Fee	(1,000,000)	(250,000)	(500,000)
31	Contractor and Lease Fees	Annual Pmts	-	(30,000,000)	(60,000,000)
32	Annual Changes	Equipment Changes	-	(250,000)	(500,000)
34	Total		(1,000,000)	1,000,000	2,000,000

Fig 5.3

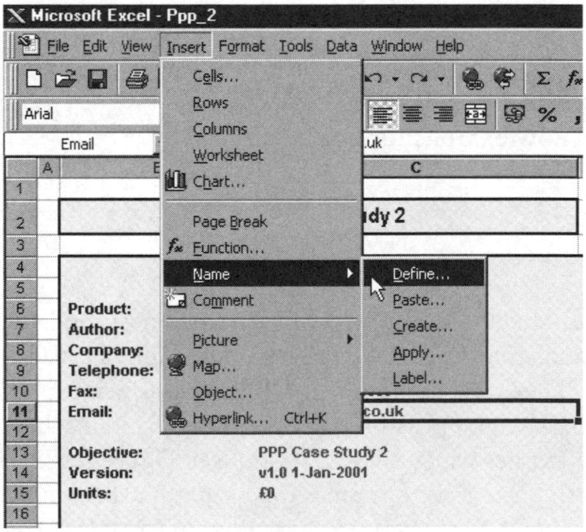

Fig 5.4

This is a list of names in the workbook:

Author	=Menu!$C$7
Company	=Menu!$C$8
Contact	=Menu!$B$27
Email	=Menu!$C$11
Fax	=Menu!$C$10
Objective	=Menu!$C$13
Product	=Menu!$C$6
Telephone	=Menu!$C$9
Units	=Menu!$C$15
Version	=Menu!$C$14

Formatting

The model follows:

- formats;
- number formats;
- lines and borders;
- colour and patterns;
- specific colour for inputs (blue), totals (green) and results (red).

There are specific formats up as custom formats such as in cell E23 (see Figure 5.5).

Functions

The model needs to calculate the answer to the discounted cash flows as:

$$\frac{Cash\_Flow}{(1 + Interest\_Rate)^{Period\_Number}}$$

Fig 5.5

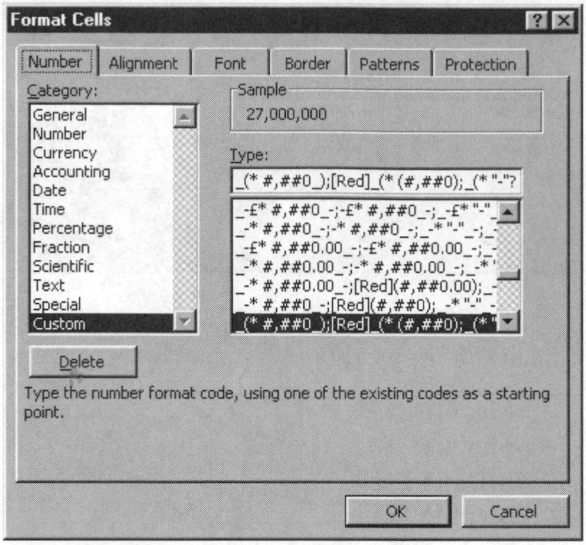

Cell G6 uses the function, NPV as:

```
=NPV($C$13,E34:N34)+D34
```

Comments

Comments are useful to assist users and explain calculations (see Figure 5.6).

Fig 5.6

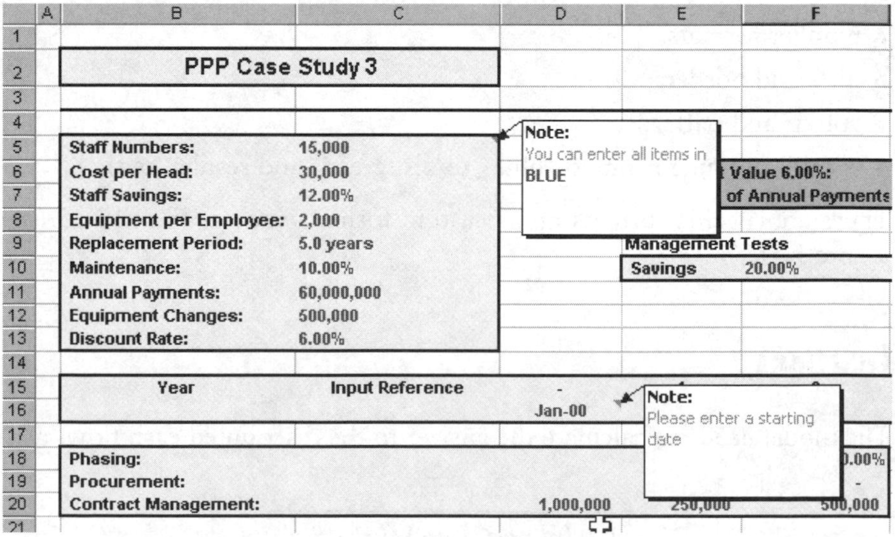

Validation

Data Validation is used in cell C7 to ensure that the users insert a percentage which is between minus 100% and plus 100% (see Figure 5.7).

Fig 5.7

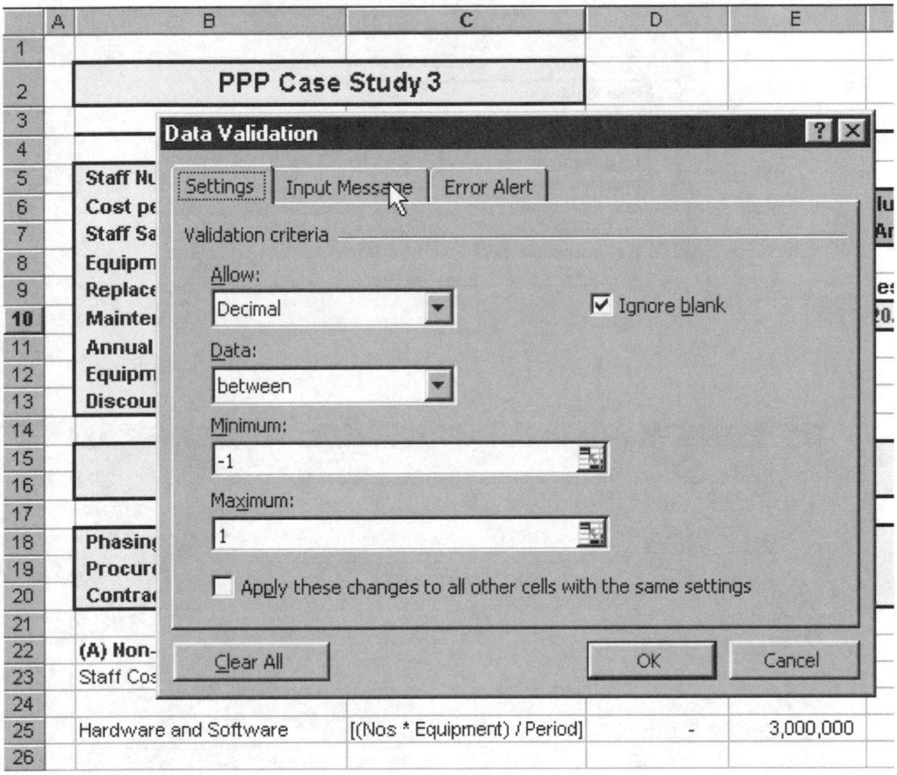

Conditional formatting

As shown in Figure 5.8, you can set up a condition to decide if the NPV is high enough, e.g. cell G10:

```
=IF(G7>F10,"Yes","No")
```

The next stage is to use conditional formatting in cell G10 to format the answer. The formatting is green if the project passes the test and pink if it fails (see Figure 5.9).

Fig 5.8

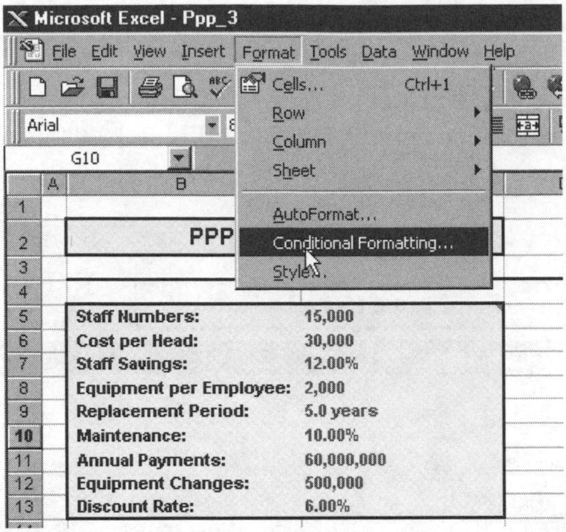

Fig 5.9

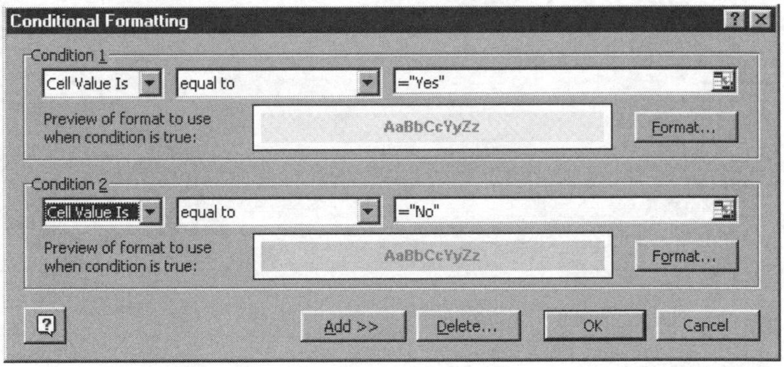

Printing

The application needs to be set up for printing since it is annoying for a user to have to sort this out. Go to `File`, `Page Setup`. The tabs are:

- Sheet – select the cells (see Figure 5.10).
- Page – landscape and reduced to fit on the page.
- Custom headers and footers (see Figure 5.11).

  The custom headers and footers are set as follows:

  Header: File Name Sheet Name : Data Time inserted as: &F &A &D &T

  Footer: Sheet Name : Page Number inserted as &A : Page &P

Fig 5.10

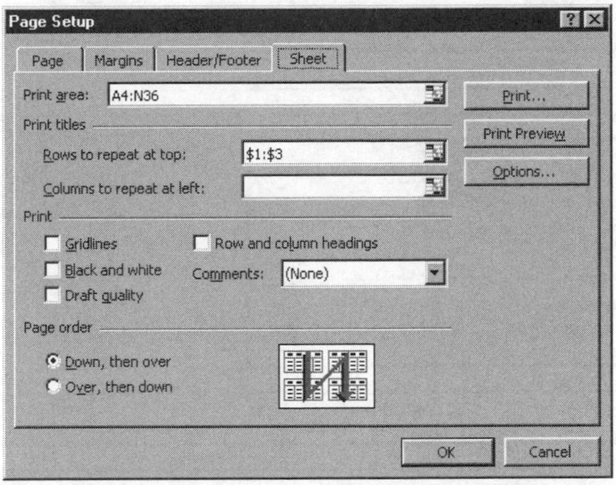

Fig 5.11

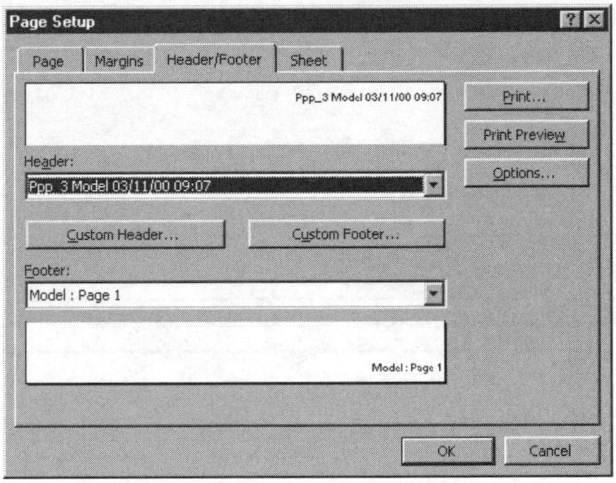

5. PPP 3

The completed file PPP 3 is a basic model (see Figure 5.12), which provides a single answer. In particular, there is:

- no automation;
- no menu system;
- no risk analysis or testing of the model parameters.

Fig 5.12

	A	B	C	D	E	F
1						
2		PPP Case Study 3				
3						
4						
5		Staff Numbers:	15,000		Results	
6		Cost per Head:	30,000		Net Present Value 6.00%:	
7		Staff Savings:	12.00%		Percentage of Annual Payments	
8		Equipment per Employee:	2,000			
9		Replacement Period:	5.0 years		Management Tests	
10		Maintenance:	10.00%		Savings	20.00%
11		Annual Payments:	60,000,000			
12		Equipment Changes:	500,000			
13		Discount Rate:	6.00%			
14						
15		Year	Input Reference	-	1	2
16				Jan-01	Jan-02	Jan-03
17						
18		Phasing:			50.00%	100.00%
19		Procurement:			-	-
20		Contract Management:		1,000,000	250,000	500,000
21						
22		(A) Non-adjusted costs and savings				
23		Staff Costs	Nos * Cost * Percent	-	27,000,000	54,000,000
24						
25		Hardware and Software	[(Nos * Equipment) / Period]	-	3,000,000	6,000,000
26						
27		Maintenance	Nos * Equipment * Saving	-	1,500,000	3,000,000
28						
29		Contract Management	Mgt Fee	(1,000,000)	(250,000)	(500,000)
30						
31		Contractor and Lease Fees	Annual Pmts	-	(30,000,000)	(60,000,000)
32		Annual Changes	Equipment Changes	-	(250,000)	(500,000)
33						
34		Total		(1,000,000)	1,000,000	2,000,000
35						

6. PPP 4

Further improvements are needed to turn the model into a more rounded application for management purposes, for example:

- menu
- combo boxes
- scenarios
- risk analysis
- documentation
- testing
- protecting.

These are detailed in the files PPP_4 to PPP_6.

Menu system

A Menu system can direct users and provide a structure for the application. This is on the Menu sheet on PPP 4 where a combo box is populated from cells B51 to B70. The cell link is cell C50 (see Figure 5.13). This is the same methodology as the Investment Model in the previous chapter and shows a consistency of approach.

The GetSheetNames macro is assigned to the control so that every time you click the control, the macro counts the sheets in the workbook and populates the cells B51 to B70 with the names. It then displays the sheet number corresponding to the index number in cell C50. Excel uses an index number for each sheet, so the Menu is Sheet 1 and the Model Sheet 2.

A simpler form of this macro is in the file Menu_Structure. Here you populate the workings for the combo box manually with the sheet names. The macro selects the sheet number returned by the combo box.

Fig 5.13

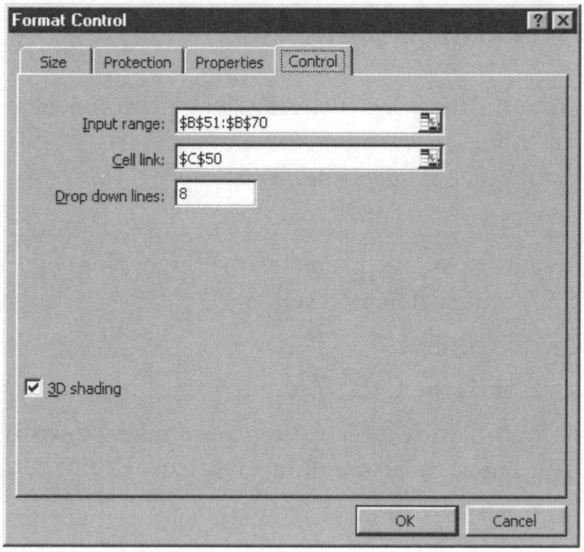

Simple macros and buttons

Simple macros are easily recorded by:

- going to `Tools, Macros, Record New Macro`;
- providing a name for the macro;
- recording the key strokes;

- pressing the `Stop Recording` button;
- assigning the macro to the button;
- viewing the Forms toolbar and choosing Buttons.

There is a macro in the file called PrintSetUp, which is a utility macro for setting up the printing with custom headers and footers. To access this quickly, this is assigned to a button on the Spare sheet. You can also view macros by accessing:

- `Tools`, `Macros`, selecting a name and then `Edit`;
- `Tools`, `Visual Basic Editor` and then looking for the File Name and then the Modules in the Project Window. The PrintSetUp macro is in Module 3.

7. PPP 5

Combo boxes for defined entries

The discount rate on the Model sheet is better served by a combo box help to control inputs. This again uses a standard layout with workings at the bottom of the schedule. The steps to insert the control are as follows:

- Cut the discount rate and paste into the workings at cell C90 and change its colour to a calculated cell.
- Draw and size the control.
- Right click to format the Control.
- Provide the Control with information to populate it with and a cell to update with an index (selection number):
  - Populate range = Input range.
  - Index number = Cell link.

The Combo box populates itself with B93:B100 and updates C89 (see Figure 5.14).

The completed formula at cell C90 is in the file PPP 5 `=OFFSET(B92,C89,0)`. The index number is five so the result is five cells down from cell B92, which is 6.00%.

Fig 5.14

	A	B	C
84			
85			
86		**Workings**	
87		**Interval**	**0.25%**
88		**Starting Rate**	**5.00%**
89		**Index Number**	5
90		**Result**	
91			
92		**Values**	
93		5.00%	
94		5.25%	
95		5.50%	
96		5.75%	
97		6.00%	
98		6.25%	
99		6.50%	
100		6.75%	
101			
102			
103			

Scenarios

So far, the model has produced one set of answers. However, you may want to store other views of the future as scenarios. In order to reduce code, you would not want to produce multiple spreadsheets which simply repeat the same programming. Enter scenarios using:

- Tools, Scenarios.
- Add a Scenario – Base Case (see Figure 5.15).
- Select multiple groups of cells using commas for each of the selections.
- If input cells are in a particular colour then it is easy to find all the inputs.

If you have more than one Scenario, you can click Summary and Excel produces a management report as in Figure 5.16.

If cells are named, then names rather than cell references are shown. The results of the other scenarios demonstrate that the net present value of 12,776,778 is easily turned into a negative figure. In particular, the model seems sensitive to changes in the anticipated cost savings.

Fig 5.15

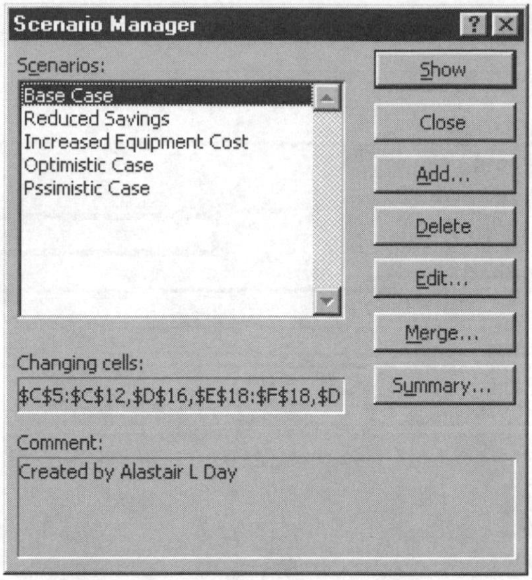

Fig 5.16

	A	B	C	D	E	F	G	H	I
1									
2		**Scenario Summary**							
3				**Current Values:**	**Base Case**	**Reduced Savings**	**Increased Equipment Cost**	**Optimistic Case**	**Pessimistic Case**
5		**Changing Cells:**							
6			**$C$5**	15,000	15,000	15,000	15,000	15,000	15,000
7			**$C$6**	25,000	30,000	25,000	25,000	30,000	25,000
8			**$C$7**	10.00%	12.00%	11.00%	10.00%	13.00%	10.00%
9			**$C$8**	1,750	2,000	1,750	2,250	2,000	1,750
10			**$C$9**	5.0 years	5.0 years	5.0 years	5.0 years	5.0 years	5.0 years
11			**$C$10**	8.00%	10.00%	8.00%	8.00%	12.00%	8.00%
12			**$C$11**	62,000,000	60,000,000	62,000,000	62,000,000	59,000,000	62,000,000
13			**$C$12**	600,000	500,000	600,000	600,000	400,000	600,000
14			**$D$16**	Jan-00	Jan-00	Jan-00	Jan-00	Jan-00	Jan-00
15			**$E$18**	50.00%	50.00%	50.00%	50.00%	50.00%	50.00%
16			**$F$18**	100.00%	100.00%	100.00%	100.00%	100.00%	100.00%
17			**$D$20**	1,000,000	1,000,000	1,000,000	1,000,000	1,000,000	1,000,000
18			**$E$20**	250,000	250,000	250,000	250,000	250,000	250,000
19			**$F$20**	500,000	500,000	500,000	500,000	500,000	500,000
20			**$B$41**	0.50%	0.50%	0.50%	0.50%	0.50%	0.50%
21			**$C$41**	9.0%	9.0%	9.0%	9.0%	9.0%	9.0%
22			**$B$62**	0.50%	0.50%	0.50%	0.50%	0.50%	0.50%
23			**$C$62**	5.0%	5.0%	5.0%	5.0%	5.0%	5.0%
24			**$C$87**	0.25%	0.25%	0.25%	0.25%	0.25%	0.25%
25			**$C$88**	5.00%	5.00%	5.00%	5.00%	5.00%	5.00%
26			**$C$89**	5	5	5	5	5	5
27		**Result Cells:**							
28			**$G$6**	(126,713,098)	12,776,778	(100,881,640)	(112,247,481)	55,484,789	(126,713,098)
29			**$G$7**	-202.42%	21.12%	-161.15%	-179.31%	93.41%	-202.42%
30			**$G$10**	No	Yes	No	No	Yes	No
31		Notes: Current Values column represents values of changing cells at							
32		time Scenario Summary Report was created. Changing cells for each							
33		scenario are highlighted in gray.							
34									

Data tables and risk

Data tables may be a more useful method of testing important variables and displaying multiple answers. This may illuminate risk factors or other considerations. PPP 4 has the templates set up at the bottom of the schedule to insert data tables for staff savings and the discount rate as one-dimensional tables.

The data tables are inserted using the method in the previous chapter. The layout is standard with the interval input marked in blue. One of the row headers has to be an input cell and not a formula, and here this is cell C41.

It is useful to see how changes in important variables 'flex' the answer. For example, what happens if the savings are not 12%? In the example, the net present value falls sharply if the planned savings are not achieved. The difference is far more than the reduction due to an increase in the discount rate. The charts show the effect of the changes clearly (see Figure 5.17). Data tables provide a greater understanding of what can go wrong by testing the inputs and providing multiple answers.

Fig 5.17

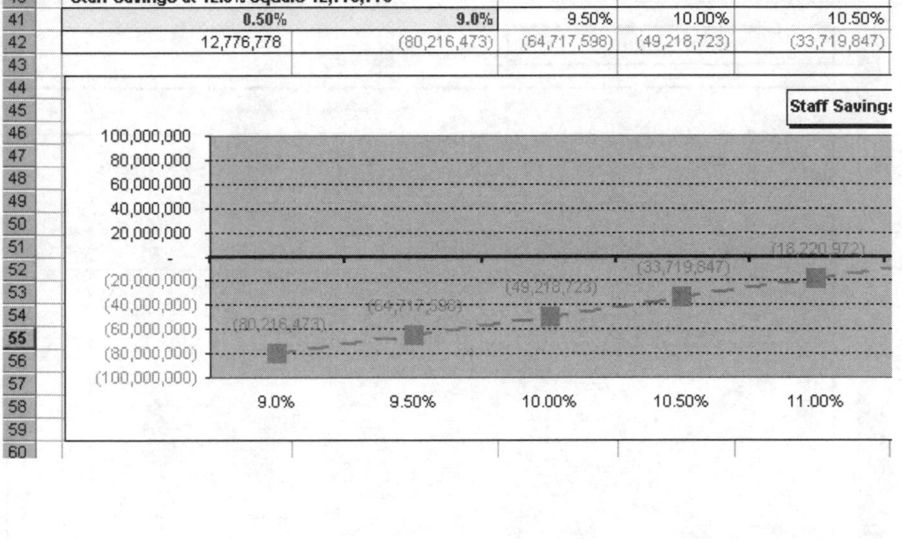

A single answer should always be tested since management needs to know if the current view of the future or scenario is reasonable and attainable. By testing assumptions, you can try to understand the behaviour of variables.

There are various techniques, covered later in the book, which also cover risk:

- dispersion and variation;
- standard deviation;
- coefficient of variation;
- simulation;
- Monte Carlo simulation using the products Crystal Ball or @RISK.

8. DOCUMENTING, TESTING AND PROTECTING

You always need to document workings and their application (see Figure 5.18). Some questions are:

- what are the important calculations;
- the background behind some of the costs, for example the phasing of the costs;
- if you distribute the model, would a colleague understand the calculations;
- will you understand what you did in a year's time?

Fig 5.18

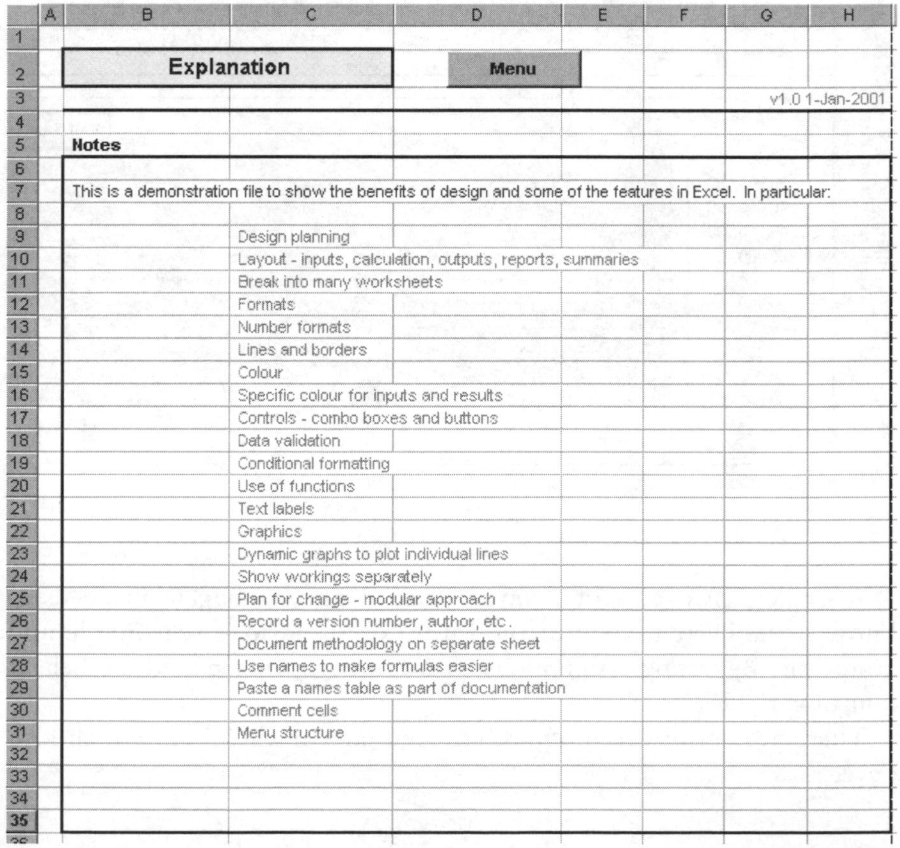

You could also paste a Names list and macros as part of documentation. This is on the Spare sheet.

The row and column headers and grid lines are removed using `Tools, Options, View`. This makes the interface look less cluttered and, on completion, you do not need this information.

The straightforward methods of testing the model are using test data and checking the answer with a business or financial calculator. Calculators such as the Hewlett-Packard HP17BII have built in programs for discounted cash flow problems such as net present value. Other methods include:

- audit toolbar;
- pattern matching using `Edit, Goto Special`;
- `Tools, Options, View` – show formulas (see Figure 5.19). Alternatively, toggle using `Cntrl + ``.

When the model is finished, use protection to avoid unnecessary overwriting or changes to the structure of the workbook (see Figure 5.20).

Fig 5.19

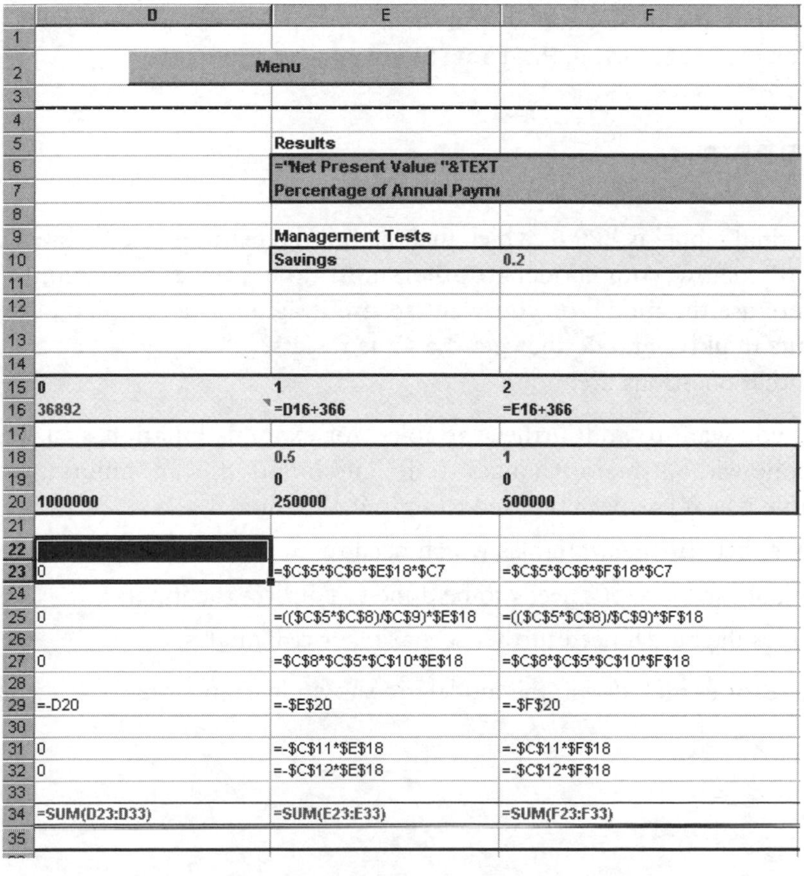

	D	E	F
1			
2	Menu		
3			
4			
5		Results	
6		="Net Present Value "&TEXT	
7		Percentage of Annual Paym	
8			
9		Management Tests	
10		Savings	0.2
11			
12			
13			
14			
15	0	1	2
16	36892	=D16+366	=E16+366
17			
18		0.5	1
19		0	0
20	1000000	250000	500000
21			
22			
23	0	=$C$5*$C$6*$E$18*$C7	=$C$5*$C$6*$F$18*$C7
24			
25	0	=(($C$5*$C$8)/$C$9)*$E$18	=(($C$5*$C$8)/$C$9)*$F$18
26			
27	0	=$C$8*$C$5*$C$10*$E$18	=$C$8*$C$5*$C$10*$F$18
28			
29	=-D20	=-$E$20	=-$F$20
30			
31	0	=-$C$11*$E$18	=-$C$11*$F$18
32	0	=-$C$12*$E$18	=-$C$12*$F$18
33			
34	=SUM(D23:D33)	=SUM(E23:E33)	=SUM(F23:F33)
35			

Fig 5.20

- Protect all cells (click between row 1 and column A to select whole sheet) and then unprotect cells that need inputs. Use `Format, Cells, Protection`. (This is one of the reasons for colour coding the inputs and changing the colour if the status changes.)
- Protect the workbook to stop others amending the structure.
- If you use passwords you have to write them down – you cannot remove the protection of the sheet or workbook without them. Use `Tools, Protection, Protect Sheet or Workbook`.

9. PPP 6

The final model is PPP 6, which includes all the features (see Figure 5.21). Finally, show your model to others and take advice. For example, if others use the model or you want to use it again as a template, are the inputs intuitive and do they get the same results?

Other questions are:

- If you want to add further variables, for example inflation, can this be done without major changes to design? Inflation is an important variable which has been omitted to simplify the model.
- Are there further variables which need to be modelled?
- What further work needs to be done to confirm the inputs?
- Does the model need further scenarios or risk analysis?

The features included in the model are shown in Figure 5.22.

Fig 5.21

	A	B	C	D	E	F	G
1							
2		PPP Case Study 6		Menu			
3							
4							
5		Staff Numbers:	15,000		Results		
6		Cost per Head:	30,000		Net Present Value 6.00%:		12,776,778
7		Staff Savings:	12.00%		Percentage of Annual Paymen		21.12%
8		Equipment per Employee	2,000				
9		Replacement Period:	5.0 years		Management Tests		
10		Maintenance:	10.00%		Savings	20.00%	Yes
11		Annual Payments:	60,000,000				
12		Equipment Changes:	500,000				
13		Discount Rate:	6.00%				
14							
15		Year	Input Reference	-	1	2	3
16				Jan-01	Jan-02	Jan-03	Jan-04
17							
18		Phasing:			50.00%	100.00%	
19		Procurement:			-	-	
20		Contract Management:		1,000,000	250,000	500,000	
21							
22		(A) Non-adjusted costs and savings					
23		Staff Costs	Nos * Cost * Percent	-	27,000,000	54,000,000	54,000,000
24							
25		Hardware and Software	[(Nos * Equipment) / Perioc	-	3,000,000	6,000,000	6,000,000
26							
27		Maintenance	Nos * Equipment * Saving	-	1,500,000	3,000,000	3,000,000
28							
29		Contract Management	Mgt Fee	(1,000,000)	(250,000)	(500,000)	(500,000)
30							
31		Contractor and Lease Fees	Annual Pmts	-	(30,000,000)	(60,000,000)	(60,000,000)
32		Annual Changes	Equipment Changes	-	(250,000)	(500,000)	(500,000)
33							
34		Total		(1,000,000)	1,000,000	2,000,000	2,000,000
35							

Fig 5.22

PPP Case - Design Features

No	Item	Included
1	Formats	Yes
2	Number formats	Yes
3	Lines and borders	Yes
4	Colour and patterns	Yes
5	Specific colour for inputs and results	Yes
6	Data validation	Yes
7	Controls - combo boxes and buttons	Yes
8	Conditional formatting	Yes
9	Use of functions and types of functions	Yes
10	Add-ins for more functions	No
11	Text and updated labels	Yes
12	Record a version number, author, etc.	Yes
13	Use names to make formulas easier	Yes
14	Paste a names table as part of documentation	Yes
15	Comment cells	Yes
16	Graphics	Yes
17	Dynamic graphs to plot individual lines	No
18	Data tables	Yes
19	Scenarios	Yes
20	Goalseek	No
21	Solver	No
22	Use of templates	Yes
23	Plan for change - modular approach	Yes
24	Menu structure	Yes

10. SUMMARY

The chapter has reviewed a case study of an outsourcing example as a vehicle to demonstrate the stages in layering Excel features and techniques. The seven stages illustrate:

- design layout;
- calculation;
- formatting, functions, comments, validation and printing;
- menus, combo boxes, macros and buttons;
- scenarios, data tables and risk;
- documentation, testing and protecting;
- user comment and areas for improvement.

Part

B

Applications

Part B introduces a number of applications by outlining first the theory and then the application in the financial model. Each model follows the design procedure outlined in Part A to provide templates for study and further development.

The chapters in Part B are:

6 Analysing performance

7 Cash flow

8 Forecasting models

9 Forecasting financials

10 Variance analysis

11 Breakeven analysis

12 Portfolio analysis

13 Cost of capital

14 Bonds

15 Investment analysis

16 Risk analysis

17 Depreciation

18 Leasing

19 Company valuation

20 Optimization

21 Decision trees

22 Risk management

23 Modelling checklist

Analysing performance

This chapter introduces models for reviewing performance and understanding financial information. The starting point is the publicly available information organizations produce in the form of annual reports. Annual reports for public companies consist of:

- directors' report – qualitative report of the previous accounting period;
- auditor's report – third-party report on the results;
- profit and loss statement – revenue and costs;
- balance sheet – snapshot of what the company owns and owes to bankers, government and shareholders;
- cash flow statement – cash generated from operations and other sources and uses of cash;
- notes to the accounts – detail to the statements above as required by the UK or overseas Companies Acts.

The level of detail depends on corporate governance and legal requirements in the country where the company resides. Private companies often produce very little information and indeed the trend in the UK is to demand less information and even dispense with a third-party audit.

The report also details the accounting standards and conventions used by the company in drafting the report and accounts. This is important since it is often difficult to compare companies across borders due to differing standards. For example, accounting profit can be enhanced by increasing the depreciation period for assets or changing the method of valuing stock.

Analysing performance depends on standardizing the information available so that the raw data can be processed to provide information on the performance of the company. The analysts need to review the company in terms of its peer group, shareholders want to understand if their investment is safe and likely to rise in value, and other stakeholders may want more information on the organization's progress. Unfortunately, the information usually lies in a number of sections. For example, there is usually a total for debtors (accounts receivable) or stock (inventory) on the face of the balance sheet, while the detail is contained in the notes at the back of the report. To understand the figures, you have to continually flip from one section to another.

The figures tend to overpower the reader with the wealth of detail. Most people are not proficient at handling large quantities of numbers and immediately understanding the relationships between them. If you are going to lend money to the company or understand its performance, you need to decide if the organization is becoming more or less risky. One solution is to 'spread' the accounts in a standardized form in order to understand the figures more fully. The process is:

- Identify sources of risk.
- Describe qualitatively.
- Analyse by spreading the accounts and reviewing the results.
- Mitigate.
- Result – is the risk increasing or decreasing?

The accounts in a standardized form allow you to:

- scan the results for unusual numbers;
- review the trends in the absolute numbers;
- calculate financial and other ratios, e.g. profit margin – profit may be increasing, but this ratio tells you if they are making more or less money for every $1 of sales generated;
- highlight areas for further analysis or investigation.

The base information will also provide the data for further information on cash flow, forecasting and company valuation. The company is the fictitious organization Technology Sales Limited.

The first stage of the exercise is to produce a model which contains schedules for the income statement and balance sheet. The model allows up to five years of results in order to ascertain the trends. If you were lending for five years, then you would need more than two years' figures for the analysis. The cash flow and some ratios can be derived from this information. This is based on the Application_Template, which immediately provides a menu structure and housekeeping macros to automate basic tasks. The model also tries to build on the good practice discussed in the first five chapters.

The model template used in this chapter is called Financial_Analysis.

1. PROFIT AND LOSS

The structure of the profit and loss or income statement follows traditional lines (see Figure 6.1), although it is simplified for ease of understanding. However, it could be made more complex with the addition of more lines to display an increased level of detail.

Fig 6.1

Income statement.

	A	B	C	D	E	F	G	H	I	J	K
6		Client: FinAnalysis									
8		**No**		**Item**	**£'000**				**Dec-96**	**Dec-97**	**Dec-98**
9											
10		P10		Sales					16,567.0	22,154.0	29,124.0
11		P11		Cost of Goods Sold					(14,987.0)	(20,123.0)	(25,760.0)
12		P12	**Gross Margin**						**1,580.0**	**2,031.0**	**3,364.0**
13		P13		Depreciation		Manufacturer			(245.0)	(400.0)	(625.0)
14		P14				Amortisation/Other			-	-	-
15		P15		Sales, General &Administration Overheads					(756.0)	(900.0)	(1,290.0)
16		P16	**Net Operating Profit (NOP)**						**579.0**	**731.0**	**1,449.0**
17		P17		Interest Expense					(79.0)	(125.0)	(287.0)
18		P18		Interest Income					-	-	-
19		P19		Other Financial Income					-	-	-
20		P20	**Profit after Financial Items**						**500.0**	**606.0**	**1,162.0**
21		P21		Exceptional Expense					-	-	-
22		P22	**Profit before Tax**						**500.0**	**606.0**	**1,162.0**
23		P23		Tax					-	-	-
24		P24	**Net Profit after Tax (NPAT)**						**500.0**	**606.0**	**1,162.0**
25		P25		Minority Interest					-	-	-
26		P26		Dividends					-	-	-
27		P27	**Profit or (Loss) for the Financial Year**						**500.0**	**606.0**	**1,162.0**
28											

The dates are based on the named cell 'Enddate' at the Menu cell C20 and use a function called EDATE to count back from the last date to ensure that the dates are correct. The input cells are marked blue and the totals are in bold green. The latter cells only add up the cells above, which all adhere to the cash flow rule. Cash received is positive while cash outflows are entered as negative numbers. Numbers are formatted using accounting formats so that zeros display as a '-' to make the schedule easier to understand.

Excel does not allow you to 'drill down' to the answers from one schedule to another. It can be a problem understanding the source of the cell results. The model uses a numbering system, for example 'P' for profit and loss or 'B' for balance sheet, when referring to this data in the calculation schedules.

The levels of profit are clearly marked as in Table 6.1.

Table 6.1

Levels of profit.

Label	Alternative
Gross Profit	Gross Margin
Net Operating Profit	Earnings or Profit before Interest and Tax (EBIT, PBIT)
Profit after Financial Items:	
Profit before Tax	Earnings before Tax
Net Profit after Tax	Earnings or Profit after Tax (EAT, PAT)
Retained Earnings	Retained Profit

For completeness, the percentages are also calculated on the right-hand side (see Figure 6.2).

Fig 6.2

Income statement – percentages.

	N	O	P	Q	R	S
6		Percentages Comparison				
8		Dec-96	Dec-97	Dec-98	Dec-99	Dec-00
9						
10		100.0	100.0	100.0	100.0	100.0
11		90.5	90.8	88.4	85.9	87.7
12		9.5	9.2	11.6	14.1	12.3
13		1.5	1.8	2.1	2.6	2.4
14		-	-	-	-	-
15		4.6	4.1	4.4	4.9	6.7
16		3.5	3.3	5.0	6.6	3.2
17		0.5	0.6	1.0	0.7	0.5
18		-	-	-	-	-
19		-	-	-	-	-
20		3.0	2.7	4.0	5.9	2.8
21		-	-	-	-	-
22		3.0	2.7	4.0	5.9	2.8
23		-	-	-	-	-
24		3.0	2.7	4.0	5.9	2.8
25		-	-	-	-	-
26		-	-	-	1.3	1.0
27		3.0	2.7	4.0	4.6	1.8
28						

2. BALANCE SHEET

The balance sheet shows the assets and liabilities of the company at each year end. Again the format corresponds to international notation and is split into current and fixed assets (see Figure 6.3) followed by current liabilities, long-term debt and shareholders' funds, which is split into shares and retained profit and loss (see Figure 6.4). Again, you could increase the detail by adding columns for more share types such as preference shares.

Fig 6.3

Assets.

	A	B	C–H	I	J	K
6		Client: FinAnalysis				
8		No	Assets £'000	Dec-96	Dec-97	Dec-98
9						
10		B10	Cash and Deposits	78.0	123.0	308.0
11		B11	Marketable Securities	-	-	-
12		B12	Trade Receivables (Debtors):	3,756.0	4,678.0	5,238.0
13		B13	Inventory	-	-	-
14		B14	Sundry Current Assets	1,123.0	1,567.0	3,373.0
15		B15	**Current Assets**	**4,957.0**	**6,368.0**	**8,919.0**
16		B16	Land and Buildings - Freehold	1,350.0	1,350.0	1,350.0
17		B17	Plant and Machinery	300.0	4,567.0	6,918.0
18		B18	Depreciation	(357.0)	(457.0)	(674.0)
19		B19	**Net Property, Plant and Equipment**	**1,293.0**	**5,460.0**	**7,594.0**
20		B20	Other Investments	-	-	-
21		B21	Intangibles/Goodwill	-	-	-
22		B22	**Non Current and Fixed Assets**	**1,293.0**	**5,460.0**	**7,594.0**
23		B23				
24		B24	**Total Assets**	**6,250.0**	**11,828.0**	**16,513.0**

The total assets are given for each year and there is again a percentage split. There is no real programming here and Excel is used to ensure that the columns add correctly. The formatting of the numbers, colours, columns and general appearance is common throughout the application. Similarly, all reports are formatted ready for printing with custom headers and footers inserted using a macro called SetUpSheet.

Liabilities.

Fig 6.4

	No	Liabilities	£'000	Dec-96	Dec-97	Dec-98
25						
26	No	Liabilities	£'000	Dec-96	Dec-97	Dec-98
27						
28	B28	Short Term Bank Loans		500.0	900.0	1,439.0
29	B29	Trade Creditors (Receivables)		638.0	3,256.0	3,475.0
30	B30	Other Creditors		678.0	890.0	990.0
31	B31	Other Current Liabilities		2,679.0	3,568.0	4,311.0
32	B32	**Current Liabilities**		**4,495.0**	**8,614.0**	**10,215.0**
33	B33	Long Term Bank Loans		1,200.0	2,500.0	3,413.0
34	B34	**Long Term Liabilities**		**1,200.0**	**2,500.0**	**3,413.0**
35	B35	Deferred Taxation		-	-	342.0
36	B36	**Long Term Liabilities and Provisions**		**1,200.0**	**2,500.0**	**3,755.0**
37	B37	Ordinary Shares (Common Stock)		100.0	100.0	1,365.0
38	B38	Profit and Loss Reserve (Retained Earnings)		455.0	614.0	1,178.0
39	B39	**Shareholders' Funds**		**555.0**	**714.0**	**2,543.0**
40	B40					
41	B41	**Total Liabilities and Equity**		**6,250.0**	**11,828.0**	**16,513.0**
42						
43		CheckSum:	No Errors	-	-	-

The schedule includes a 'CheckSum' to check that assets equal liabilities (see Figure 6.4). If they do not, then cell E43 displays a warning message:

```
=IF(SUM(I43:M43)<>0,"Errors","No Errors")
```

Together the income statement and balance sheet constitute the basic inputs to the model. In this form, you can look along the rows and try to pick out trends. The percentage views assist, but eventually you need to look more closely by calculating ratios which can be tedious with a pocket or financial calculator. However, this process is straightforward using Excel.

3. RATIOS

The purpose of this section is to outline some of the ratios used by analysts and their purpose rather than an in-depth analysis of the accounts in the example. In this context, some companies are more successful than others in the industry through better use of resources and management, or perhaps sometimes because of good luck. Financial analysts tend to discount luck and concentrate on the results through ratio analysis. Figure 6.5 is a stylized map of the process of interpreting company results:

Fig 6.5 **Risk.**

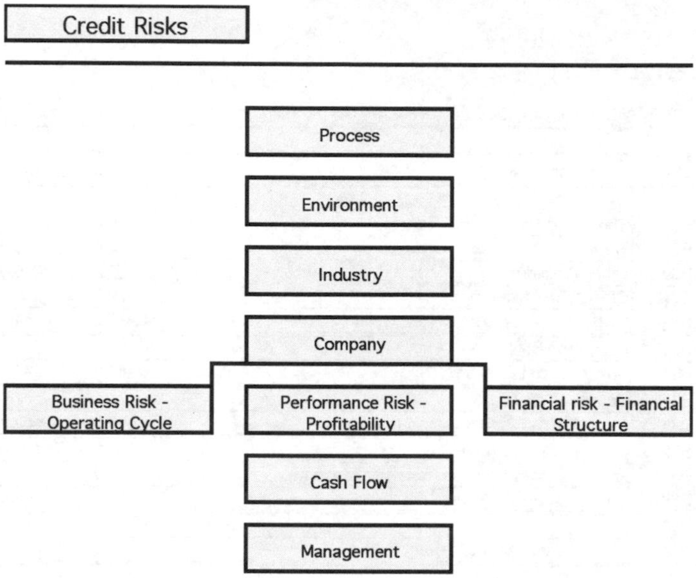

The first stage is to define the purpose of the investigation. The diagram proceeds to the environment, which covers factors beyond the company's control, for example:

- social trends;
- technological developments;
- economic cycles, growth or decline;
- environmental issues;
- political developments as they affect the organization;
- values and changes in the way certain business ethics are viewed.

The problem is to decide if the company can survive and generate earnings, so next one would study the industry and its competitive position. Some industries can build barriers around them that ensure that they can generate profits over a long period. Other industries possess advantages such as patents or brands which enable them to produce superior profits over time. Companies such as Microsoft would fall into this category, where its position, as a dominant player, has allowed it to grow quickly over the last decade and protect many of its markets from competition.

After consideration of the macro and industrial context, you are in a superior position to consider the company. Ratios help this process, but bear in mind the following:

- There is no right or wrong answer.
- The absolute numbers are not important.
- Ratios vary widely between different sectors such as retailers, manufacturers and service companies.
- Trends need to be considered against prevailing economic conditions.
- Ratios are backward looking and it usually takes companies some months to report and file accounts.
- Analysis against a peer group can highlight areas where the company fares better or worse than the group members.

There are three main issues to be considered:

- operating risk – the operating cycle (see Figure 6.6);
- performance risk – profitability;
- financial risk – financial structure.

The three areas of risk determine the quality and quantity generated by the organization. The decisions of what and how much to produce are underpinned by the management.

Fig 6.6

Operating cycle.

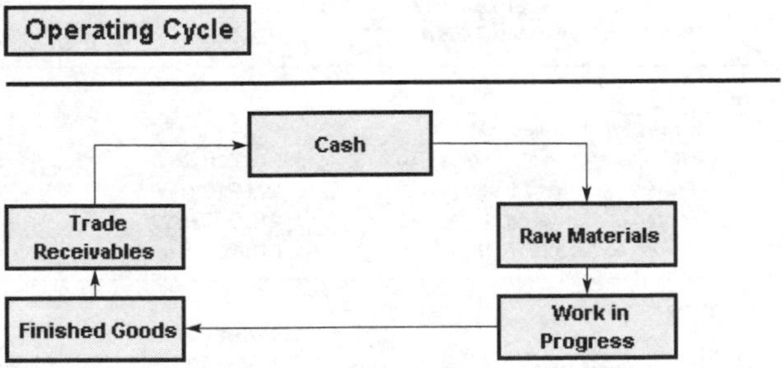

Cash is used to purchase raw materials which move through the production process into finished goods (see Figure 6.6). The company delivers the goods, invoices its customers and has to wait for the customer to pay. It is a measure of management ability how fast it can 'turn' this cycle. If it cannot sell its goods, then they will sit in the warehouse and have to be funded from the operating cycle, bank finance or new equity. More borrowings will increase the company's costs and reduce profits. This is termed business risk.

Performance risk means profitability, which in turn usually equates to cash flow. Companies need to generate profits in order to invest in equipment and growth opportunities. In the long term, a lack of profits usually means that a company will be uncompetitive, go bust or will be taken over by businesses that are more aggressive.

Where you have profits, but no cash, then you need to examine the accounting standards used or investigate creative accounting practices. For example, costs moved to the balance sheet such as research and development mean that cash has been spent, but is being recorded in the profit and loss account over a number of periods. This increases profits in the short term at the expense of the long term.

Financial risk is concerned with the structure of the balance sheet together with who provides the finance facilities to the company. The essential difference between debt and equity is that dividends do not have to be paid, while bankers require payment. As the proportion of debt increases, so does the interest burden and therefore the amount of financial risk. Ratios in this section illustrate the proportion of the company owned by the shareholders and degree of financial burden.

The ratios considered in this book are listed in Figure 6.7.

Fig 6.7

Ratios.

Client: FinAnalysis

Line	Item £000	Reference	Dec-00	Action
	Core Ratios			
R11	Return on Sales (NPAT/Sales %)	P24/P10	2.76	Worse
R12	Asset Turnover (Sales / Total Assets)	P10/B24	1.55	Worse
R13	Asset Leverage (Total Assets/Equity)	B23/B39	5.28	OK
R14	Return on Equity (NPAT/Equity %)	P24/B39	22.52	Worse
	Profitability			
R18	Gross Profit / Sales (%)	P12/P10	12.31	OK
R19	Net Operating Profit / Sales (%)	P16/P10	3.23	Worse
R20	Profit before Tax / Sales (%)	P22/P10	2.76	Worse
R21	Return on Capital Employed (ROCE)	P16/B39+B33	10.20	Worse
R22	Return on Assets (ROA)	P16/B24	4.99	Worse
	Operating Efficiency			
R26	Inventory Days	B13/P11	3.07	N/A
R27	Trade Receivables (Debtor) Days	B12/P10	55.09	OK
R28	Creditors Days	B29/P11	33.33	Worse
R29	Funding Gap Debtors+Inventory-Creditors		24.83	Worse
	Financial Structure			
R33	Current Ratio	B15/B32	1.58	Better
R34	Quick Ratio (Acid Test)	B15-B13/B32	1.56	Better
R35	Working Capital (Thousands)	B15-B32	8,164	OK
R36	Gross Gearing (%)	B28+B33/B39	165.10	OK
R37	Net Gearing (%)	B28+B33-P10+11/B39	165.06	OK
R38	Solvency	P16/P17	6.90	OK
	Cashflow Ratios			
R42	EBITDA / Sales (%)	C12/P10	5.62	Worse
R43	Net Operating Cash Flow/Sales	C17/P10	(7.84)	Worse
R44	Cash Flow before Financing/Sales	C42/J10	(14.26)	OK

Du Pont ratios (core ratios)

One short cut to calculating pages of ratios is to look at the core ratios which make up the return on equity. This is considered the most important since this ratio computes the return to shareholders who risk their capital in the enterprise.

The return on equity is Net profit after tax / Shareholders' equity and this can be subdivided into:

Return on Sales	(NPAT / Sales)	Profitability	P24/P10
Asset Turnover	(Sales / Total Assets)	Operating Efficiency	P10/B24
Asset Leverage	(Total Assets / Equity)	Financial Structure	B23/B39

These three ratios, when multiplied together, equal the return on equity.

NPAT / Equity = Sales / Total Assets * Total Assets / Equity * NPAT / Sales

The ratios in this section are multiplied out to show the composition of the return on equity. This has declined over the period and the model uses functions to determine if last year is better than the two previous years ('Better'), ahead of one year ('OK') or worse than both years ('Worse'). This directs the user at the lines that need investigation or further attention. The formula in cell L11 is:

```
=IF(K11=0,"N/A",IF(J11=0,"N/A",IF(AND(L11/K11>1,L11/J11>
1),"Better",IF(OR(L11/K11>1,L11/J11>1),"OK","Worse"))))
```

Inventory and receivable days together with the funding gap use opposite logic. If the number of days or the gap increases, this means that the company has to find more resources to fund the cycle. The funding gap increases in the two previous periods and so the cell formula returns 'Worse'.

In each formula, the possibility of an error caused by a zero number is handled by an IF statement. This is Ratios cell L11:

```
=IF(Income!M10<>0,(Income!M24/Income!M10)*100,0)
```

An alternative would be to use ISERROR to force zero if Excel cannot calculate an answer. The answer is multiplied by 100 since the application standardizes on numbers rather than a mixture of numbers and percentages.

```
=IF(ISERROR(Income!M24/Income!M10),0,(Income!M24/Income!
M10)*100)
```

The ratios demonstrate the levers that management can use to extract performance from the business:

- earnings from each $1 of sales – profit margin (income statement);
- sales for each $1 of assets – asset turnover (asset side of balance sheet);
- equity used to finance each $1 of assets – financial or asset leverage (liabilities side of balance sheet).

Performance measurement in the form of 'what gets measured gets managed' can be summarized as:

- economy – how well the company buys in the factors of production, i.e. labour, materials, knowledge;
- efficiency – how well the company turns the 'raw materials' into goods and services for sale;
- effectiveness – how well the company rewards the key stakeholders including shareholders;
- environment – the company's responsibilities in the wider world;
- ethics – ethical goals such corporate governance.

Return on equity is often considered to be the most important return measure; however, you need also to bear in mind the following:

- The return on equity (ROE) is backward looking and historic yet management has to take strategic decisions on a scenario view of the future.
- The calculation does not include a measure of the risk profile of the industry and company. More risk should demand a greater return to shareholders.
- The ROE is an accounting measure and is based on book values. The value of equity may be better presented by the market value of debt and the market value of equity (enterprise value).

Profitability depends on strategy and the market. Competition means that companies are not free to make as much profit as they wish. Companies with strong brands can be expected to produce superior profits whereas small companies are often dependent on one or two products or on subcontracts from a larger company.

Asset turnover depends on the sector and the assets needed in the business. Software houses invest in people as the major asset in developing competitive advantage as opposed to a car manufacturing company that requires a high level of fixed plant and equipment.

Asset leverage depends on the uncertainty of cash flows. In a risky business, such as pharmaceuticals, shareholders are normally expected to fund research and development. British Biotechnology plc has returned to the market several times since inception in the mid 1980s in order to fund new product development.

Profitability

The profitability ratios show the profit from operations and the profit lines available to debt and equity providers. As alternative return measures, the return on capital employed and the return on assets are included.

Ratio	*Calculation*	*Reference*
Gross Profit / Sales (%)	Gross Margin	P12/P10
Net Operating Profit / Sales (%)	Profit before Tax and Interest	P16/P10
Profit before Tax / Sales (%)	Profit after Interest Payments	P22/P10
Return on Capital Employed (ROCE)	Pre-tax Profit / Long-term Debt plus Equity	P16/B39+B33
Return on Invested Capital (ROIC)	Pre-tax Profit * (1 – Tax) / Debt + Equity	P16*(1–T) /B28+33+39
Return on Assets (ROA)	Pre-tax Profit / Total Assets	P16/B24

Operating cycle

The liquidity ratios show the days inventory held, the length of time it takes customers to pay and the credit extended by suppliers. The funding gap is the number of days that need to be funded by cash or overdraft. If the funding gap is long then potentially the risk of default is greater. In this business, the gap has increased to over 20 days.

Inventory Days	Inventory / Cost of Goods Sold *365	B13/P11
Trade Receivables (Debtor) Days	Receivables / Sales * 365	B12/P10
Creditors Days	Inventory / Cost of Goods Sold *365	B29/P11
Funding Gap	Debtor Days + Inventory Days – Creditor Days	

Leverage, capital structure and coverage on interest

These ratios show the liquidity and financial structure. Negative working capital is common in food retailing and therefore is not always a problem. On the other hand, small companies are often illiquid and highly geared with large borrowing relative to the owners' funds. This is likely to be a source of risk. In the example company, the structure ratios have improved over the period as the company matures.

Current Ratio	Current Assets / Current Liabilities	B15/B32
Quick Ratio (Acid Test)	Current Assets – Stock / Current Liabilities	B15–B13/B32
Working Capital (Thousands)	Current Assets – Current Liabilities	B15–B32
Gross Gearing (%)	Short + Long-term Debt / Equity	B28+B33/B39
Net Gearing (%)	Short + Long-term Debt – Cash – Securities / Equity	B28+B33–P10+ 11/B39
Solvency	Operating Profit / Interest	P16/P17

Table 6.2

Ratio analysis for example company

Item	Dec-96	Dec-97	Dec-98	Dec-99	Dec-00	Action
Core ratios						
Return on Sales (NPAT / Sales %)	3.02	2.74	3.99	5.90	2.76	Worse
Asset Turnover (Sales / Total Assets)	2.65	1.87	1.76	1.86	1.55	Worse
Asset Leverage (Total Assets / Equity)	11.26	16.57	6.49	4.80	5.28	OK
Return on Equity (NPAT / Equity %)	90.09	84.87	45.69	52.80	22.52	Worse
Profitability						
Gross Profit / Sales (%)	9.54	9.17	11.55	14.11	12.31	OK
Net Operating Profit / Sales (%)	3.49	3.30	4.98	6.60	3.23	Worse
Profit before Tax / Sales (%)	3.02	2.74	3.99	5.90	2.76	Worse
Return on Capital Employed (ROCE)	32.99	22.74	24.33	26.95	10.20	Worse
Return on Invested Capital (ROIC)	25.68	17.77	19.59	25.61	9.94	Worse
Return on Assets (ROA)	9.26	6.18	8.77	12.29	4.99	Worse
Operating efficiency						
Inventory Days	–	–	–	3.99	3.07	N/A
Trade Receivables (Debtor) Days	82.75	77.07	65.65	35.97	55.09	OK
Creditors Days	15.54	59.06	49.24	37.46	33.33	Worse
Funding Gap Debtors + Inv. – Creditors	67.21	18.01	16.41	2.49	24.83	Worse
Financial structure						
Current Ratio	1.10	0.74	0.87	1.48	1.58	Better
Quick Ratio (Acid Test)	1.10	0.74	0.87	1.44	1.56	Better
Working Capital (Thousands)	462	(2,246)	(1,296)	5,689	8,164	OK
Gross Gearing (%)	306.31	476.19	190.80	130.45	165.10	OK
Net Gearing (%)	292.25	458.96	178.69	55.36	165.06	OK
Solvency	7.33	5.85	5.05	9.49	6.90	OK

4. TREND ANALYSIS

Trend analysis is difficult from annual reports. However, you can begin to gain a better picture of the key areas of profitability, structure and operating efficiency by looking at the trends. The three approaches involve looking at the individual ratios to ascertain if they are 'sensible', comparing against industry averages and using trend analysis to see how they change over time.

This company is clearly producing a lower return on equity and is failing to maintain its profitability. All the return measures of return on equity, assets and capital employed are declining. In addition, the debtor days are increasing while the creditor days are declining.

The ratios for the example are shown in Table 6.2 formatted to two decimal places.

To illustrate these trends more clearly, the model also makes use of the dynamic graph feature discussed in Chapter 3 and demonstrated in the model Dynamic_Graph. There is a further example in Dynamic_Graph_Ratios, which is a copy of some data in the example model, a combo box control and a chart (see Figure 6.8).

Ratios graph.

Fig 6.8

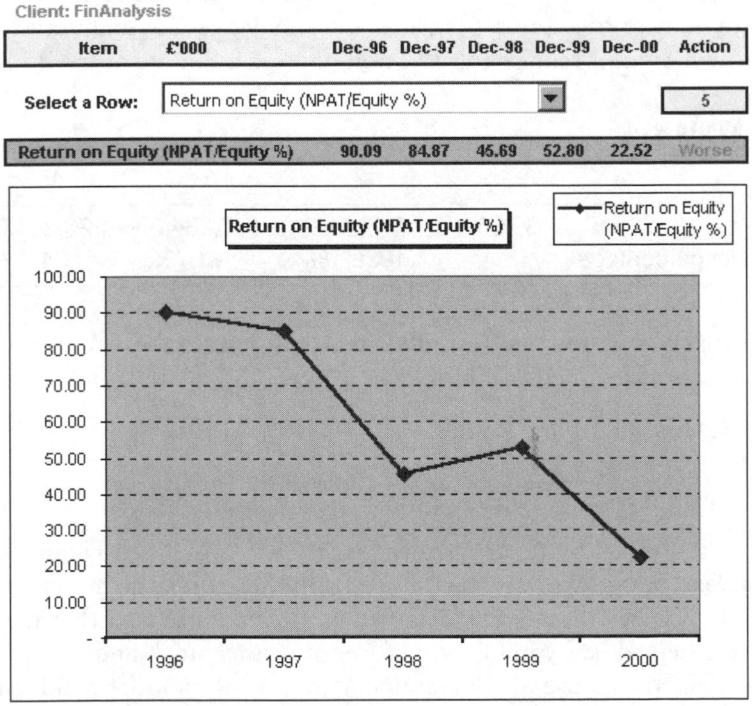

The three statements of profit and loss, balance sheet and ratios constitute a working summary of the five annual reports. The analysis in the Excel model shows a company under financial pressure; however, sales grew strongly in the previous period and levelled in the last period. The next part of the analysis reviews the growth and sustainability.

5. SUSTAINABILITY

Two areas of management are particularly tricky: these are growth and decline. In the latter case management is often not swift enough in taking decisive action and can be overtaken by events. If management follows a more successful strategy, it can withdraw from unprofitable markets and move over a period into other areas where its competencies better fit the market conditions.

Sales growth presents its own problems, since scarce resources are strained in funding greater stocks, work in progress and debtors. Small companies are particularly susceptible to overtrading or growth problems. Companies can be profitable and still go bust due to a lack of liquid resources. You need cash to make money and therefore one area of analysis could be to calculate how quickly a company should grow or what growth can be funded from retained profits.

This is a public company, which experienced high rates of growth in the software market (see Table 6.3). It is a 'knowledge' company and therefore growth did not require the addition of large amounts of fixed plant.

Table 6.3 **Company growth**

	1	2	3	4
Sales	3,706.0	75,531.0	137,234.0	226,284.0
Growth percentage		1938.1%	81.7%	64.9%

The model contains two formulas: the first defines the amount of sales generated from retained earnings:

R = Retained Earnings / Sales
G = Sales Growth %
T = Current Assets / Sales

The growth funded by retained earnings is = R / G * T (see Figure 6.9). In the last year, the growth rate has slowed and therefore a higher proportion of growth has been funded by retained earnings. Note also that the company has received new capital in the form of further stock and new loans.

The calculations use an IF statement to stop the model producing an error by dividing by zero. The references show the source of the figures to help with auditing.

Fig 6.9

Growth formulas.

8	Line	Item £'000	Reference	Dec-96	Dec-97
48		Growth Formulas			
49	R49	R = Retained Earnings / Sales	P27/P10	3.02	2.74
50	R50	G = Sales Growth %	Change in P10	-	33.72
51	R51	T = Current Assets / Sales	B15/P10	29.92	28.74
52	R52	Growth funded by RE = R / G * T		-	28.22
53					
54	R54	Profit Margin (P)	P24/P10	3.02	2.74
55	R55	Retained Earnings (R)	P27/P24	100.00	100.00
56	R56	Asset Turnover (A)	R12	2.65	1.87
57	R57	Asset Equity (T)	B24/B29	-	21.31
58	R58	Sustainable Growth (PRAT)		-	109.19
59					

The second set of formulas derive the sustainable growth by multiplying out the drivers detailed in column G:

- Profit Margin (P)
- Retained Earnings (R)
- Asset Turnover (A)
- Asset Equity (T).

The sustainable growth is lower in the final periods as the balance sheet has weakened. For example, the cash in the business at balance sheet line 10 has reduced in one year from 3,452.0 to 2.0. Again the final column uses IF, AND and OR functions to determine if the formulas are more or less favourable.

The growth formulas confirm that either earnings, new equity or new debt has to fund growth. This company has been growing quickly. Sales growth has reduced in the final period and profitability ratios have declined leading to less efficiency and worsening financial ratios.

6. SUMMARY

The basic financial statements of profit and loss and balance sheet can be used to produce a ratio analysis of a company. This chapter took the basic Application_Template and built the statements around the menu system to reduce development time. The model conforms to the design criteria laid out in the first chapters and is a platform for further analysis such as cash flow and forecasting. The ratios have highlighted some areas for investigation and cash flow analysis will assist further making the analysis model more usable.

7

Cash flow

While the balance sheet and income statement are based on accounting standards and conventions, cash is 'real' and cannot be varied so much by management decisions about presentation. Bankers want to understand cash flows since the priorities are that the company survives and generates sufficient cash to repay loans, lease rentals and other forms of borrowing. Corporate finance today concentrates more on cash as an international measure for assessing performance.

The model introduced in the last chapter, Financial Analysis, reconciles the income statement and balance sheet back to change in cash.

Starting cash balance
+ Cash generated from operations and other sources
– Cash used to fund operations, investment, research, etc.
= Ending cash balance

The model uses a layout which calculates the trading cash or net operating cash flow (NOCF) and then the uses of the cash together with the new capital introduced into the business to reconcile back to bank. As with the balance sheet, the spreadsheet must self-check to rule out any mathematical errors.

The important lines are:

EBITDA	Net operating profit adding back non cash items such as depreciation of fixed assets and amortization of goodwill
Net operating cash flow	Trading cash produced from the trading of the company
Cash flow before financing	Cash before new capital. (This links to the growth formulas in the previous chapter.)

Fig 7.1

Cash flow method.

Cash Flow Method

v1.0 1-Jan-2001

Item	Comment
Net Operating Profit (NOP)	Income Statement
Depreciation / Amortisation	Non cash items
Earnings before Interest, Tax, Depreciation and Amortisation (EBITDA)	
Operating Items	
(+)/- Current Assets	Inc = negative, Dec = positive
+/(-) Current Liabilities	Inc = Positive, Dec = negative
Net Operating Cash Flow (NOCF)	EBITDA + change in working capital
Returns on Investment and Servicing of Finance	
Interest Received	Income statement
Interest Paid	Income statement
Dividends	Income statement
Net Cash Outflow from Returns on Investments and Servicing of Finance	
Taxation	
Taxes Paid	Income statement
Deferred Tax	Change in balance sheet
Net Cash Outflow for Taxation	
Investing Activities	
Expenditure on Property, Plant and Equipment	Change in balance sheet + depreciation in P&L
Expenditure on Investments & Intangibles	Change in balance sheet
Marketable Securities	Change in balance sheet
Net Cash Outflow for Capital Expenditure and Financial Investment	
Exceptional and Minority Items	
Exceptional Income and Expense	Income statement and balance sheet (if applicable)
Net Cash Outflow from Exceptional and Minority Items	
Reconciliation	
Reconciliation Figure	Difference between RE on P&L and balance sheet
Total Cash (Outflow)/Inflow before Financing	Addition
Financing	
Share Capital and Reserves	Change in balance sheet
Short Term Debt and Provisions	Change in balance sheet
Long Term Debt and Provisions	Change in balance sheet
Net Cash Inflow/(Outflow) from Financing	
Increase / (Decrease) in Cash	Addition
Reconciliation of Net Cash Flow to Bank	
Cash	Change in balance sheet
CheckSum:	

Figure 7.1 illustrates the derivation of the lines in the cash flow. This is particularly useful where the information is derived from the change in balance from the beginning to the end of the year in the balance sheet and the amounts passed through the income statement.

1. DERIVING CASH FLOW

There is a model called Cash_Flow_Statement, which demonstrates how the cash flow for the final period is calculated. This contains a copy of the data for the income statement and balance sheet and derives the cash flow statement (see Figure 7.2).

Fig 7.2

Cash flow.

Cash Flow — *Systematic Finance plc*

v1.0 1-Jan-2001

Client: FinAnalysis

Line	Item £'000	Reference	Dec-00
C10	**Net Operating Profit (NOP)**		**1,379.0**
C11	Depreciation / Amortisation	P13.14	1,023.0
C12	**Earnings before Interest, Tax, Depreciation and Amortisation (EBITDA)**		**2,402.0**
	Operating Items		
C15	(+)/- Current Assets	B12.14	(8,112.0)
C16	(+)/- Current Liabilities	B29.31	2,356.0
C17	**Net Operating Cash Flow (NOCF)**		**(3,354.0)**
	Returns on Investment and Servicing of Finance		
C20	Interest Received	P18	-
C21	Interest Paid	P17	(200.0)
C22	Dividends	P26	(420.0)
C23	**Net Cash Outflow from Returns on Investments and Servicing of Finance**		**(620.0)**
	Taxation		
C26	Taxes Paid	P23	-
C27	Deferred Tax	B35	(60.0)
C28	**Net Cash Outflow for Taxation**		**(60.0)**
	Investing Activities		
C31	Expenditure on Property, Plant and Equipment	B19+P13+P14	(1,941.0)
C32	Expenditure on Investments, LT Assets & Intangibles	B20.21+P19	-
C33	Marketable Securities	B11	-
C34	**Net Cash Outflow for Capital Expenditure and Financial Investment**		**(1,941.0)**
	Exceptional and Minority Items		
C37	Exceptional Income and Expense	P21+P25	-
C38	**Net Cash Outflow from Exceptional and Minority Items**		-
	Reconciliation		
C41	Reconciliation Figure		(121.0)
C42	**Total Cash (Outflow)/Inflow before Financing**		**(6,096.0)**
	Financing		
C45	Share Capital and Reserves	B37	-
C46	Short Term Debt and Provisions	B28	(169.0)
C47	Long Term Debt and Provisions	B33	2,815.0
C48	**Net Cash Inflow/(Outflow) from Financing**		**2,646.0**
C49			
C50	**Increase / (Decrease) in Cash**		**(3,450.0)**
	Reconciliation of Net Cash Flow to Bank		
	Cash	B10	(3,450.0)
	CheckSum: No Errors		-

The balance sheet calculates the differences between each of the years. On the asset side of the balance sheet, an increase means that cash is being consumed, while a reduction is a source of cash. If debtors increase, then the company is less efficient in collecting cash and therefore needs more cash to fund the operating cycle. The opposite is true with creditor items. If the creditors rise, then more credit is being extended to the company and this increases cash resources.

Certain items such as fixed assets require items from the balance sheet and income statement. This is the change in net fixed assets plus the depreciation in the income statement. The reconciliation section at the bottom assist with the coding of the cells, since the difference must disappear when all the rows have been included in the calculations. As part of the checking of such a model, you need to try several companies to ensure that all lines are included. For example, this company does not have any investment in intangibles and you need to ensure that the model still works if you do enter values for these items.

The reconciliation item catches any differences between the retained earnings in the income statement and the amount actually added to the reserves in the balance sheet. These could consist of prior year adjustments, translation adjustments, shares issued for scrip dividends, goodwill write-offs or other adjustments.

2. NET OPERATING CASH FLOW (NOCF)

The statement illustrates the reduction in profitability in the last period since the operating cash flow is minus 3.3 million, which is greater than in any previous period. While the company is still profitable, the trading activity is consuming rather than producing cash. When investment in capital equipment is taken into account, the outflow is over 6 million. This is restored in part by new debt so that the final change in cash is minus 3.4 million. These findings add weight to the ratio analysis since the company's performance has declined and this has had an abrupt effect on cash reserves. Anybody lending to this company would want to be certain that the company could fund its existing and new debt out of trading. It is no use borrowing to pay the interest on current commitments.

The ratios schedule contains cash flow ratios at the bottom calculated by dividing different cash measures back into sales:

- EBITDA / Sales (%)
- Net Operating Cash Flow/Sales
- Cash Flow before Financing/Sales.

Cell L43 divides the cash flow by the sales figure:

```
=IF(Income!M10<>0,Cashflow!M12/Income!M10*100,0)
```

3. FREE CASH FLOW

There are many definitions of cash flow and a further definition is free cash flow. This is the cash flow available to pay debt providers and equity holders. It is defined as:

Operating Profit (NOP)
  + Depreciation / Amortization / Non-cash Items
Earnings before Interest, Tax, Depreciation and Amortization (EBITDA)
  +/– Changes in Net Working Assets
Net Operating Cash Flow (NOCF)
  – Expenditure on Property, Plant and Equipment / Proceeds of Sale
  – Net Cash Outflow for Taxation
Operating Free Cash Flow

There is a schedule in the Financial_Analysis model called Free_Cash_Flows. This obtains the information from the cash flow schedule (see Figure 7.3). The free cash outflow is even more marked at over 5 million due to the heavy investment in plant and equipment.

Fig 7.3 **Free cash flow.**

	A	B	C	D	E	J
6		Client: FinAnalysis				
8		Line		Reference	£'000	Dec-00
9						
10		FC10	Free Cash Flow			
11		FC11	Operating Profit (NOP)		C10	1,379.0
12		FC12	Depreciation / Amortisation / Non-cash Items		C11	1,023.0
13		FC13	Earnings before Interest, Tax, Depreciation and Amortisation (EBITDA)		FCF11.12	2,402.0
14		FC14	Changes in Net Working Assets		C15.16	(5,756.0)
15		FC15	Net Operating Cash Flow (NOCF)		FCF13.14	(3,354.0)
16		FC16	Expenditure on Property, Plant and Equipment /Proceeds of Sale		C31	(1,941.0)
17		FC17	Net Cash Outflow for Taxation		C28	(60.0)
18		FC18	Operating Free Cashflow		FCF15.17	(5,355.0)
19						

4. COVER RATIOS

The free cash schedule also includes loan cover. An annual rental is calculated based on a period, nominal interest rate, capital value and terminal or future value. The model computes the annual rental and then cover created by the different cash flow lines (see Figure 7.4). This is just the cash that has to be found rather than loan amortization plus interest. For example, a leasing company needs to understand the sensitivity and uncertainty in the cash flow and this method seeks to highlight the risk. Here a loan of 2 million is extra risk and not covered by the trading history in the last period.

Cell F29 calculates the annual payment using the PMT function:

```
=IF(SUM(F23:F26)<>0,PMT(F24,F23,-ABS(F25),F26,D89),0)
```

Fig 7.4

Loan cover.

	A	B	C	D	E	F
6		Client: FinAnalysis				
8		Line		Reference	£'000	Dec-97
21						
22			Loan Calculation			
23		FC23	Period (Years)	N		5.00 yrs
24		FC24	Interest Rate	I		10.00%
25		FC25	Capital Value £'000	PV		2,000.00
26		FC26	Future or Terminal Value	FV		0.00
27		FC27	Advance or Arrears Payments		Arrears	
28						
29		FC29	Annual Rental £'000			527.6
30						
31						
32						
33			Free Cash Flow			
34		FC34	Operating Profit (NOP) : Times Cover			1.39
35		FC35	Earnings before Interest, Tax, Depreciation and Amortisation (EBITDA) : Times Cover			2.14
36		FC36	Net Operating Cash Flow (NOCF) : Times Cover			6.60
37		FC37	Operating Free Cashflow : Times Cover			(2.05)
38						

5. SUMMARY

Cash is the lifeblood of a company and a model to calculate ratios would be incomplete without a derivation of cash flow. While there are a number of ways of presenting the sources and uses of funds, this method outlines the trading and non-trading uses. The method also computes different levels of cash flow available to different classes of stakeholder and the cover ratios.

8

Forecasting models

Management is concerned with predicting the future whether in strategic planning or annual budgeting. The level of risk or uncertainty may not be known in advance; however, a forecast is an attempt to describe and analyse all the factors that may affect the final outcome. In Excel, you often want to forecast sales or cost figures and this chapter discusses some methods of forecasting.

Examples of forecasting models include:

- production planning and materials scheduling;
- manpower planning;
- project or investment analysis;
- cash budgeting.

Quantitative forecasts start with historic data and pass through these stages:

- purpose of the forecast and the audience and level of detail required;
- time horizon, bearing in mind that the level of uncertainty increases with longer forecasts;
- identification of assumptions or areas of uncertainty;
- applicable techniques;
- application of sensitivity and scenario analysis to test the results;
- monitoring and attempting to improve on the assumptions.

It is worth noting that people often 'believe' Excel-based forecasts since they are well presented and difficult to disprove without auditing the whole model. Without a defined modelling procedure, there are many possibilities of error and, therefore, forecasts should always be checked for mathematical and procedural errors. This is the reason for auditing commercial models to ensure that the model produces the correct results.

1. HISTORIC FORECASTS

Historic or naïve models are based on the relationships within a single set of variables. There is no understanding or attempt to analyse the variables. The relationship in the future will only hold if none of the underlying variables change in value and importance. This is unlikely in the real world and therefore a margin of error must be expected. Indeed the future rarely equals the past.

There are a number of methods in Excel for forecasting forward a set of data. Open the file Forecast_Trends and select the Trends sheet. This shows a set of sales data in blue from the Financial_Analysis model. To forecast the data you could highlight it and drag the numbers forward for the next five years. Excel understands the progressions in numbers or data lists, for example the days in the week, by this same method. You can check the lists or add new ones at `Tools`, `Options`, `Custom Lists`.

Another way of forecasting would be to use the function trend. This uses known Xs and Ys and allows you to specify a new X. The formula in cell I12 uses I8 as the date for the next column.

```
=TREND($D$10:$H$10,$D$8:$H$8,I8)
```

The advantage of this simple forecasting approach is that these plots are easy to produce using the Chart Wizard. Drawing a chart allows you to check that the result looks satisfactory. The chart in Figure 8.1 is a scattergraph with interconnecting lines. Cell H12 looks up the last historic value and the historic and forecast series are drawn so that they appear to connect.

2. TREND LINES

The chart in Figure 8.1 shows another way of forecasting the historic sales data. A simple trend line can be added by right clicking the historic series. Using Options, the trend is projected forward by 1,850 units. The data in row 8 is a time series and therefore delineated in days. Five years equated to approximately 1,850 units.

The trend line matches almost precisely the forecasts produced by dragging the data and the Trend function. One of the options on the trend line is to display the R^2 fit and series equation. The former provides a measure of fit, which in this case is 0.9629. Since 1 is a perfect fit, this represents a good measure.

A linear trend is represented by the equation $y = mx + b$. This is calculated in row 14 as a further forecasting measure.

Fig 8.1 **Trends.**

Client: FinAnalysis

No	Item	Dec-96	Dec-97	Dec-98	Dec-99	Dec-00	Dec-01	Dec-02	Dec-03
P10	(1) Sales	**16,567.0**	**22,154.0**	**29,124.0**	**41,122.0**	**42,758.0**	51,750.0	58,885.0	66,020.0
	(2) Trend Function					42,758.0	51,752.4	58,883.0	66,013.5
	(3) Formula: mx-b						51,758.2	58,888.9	66,019.5

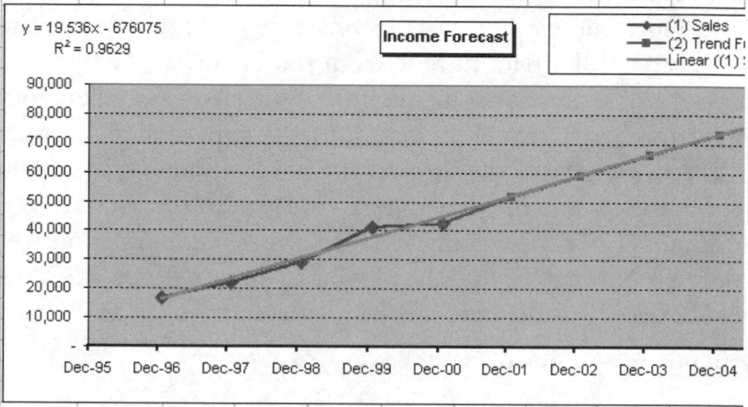

3. TREND LINES FOR ANALYSIS

Trend lines can be combined with controls to provide advanced analysis allowing you to analyse several lines in a table.

As part of the package, Financial_Analysis includes two report schedules, Management_Summary and Management_Analysis. The latter schedule contains three graphs which chart a single line looked up from a block of data below in rows 79 to 214. This is data looked up from the income statement, balance sheet, cash flow, ratios and valuation sheets and includes the forecast dealt with in a later chapter.

The technique is simply to concatenate columns C and D in column Q, for example cell Q79, to provide a list of inputs to the combo box control:

```
=CONCATENATE(C79,D79)
```

The update cell then becomes the input for OFFSET functions across the page to return each of the columns. Therefore, as the user selects a row, to analyse the results in row 16, update and the charts use this data. The labels in cells C16 and C11 also update to make the whole process 'dynamic'. The cell formula in cell F16 is:

```
=OFFSET(F$78,$K$13,0)
```

Dynamic chart.

Fig 8.2

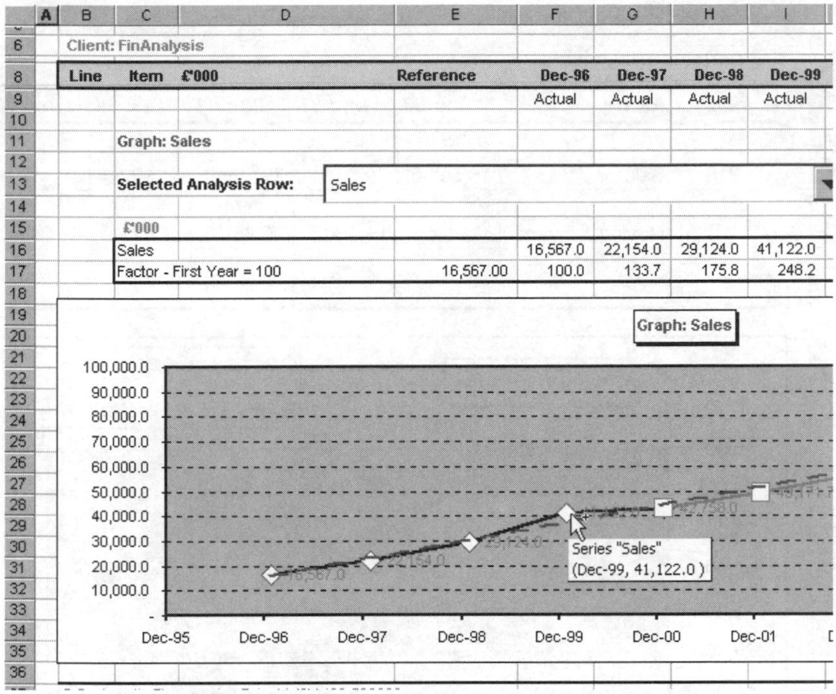

The first graph is a scattergraph, which plots columns F to K as the first series and the forecast from K to O so that the two appear to join. A trend line can then be drawn through the first series and then using the trend line options extended for a further five years (see Figure 8.2). The advantage to the user is the ability to see if the forecast is above or below the trend for the previous periods.

4. DATA SMOOTHING

There are two techniques included in the file, Forecast_Trend. Often data do not seem to fit due to periodic, seasonal or cyclical variations. The two techniques are moving averages and exponential smoothing.

Moving averages simply remove the variation by taking an average of two or more data points. You can do this manually as demonstrated on the Moving_Averages sheet or use a trend line (see Figure 8.3).

This method is easy to understand and requires limited mathematics. The main disadvantage is that all data is weighted equally whereas logically the most recent should carry greater weight. This is addressed by the second method called exponential smoothing, which uses a weighted average of historic data. The future is more likely to be based statistically on the most recent past rather than older results.

Fig 8.3 **Moving averages.**

Client: FinAnalysis						
No	**Item**	**Dec-96**	**Dec-97**	**Dec-98**	**Dec-99**	**Dec-00**
P10	Sales	16,567.0	22,154.0	29,124.0	41,122.0	42,758.0
	Moving Average		19,360.5	25,639.0	35,123.0	41,940.0

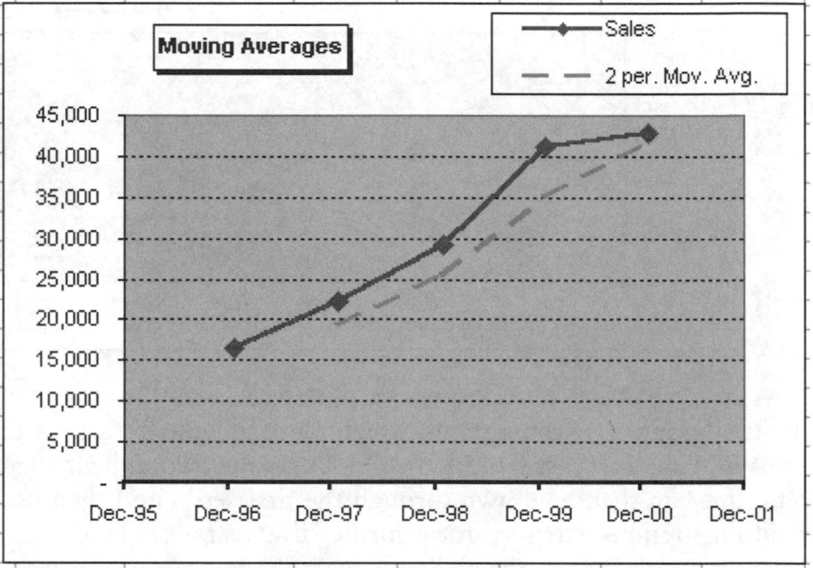

The formula is:

$$y_{new} = Ay_{old} + (1 - A)y_{forecast}$$

y_{new} = smoothed average used as the forecast
y_{old} = last historic data
$y_{forecast}$ = last smoothed forecast
A = smoothing constant.

The model uses Excel Solver in the toolbar `Tools`, `Solver` to minimize the error and recalculate the smoothing constant. The differences between the forecast and the actual are squared and added in cell G23. The result is then square rooted in cell C27 (see Figure 8.4).

Solver calculates the constant as 1.63 and this minimizes the mean squared error in cell C27. The process has been programmed in Visual Basic and the code is:

```
Sub Solver()
SolverReset
SolverOptions precision:=0.001
SolverAdd CellRef:=Range("d6"), Relation:=3, FormulaText:=0
SolverOk SetCell:="$C$27", MaxMinVal:=2, ValueOf:="0",
ByChange:="$D$6"
SolverSolve userFinish:=True
End Sub
```

This resets and clears Solver and first adds the constraint that the constant must be greater than zero. Secondly the code invokes Solver to set cell C27 (mean squared error) to a minimum by changing cell D6 (the constant). `UserFinish:=True` suppresses the Solver dialog box at the end of the process. If you use Solver in macros, you have to ensure that you register it in the Visual Basic editor by accessing `Tools`, `References`. You can then tick Solver so that Excel knows to load Solver every time you open the file (see Figure 8.5).

Fig 8.4

Exponential smoothing.

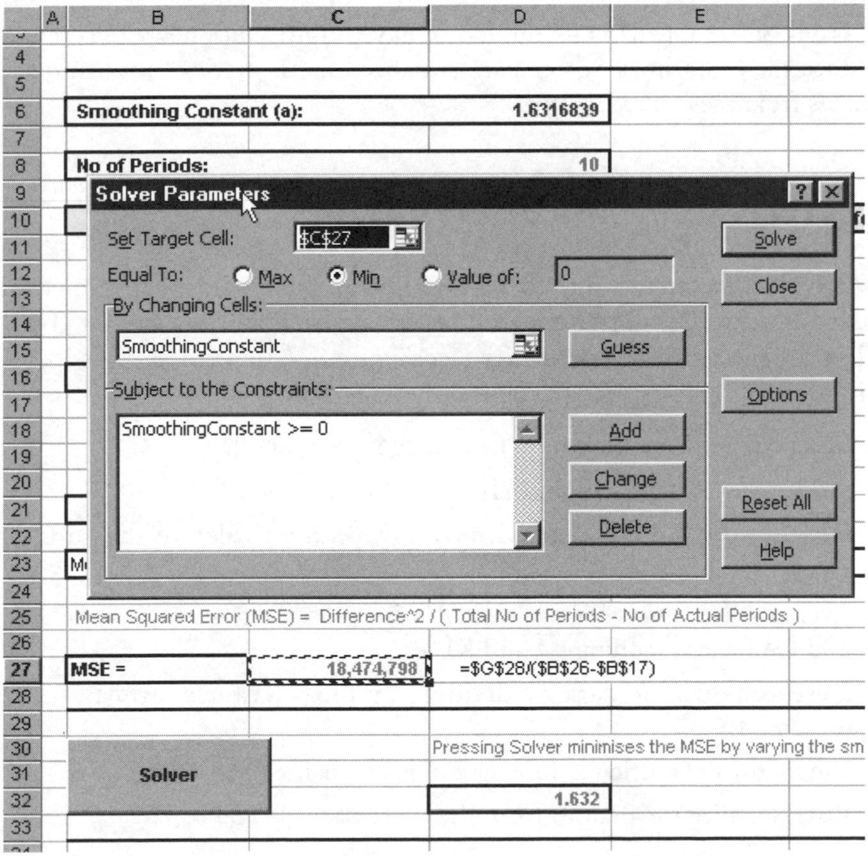

Fig 8.5 **Solver references dialog.**

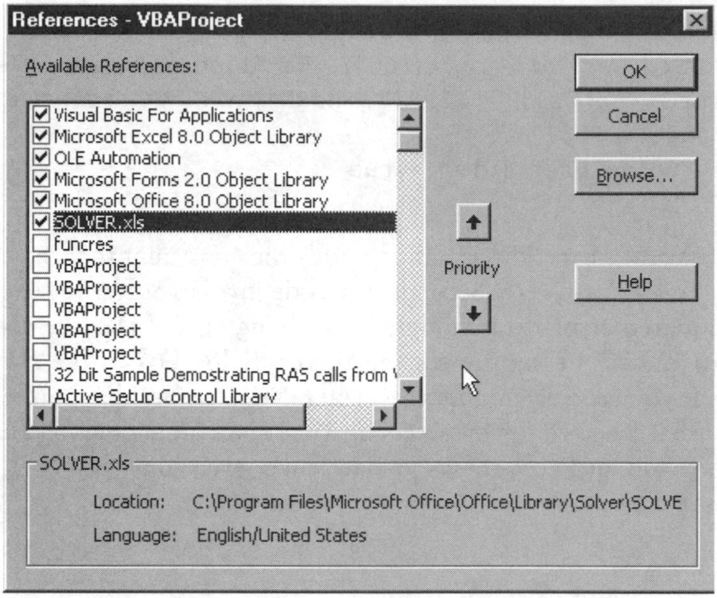

Using Solver means that you do not have to introduce new constants to reduce the error since Solver uses advanced mathematics to work backwards from the desired answer.

5. CYCLICALITY AND SEASONALITY

When data fluctuates due to seasonality or cyclicality, then a method called classical decomposition can be used. This is in the Forecast_Trend file on a sheet called Seasonality (see Figure 8.6). The method is as follows:

- Calculate a four-period moving average (column G).
- Centre the average (column H).
- Divide Sales by the centred moving average to derive the random factor (column I).
- Average the factors for each quarter by averaging all the Q1, Q2, Q3 and Q4 factors (columns J and K).
- Deseasonalize the data by dividing by the relevant quarterly factor (column L).
- Use a Growth Function to forecast the deseasonalized data (cells L34 to L37).
- Reseasonalize the data to form the forecast (cells F34 to F37).

Seasonality.

Fig 8.6

	D	E	F	G	H	I	J	K	L
6	Period = t	Sales	Input Sales	Four Quarter Moving Average	Centred Moving Average	Seasonal Random	Seasonal Factor	Adjusted Seasonal Factor	De seasonalised Data
8			Sales		TC	SR=Sales/ TC		S	Sales/S
9	1	16,567.00	5,000.00				0.9345	0.8850	5,649.67
10	2		3,000.00	4,141.75			0.5836	0.5527	5,427.60
11	3		4,000.00	4,266.75	4,204.25	0.951	1.0328	0.9781	4,089.50
12	4		4,567.00	4,416.75	4,341.75	1.052	1.6727	1.5841	2,882.94
13	5	22,154.00	5,500.00	4,666.75	4,541.75	1.211		0.8850	6,214.64
14	6		3,600.00	5,538.50	5,102.63	0.706		0.5527	6,513.12
15	7		5,000.00	5,663.50	5,601.00	0.893		0.9781	5,111.87
16	8		8,054.00	5,513.50	5,588.50	1.441		1.5841	5,084.13
17	9	29,124.00	6,000.00	6,013.50	5,763.50	1.041		0.8850	6,779.61
18	10		3,000.00	7,281.00	6,647.25	0.451		0.5527	5,427.60
19	11		7,000.00	7,531.00	7,406.00	0.945		0.9781	7,156.62
20	12		13,124.00	8,281.00	7,906.00	1.660		1.5841	8,284.59
21	13	41,122.00	7,000.00	9,281.00	8,781.00	0.797		0.8850	7,909.54
22	14		6,000.00	10,280.50	9,780.75	0.613		0.5527	10,855.20
23	15		11,000.00	10,330.50	10,305.50	1.067		0.9781	11,246.12
24	16		17,122.00	10,330.50	10,330.50	1.657		1.5841	10,808.34
25	17	42,758.00	7,200.00	10,580.50	10,455.50	0.689		0.8850	8,135.53
26	18		6,000.00	10,689.50	10,635.00	0.564		0.5527	10,855.20
27	19		12,000.00	8,889.50	9,789.50	1.226		0.9781	12,268.49
28	20		17,558.00	9,286.06	9,087.78	1.932		1.5841	11,083.57
30	210		7,586.25	7,525.37	7,570.45		4.2235	4.0000	109,441.07
34	21		11273.63					0.8850	12738.47
35	22		7444.69					0.5527	13468.93
36	23		13929.62					0.9781	14241.29
37	24		23853.97					1.5841	15057.93

Seasonality chart.

Fig 8.7

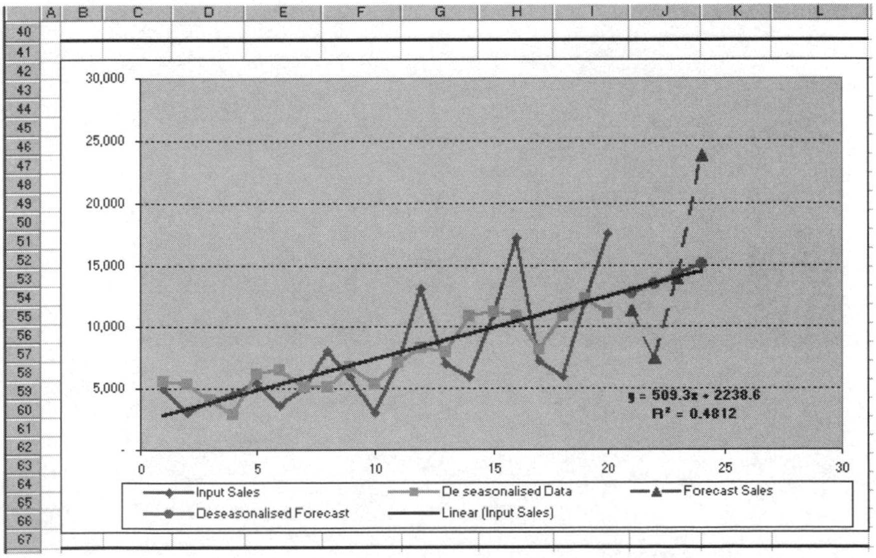

The resulting chart shown in Figure 8.7 shows:

- actual and smoothed historic data;
- forecast smoothed and seasonal series;
- trend line through the sales data.

6. SUMMARY

This chapter has introduced forecasting methods based simply on previous results together with more advanced methods such as exponential smoothing, moving averages and time series decomposition. Whatever method is chosen, you need to look carefully at the basis for the forecast and ensure that there is sufficient underlying data for some measure of confidence in the results. For example, consider the source and reliability of the data, the possible bias or presence of random factors and the likelihood that the forecast can be achieved. This is particularly important for sales forecasts since they need to be linked to strategy and decisions about resources.

9

Forecasting financials

The last chapter introduced statistical methods for forecasting sales and other variables. This chapter outlines methods for redrawing the historic income statement for future periods using the file Financial_Analysis. Companies forecast for strategic planning and bankers are interested in calculating the future cash flows of a company for underwriting a loan or project finance. Since the ratio and cash flow analysis was historic, forecasting provides an opportunity for estimating future performance.

Since a model exists in the form of the Financial_Analysis application, the techniques have been layered onto the existing schedules. The advantages are:

- the framework already exists for all the financial statements;
- the resulting model will be more comprehensive and useful;
- this approach saves the user from learning a new format.

The completed model should answer a number of questions, for example:

- Does the company possess sufficient facility to fund the anticipated growth?
- Will the company's balance sheet strengthen or weaken?
- Are there other areas which require investigation?

The method is to review the 'drivers' or important variables in the historic statements and then use the percentages to 'drive' a pro-forma income statement and balance sheet forward. With these schedules in place, the model can derive the cash flow and ratios. Comparisons are than possible between the historic and future projections. In addition, modelling allows you to examine the behaviour and sensitivity of variables, especially how changes 'flex' the result.

This chapter works through a forecast for Technology Sales Limited and produces its pro-forma statements. This could be an internal analysis or a forecast to support new borrowings in order to convince a banker of the quality and quantity of cash flow.

1. KEY DRIVERS

This approach is sometimes called percent of sales forecasting. It involves calculating:

- profit and loss items as a percentage of sales;
- balance sheet items as a percentage of sales;
- drawing the profit and loss;
- drawing the balance sheet;
- use cash or short-term overdraft as the 'plug' to make the balance sheet add up.

Figure 9.1 is an extract from the Forecast sheet showing the historic percentages.

Fig 9.1

Key drivers.

	A	B	C	D	E	H	I	J
6		Client: FinAnalysis						
8		Line	Item	£'000	Reference	Dec-98	Dec-99	Dec-00
9						Actual	Actual	Actual
10			Forecast					
11		F11	Initial sales		P10	29,124.0	41,122.0	42,758.0
12		F12	Sales growth		Change P10	31.5%	41.2%	4.0%
13		F13	Costs of goods sold/Sales		P11/P10	88.4%	85.9%	87.7%
14		F14	Depreciation rate		P13.P14/B19	8.2%	24.5%	19.1%
15		F15	SG&A/Sales		P15/P10	4.4%	4.9%	6.7%
16		F16	Interest paid on debt		P17/B28+B33	5.9%	4.8%	2.3%
17		F17	Interest earned on cash		P18.19/B10.11	-	-	-
18		F18	Exceptionals/Sales		P21/F11	-	-	-
19		F19	Marginal tax rate		P23/P22	-	-	-
20		F20	Dividend payout ratio		P26/P24	-	22.6%	35.6%
21		F21	Net fixed assets/Sales		B19/F11	26.1%	10.8%	12.5%
22		F22	Intangibles/Sales		B20.21/F11	-	-	-
23		F23	Current assets/Sales		B12.14/F11	29.6%	34.5%	52.2%
24		F24	Current liabilities/Sales		B32-B28/F11	30.1%	27.8%	32.2%
25		F25	Debt/Sales		B33+B28/F11	16.7%	14.6%	20.2%
26		F26	Deferred tax/Sales		B35/F11	1.2%	0.1%	-
27		F27	New Equity		B37	1,265	635	-
28								

Since most variables are assumed to have a linear relationship to sales, the only difficulties are interest payments, receipts and depreciation. These require information from the income statement and balance sheet as detailed in Figure 9.2. New equity is an actual amount rather than a percentage.

Fig 9.2

Variables.

Item	Reference	
Forecast		
Initial sales	P10	Use last year as the base
Sales growth	Change P10	Sales growth
Costs of goods sold/Sales	P11/P10	
Depreciation rate	P13.P14/B19	Depreciation on previous year's fixed asset in balance sheet
SG&A/Sales	P15/P10	
Interest paid on debt	P17/B28+B33	Interest paid on debt in balance sheet
Interest earned on cash	P18.19/B10.11	Interest received on marketable securities in balance sheet
Exceptionals/Sales	P21/F11	
Marginal tax rate	P23/P22	Tax paid / Profit before tax
Dividend payout ratio	P26/P24	Dividends / Profit after tax
Net fixed assets/Sales	B19/F11	
Intangibles/Sales	B20.21/F11	
Current assets/Sales	B12.14/F11	
Current liabilities/Sales	B32-B28/F11	
Debt/Sales	B33+B28/F11	
Deferred tax/Sales	B35/F11	
New Equity	B37	Actual amount

Sales growth is usually the most important variable since it propels the company forward. The growth rate in cell G12 of 33.7% is based on this formula. In all cases, the model will display zero if there are no sales in the previous period, and it will suppress mathematical errors.

```
=IF(F11=0,0,(G11-F11)/F11)
```

Columns K to O are inputs for the five years of the forecast. The user simply reviews the previous five-year period and after investigation selects a percentage for each of the variables (see Figure 9.3). It is a good idea to establish a 'Base Case' and save it as a scenario using `Tools`, `Scenarios`, Add. It is likely that you would want to test various views of the future and scenarios are a good way of recording the 'audit trail'.

The percentages are all in blue as input cells. You can then develop the answers by changing individual years. There is no rule that sales growth or depreciation has to be the same each year.

Fig 9.3

Forecast variables.

	A	B	C	D	E	J	K	L	M
6		Client: FinAnalysis							
8		Line	Item	£'000	Reference	Dec-00	Dec-01	Dec-02	Dec-03
9						Actual	Forecast	Forecast	Forecast
10			Forecast						
11		F11	Initial sales		P10	42,758.0	49,171.7	56,547.5	65,029.6
12		F12	Sales growth		Change P10	4.0%	15.0%	15.0%	15.0%
13		F13	Costs of goods sold/Sales		P11/P10	87.7%	87.0%	87.0%	87.0%
14		F14	Depreciation rate		P13.P14/B19	19.1%	15.0%	15.0%	15.0%
15		F15	SG&A/Sales		P15/P10	6.7%	6.5%	6.5%	6.5%
16		F16	Interest paid on debt		P17/B28+B33	2.3%	4.0%	4.0%	4.0%
17		F17	Interest earned on cash		P18.19/B10.11	-	2.0%	2.0%	2.0%
18		F18	Exceptionals/Sales		P21/F11	-	0.0%	0.0%	0.0%
19		F19	Marginal tax rate		P23/P22	-	20.0%	20.0%	20.0%
20		F20	Dividend payout ratio		P26/P24	35.6%	40.0%	40.0%	40.0%
21		F21	Net fixed assets/Sales		B19/F11	12.5%	8.0%	8.0%	8.0%
22		F22	Intangibles/Sales		B20.21/F11	-	0.0%	0.0%	0.0%
23		F23	Current assets/Sales		B12.14/F11	52.2%	50.0%	50.0%	50.0%
24		F24	Current liabilities/Sales		B32-B28/F11	32.2%	35.0%	35.0%	35.0%
25		F25	Debt/Sales		B33+B28/F11	20.2%	15.0%	15.0%	15.0%
26		F26	Deferred tax/Sales		B35/F11	-	0.0%	0.0%	0.0%
27		F27	New Equity		B37	-	1,000	500	-
28									

Fig 9.4

	A	B	C	D	E	J	K	L	M
6		Client: FinAnalysis							
8		Line	Item	£'000	Reference	Dec-00	Dec-01	Dec-02	Dec-03
9						Actual	Forecast	Forecast	Forecast
20		F20	Dividend payout ratio		P26/P24	35.6%	40.0%	40.0%	40.0%
21		F21	Net fixed assets/Sales		B19/F11	12.5%	8.0%	8.0%	8.0%
22		F22	Intangibles/Sales		B20.21/F11	-	0.0%	0.0%	0.0%
23		F23	Current assets/Sales		B12.14/F11	52.2%	40.0%	40.0%	50.0%
24		F24	Current liabilities/Sales		B32-B28/F11	32.2%	30.0%	30.0%	35.0%
25		F25	Debt/Sales		B33+B28/F11	20.2%	15.0%	15.0%	15.0%
26		F26	Deferred tax/Sales		B35/F11	-	0.0%	0.0%	0.0%
27		F27	New Equity		B37	-	1,000	500	-
28									
29									
30			Results						
31		F31	Net Operating Profit (NOP)		P16	1,379	2,393	3,086	3,548
32		F32	Shareholders' Funds		B39	5,235	7,225	9,119	10,731
33		F33	Net Operating Cash Flow (NOCF)		C17	(3,354.00)	6,425	2,882	(19.92)
34		F34	Return on Equity (NPAT/Equity %)		R14	23	23	25	25
35									

The model provides the user with immediate feedback as each variable is changed. You do not want to have to select the forecast statement to see the answer every time you change an input cell. Below the main table, there is a table of results showing the net operating profit, shareholders' funds, net operating cash flow and the return on equity (see Figure 9.4).

Table 9.1 gives details of the construction of the financial statements.

Construction of the financial statements.

Table 9.1

Item	Calculation
Sales	Calculate using sales growth
Costs of goods sold	Gross profit margin in Forecast
Depreciation	Use depreciation rate on last year's fixed assets
Net operating profit (NOP)	
Interest paid on debt	Use interest % on beginning of year debt
Interest earned on cash	Interest % in Forecast
Exceptional items	Include actual from Forecast
Profit before tax (EBT)	Sum
Taxes	Tax payout ratio in Forecast
Profit after tax (EAT)	Sum
Dividends	Dividend payout ratio in Forecast
Retained earnings (RE)	
Balance sheet	
Cash and marketable securities	Derived by deduction of assets and liabilities
Current assets:	
Debtors	Debtor / Sales in Forecast
Inventory	Inventory / COGS in Forecast
Fixed assets:	FA / Sales in Forecast
At cost	
Depreciation	Depreciation rate on starting FA in forecast
Net fixed assets	
Intangibles	Input if relevant
Total assets	
Current liabilities	Creditors / COGS in Forecast
Tax	
Debt	Debt / Sales in Forecast
Stock/equity	Input increase or decrease in Forecast
Accumulated retained earnings	Add retained earnings from income statement to balance sheet
Total liabilities and equity	

2. DERIVING FINANCIAL STATEMENTS

The model produces the income statement and balance sheet by applying the ratio percentages to the enhanced sales (see Figure 9.5). These are called FIncome and FBalance and follow exactly the framework of the historic sheets. The past results are repeated together with the future values.

Colour coding in the form of shaded cells is also used to highlight the forecast. The method to create the sheets was as follows:

- Insert a worksheet.
- Run the SetUpSheet to format the sheet and write the header and footers for printing.
- Change the name to 'F', e.g. FIncome.
- Copy the income statement and paste into the new sheet.
- Code the labels in columns B to G to look up the historic sheet (this means that if you change anything on the Income sheet it will update on the forecast).
- Insert the formulas in the historic cells to look up the values in the historic sheet.
- Insert the formulas by multiplying out from the Forecast sheet.
- Check the results including the signs (negative or positive).

The formulas use the forecast sheet to derive the new values, as with the detail for column N shown in Figure 9.6. In rows 17 and 18, the logic checks if cash is positive or negative and only applies funding interest on negative balances. The cash rules are followed and costs are all negative.

Fig 9.5

Income statement.

	A	B	C	D	E	F	G	N	O	P	Q
6		Client: FinAnalysis									
8		No		Item	£'000			Dec-01	Dec-02	Dec-03	Dec-04
9								Forecast	Forecast	Forecast	Forecast
10		P10		Sales				49,171.7	56,547.5	65,029.6	74,784.0
11		P11		Cost of Goods Sold				(42,779.4)	(49,196.3)	(56,575.7)	(65,062.1)
12		P12	Gross Margin					6,392.3	7,351.2	8,453.8	9,721.9
13		P13		Depreciation		Manufacturer		(603.3)	(590.1)	(678.6)	(780.4)
14		P14				Amortisation/Other		-	-	-	-
15		P15		Sales, General &Administration Overheads				(3,196.2)	(3,675.6)	(4,226.9)	(4,861.0)
16		P16	Net Operating Profit (NOP)					2,392.9	3,085.5	3,548.4	4,080.6
17		P17		Interest Expense				(331.4)	(295.0)	(339.3)	(390.2)
18		P18		Interest Income				0.0	115.0	148.5	110.6
19		P19		Other Financial Income				-	-	-	-
20		P20	Profit after Financial Items					2,061.6	2,905.5	3,357.5	3,801.0
21		P21		Exceptional Expense				-	-	-	-
22		P22	Profit before Tax					2,061.6	2,905.5	3,357.5	3,801.0
23		P23		Tax				(412.3)	(581.1)	(671.5)	(760.2)
24		P24	Net Profit after Tax (NPAT)					1,649.3	2,324.4	2,686.0	3,040.8
25		P25		Minority Interest				-	-	-	-
26		P26		Dividends				(659.7)	(929.8)	(1,074.4)	(1,216.3)
27		P27	Retained Profit for the Year					989.6	1,394.6	1,611.6	1,824.5
28											

The balance sheet follows the same pattern using the drivers from the Forecasting sheet (see Figure 9.7). Where necessary, the model apportions the forecast percentage between different rows. The current assets percentage is 40% and this is split between debtors, inventory and sundry current assets in rows 12 to 14.

```
=(Forecast!K$11*Forecast!K$23)*(M12/SUM(M$12:M$14))
```

Cash and short-term debt are used to balance the assets and liabilities as the model 'plug'. The model includes workings at row 47 on the forecast balance sheet which compare the assets without cash to the liabilities without short-term debt. If the assets are greater than the liabilities, the model assumes there is a requirement for loans. In the event that liabilities are greater than assets, the model adds the balance to cash.

Cell logic.

Fig 9.6

	N
6	
8	**=EDATE(M8,12)**
9	=IF(N8<=EndDate,"Actual","Forecast")
10	=Forecast!K11
11	=-N10*Forecast!K13
12	**=SUM(N10:N11)**
13	=-Forecast!K14*FBalance!M19
14	=M14
15	=-Forecast!K15*Forecast!K11
16	**=SUM(N12:N15)**
17	=-FBalance!M33*Forecast!K16+IF(FBalance!M10<0,FBalance!M10*Forecast!K16,0)
18	=(IF(FBalance!M10<0,0,FBalance!M10)+FBalance!M11)*Forecast!K17
19	=M19
20	**=SUM(N16:N19)**
21	=Forecast!K18*Forecast!K11
22	**=SUM(N20:N21)**
23	=-Forecast!K19*FIncome!N22
24	**=SUM(N22:N23)**
25	=M25
26	=IF(N24>0,-Forecast!K20*FIncome!N24,0)
27	**=SUM(N24:N26)**
28	

The balance sheet self-checks and there are no errors at the bottom in row 43. If there are errors of addition, an error message is displayed.

With the completed financial statements, you can review the figures for obvious logic and formula errors and then examine the trends in the figures. The sales growth has to be financed and therefore you would expect to see changes in the structure of the balance sheet:

- fixed assets – new and replacement assets;
- debtors + inventory – creditors = funding gap;
- discretionary funding = new loans and equity.

Fig 9.7

Balance sheet.

	A	B	C D E F	G H	N	O	P	Q
6		Client: FinAnalysis						
8		No	Assets £'000		Dec-01	Dec-02	Dec-03	Dec-04
9					Forecast	Forecast	Forecast	Forecast
10		B10	Cash and Deposits		5,749.4	7,422.8	5,528.4	6,572.6
11		B11	Marketable Securities		-	-	-	-
12		B12	Trade Receivables (Debtors):		5,691.7	6,545.4	9,409.1	10,820.4
13		B13	Inventory		277.8	319.5	459.2	528.1
14		B14	Sundry Current Assets		13,699.2	15,754.1	22,646.5	26,043.5
15		B15	**Current Assets**		**25,418.1**	**30,041.8**	**38,043.2**	**43,964.6**
16		B16	Land and Buildings		1,254.7	1,442.9	1,659.3	1,908.2
17		B17	Plant and Machinery		4,170.3	4,795.8	5,515.2	6,342.5
18		B18	Depreciation		(1,491.2)	(1,714.9)	(1,972.1)	(2,268.0)
19		B19	**Net Property, Plant and Equipment**		**3,933.7**	**4,523.8**	**5,202.4**	**5,982.7**
20		B20	Other Investments		-	-	-	-
21		B21	Intangibles/Goodwill		-	-	-	-
22		B22	**Non Current and Fixed Assets**		**3,933.7**	**4,523.8**	**5,202.4**	**5,982.7**
23		B23						
24		B24	**Total Assets**		**29,351.8**	**34,565.5**	**43,245.6**	**49,947.3**
25								
26		No	Liabilities £'000		Dec-01	Dec-02	Dec-03	Dec-04
27								
28		B28	Short Term Bank Loans		-	-	-	-
29		B29	Trade Creditors (Receivables)		3,664.9	4,214.6	5,654.6	6,502.8
30		B30	Other Creditors		2,851.4	3,279.1	4,399.5	5,059.4
31		B31	Other Current Liabilities		8,235.2	9,470.5	12,706.3	14,612.2
32		B32	**Current Liabilities**		**14,751.5**	**16,964.2**	**22,760.4**	**26,174.4**
33		B33	Long Term Bank Loans		7,375.8	8,482.1	9,754.4	11,217.6
34		B34	**Long Term Liabilities**		**7,375.8**	**8,482.1**	**9,754.4**	**11,217.6**
35		B35	Tax/Deferred Taxation		-	-	-	-
36		B36	**Long Term Liabilities and Provisions**		**7,375.8**	**8,482.1**	**9,754.4**	**11,217.6**
37		B37	Ordinary Shares (Common Stock)		3,000.0	3,500.0	3,500.0	3,500.0
38		B38	Profit and Loss Reserve (Retained Earnings)		4,224.6	5,619.2	7,230.8	9,055.3
39		B39	**Shareholders' Funds**		**7,224.6**	**9,119.2**	**10,730.8**	**12,555.3**
40		B40						
41		B41	**Total Liabilities and Equity**		**29,351.8**	**34,565.5**	**43,245.6**	**49,947.3**

The new funding requirement, expressed simply in this model as cash, is either positive or negative and makes the balance sheet assets equal liabilities. These are the cash workings in N10, which represent liabilities and equity and all the asset rows except cash:

```
=N41-SUM(N20:N21)-SUM(N16:N18)-SUM(N11:N14)
```

The second stage of the forecast is to copy forward cash flow and ratios information to new worksheets. You can then update the cell formulas to point at FIncome and FBalance. Since the logic on the cash flow worked with the historic sheet, it must also work when using data from the forecast.

The formula in cell N15, change in current assets, calculates the difference between the two balance sheet dates:

```
=SUM(FBalance!M12:FBalance!M14)–SUM(FBalance!N12:FBalance!N14)
```

The other cells all follow exactly the logic in the Cashflow sheet (see Figure 9.8). The advantage is now a longer period to view:

- Earnings before Interest, Tax, Depreciation and Amortization (EBITDA);
- Net Operating Cash Flow;
- Cash Flow before Financing.

Fig 9.8

Forecast cash flow.

Client: FinAnalysis

Line	Item £'000	Dec-01	Dec-02	Dec-03	Dec-04
		Forecast	Forecast	Forecast	Forecast
C10	**Net Operating Profit (NOP)**	**2,392.9**	**3,085.5**	**3,548.4**	**4,080.6**
C11	Depreciation / Amortisation	803.3	590.1	678.6	780.4
C12	**Earnings before Interest, Tax, Depreciation and**	**3,196.2**	**3,675.6**	**4,226.9**	**4,861.0**
C14	**Operating Items**				
C15	(+)/- Current Assets	2,634.3	(2,950.3)	(9,895.8)	(4,877.2)
C16	+/(-) Current Liabilities	969.5	2,212.7	5,796.1	3,414.1
C17	**Net Operating Cash Flow (NOCF)**	**6,800.0**	**2,938.0**	**127.2**	**3,397.8**
C19	**Returns on Investment and Servicing of Finance**				
C20	Interest Received	0.0	115.0	148.5	110.6
C21	Interest Paid	(331.4)	(295.0)	(339.3)	(390.2)
C22	Dividends	(659.7)	(929.8)	(1,074.4)	(1,216.3)
C23	**Net Cash Outflow from Returns on Investments**	**(991.0)**	**(1,109.8)**	**(1,265.2)**	**(1,495.9)**
C24	**Taxation**				
C25	Taxes Paid	(412.3)	(581.1)	(671.5)	(760.2)
C26	Deferred Tax	-	-	-	-
C27	**Net Cash Outflow for Taxation**	**(412.3)**	**(581.1)**	**(671.5)**	**(760.2)**
C29	**Investing Activities**				
C30	Expenditure on Property, Plant and Equipmen	618.0	(1,180.1)	(1,357.1)	(1,560.7)
C31	Expenditure on Investments, LT Assets & Int	-	-	-	-
C32	Marketable Securities	-	-	-	-
C33	**Net Cash Outflow for Capital Expenditure and Fin**	**618.0**	**(1,180.1)**	**(1,357.1)**	**(1,560.7)**
C35	**Exceptional and Minority Items**				
C36	Exceptional Income and Expense	-	-	-	-
C37	**Net Cash Outflow from Exceptional and Minority**	-	-	-	-
C39	**Reconciliation**				
C40	Reconciliation Figure	-	-	-	-
C41	**Total Cash (Outflow)/Inflow before Financing**	**6,014.7**	**67.0**	**(3,166.6)**	**(419.0)**

The ratios are forecast using the same method in FRatios, by copying forward and then using `Edit`, `Replace` to update the cells and then copy to the right (see Figure 9.9).

The text on the right refers to the last two years actual and the first year of the forecast to provide some information on the direction of the ratios. If the forecast is better than the last two, the cell displays 'Better', and if an improvement over one of two, displays 'OK'. If the ratio has deteriorated, the cell reads 'Worse'. The formula in cell R11 reads:

```
=IF(K11=0,"N/A",IF(L11=0,"N/A",IF(AND(M11/L11>1,M11/K11>
1),"Better",IF(OR(M11/L11>1,M11/K11>1),"OK","Worse"))))
```

Fig 9.9 **Forecast ratios.**

	A	B	C	D	E	F	M	N	O	R
6		Client: FinAnalysis								
8		Line		Item	£'000		Dec-01	Dec-02	Dec-03	Dec-01
9							Forecast	Forecast	Forecast	Forecast
10			Core Ratios							
11		R11		Return on Sales (NPAT/Sales %)			3.35	4.11	4.13	OK
12		R12		Asset Turnover (Sales / Total Assets)			1.68	1.64	1.50	OK
13		R13		Asset Leverage (Total Assets/Equity)			4.06	3.79	4.03	Worse
14		R14		Return on Equity (NPAT/Equity %)			22.83	25.49	25.03	OK
17			Profitability							
18		R18		Gross Profit / Sales (%)			13.00	13.00	13.00	OK
19		R19		Net Operating Profit / Sales (%)			4.87	5.46	5.46	OK
20		R20		Profit before Tax / Sales (%)			4.19	5.14	5.16	OK
21		R21		Return on Capital Employed (ROCE)			16.39	17.53	17.32	OK
22		R22		Return on Invested Capital (ROIC)			19.67	21.04	20.79	OK
23		R23		Return on Assets (ROA)			8.15	8.93	8.21	OK
26			Operating Efficiency							
27		R27		Inventory Days			2.37	2.37	2.96	Better
28		R28		Trade Receivables (Debtor) Days			42.25	42.25	52.81	OK
29		R29		Creditors Days			31.27	31.27	36.48	Worse
30		R30		Funding Gap Debtors+Inventory-Creditors			13.35	13.35	19.29	OK
33			Financial Structure							
34		R34		Current Ratio			1.72	1.77	1.67	Better
35		R35		Quick Ratio (Acid Test)			1.70	1.75	1.65	Better
36		R36		Working Capital (Thousands)			10,667	13,078	15,283	Better
37		R37		Gross Gearing (%)			102.09	93.01	90.90	Worse
38		R38		Net Gearing (%)			22.51	11.62	39.38	Worse
39		R39		Solvency			7.22	10.46	10.46	OK
42			Cashflow Ratios							
43		R43		EBITDA / Sales (%)			6.50	6.50	6.50	OK
44		R44		Net Operating Cash Flow/Sales			13.83	5.20	0.20	OK
45		R45		Cash Flow before Financing/Sales			12.23	0.12	(4.87)	OK
46										

3. ALTERNATIVE APPROACHES

There are other methods of forecasting the financial statements which are more complex than the method outlined in this chapter. One is to use ratios and actual figures rather than percentages as in Table 9.2.

Again, cash or short-term debt is used to balance the assets and liabilities. The model could be made iterative such that negative cash could be added to short-term debt, while cash is shown with current assets. This approach has not been adopted with the example model in order to keep the construction as simple as possible.

Table 9.2

Alternative forecasting method

Item	Calculation
Sales	Calculate using sales growth
Cost of goods sold	Calculate using gross profit margin
Depreciation	Use Depreciation. / Average fixed assets ratio
Net operating profit (NOP)	
Interest paid on debt	Use interest % on average debt (beginning plus end of year / 2)
Interest earned on cash	Simplify and use above figure
Exceptional items	Include actual from forecast
Profit before tax (EBT)	Sum
Taxes	Use tax payout ratio
Profit after tax (EAT)	Sum
Dividends	Use dividend payout ratio
Retained earnings (RE)	
Balance sheet	
Cash and marketable securities	Derived by deduction of assets and liabilities
Current assets:	
Debtors	Use debtor days based on sales
Inventory	Use inventory days based on cost of goods sold
Fixed assets:	Add CAPEX to fixed assets
At cost	
Depreciation	Add P&L depreciation to balance
Net fixed assets	
Intangibles	Input if relevant
Total assets	
Current liabilities	Use creditor days based on goods sold
Tax	
Debt	Add new long-term debt
Stock/equity	Add equity increase or decrease
Accumulated retained earnings	Add retained earnings to balance
Total liabilities and equity	

4. FINANCIAL ANALYSIS

The qualitative analysis shows an improving position with solid cash flow over the forecast period. It is, in the experience of the author, possible to be extraordinarily bullish in a spreadsheet and somehow to lose touch with reality on how the forecast result could be achieved. Certainly, this company expects a dramatic improvement in its fortunes!

There are two more schedules in the application to assist with analysis, called Management_Summary and Management_Analysis. The first looks up important lines in the other schedules and puts together the summary of the income statement, balance sheet, cash flow and ratios (see Figure 9.10). The tests on the right try to assist with pinpointing the rows for management attention in the first year of the forecast.

Fig 9.10 **Management summary.**

	A	B	C	D	K	L	M	N
6		Client: FinAnalysis						
8		Line	Item	£'000	Dec-01	Dec-02	Dec-03	Dec-04
9					Forecast	Forecast	Forecast	Forecast
10		S10	Sales		49,171.7	56,547.5	65,029.6	74,784.0
11		S30	Sales growth		15.0%	15.0%	15.0%	15.0%
12		S11	Gross Margin		6,392.3	7,351.2	8,453.8	9,721.9
13		S12	Net Operating Profit (NOP)		2,392.9	3,085.5	3,548.4	4,080.6
14		S13	Net Profit after Tax (NPAT)		1,649.3	2,324.4	2,686.0	3,040.8
15								
16		S15	Current Assets		25,418.1	30,041.8	38,043.2	43,964.6
17		S16	Non Current and Fixed Assets		3,933.7	4,523.8	5,202.4	5,982.7
18		S17	Current Liabilities		14,751.5	16,964.2	22,760.4	26,174.4
19		S18	Long Term Liabilities and Provisions		7,375.8	8,482.1	9,754.4	11,217.6
20		S19	Shareholders' Funds		7,224.6	9,119.2	10,730.8	12,555.3
21								
22		S21	Net Operating Cash Flow (NOCF)		6,800.0	2,938.0	127.2	3,397.8
23		S22	Total Cash (Outflow)/Inflow before Financ		6,014.7	67.0	(3,166.6)	(419.0)
24		S23	Increase / (Decrease) in Cash		5,747.4	1,673.4	(1,894.3)	1,044.1
25								
26		S25	Return on Sales (NPAT/Sales %)		3.35	4.11	4.13	4.07
27		S26	Asset Turnover (Sales / Total Assets)		1.68	1.64	1.50	1.50
28		S27	Asset Leverage (Total Assets/Equity)		4.06	3.79	4.03	3.98
29		S28	Return on Equity (NPAT/Equity %)		22.83	25.49	25.03	24.22
30								

The Management_Analysis looks up each line from the four forecast schedules in rows 79 to 214 and uses a combo control and an OFFSET function to form a dynamic graph. This enables you to analyse a line on three graphs:

- line graph with three series: historic, forecast and historic trend line extrapolated by five years;
- block graph of the historic and forecast figures;
- block graph of the factors where the first period is equal to 100.

An example of the historic and forecast net operating cash flow is shown in Figure 9.11. This method illustrates clearly the reduction in cash flow in year 4. The forecast is above the mathematical linear trend line and therefore merits further investigation.

Fig 9.11

Dynamic graph.

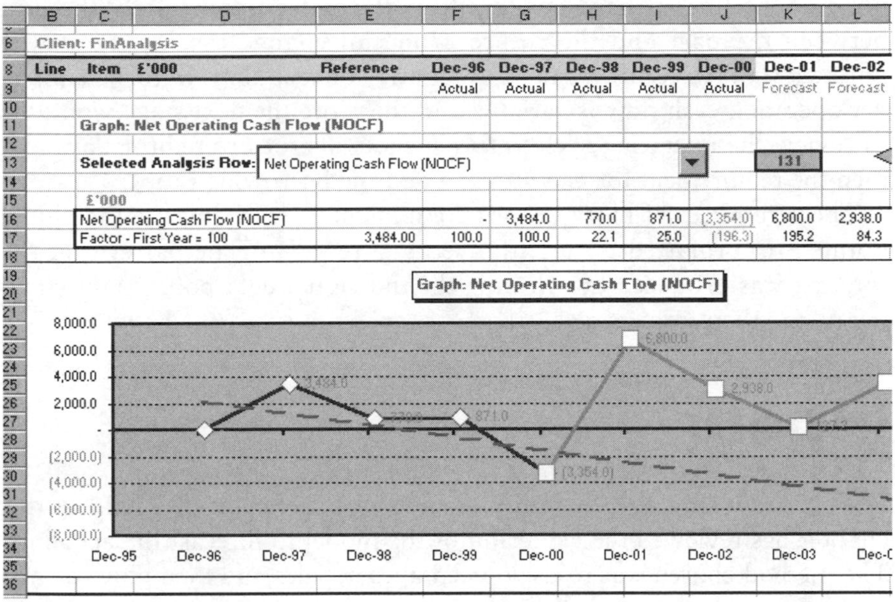

Fig 9.12

Block charts.

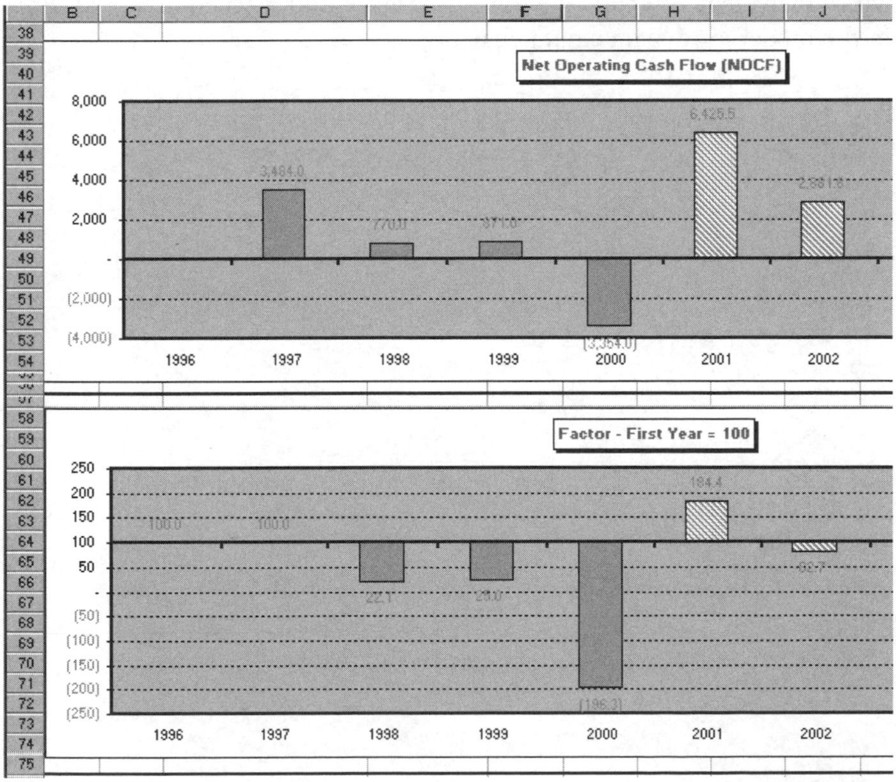

The advantage of this method is that you can view each line because none of the lines is hard coded and you can see immediately the link between the past and the future. You can change the inputs on the Forecast sheet to see the result on the ratios or cash flow. In this example, net operating cash flow is variable and therefore the next stage would be to review the operating cycle ratios such as debtor or creditor days and then the requirement for new funding and the borrowing ratios.

The second set of block graphs contains one series, but the individual points are formatted differently (see Figure 9.12). The pattern on the forecast was produced by selecting the individual data point, right clicking it, and then formatting patterns.

5. SUMMARY

With the raw data already in the accounts model Financial_Analysis, this chapter has reviewed the extension of the model to forecast the accounts. The method chosen was to use percentages of sales and then plug the gap with cash or borrowings. The accounts can then be drawn forward to produce composite statements of past and future. The schedules self-check themselves as far as possible and provide management information. More management analysis is on a summary and a schedule for all lines in the model for dynamic data charting.

10

Variance analysis

Variance analysis compares standard or budget performance to actual performance. The previous chapter was concerned with forecasting and projecting financial statements whereas this chapter deals with pinpointing significant variances for management attention. Normally data is processed at the end of an accounting period and is already out of date before management can take corrective action. The process attempts to pick out only those variances, which are large enough to merit extra action over and above repetitive minor differences.

The advantages of this approach are:

- fixed and variable cost control;
- management by exception focuses attention on problem areas;
- assistance with planning and next year's budget;
- assistance with future decision making.

Excel as used by many is an adding machine for budgets and other accounting tasks. The grid of cells and formulas is particularly effective at manipulating columns and rows of figures. Two files are available for this chapter, which offer more analysis techniques:

Cash_Flow	Simple budget of income statement, balance sheet, cash flow and ratios.
Cash_Flow_Budget	Layered as above, but with sheets for 'actual' results and then a comparison.

1. CASH FLOW BUDGETS

Both files used the application template as a base and were created by extending the Financial_Analysis application. This backs up the points regarding reusable chunks of code made in earlier chapters as a way of speeding up development. The application covers 12 months as opposed to five years of historic and forecast data. The complexity was added in layers and the same basic layout was followed on all schedules:

- Menu
- Income statement
- Balance sheet
- Ratios
- Cashflow
- Management analysis
- Management summary.

The menu for the basic cash flow model is shown in Figure 10.1.

Fig 10.1 **Menu.**

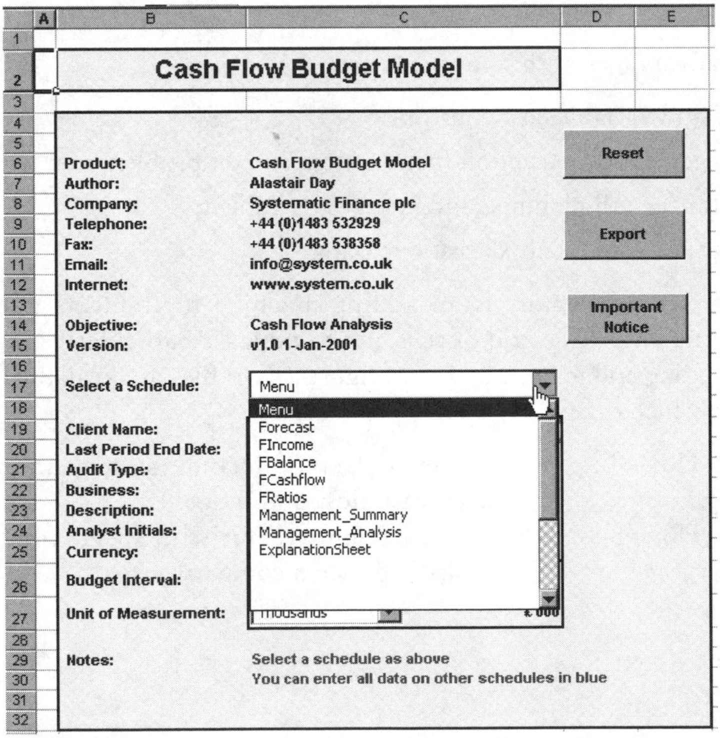

The Forecasting sheet follows the format in the Financial_Analysis application and uses the final period in the previous year as the base for sales growth. The Income and Balance sheets display inputs for the last period figures and, together with the forecast percentages (see Figure 10.2), the model generates the forecast statements.

Fig 10.2

Forecast.

Forecasting

Main Menu

Client: CashBudget

Line	Item	£000	Reference	Dec-00	Jan-01	Feb-01	Mar-01
				Future	Future	Future	Future
	Forecast						
F11	Initial sales		P10	2,000.0	2,520.0	3,024.0	3,628.8
F12	Sales growth		Change P10	-	26.00%	20.00%	20.00%
F13	Costs of goods sold/Sales		P11/P10	78.0%	87.00%	87.00%	87.00%
F14	Depreciation rate		P13.P14/B19	1.9%	0.72%	0.72%	0.72%
F15	SG&A/Sales		P15/P10	10.0%	6.50%	6.50%	6.50%
F16	Interest paid on debt		P17/B28+B33	0.2%	0.35%	0.35%	0.35%
F17	Interest earned on cash		P18.19/B10.11	-	0.00%	0.00%	0.00%
F18	Exceptionals/Sales		P21/F11	-	0.00%	0.00%	0.00%
F19	Marginal tax rate		P23/P22	25.0%	20.00%	20.00%	20.00%
F20	Dividend payout ratio		P26/P24	-	39.99%	39.99%	39.99%
F21	Net fixed assets/Sales		B19/F11	267.8%	250.00%	250.00%	250.00%
F22	Intangibles/Sales		B20.21/F11	-	0.00%	0.00%	0.00%
F23	Current assets/Sales		B12.14/F11	1115.2%	550.00%	550.00%	550.00%
F24	Current liabilities/Sales		B32-B28/F11	689.1%	450.00%	450.00%	450.00%
F25	Debt/Sales		B33+B28/F11	432.2%	150.00%	150.00%	150.00%
F26	Deferred tax/Sales		B35/F11	-	0.00%	0.00%	0.00%
F27	New equity		B37	-	-	-	-

In each month, cash is used to ensure that assets and liabilities balance. The cash flow uses the same framework and the format is copied across the page. The cash flow is derived from the income statement and balance sheet and it must therefore balance. The accounting statements also provide control totals for comparison with a formal financial accounting system.

The ratios use a base of 30 days rather than 360 days and there is a totals column to compare the ratios for the year. The use of the existing programming means a much shorter development time for the application with fewer programming errors.

A summary is available in the form of a Management Summary and analysis through charts on the Management_Analysis schedule (see Figures 10.3 and 10.4).

Fig 10.3

Summary.

Client: CashBudget

Line	Item	£'000	Reference	Jan-01	Feb-01	Mar-01	Apr-01
				Future	Future	Future	Future
S10	Sales		P10	2,520.0	3,024.0	3,628.8	4,354.6
S30	Sales growth		F12	26.0%	20.0%	20.0%	20.0%
S11	Gross Margin		P12	327.6	393.1	471.7	566.1
S12	Net Operating Profit (NOP)		P16	125.2	151.1	181.4	217.7
S13	Net Profit after Tax (NPAT)		P24	77.2	110.4	132.5	159.0
S15	Current Assets		B15	14,101.3	16,632.0	19,958.4	23,950.1
S16	Non Current and Fixed Assets		B22	6,300.0	7,560.0	9,072.0	10,886.4
S17	Current Liabilities		B32	11,340.0	14,308.4	18,160.1	22,782.1
S18	Long Term Liabilities and Provisions		B36	3,780.0	4,536.0	5,443.2	6,531.8
S19	Shareholders' Funds		B39	5,281.3	5,347.6	5,427.1	5,522.5
S21	Net Operating Cash Flow (NOCF)		C17	6,164.8	(307.5)	(368.9)	(442.7)
S22	Total Cash (Outflow)/Inflow before Financ		C42	5,102.3	(1,697.7)	(2,037.3)	(2,444.7)
S23	Increase / (Decrease) in Cash		C50	239.3	(241.3)	(0.0)	-
S25	Return on Sales (NPAT/Sales %)		P24/P10	3.06	3.65	3.65	3.65
S26	Asset Turnover (Sales / Total Assets)		P10/B24	0.12	0.13	0.13	0.13
S27	Asset Leverage (Total Assets/Equity)		B23/B39	3.86	4.52	5.35	6.31
S28	Return on Equity (NPAT/Equity %)		P24/B39	1.46	2.07	2.44	2.88

Fig 10.4

Charts.

Management Analysis Charts

Main Menu

Client: CashBudget

Line	Item	£'000	Reference	Jan-01	Feb-01	Mar-01	Apr-01	Ma
				Future	Future	Future	Future	F

Graph: Earnings before Interest, Tax, Depreciation and Amortisation (EBITDA)

Selected Analysis Row: Earnings before Interest, Tax, Depreciation and Amortisation (EBITDA

£'000

Earnings before Interest, Tax, Depreciation and Amortisat		163.8	196.5	235.9	283.0	
Factor - First Period = 100	163.79	100.0	120.0	144.0	172.8	

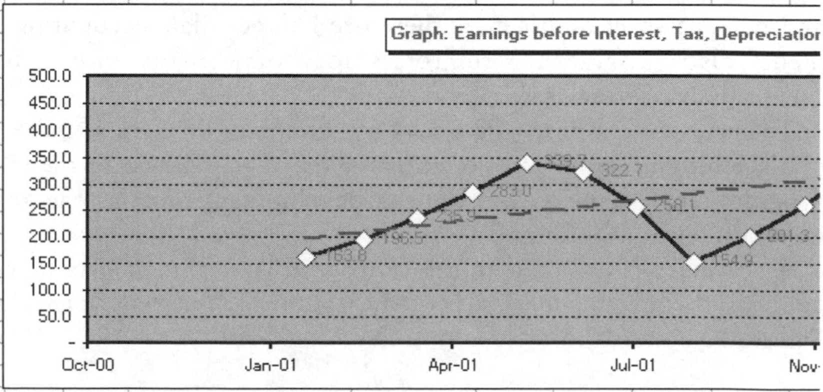

2. MONTHLY CASH MODEL

The model Cash_Flow_Budget extends the simple budget model by adding further sets of schedules for actual results and variance. As stated in the earlier chapters, a simple budget model has limited usefulness, but an application comparing actual to budget performance is much more usable to management to support decision making. The idea is to enter the actual figures progressively throughout the year and then be able to compare the results against the budget.

The method for the income statement was as follows:

- Copy the forecast sheets and paste onto new sheets.
- Change the new sheet name to, for example, AIncome.
- Find and replace the references to the forecast and replace them with actual. This includes FIncome, FBalance, FRatios and FCash.
- Update the title and change the colour scheme.
- Add in IF statements to ensure that nothing is displayed if there is no 'actual' data.
- Repeat procedure for the balance sheet, ratios and cash flow.

Actual income statement.

Fig 10.5

Actual Income Statement | **Main Menu**

Client: CashAnalysis

Line	Item £'000		Dec-00	Jan-01	Feb-01	Mar-01	Apr-01
			Future	Future	Future	Future	Future
P10	Sales		1,900.0	2,356.0	3,100.0	3,545.0	-
P11	Cost of Goods Sold		(1,600.0)	(2,200.0)	(2,789.0)	(2,999.0)	-
P12	**Gross Margin**		300.0	156.0	311.0	546.0	-
P13	Depreciation	Manufacturer	(122.0)	(38.0)	(45.0)	(55.0)	-
P14		Amortisation/Other	-	-	-	-	-
P15	Sales, General &Administration Overheads		(204.0)	(161.0)	(200.0)	(236.0)	-
P16	**Net Operating Profit (NOP)**		(26.0)	(43.0)	66.0	255.0	-
P17	Interest Expense		(22.0)	(28.7)	(13.1)	(18.1)	-
P18	Interest Income		-	-	-	-	-
P19	Other Financial Income		-	-	-	-	-
P20	**Profit after Financial Items**		(48.0)	(71.7)	52.9	236.9	-
P21	Exceptional Expense		-	-	-	-	-
P22	**Profit before Tax**		(48.0)	(71.7)	52.9	236.9	-
P23	Tax		(29.0)	(18.0)	(29.0)	(33.0)	-
P24	**Net Profit after Tax (NPAT)**		(77.0)	(89.7)	23.9	203.9	-
P25	Minority Interest		-	-	-	-	-
P26	Dividends		-	(32.0)	(45.0)	(53.0)	-
P27	**Retained Profit for the Year**		(77.0)	(121.7)	(21.1)	150.9	-

- Manually change the references on the chart since series references do not automatically update when you copy from one sheet to another.
- Change the formatting of the cells to accept numbers, colour coding and protections using `Format Cells`. Figure 10.5 shows the inputs and totals clearly.

The Variance sheets were set up in the same way with the syntax in the form of 'Actual – Budget'. This is cell J10 on the VCashflow sheet. It is set to display zero unless there is data in the relevant Actual Cashflow sheet cell J10.

```
=IF(AIncome!J10=0,0,ACashFlow!J10-FCashflow!J10)
```

The menu system is extended to include new inputs for budget interval and the month number (see Figure 10.6). This is to extend the model to cope with monthly, quarterly, biannual and annual periods. The month number records the final period with actual figures.

Fig 10.6 **Budget menu.**

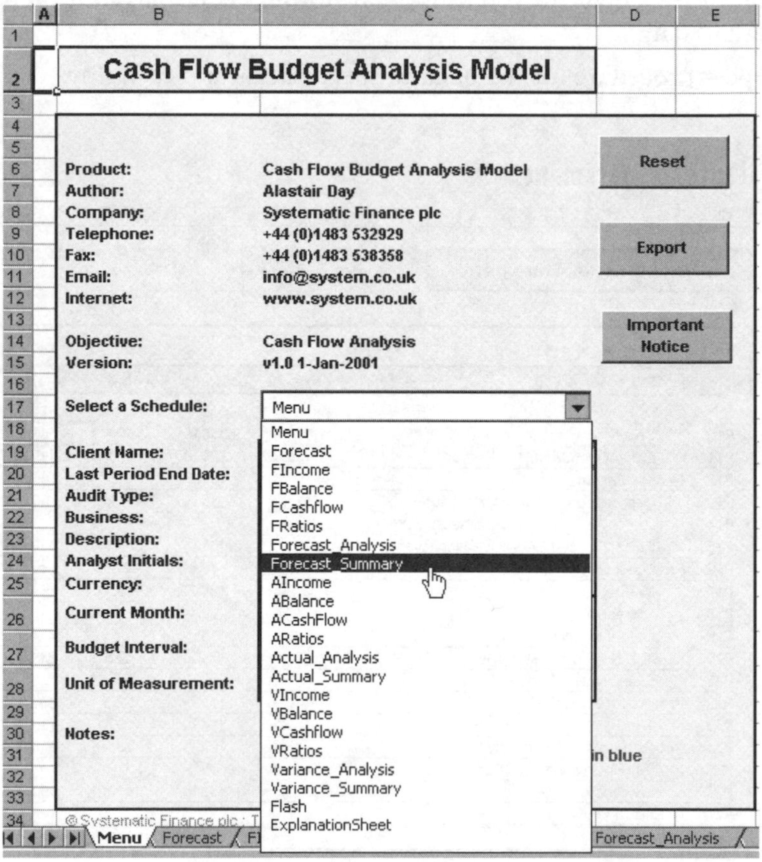

3. 'FLASH' REPORT AND GRAPHICS

The management reports would not be complete without a 'Flash' report detailing the key actual versus budget results for a single month (see Figure 10.7). This schedule looks up data from the budget and actual sheets and presents it in columnar form. The user selects the relevant month using the combo control at the top and a graph is placed at the bottom for picking out and charting individual lines (see Figure 10.8).

Flash report.

Fig 10.7

Select Month: 3: 31-Mar-2001 | 3 | Main Menu

Client: CashAnalysis

Line	Item	£'000 Reference	Budget	Actual	Variance	%
S10	Sales	P10	3,628.8	3,545.0	(83.8)	(2.3)
S30	Sales growth	F12	20.0	12.6	(7.4)	(37.2)
S11	Gross Margin	P12	471.7	546.0	74.3	15.7
S12	Net Operating Profit (NOP)	P16	181.4	255.0	73.6	40.6
S13	Net Profit after Tax (NPAT)	P24	132.5	203.9	71.3	53.8
S15	Current Assets	B15	19,958.4	19,780.0	(178.4)	(0.9)
S16	Non Current and Fixed Assets	B22	9,072.0	9,072.0	-	-
S17	Current Liabilities	B32	18,160.1	18,133.0	(27.1)	(0.1)
S18	Long Term Liabilities and Provisions	B36	5,443.2	5,374.0	(69.2)	(1.3)
S19	Shareholders' Funds	B39	5,427.1	5,345.0	(82.1)	(1.5)
S21	Net Operating Cash Flow (NOCF)	C17	(368.9)	(243.5)	125.4	34.0
S22	Total Cash (Outflow)/Inflow before Financing	C42	(2,037.3)	(1,721.5)	315.8	15.5
S23	Increase / (Decrease) in Cash	C50	(0.0)	-	0.0	100.0
S25	Return on Sales (NPAT/Sales %)	P24/P10	3.7	5.8	2.1	57.5
S26	Asset Turnover (Sales / Total Assets)	P10/B24	0.1	0.1	(0.0)	(1.7)
S27	Asset Leverage (Total Assets/Equity)	B23/B39	5.3	5.4	0.0	0.9
S28	Return on Equity (NPAT/Equity %)	P24/B39	2.4	3.8	1.4	56.2

The percentage column presents a problem since negative numbers can result in the wrong answer. The formula in K13 multiplies the result by –1 if the signs for the actual and budget figures are negative:

```
=IF(F13<>0,(H13-F13)/F13*100,0)*IF(AND(SIGN(F13)<1,SIGN
(H13)<1),-1,1)
```

The chart uses an Index function linked to a control to graph the individual line. It is usually beneficial to allow analysis of individual lines rather than hard coding, for example, a sales or profits graph.

Fig 10.8 **Flash report chart.**

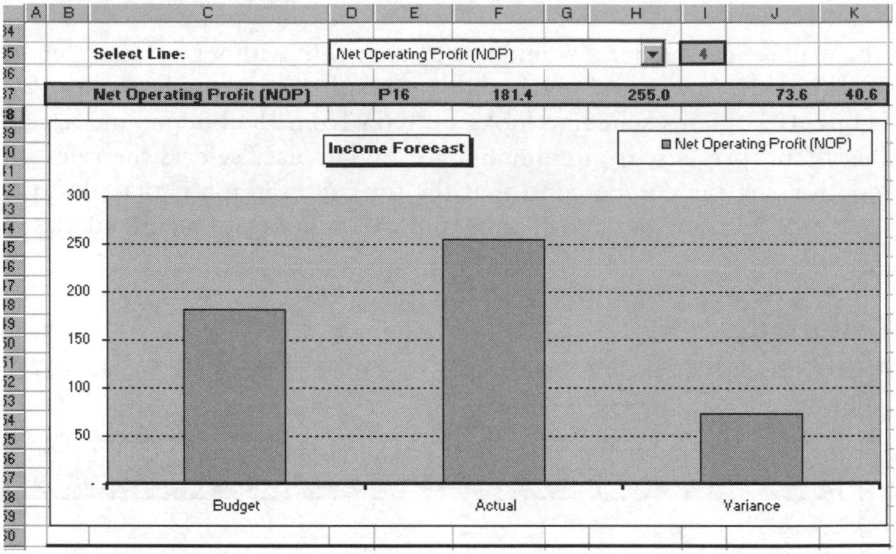

4. SUMMARY

This chapter introduces two cash flow models, which use an income statement and balance sheet together with forecast percentages to construct a monthly set of accounting statements including ratios and a cash flow statement. For ease of understanding, the models use the same format throughout and develop the method in the earlier model Financial_Analysis. The complexity is layered and the final model contains sheets for recording the actual results through the year and variance sheets for management review.

11

Breakeven analysis

Managers often want to know what quantity of a particular product has to be made in order to break even or produce a specific profit. This methodology divides costs into fixed and variable and seeks to find a level of production, which results in a break-even state. A model can help by applying the formulas and adding sensitivity analysis. As a related activity, the degree of operating leverage refers to the change in earnings to each $1 of sales.

The file used in this chapter is 'Leverage'.

1. BREAKEVEN

Costs are divided into:

- fixed costs that are constant and not dependent on quantity, for example administration overheads;
- variable costs that depend on the level of production.

As production increases, the amount of fixed cost per unit declines to the point where a production quantity results in zero earnings. The chart shown in Figure 11.1 is on the Costs sheet and demonstrates the key lines of:

- cost of sales (variable cost);
- fixed cost;
- total cost (fixed plus variable cost);
- sales.

The sales line crosses the total cost line at 40,000 units, confirming that earnings are zero at this level of production.

Fig 11.1 **Costs.**

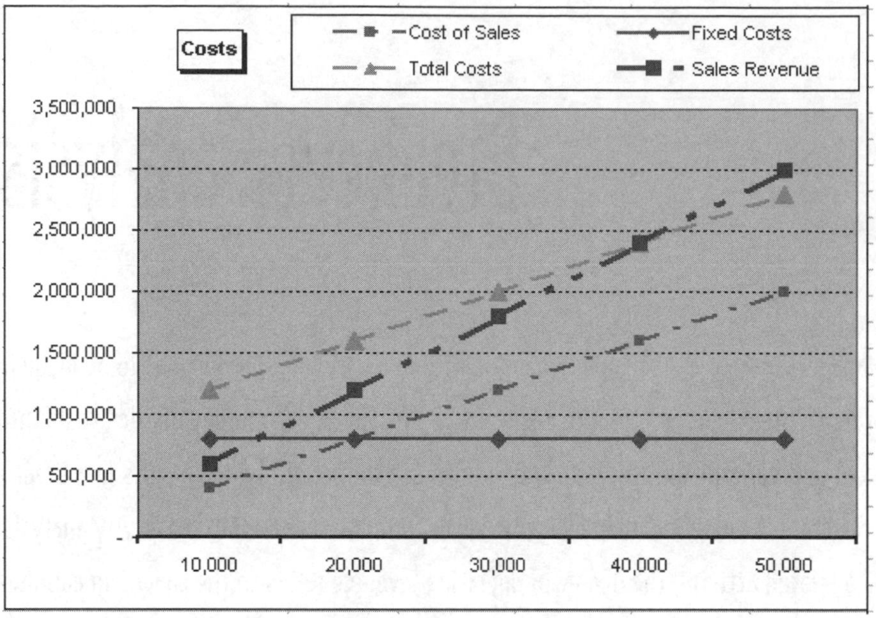

The full details for this example are on the Costs sheet in the Leverage model. This follows the design method in setting out areas of the schedule and using the Application_Template file as a base. The model sheet uses an initial investment and then plots the income statement over five years. This basic model will be used again in Chapter 15 on investment analysis.

The model assumes differing sales volumes and price erosion over the period (see Figure 11.2). In contrast, there is a variable cost per unit which is reduced in each of the periods. Selling and administration costs also vary in each year. To complete the financial statements, there is also a balance sheet and cash flow, which both self-check for accuracy.

The formulas for working out the breakeven are:

- P = price per unit
- Q = quantity produced and sold
- V = variable cost per unit
- F = fixed cost.

The definition is:

$$Q(P - V) - F = Earnings$$

This can be rewritten as:

$$Break\_Even\_Q = \frac{F}{(P - V)}$$

Model inputs.

	A	B	C	D	E	F	G
5							
6		**Start Date:**		**1-Jan-01**			
7		**Initial Investment:**		**2,500,000**			
8		**Initial Sales Price per Unit:**		**60.00**			
9		**Annual Price Change:**		**(5.00%)**			
10		**Initial Cost per Unit:**		**40.00**			
11		**Annual Cost Improvement:**		**10.00%**			
12		**Project Life:**		**5.00 yrs**			
13		**Working Capital as % of Sales:**		**10.00%**			
15				**Year 0**	**1**	**2**	**3**
16				**Jan-01**	**Jan-02**	**Jan-03**	**Jan-04**
17							
18		Sales Volume			**50,000**	**55,000**	**45,000**
19		Price per Unit			60.00	57.00	54.15
20							
21		Sales Revenue			3,000,000	3,135,000	2,436,750
22							
23		Annual Cost per Unit			40.00	36.00	32.40
24		Manufacturing Cost			(2,000,000)	(1,980,000)	(1,458,000)
25							
26							
27		**Profit and Loss Account**					
28		Sales Revenue			3,000,000	3,135,000	2,436,750
29		Cost of Sales			(2,000,000)	(1,980,000)	(1,458,000)
30		Contribution			1,000,000	1,155,000	978,750
31		Selling and Administration Costs			**(300,000)**	**(200,000)**	**(150,000)**
32		Other			(500,000)	(500,000)	(500,000)
33		**Profit/(Loss)**			200,000	455,000	328,750
34							

In the first year, the fixed costs are 800,000. The selling cost per unit is 60.0 and the variable cost 40.0. Therefore:

$$Break\_Even\_Q = \frac{800,000}{(60-40)} = 40,000\_units$$

The revenue is 40,000 * 60 = 2,400,000.

Contribution is the price minus variable cost as the *contribution* towards fixed costs. Row 33 computes the contribution percentage as:

$$\frac{(P-V)}{P} = \frac{(60-40)}{60} = 33.33\%$$

Dividing the fixed costs by the contribution percentage produces the breakeven sales revenue of 2,400,000 in the first year. Lines 35 and 36 show the cover in terms of number of units and revenue (see Figure 11.3).

Breakeven revenue and volume varies in each of the periods as cost improvements feed through to contribution (see Figure 11.4). The contribution percentage increases from 33% to 46% in year 5.

Fig 11.3

Breakeven analysis.

B	C	D	E	F
	Year 0	1	2	3
	Jan-01	Jan-02	Jan-03	Jan-04
Sales Volume		50,000	55,000	45,000
Price per Unit		60.00	57.00	54.15
Sales Revenue		3,000,000	3,135,000	2,436,750
Variable Costs				
Annual Cost per Unit		40.00	36.00	32.40
Manufacturing Cost		(2,000,000)	(1,980,000)	(1,458,000)
Contribution		**1,000,000**	**1,155,000**	**978,750**
Fixed Costs				
Selling and Administration Costs		(300,000)	(200,000)	(150,000)
Other		(500,000)	(500,000)	(500,000)
Total Fixed Costs		**(800,000)**	**(700,000)**	**(650,000)**
Earnings before Interest and Tax (EBIT)		**200,000**	**455,000**	**328,750**
Break Even				
Break even volume	Q = F / (P-V)	40,000	33,333	29,885
Break even revenue	Q * P	2,400,000	1,900,000	1,618,276
Contribution percentage	(P - V) / P	33.33	36.84	40.17
Excess/(Deficit) Units		10,000	21,667	15,115
Excess/(Deficit) Revenue		600,000	1,235,000	818,474

Fig 11.4

Breakeven chart.

Selected: Break even volume

Graph line Break even volume 21

B	C	D	E	F	G	H	I
Break even volume	**Q = F / (P-V)**	**40,000**	**33,333**	**29,885**	**28,722**	**27,844**	**31,957**

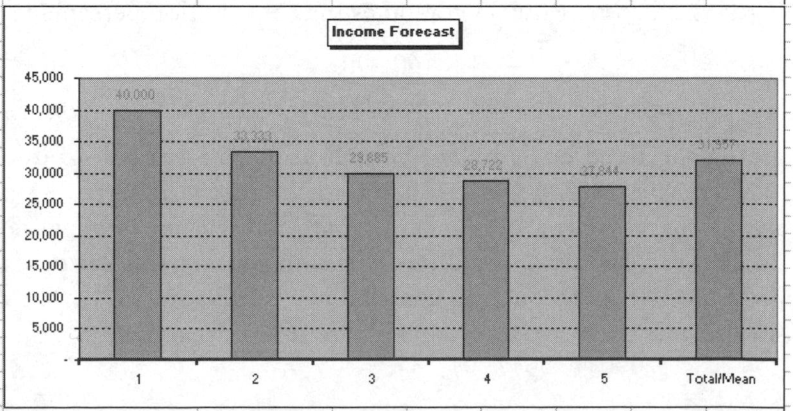

The model also includes the facility to target an earnings figure (see Figure 11.5). The input in cell C5 is 62,500 and rows 39 and 40 show the:

$$Target\_Q = \frac{(F + Target\_EBIT)}{(P - V)}$$

Breakeven targets.

Fig 11.5

	A	B	C	D	E	F
7						
8			Year 0	1	2	3
9			Jan-01	Jan-02	Jan-03	Jan-04
38						
39		Target EBIT of 62,500	Q = (F + EBIT) / (P-V)	43,125	36,310	32,759
40		Revenue including target EBIT	Q * P	2,587,500	2,069,643	1,773,879
41						
42		Excess/(Deficit) Units		6,875	18,690	12,241
43		Excess/(Deficit) Revenue		412,500	1,065,357	662,871
44						
45						
46		Cash break even	Q = (F - Deprn) / (P-V)	15,000	9,524	6,897
47		Cash revenue	Q * P	900,000	542,857	373,448
48						
49		Excess/(Deficit) Units		35,000	45,476	38,103
50		Excess/(Deficit) Revenue		2,100,000	2,592,143	2,063,302
51						

An alternative is to calculate the cash breakeven (see Figure 11.6) since the formulas above include depreciation, which is a non-cash item. Depreciation here is 500,000 per annum out of total fixed costs of 800,000.

$$Cash\_Q = \frac{(F - Non\_Cash\_Items)}{(P - V)}$$

The year 1 answer in cell D46 is 15,000, which results in revenue of 900,000. Again the breakeven point declines in future years; however, the reduction is more marked without the depreciation.

When more than one product is involved, you need to adopt a different method as shown on the Product_Mix sheet (see Figure 11.7). Different selling prices and variable cost produce different contribution margins. Breakeven points vary with the number of units sold. The method is to determine the sales mix and then derive a weighted-average contribution margin.

The production quantities, selling prices, variable cost per unit and overall fixed cost is set out in an inputs box. The sales and variable cost are calculated out to show the contribution from each product line. The mix of sales is also calculated as in cell D19:

```
=IF($G17<>0,D17/$G17,0)*100
```

Fig 11.6

Cash breakeven.

	Year 0	1	2	3	4	5	Total/Mean
	Jan-01	Jan-02	Jan-03	Jan-04	Jan-05	Jan-06	
Selected: Cash revenue							
Graph line	Cash revenue				37		
Cash revenue	Q * P	900,000	542,857	373,448	323,211	280,785	484,060

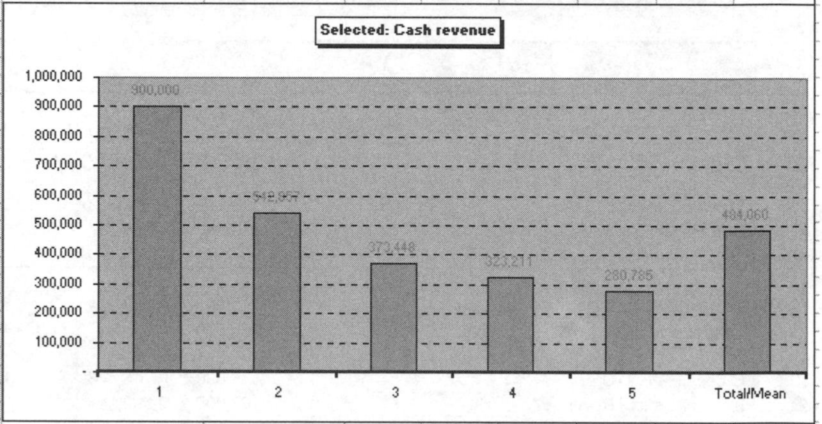

Fig 11.7

Product mix.

Products		A	B	C	Total
Quantity		500.00	1,000.00	750.00	2,250.00
Selling Price		40.00	70.00	30.00	46.67
Variable Cost		16.00	35.00	8.00	19.67
Fixed Cost		30,000.00			
Sales		20,000.00	70,000.00	22,500.00	112,500.00
Mix		17.78	62.22	20.00	100.00
Variable Cost		(8,000.00)	(35,000.00)	(6,000.00)	(49,000.00)
Contribution Margin	**Sales - VC**	**12,000.00**	**35,000.00**	**16,500.00**	**63,500.00**
Ratio	Contrib / Sales	60.00	50.00	73.33	56.44
Contribution Ratio		56.44			
Break Even Revenue	FC / Contrib Ratio	53,149.61			
Break Even	**BE * Mix**	**9,448.82**	**33,070.87**	**10,629.92**	**53,149.61**
Variance	Sales - BE	10,551.18	36,929.13	11,870.08	59,350.39
Number of Units		236	472	354	1,063
Variance - Units		264	528	396	1,187

The breakeven revenue of 56.44% is:

$$Break\_Even\_Revenue = \frac{Fixed\_Cost}{Contribution\_Margin\_Ratio} = \frac{30{,}000}{\left(\frac{63{,}500}{112{,}500}\right)}$$

The breakeven revenue is then multiplied by the sales percentage of each product to find the breakeven revenue for each product. Dividing by the sale price per unit calculates the number of units required.

2. OPERATING LEVERAGE

The model also calculates operating leverage on the Leverage sheet. This is defined as the variability of earnings to corresponding changes in revenue. This variability results from a high level of fixed costs and makes the company dependent on volume for covering the fixed costs. This risk is usually defined as business risk and is governed by:

Leverage.

Fig 11.8

		D	E	F
5	**Borrowings**	**250,000**		
6	**Interest Rate**	**10.0%**		
7	**Tax**	**30.0%**		
8	**Number of Shares**	**10,000**		
10		**1**	**2**	**3**
11		**Jan-02**	**Jan-03**	**Jan-04**
13	Sales	3,000,000	3,135,000	2,436,750
15	Earnings before interest and tax	200,000	455,000	328,750
17	Interest	(25,000)	(25,000)	(25,000)
19	Earnings before tax	175,000	430,000	303,750
21	Tax	(52,500)	(129,000)	(91,125)
23	Earnings after tax (EAT)	122,500	301,000	212,625
25	Earnings per share (EPS)	12.25	30.10	21.26
28	**Operating Leverage**			
29	Change in EBIT		127.50	(27.75)
30	Change in sales		4.50	(22.27)
32	Operating leverage (DOL)	EBIT/Sales	28.33	1.25

- macro factors such as the economic and political climate;
- industry factors such as the fixed asset and cost requirements, as in, for example heavy industries such as cement making or car production;
- company factors defined by management action and strategy, for example the structure of costs.

This analysis requires more input information (see Figure 11.8). The sales and earnings information is looked up from the Model sheet. The formula for operating leverage is:

$$Operating\_Leverage = \frac{\%Change\_in\_EBIT}{\%Change\_in\_Sales}$$

In each case the breakeven point does not change as this is driven by fixed costs. If sales decline, a high degree of operating leverage will result in an even faster decline in earnings.

3. FINANCIAL LEVERAGE

Financial leverage is the change in the earnings per share relative to changes in earnings. This is affected directly by management decisions about the structure of the organization and the level of debt financing. The formula is:

$$Financial\_Leverage = \frac{\%Change\_in\_EPS}{\%Change\_in\_EBIT}$$

The Leverage sheet includes the debt servicing and number of shares as input cells (see Figure 11.9).

Fig 11.9

Financial leverage.

	A	B	C	D	E	F
4						
5		**Borrowings**		**250,000**		
6		**Interest Rate**		**10.0%**		
7		**Tax**		**30.0%**		
8		**Number of Shares**		**10,000**		
10				**1**	**2**	**3**
11				**Jan-02**	**Jan-03**	**Jan-04**
34						
35		**Financial Leverage**				
36		Change in EPS			145.71	(29.36)
37		Change in EBIT			127.50	(27.75)
38						
39		Degree of financial leverage (DFL)		EPS/EBIT	1.14	1.06
40						

In the first year, the earnings per share will increase by a factor of 1.14 for each unit change in earnings before interest and tax. When earnings are rising the effect is beneficial; however, the same effect will result from reducing earnings.

4. COMBINED LEVERAGE

The model also calculates the combined leverage of financial and operating measures. Management is using both kinds to leverage the earnings per share. This ratio is defined as:

$$Combined\_Leverage = \frac{\%Change\_in\_EPS}{\%Change\_in\_Sales}$$

This can be rewritten as:

$$Combined\_Leverage = Operating\_Leverage * Financial\_Leverage$$

To display the results clearly, the three types of leverage are shown on a simple line graph at the bottom of the schedule (see Figure 11.10).

Fig 11.10

Combined leverage.

		1 Jan-02	2 Jan-03	3 Jan-04	4 Jan-05	5 Jan-06	Total
Combined Leverage							
Change in EPS			145.71	(29.36)	(62.18)	(79.29)	(6.28)
Change in sales			4.50	(22.27)	(26.11)	(18.57)	(15.61)
Degree of combined leverage	EPS/Sales		32.38	1.32	2.38	4.27	8.07
Check: DOL * DFL			-	-	-	-	-

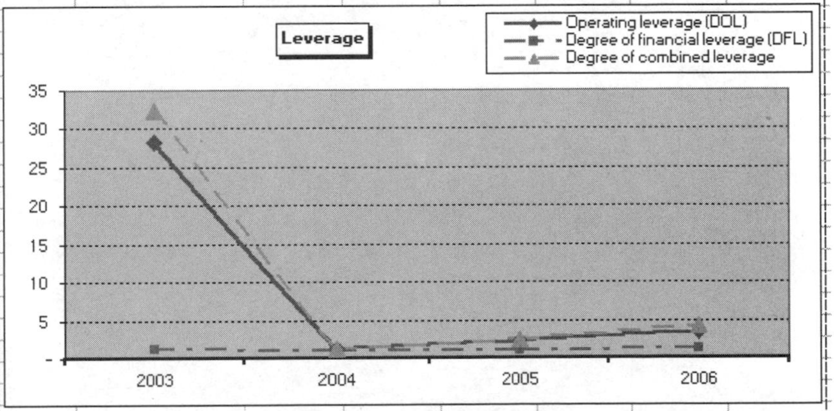

Costs and contribution vary with each year and therefore the relationships are not constant. The increase in profitability in the first year is not sustained and both sales and earnings per share decline in future periods.

5. SUMMARY

Breakeven analysis seeks to understand the nature of costs and their behaviour. The model used in this chapter calculates the breakeven for single and multiple products. The second section shows the operating and financial leverage with the combined leverage as a further set of management ratios.

12

Portfolio analysis

This chapter and the next, model fundamental finance theories on diversification and the cost of capital. This chapter discusses diversification as encapsulated by portfolio theory developed by Harry Markowitz from his original 1952 paper. The theory seeks to answer how risk varies when you combine shares or other risky assets in a portfolio. The important finance variables for shares are their return and volatility, the latter of which is measured by the standard deviation of the shares. A rational investor wants to earn as much as possible while controlling risk, and he wants to know what weights of securities should be held in order to maximize return. While random holding of a number of shares reduces risk substantially, this theory attempts a more systematic method of allocating shares. In the file called Portfolio the following sections model some of the important theories.

1. FORMULAS

The assumptions for portfolio theory are:

- investors are risk-averse and require a greater return for taking more risk;
- investors are rational and decide purely based on risk and return;
- investors want to make money rather than lose money.

Based on historic data, you want to determine the optimum holdings of two securities. You could leave your money in government bonds with little or no risk or buy all of one share; however, a mix of the two shares could increase return and 'manage' risk.

The file called Portfolio contains all the workings on a sheet called Model. The two items to be calculated are the risk and return on the portfolio at various weightings. By varying the holdings and using the historic data, it should be possible to find the weighting which offers the greatest return for the lowest risk.

The initial weightings are 50:50 and Figure 12.1 provides the monthly returns on each of the two securities. In practice, it would obviously be better to have more data, but this will suffice for demonstrating the technique. The mean in column E is simply the weighted return. The formula in cell E13 is:

```
=(C13*Weighting_A+D13*Weighting_B)/100
```

Fig 12.1 **Portfolio inputs.**

	A	B	C	D	E
4					
5		**Starting Period**	**Jan-00**		
6		**Interval (Months)**	**1**		
7		**Weighting Security A**	**50.00**		
8		**Weighting Security B**	**50.00**		
9					
10		**Risk free rate**	**4.00**		
11					
12		**Period**	**A**	**B**	**Mean**
13		Jan-00	**2.54**	**3.84**	3.19
14		Feb-00	**3.93**	**5.37**	4.65
15		Mar-00	**2.27**	**7.50**	4.89
16		Apr-00	**12.28**	**8.00**	10.14
17		May-00	**6.21**	**2.48**	4.35
18		Jun-00	**5.66**	**14.19**	9.93
19		Jul-00	**7.97**	**5.02**	6.50
20		Aug-00	**9.99**	**2.30**	6.15
21		Sep-00	**3.09**	**14.19**	8.64
22		Oct-00	**5.56**	**10.40**	7.98
23		Nov-00	**3.74**	**10.46**	7.10
24		Dec-00	**3.37**	**12.34**	7.86
25					
26		Average Return 1-00 to 12-00	5.55	8.01	6.78
27					
28		Standard Deviation	3.00	4.12	2.14
29					
30		Correlation A:B	(0.31)		
31					

The average returns are in row 26 and formula for the expected portfolio return is:

$$\text{Weighting}_A * \text{Return}_A + \text{Weighting}_B * \text{Return}_B$$

The risk or volatility is defined by standard deviation and this is achieved in two ways on the sheet. It is calculated using the functions for standard deviation and correlation and then calculated using the formula in cell E30:

```
=SQRT(((Weighting_A)^2)*(SDev_A)^2+((Weighting_B)^2)*(SD
ev_B)^2+2*Weighting_A*SDev_A*Weighting_B*SDev_B*
Correlation)/100
```

The standard deviations are in cells C28 and D28 using the function SDEVP for the whole population rather than a sample:

```
=STDEVP(C13:C24)
```

Correlation is provided by the function CORREL in cell C30:

```
=CORREL(C13:C24,D13:D24)
```

The calculated returns for A and B are shown in Figure 12.2.

Returns for A and B.

Fig 12.2

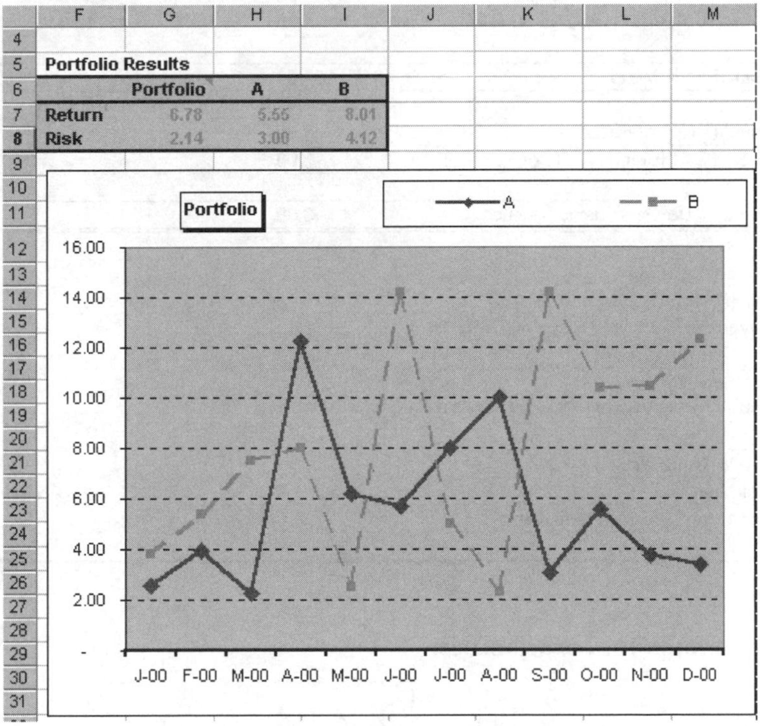

If you want to see all the statistical functions you can always access Excel Help, select a statistical function and then press 'See also' at the top of the notes to see a linked list of all related functions. You can then 'jump' and review each of the possibilities.

At the bottom, there is a workings section, which calculates standard deviation, covariance, correlation and the portfolio risk from its constituents (see Figure 12.3).

Fig 12.3 **Workings.**

	B	C	D	E	F	G
103						
104	**(A) Standard Deviation**					
105	Number of Results	12.00				
106						
107		**A-Aa**	**(A-Aa)^2**		**B-Bb**	**(B-Bb)^2**
108	1-Jan-00	(3.01)	9.06		(4.17)	17.37
109	1-Feb-00	(1.62)	2.63		(2.64)	6.96
110	1-Mar-00	(3.28)	10.76		(0.51)	0.26
111	1-Apr-00	6.73	45.28		(0.01)	0.00
112	1-May-00	0.66	0.43		(5.53)	30.55
113	1-Jun-00	0.11	0.01		6.18	38.22
114	1-Jul-00	2.42	5.85		(2.99)	8.93
115	1-Aug-00	4.44	19.71		(5.71)	32.58
116	1-Sep-00	(2.46)	6.06		6.18	38.22
117	1-Oct-00	0.01	0.00		2.39	5.72
118	1-Nov-00	(1.81)	3.28		2.45	6.01
119	1-Dec-00	(2.18)	4.76		4.33	18.77
120						
121	Sum: (Result-Mean)	(0.00)	107.84		-	203.59
122						
123	Sum * (1 / No of Results)		8.99			16.97
124	SDev = Sqrt [Sum * (1 / No of Results)]		3.00			4.12
125						
126	Standard Deviation using function		3.00			4.12
127						
128	**(B) Covariance**					
129	Sum[(A-Aa)*(B-Bb)]		(46.18)			
130	Covariance = [1/No] * Sum[(A-Aa)*(B-Bb)]		(3.85)			
131						
132	**(C) Correlation**					
133	Correlation = Covar / (SDevA * SDevB)		(0.31)			
134						
135	**(D) Portfolio Risk**					
136	Risk formula		45638.40			
137	**Portfolio Standard Deviation**		**2.14**			
138						

The formula for covariance is:

$$\sigma = \sqrt{\frac{1}{n} \sum (A_i - A)^2}$$

The sum of the (Result – Mean) is in row 121 and this is multiplied by the inverse of the number of results. The standard deviation is the square root in row 126. This is compared with the result using the SDEVP function.

Covariance returns the relationship between two data sets and this is needed to calculate correlation. The formula is:

$$Covar = \frac{1}{n} \sum_{i=1}^{n} (A - AverageA)\,(B - AverageB)$$

A = return on share A in the time period
B = return on share B in the time period
n = number of periods
$AverageA$ = average return on share A
$AverageB$ = average return on share B.

Correlation is:

$$Correlation = \frac{Covariance}{SDevA * SDevB}$$

$SDevA$ = standard deviation for share A calculated above
$SDevB$ = standard deviation for share B.

These components are then inserted in the portfolio risk calculation in cells D136 and D137 to produce the answer 2.14. The model has a management summary at the top of the page to show the reduction in risk from holding the two securities.

2. OPTIMUM PORTFOLIO

The next stage of the problem is to understand how risk and return change as percentage holdings of each security vary. To display all the answers, there are two data tables, one for risk and the other return. This is a convenient way of showing all the portfolios and then Excel can be used to pick out the optimum weightings of the two shares.

The process is in three stages:

- Calculate the possible portfolio weightings at 10% intervals for return and standard deviation.
- Look up each of the possible portfolios.
- Draw a scatter chart with joined lines of the possible portfolios.

The data table follows the standard layout as detailed in earlier chapters (see Figure 12.4). The intervals are separate inputs at the top and the single input cells for the column and row are clearly marked in blue.

Cells B37 and B51 point to the named cells Portfolio_Risk and Portfolio_Return respectively. The result is a grid, which includes the answer at 50% of each security. Conditional formatting is used to show up the answer in each table (see Figure 12.5).

The next stage is to pick out the possible portfolios, for example, 100 : 0, 90 : 10, 80 : 20. The next table uses the LOOKUP function called INDEX to find values progressively across and down the data table grid.

Fig 12.4

Data tables.

	A	B	C	D	E	F	G	H
32								
33		Data Table: Standard Deviation with A across and B down						
34		Interval Across	10.00					
35		Interval Down	10.00					
36								
37		2.14	-	10.00	20.00	30.00	40.00	50.00
38		100.00	4.12	4.04	3.97	3.93	3.91	3.92
39		90.00	3.71	3.62	3.57	3.53	3.52	3.54
40		80.00	3.30	3.21	3.16	3.13	3.14	3.17
41		70.00	2.88	2.80	2.76	2.74	2.76	2.80
42		60.00	2.47	2.39	2.35	2.35	2.39	2.46
43		50.00	2.06	1.99	1.96	1.97	2.03	2.14
44		40.00	1.65	1.58	1.57	1.61	1.71	1.85
45		30.00	1.24	1.18	1.19	1.28	1.43	1.62
46		20.00	0.82	0.78	0.85	1.01	1.23	1.47
47		10.00	0.41	0.43	0.61	0.86	1.14	1.43
48		-	-	0.30	0.60	0.90	1.20	1.50
49								
50		Data Table: Return with A across and B down						
51		6.78	-	10.00	20.00	30.00	40.00	50.00
52		100.00	8.01	8.56	9.12	9.67	10.23	10.78
53		90.00	7.21	7.76	8.32	8.87	9.43	9.98
54		80.00	6.41	6.96	7.52	8.07	8.63	9.18
55		70.00	5.61	6.16	6.72	7.27	7.83	8.38
56		60.00	4.80	5.36	5.91	6.47	7.02	7.58
57		50.00	4.00	4.56	5.11	5.67	6.22	6.78
58		40.00	3.20	3.76	4.31	4.87	5.42	5.98
59		30.00	2.40	2.96	3.51	4.07	4.62	5.18
60		20.00	1.60	2.16	2.71	3.27	3.82	4.38
61		10.00	0.80	1.36	1.91	2.47	3.02	3.58
62		-	-	0.56	1.11	1.67	2.22	2.78

Fig 12.5

Conditional formatting.

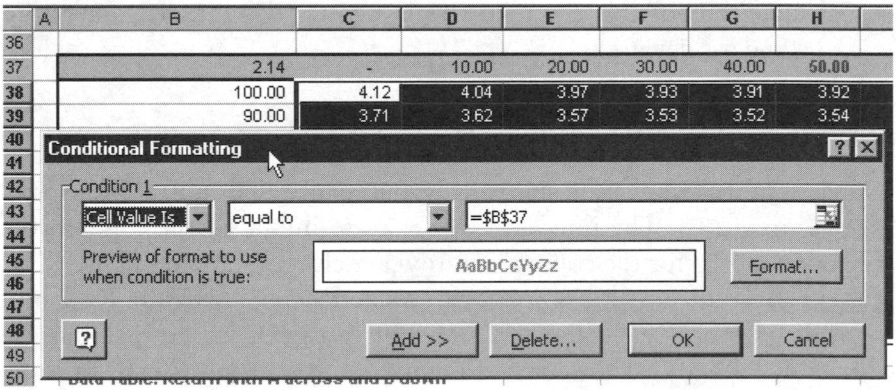

The formula in cell C66 is:

```
=INDEX($C$38:$M$48,C$65,C$65)
```

Cells C38:M48 are the whole of the standard deviation data table. It finds 4.12 as the value one down and one across. As the function in cell C66 is copied across, the across and down value augments by one. The result shown in Figure 12.6 finds all the possible portfolios at 10% intervals. The same procedure is repeated for the returns data table.

Index.

Fig 12.6

	A	B	C	D	E	F	G	H
63								
64		Portfolio: Risk Return Chart						
65			1	2	3	4	5	6
66		Standard Deviation	4.12	3.62	3.16	2.74	2.39	2.14
67		Average Return	8.01	7.76	7.52	7.27	7.02	6.78
68								
69		Standard Deviation	-	2.03				
70		Market Line	4.00	6.53		Match	7	

The table also finds the minimum standard deviation in cell D69 and then uses a MATCH function in cell G70 to work out which period it relates to. This function is used since LOOKUP and its derivatives need data in an ascending order.

```
Cell D69 =MIN(C66:M66)
Cell G70 =MATCH(D69,C66:M66,0)
```

Cell D70 then uses an OFFSET function to start at the left side of the data in row 67 and move across by the value returned by the MATCH function. This will enable an example market line to be plotted from the risk-free rate to the point on the graph with the least standard deviation. This is the extension of the theory into the Capital Assett Pricing model discussed in the next chapter.

```
Cell D70 =OFFSET(B67,0,G70)
```

The third stage is to plot the results on a scattergraph with joined lines. This should give the distinctive shape of a curve. The series co-ordinates are:

```
=SERIES(Model!$B$67,Model!$C$66:$M$66,Model!$C$67:$M$67,1)
```

This series is the efficient frontier and demonstrates that other weightings will suboptimize or produce a less than efficient portfolio. The graph demonstrates the highest possible level of return for a given risk or the return at the lowest possible level of risk (see Figure 12.7).

The line of the risk-free rate to the portfolio series has been extended as a trend line and formatted in red to look as if the market line has been extended. The formula for the line is also displayed using the trend line options. The result is the chart, which illustrates the trade-off between risk and return based on the historical data. This is 60% of A and 40% of B, which results in a return of 6.53 against standard deviation of 2.03.

Fig 12.7

Portfolio chart.

	B	C	D	E	F	G	H	I	J	K
64	Portfolio: Risk Return Chart									
65		1	2	3	4	5	6	7	8	
66	Standard Deviation	4.12	3.62	3.16	2.74	2.39	2.14	2.03	2.08	2.
67	Average Return	8.01	7.76	7.52	7.27	7.02	6.78	6.53	6.29	6.
68										
69	Standard Deviation	-	2.03							
70	Market Line	4.00	6.53		Match	7				

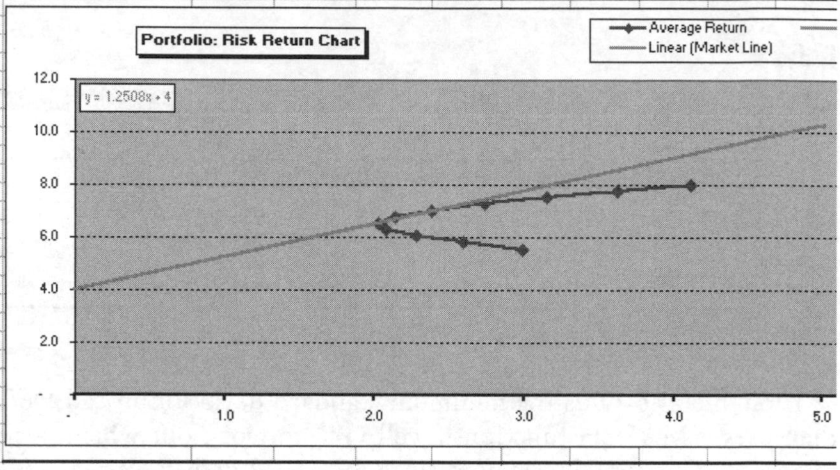

The formula for finding the weighting of A in the portfolio with the least risk more directly is:

```
[SDevB^2-SDevA*SDevB*Corr] / [SDevA^2+SDevB^2-2*SDevA
*SDevB*Corr]
```

These workings are at row 140 of the Model sheet (see Figure 12.8) and they work out the weighting and then the risk and return at these weights. The formulas for risk and return are as detailed above.

Fig 12.8

Optimum weights.

	B	C	D	E	F	G	H
138							
139	(E) Minimum Risk Portfolio						
140	[SDevB^2-SDevA*SDevB*Corr] / [SDevA^2+SDevB^2-2*SDevA*SDevB*Corr]					A:	61.86
141	Return at Optimum Weights		6.49			B:	38.14
142	Risk at Optimum Weights		2.02				
143							

As an alternative, the model also contains a Solver routine for finding the weights with the lowest risk. This is attached to the button at the top of the schedule and assigned to a macro called Solver (see Figure 12.9).

Solver.

Fig 12.9

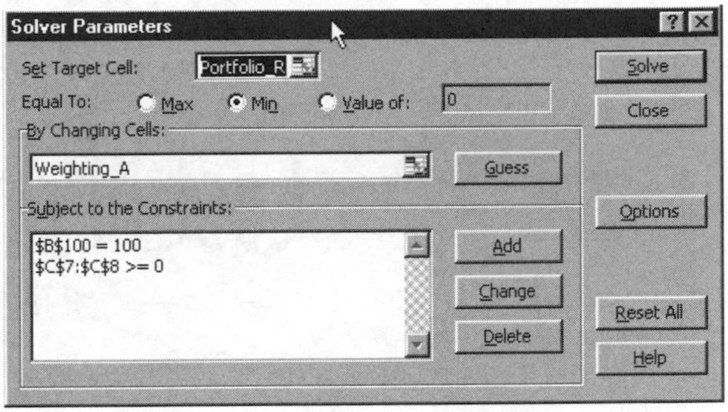

You want to minimize the risk by changing Weighting A. Weighting B is calculated as 100 minus Weighting B so this does not have to be included. The rules are:

- The sum of the weightings in cell B100 must equal 100 as a viable portfolio.
- The individual weightings must be greater than or equal to zero. This is to stop Solver assigning negative and therefore impossible values.

3. SUMMARY

This chapter introduces an important finance theory – portfolio theory – and the mathematics are set out in a model. The application makes use of functions for statistics and referencing together with data tables to produce a portfolio chart on the optimum weights of the two shares and the other possible holdings.

13

Cost of capital

This chapter introduces the cost of capital for a corporation and models the theories of the Capital Asset Pricing Model, the perpetuity model and the weighted average cost of capital. The templates are in the Portfolio file. Capital includes:

- bank financing – lines of credit, terms loans, asset-based loans and syndicated loans;
- bonds and international bonds;
- equity capital – ordinary and preferred shares and their permutations.

Each of the sources of capital carries a cost and the objective of the model is to calculate the cost of the components used to fund a company, find the proportions and then derive a merged cost of capital. The cost of capital is connected to the expectations of the lenders and investors who supply the capital. If investors require a certain rate of return, then a company must engage in projects which produce a rate of return greater than the cost of capital. If a company fails to earn a sufficient return then it cannot pay the providers of capital the expected rate.

While the cost of capital may seem to be a theoretical figure, it has a direct influence in such areas as project finance, investment appraisal and company valuation, which are considered in later chapters. As stated, the cost of capital is the minimum that a company must achieve and this is defined by the weighted average cost of capital or WACC. This chapter will concentrate on two areas of capital:

- cost of equity using the capital asset pricing model and the perpetuity or growth model;
- cost of debt.

Factors that will influence the cost of these factors are:

- interest rate environment in the short and medium term;
- risk, both market and specific since some companies and markets are inherently more uncertain than others;
- financial market conditions and the availability of capital.

1. CAPITAL ASSET PRICING MODEL

The Capital Asset Pricing Model (CAPM) is an extension of portfolio theory, where adding more shares to a portfolio means that your overall risk and return approaches market risk and return. All stock markets have an 'average' risk and this cannot be diversified away by adding more and more shares. The theory adds extra assumptions to portfolio theory:

- the possibility of a risk-free asset which carries no risk for investors, for example a government bond;
- all investors have identical expectations and views on risk.

The CAPM formula for the cost of equity can be applied to portfolios and individual shares. The formula is:

$$E(R_i) = R_f + \beta_i[E(R_m) - R_f]$$

$E(R_i)$ = expected return on share i
R_f = risk-free rate
$E(R_m)$ = expected return on the market
β_i = beta of share i.

The risk-free rate is usually cited as a government bond or undoubted debt. The market return minus the risk-free rate represents the risk premium. Investors can either accept no risk with a low rate or alternatively, through a diversified portfolio, earn a market return with increased risk. By accepting risk, the overall returns could be better or worse.

Beta.

Fig 13.1

	A	B	C	D	E	F
43		Data List				
44		Period	Date	Excess Market Returns	Excess Company Returns	Mean
45						
46		1	Apr-91	(2.2507)	(6.5645)	(4.4076)
47		2	May-91	1.3358	(5.7465)	(2.2054)
48		3	Jun-91	1.7982	6.1523	3.9752
49		4	Jul-91	1.2155	(1.3356)	(0.0601)
50		5	Aug-91	(1.6409)	(12.8990)	(7.2700)
51		6	Sep-91	1.5900	0.4679	1.0289
52		7	Oct-91	(2.8871)	(2.3701)	(2.6286)
53		8	Nov-91	7.0811	11.6574	9.3692
54		9	Dec-91	(0.9512)	0.5517	(0.1998)
55		10	Jan-92	4.3489	4.5312	4.4400
56		11	Feb-92	(4.2124)	2.1130	(1.0497)
57		12	Mar-92	8.0436	6.5692	7.3064
58		13	Apr-92	5.0739	0.1770	2.6254
59		14	May-92	(3.6594)	(3.8682)	(3.7638)
60		15	Jun-92	(3.2401)	1.3956	(0.9223)
61		16	Jul-92	(0.8665)	1.8479	0.4907
62		17	Aug-92	(1.5485)	0.1924	(0.6781)
63		18	Sep-92	(4.4662)	0.2305	(2.1179)
64		19	Oct-92	3.6531	(0.6057)	1.5237
65		20	Nov-92	3.2618	4.4744	3.8681

The beta is a measure of the variance of the share to the market. If you calculate the correlation between the share and the market together with the standard deviation, you can calculate a beta. This is demonstrated in the file Portfolio on the Returns sheet (see Figure 13.1). This models excess returns for a share against the market over 120 periods.

The formula for beta is:

$$\beta_i = \frac{S_i S_m Corr_i}{S_m} = \frac{Corr_{im} S_i}{S_m}$$

The correlation of the share to the market is calculated using the function CORREL in cell D38:

```
=CORREL(D46:D165,E46:E165)
```

The standard deviations for the share and the market are in cells D36 and E36 using:

```
=STDEV(D$46:D$165)
```

The chart plots the series for the share and the market as:

```
=SERIES(Returns!$B$2,Returns!$D$46:$D$165,Returns!$E$46:
$E$165,1)
```

The chart is a scattergraph with a trend line through the data to show the pattern (see Figure 13.2). The beta is the slope of the data as calculated using SLOPE in cell B6:

```
=SLOPE(Returns!$E$46:$E$165,Returns!$D$46:$D$165)
```

The intercept is calculated to show where the line crosses the Y-axis. The R Squared (calculated as the correlation squared) is also called the coefficient of determination. A factor of one means an exact relationship with the underlying data. Hence this is a measure of 'fit'. changes, which are related to this factor and the rest to other factors. You can display these factors directly on the graph by right clicking Options on the trend line (see Figure 13.3). This displays the equation as mx + b where m is the slope and b is the intercept. X is the value on the X-axis. Alternatively, the slope, R squared and intercept values are available as the function SLOPE, RSQ and INTERCEPT.

The beta in this example is 0.8420, which is less than one and therefore the share is less risky than the market. It is measuring relative rather than absolute risk. For instance, it does not include currency or international risk and is strictly not comparable across borders. Therefore, it follows that risky shares are likely to have a higher beta than low-risk shares. Example betas are given in Table 13.1 with more risky industries shown with higher values.

Fig 13.2

Beta calculation.

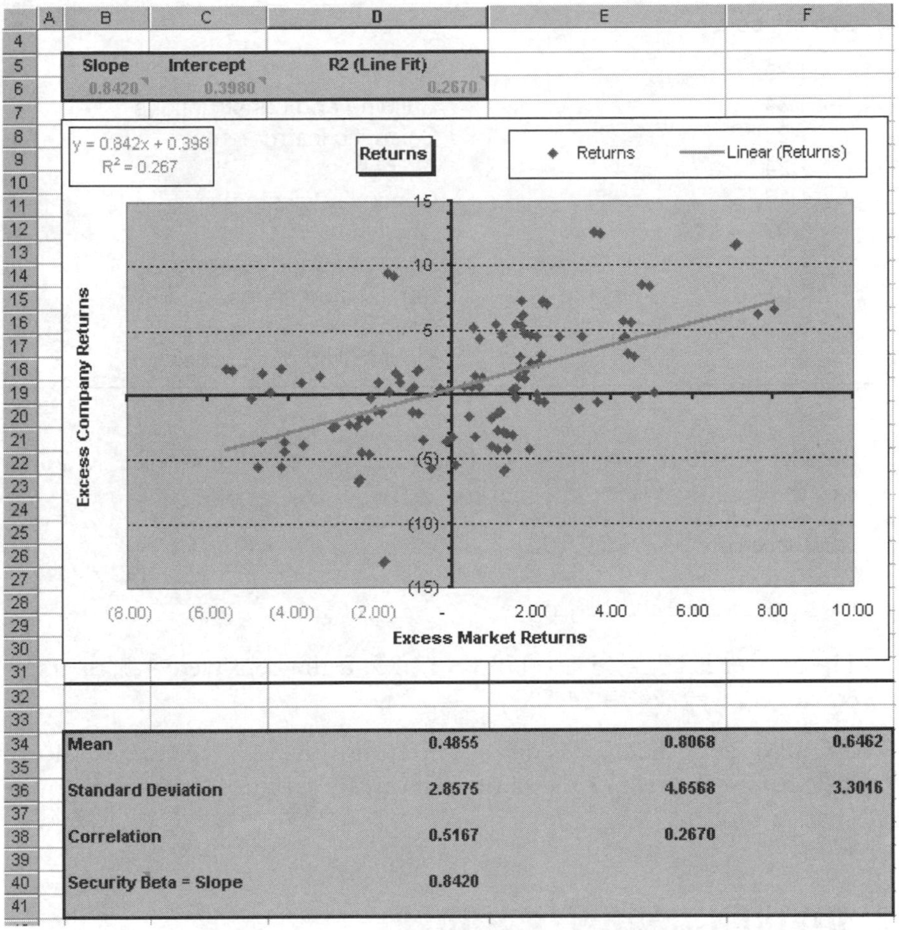

Fig 13.3

Options.

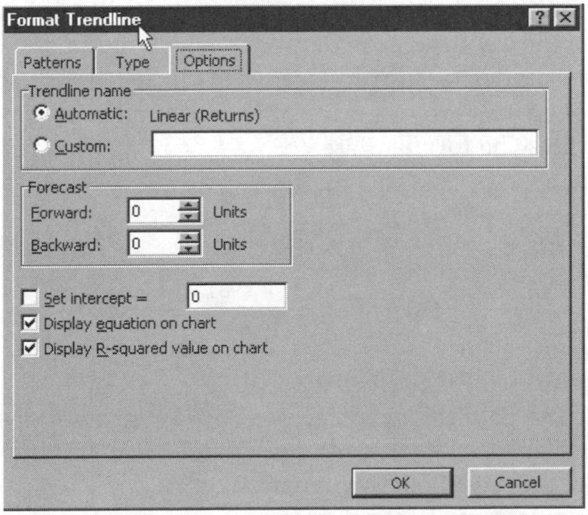

Table 13.1 **Examples of beta**

Levered beta	Industry
1.39	Hotels
1.34	Building and constructions
1.25	Scientific instruments
1.24	Airlines
1.16	General retail stores
1.09	Chemicals
1.04	Food and food retailing
1.01	Banks and finance
0.86	Petroleum refining
0.73	Electric and gas utilities

Beta encapsulates risk as per this example on the WACC schedule where the beta is close to the market:

Risk-free rate	7.00
Risk premium	5.00
Beta (β)	1.05

The answer is [7 + (5 * 1.05)] = 12.25. If the beta were 1.5, then the cost of equity rises to 14.5%.

The CAPM gives the expected rate of return if the risk-free rate is known by calculating the risk of the share in terms of variation against the overall market return.

2. DIVIDEND GROWTH MODEL

There have been criticisms of the CAPM in explaining share price movements (Fama and French, 1992). An alternative to calculating the cost of equity is to use the dividend growth model, which is sometimes known as the perpetuity model or Gordon growth model. This model simply assumes that dividends grow at a constant rate and the formula calculates the rate of return. The formulas are:

$$P_i = \frac{D_0 * (1 + g)}{(E(R_i) - g)}$$

$$E(R_i) = \frac{D_0 * (1 + g)}{P_i} + g$$

P_i = price of share i
D_0 = dividend paid this year (factored by (1 = growth) in the formula above)
$E(R_i)$ = expected return on a share based on risk
g = constant annual growth rate in dividends.

This model is on the Growth_Model sheet in the file Portfolio (see Figure 13.4). The inputs are clearly marked at the top and the only unknown input for the model is growth. The dividends for two periods are taken from annual reports and the formulas in cells C12 and C13 compute the growth between the periods. The formula is:

$$\left[\frac{FinalDividend}{StartingDividend}\right]^{(1/NumberofPeriods)}$$

The growth can also be calculated using the RATE function as in cell C13.

Cell C15 calculates the cost of equity by this method as 16.19%. Below there is a data table using the standard format outlined in earlier chapters. B20 looks at the answer in cell C15 and the intervals are driven from cell C17. The chart shows the cost of equity based on varying share prices.

Fig 13.4

Growth model.

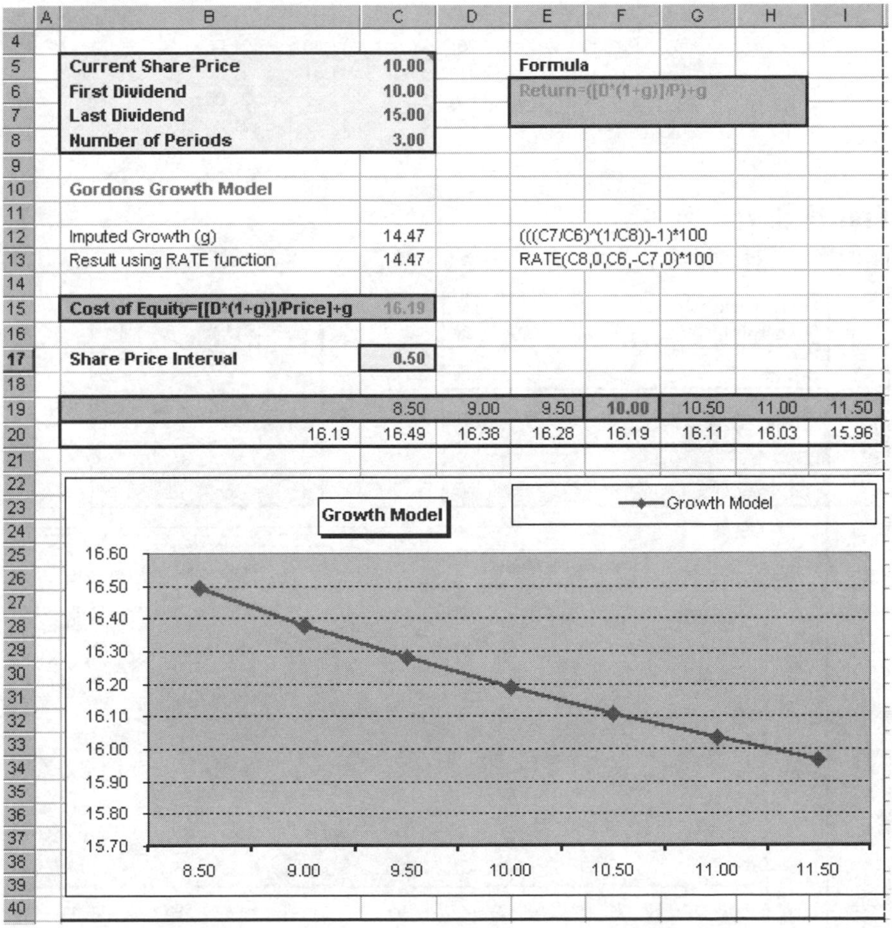

	A	B	C	D	E	F	G	H	I
4									
5		**Current Share Price**	**10.00**		**Formula**				
6		**First Dividend**	**10.00**		Return=([D*(1+g)]/P)+g				
7		**Last Dividend**	**15.00**						
8		**Number of Periods**	**3.00**						
9									
10		Gordons Growth Model							
11									
12		Imputed Growth (g)	14.47		(((C7/C6)^(1/C8))-1)*100				
13		Result using RATE function	14.47		RATE(C8,0,C6,-C7,0)*100				
14									
15		**Cost of Equity=[[D*(1+g)]/Price]+g**	16.19						
16									
17		**Share Price Interval**	**0.50**						
18									
19			8.50	9.00	9.50	**10.00**	10.50	11.00	11.50
20		16.19	16.49	16.38	16.28	16.19	16.11	16.03	15.96

Fig 13.5

Growth model proof.

Period	Dividend	PV of Flows	Value
-	-	-	21.00
1	1.05	0.95	21.00
2	1.10	1.87	21.00
3	1.16	2.74	21.00
4	1.22	3.57	21.00
5	1.28	4.36	21.00
6	1.34	5.11	21.00
7	1.41	5.84	21.00
8	1.48	6.53	21.00
9	1.55	7.18	21.00
10	1.63	7.81	21.00
11	1.71	8.41	21.00
12	1.80	8.98	21.00
13	1.89	9.53	21.00
14	1.98	10.05	21.00
15	2.08	10.55	21.00
16	2.18	11.02	21.00
17	2.29	11.48	21.00
18	2.41	11.91	21.00
19	2.53	12.32	21.00
20	2.65	12.72	21.00

Fig 13.6

Growth chart.

Interest Rate	10.00
Starting Dividend	1.00
Period	1
Growth	5.00

Growth Model at period 1	21.00
Present Value of Flows	21.00
Future Value at Period 120	20.92

Growth Model Formulas

P=[D*(1+g)]/(Return-g)

Return=([D*(1+g)]/P)+g

D=Dividend
g=Growth
Return=Expected return
P=Share price

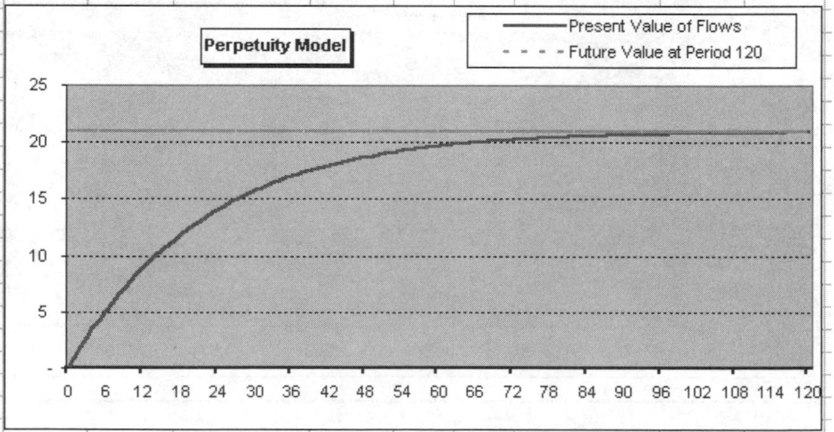

There is also a sheet to prove that this model produces a cost based on a steadily rising dividend. In the sheet called Growth_Model_Proof, the cost of equity is calculated using the formula and compared with the present value of an increasing number of dividends (see Figure 13.5). The chart shows a constant line of the equity price compared against the net present value answer.

Column C is growth at the constant rate in cell E8. The present value in column D uses the NPV formula with the number of periods in column B and the interest rate in cell E5. The result is that the present value begins to converge on the answer as shown in the chart in Figure 13.6.

If the model were allowed to calculate more than 120 periods, then the difference of 0.08 would begin to disappear.

3. COST OF PREFERENCE SHARES

Preference shares carry a fixed dividend but usually no voting powers. Thus they have features of debt and equity. For the purposes of this exercise, the dividend is known; however, the price is affected by the market price. In the example below from the WACC sheet, the cost of the debt is 8.00 / 0.90 = 8.87:

Number of preference shares	500,000
Preference share dividend	8.00
Preference market price	0.90

4. COST OF DEBT

Debt is either a known figure or it can be deduced from an annual report using the formula:

$$\frac{\textit{Interest Paid}}{\textit{Average Debt}}$$

The average debt is the opening and closing short- and long-term debt divided by two. Note that the year-end positions may not be typical balances for the whole of a year. The interest figure is on the income statement.

Bond pricing is discussed in the next chapter together with the available Excel functions.

5. WEIGHTED AVERAGE COST OF CAPITAL

The previous sections have demonstrated the calculations for different sources of capital. The WACC sheet calculates the cost of capital using these inputs entered as Example 3 on the scenarios (see Figure 13.7).

Fig 13.7 **WACC inputs.**

Row	Item	Value
5	Risk Free Rate	5.00
6	Risk Premium	7.00
7	Beta ß	1.10
8	Number of Ordinary Shares	500,000
9	Current Share Price	10.00
10	Number of Preference Shares	500,000
11	Preference Share Dividend	8.00
12	Preference Market Price	0.90
13	Average Borrowings $000	500,000
14	Cost of Borrowings	9.00
15	Tax Rate	30.00
16	First Dividend	10.00
17	Last Dividend	15.00
18	Number of Periods	4.00
19	Method of Equity Cost	CAPM

The method is:

- Calculate the cost of the individual sources of capital.
- Calculate the weights or percentages based on market (not book) values. The book value of debt is difficult to determine unless traded and therefore book value is used.
- Factor debt by (1 – Tax) if the company pays mainstream corporate tax.
- Multiply the relevant after-tax cost by its percentage.
- Add the constituents to derive the weighted average cost of capital.

The formula is:

$$WACC = \frac{D}{D+E} * R_d * (1 - Tax) + \frac{E}{D+E} * R_e$$

The calculation is shown in Figure 13.8.

The costs are derived using the methods above. Column E is the market amounts, for example the number of shares multiplied by the share price. Column F finds the percentages or weights of each source. The net of tax cost is in column H where debt is tax deductible whereas ordinary and preference shares are not. Column I multiplies out the three sources of capital to solve the WACC as 11.72%. There is also a CheckSum on the right to ensure that the answer adds up across and down.

The model is more comprehensive with the addition of a sensitivity chart together with the equity method and scenarios control (see Figure 13.9). The table uses conditional formatting to pinpoint the answer. The starting points of 12.51 and 6.30 are kept updated by a macro, which is assigned both to the button, the equity method and scenarios controls.

WACC calculation.

Fig 13.8

Capital Asset Pricing Model			
CAPM=RiskFree + Beta * Risk Premium	**12.70**		
Growth Model			
Imputed Growth (g)	10.67		(((E17/E16)^(1/E18))-1)*100
Result using RATE function	10.67		RATE(E18,0,E16,-E17,0)*100
Cost of Equity=[[D*(1+g)]/Price]+g	**12.33**		
Weighted Average Cost of Capital (WACC)			

Market Values	Market Value	%	Cost	Net of Tax Cost	
Equity selected as Average: CAPM/Growth	5,000,000	84.03	12.51	12.51	10.52
Preference	450,000	7.56	8.89	8.89	0.67
Debt	500,000	8.40	9.00	6.30	0.53
Total $000	5,950,000	100.00			
WACC=[Equity*Cost+Preference*Cost+Debt*Cost]/Total Market Value					11.72

WACC chart.

Fig 13.9

Sensitivity Table: Equity Across, Net of Tax Debt Rate Down

Interval Across	**0.10**	Update Table
Interval Down	**0.10**	

11.72	12.21	12.31	12.41	**12.51**	12.61	12.71	12.81
6.00	11.44	11.52	11.61	11.69	11.78	11.86	11.94
6.10	11.45	11.53	11.62	11.70	11.78	11.87	11.95
6.20	11.46	11.54	11.63	11.71	11.79	11.88	11.96
6.30	11.47	11.55	11.63	**11.72**	11.80	11.89	11.97
6.40	11.47	11.56	11.64	11.73	11.81	11.89	11.98
6.50	11.48	11.57	11.65	11.73	11.82	11.90	11.99
6.60	11.49	11.57	11.66	11.74	11.83	11.91	12.00

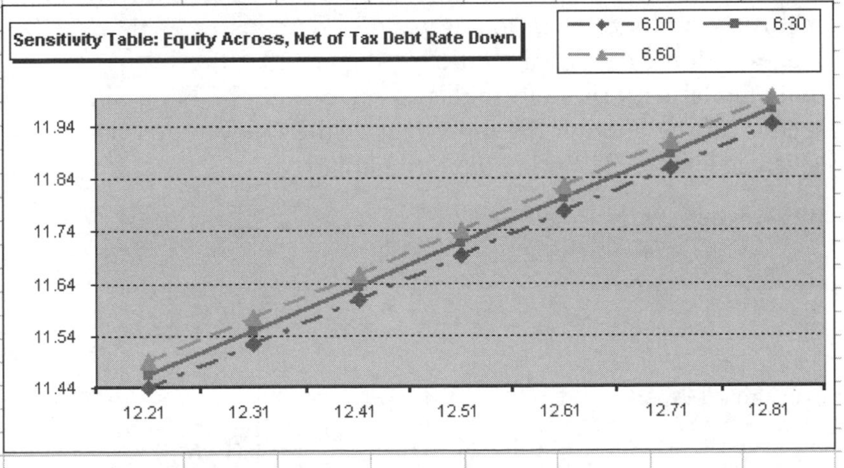

The macro simply updates cells B45 and B49 with the values in cells H33 and H35 using the Paste Special command and was recorded using the Macro Recorder in `Tools`, `Macros`, `Record New Macro`.

```
Range("H33").Select
  Selection.Copy
  Range("F45").Select
  Selection.PasteSpecial Paste:=xlValues, Operation:=xlNone,
SkipBlanks:= _False, Transpose:=False
  Range("H35").Select
  Selection.Copy
  Range("B49").Select
  Selection.PasteSpecial Paste:=xlValues, Operation:=xlNone,
SkipBlanks:= _False, Transpose:=False
```

For clarity only the upper and lower limits together with the answer are plotted on the line chart. Equity is usually less expensive than the after-tax cost of debt and since this company's debt-equity ratio is low, the resultant cost of capital is near to the cost of equity. The company is not 'leveraging' its own capital base with cheaper forms of capital and therefore needs to 'earn' more in order to reward the individual providers of capital.

6. MARGINAL WACC

The cost of capital varies depending on the amounts: a company cannot continue to borrow since bankers will demand a higher and higher premium as the perceived risk increases. Loans have to be repaid whereas a company can temporarily postpone dividend payments if there is not sufficient cash. A further sheet called Marginal_WACC uses the same general layout as the previous sheet and demonstrates that the WACC changes with the debt/equity ratio (see Figure 13.10).

The model uses these formulas to releverage the beta. Since the beta depends on the gearing the input beta is the unleveraged beta, which is releveraged in cell E23 using the formula below:

Unleveraging betas:

$$Beta_U = \frac{Beta_L}{1 + (1 - Tax)\ (\frac{Debt}{Equity})}$$

Leveraging betas:

$$Beta_L = \left[\ 1 + (1 - Tax)\ \frac{Debt}{Equity}\right] (Beta_U)$$

In this example, the cost of borrowing rises with the second facility. The inputs include a base rate and a margin. The cells in E30 to E34 calculate a weighted cost of debt and the facility usage. The WACC calculation is in row 43:

```
=IF(AND(C40),IF(AND(C38),((E38*H38)+(E39*H39)+(E40*H40))
/E41,0),0)
```

This formula ensures that cells C40 and C38 are TRUE and that the total capital is possible. If the amount exceeds the available maximum then the IF statement will return a zero result.

Marginal WACC.

Fig 13.10

	A	B	C	D	E	F	G	H	I
4									
5		**Risk Free Rate**			5.00		**Management Summary**		
6		**Risk Premium**			7.00			**Cost**	**%**
7		**Unleveraged Beta ß**			1.10		**Equity**	15.40	50.00
8		**Share Capital $000**			500,000		**Prefs**	-	-
9		**Current Share Price**			1.00		**Debt**	7.57	50.00
10		**Tax Rate**			30.00				
11		**Number of Preference Shares**			-		**WACC**	11.29	100.00
12		**Preference Share Dividend**			-				
13		**Preference Market Price**			-				
14		**Average Borrowings $000**			500,000				Units $000
15		**Basic Cost of Funds (LIBOR)**			5.00				
16		**Basic Facility Size**			300,000				
17		**Basic Margin**			2.00				
18		**Extra Facility Size**			400,000				
19		**Extra Margin**			4.00				
20									
21									
22		**Equity: Capital Asset Pricing Model**							
23		Revised Figure			1.49				
24		**CAPM=RiskFree + [Beta * Risk Premi**			**15.40**				
25									
26		**Cost of Preference Shares**							
27		**Coupon/Market Price**			-				
28									
29		**Marginal Cost of Debt**							
30		Basic Facility Usage			100.00				
31		Extra Facility Usage			50.00				
32		Basic Facility			71.43	5.00			
33		Extra Facility			28.57	2.57			
34		**Weighted Cost of Funds**				**7.57**			
35									
36		**Market Values**			**Market Value**	**%**	**Cost**	**Net of Tax Cost**	
37									
38		Equity	TRUE		500,000	50.00	15.40	15.40	7.70
39		Preference			-	-	-	-	-
40		Debt	TRUE		500,000	50.00	7.57	7.19	3.60
41		Total $000			1,000,000	100.00			
42									
43		**WACC=[Equity*Cost+Preference*Cost+Debt*Cost]/Total Market Value**							11.29

Fig 13.11

Marginal chart.

Sensitivity Table: Equity Across, Net of Tax Debt Rate Down

Interval Across	25,000	Update Table
Interval Down	50,000	

11.29	425,000	450,000	475,000	500,000	525,000	550,000	575,000
350,000	11.65	11.82	11.98	12.13	12.27	12.41	12.54
400,000	11.33	11.49	11.65	11.80	11.94	12.07	12.20
450,000	11.07	11.23	11.38	11.52	11.66	11.79	11.92
500,000	10.86	11.01	11.16	11.29	11.43	11.56	11.68
550,000	10.69	10.84	10.98	11.11	11.24	11.36	11.48
600,000	10.56	10.70	10.83	10.96	11.08	11.20	11.32
650,000	10.46	10.59	10.71	10.84	10.95	11.07	11.18

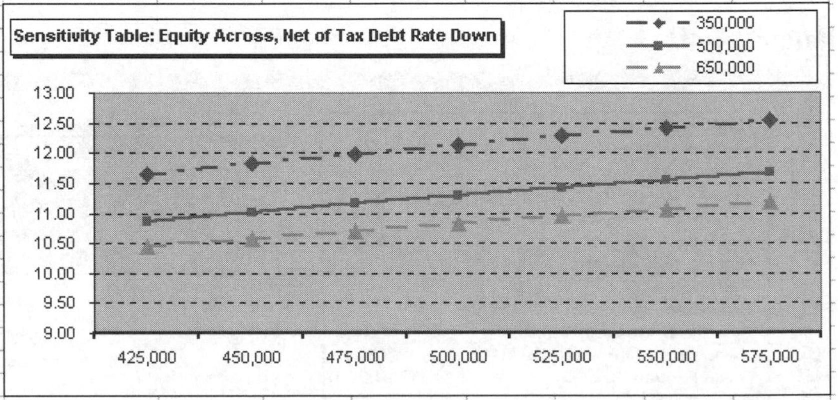

The model then uses a sensitivity table to show how the WACC flexes with varying debt/equity ratios (see Figure 13.11). The IF statement above ensures that values in the table will be zero if the total capital is not possible.

The data table shows that the cost of capital reduces as the level of debt increases by reading down the columns. At equity of 425,000, the WACC falls from 11.65% to 10.46% as debt increases from 350,000 to 650,000. Similarly the lowest WACC is at the bottom left-hand corner with the highest at the top right.

The cost of equity also increases along the rows due to the increasing proportion of equity. The chart at the bottom plots the upper, lower and middle series. The series are not parallel due to the step points in the pricing. The WACC is highest at 350,000 debt and then there is a jump at the 500,000 level due to the pricing and gearing.

7. SUMMARY

This chapter has demonstrated the basic mathematics in the Capital Asset Pricing Model, dividend growth model and the weighted average cost of capital. Each example has shown how basic models can be extended. With the use of data tables and charts the models extend the answer and provide more information. The cost of capital is the rate of return that a company must earn in order to satisfy all the providers of capital with their required rate. As shown in the last model, the WACC is not a static rate, but one that changes with risk and gearing.

14

Bonds

Bonds are securities issued by government or creditworthy companies which pay interest or coupons at regular intervals. The principal is repayable on expiry. A typical corporate bond is issued for periods between three and thirty years, while government bonds can be issued for longer periods. Bonds are transferable and valued based on current interest rates. This chapter models bonds, pricing, return and risk measures in a file called Bonds.

Bond markets use specific vocabulary:

Issue date:	Original issue date of the bond.
Settlement:	Pricing or yield date.
Maturity 3 years:	Date when principal and final coupon is due.
Redemption value:	Par value (usually 100).
Coupon %:	Interest rate fixed for the period of the bond.
Coupons per annum:	Usually paid once (annual) or twice (bi-annual) a year.
Basis:	See below.
Yield to maturity:	Inherent interest rate varies during the period based on markets.
Price:	Price of bond based on yield to maturity.

There are different bases for calculating periods and year. The price of the bond is the present value of all the cash flows (coupons and principal) calculated using discounted cash flow techniques. Since the present value goes down as the discount rises, it follows that the price of the bond falls as interest rates rise. Bond pricing assumes:

- round periods rather than actual days as used for other borrowing instruments;
- individual periods are assumed to be regular;
- pricing is the compound net present value.

If the pricing is required on the date a coupon is due, then there are no problems. Between periods, a seller expects to receive the accrued coupon within the period, while the buyer will only pay the present value of the future payments. Prices are quoted as:

- clean price = present value of the coupons and principal (dirty price – accrued coupon);
- dirty price = clean price plus the accrued interest (NPV of all cash flows).

Interest on the coupon is payable using simple interest calculations. If there are 30 days from the start of the period and it is assumed there are 360 days in the year, then the interest would be calculated as 30/360 * coupon rate. The first period could be less than the coupon periods depending on the purchase date, but thereafter coupons are payable annually, semi-annually or sometimes quarterly. The dates are the same, for example 17 January and 17 July for a semi-annual bond, and are not based on the exact number of days.

Day and year conventions vary and they are used in the various Excel functions. The methods are the number of days in the month and days in the year:

Days	Actual	Actual number of calendar days
	30 (European)	Day 31 is changed to 30
	30 (American)	If the second day is 31 but the first date is not 31 or 30, then the day is not changed from 31 to 30
Year	365	Assumes 365 days in the year
	360	Assumes 360 days in a year
	Actual	Actual including leap years

The combinations used in Excel functions are as below:

0 US (NASD) 30/360
1 Actual/actual
2 Actual/360
3 Actual/365
4 European 30/360

There are a number of defined bond functions in Excel, which are present in the Analysis Toolpak. Go to Tools, Add-ins and ensure that the add-in is ticked. The functions are used in the Bond application, in particular:

PRICE – price of a bond;
YIELD – yield to maturity;
DURATION – duration (discussed later);
MDURATION – modified duration.

1. CASH FLOWS

The file Bonds contains three bonds calculators. The sheet called cashflow sets out the flows for a bond in the form of a time line diagram. This is a useful method of graphically displaying cash flows using the convention:

Cash in = positive
Cash out = negative

This example in Figure 14.1 shows a bond with a coupon rate of 6% with six coupons remaining starting in six months' time. The price is calculated using a yield of 8% and this is a simple net present value function. The interest rate is divided by the number of coupons per annum since the function requires a periodic interest rate.

```
Cell C19 =NPV(C9/C8,D14:M14)
```

Fig 14.1 Cash flows.

	A	B	C	D	E	F	G	H	I
1									
2		Bonds Cash Flow					Menu		
3									
4									
5		Number	6		Summary				
6		Coupon Rate %	6.00		Price (NPV) at 800.0%		94.7579		
7		Redemption Value	100.00		Duration = Sum / Price		2.783 yrs		
8		Coupons per annum	2		Change per 1%		2.5357		
9		Yield %	8.00						
10									
11		Period	0	1	2	3	4	5	6
12			1-Jan-01	Jul-01	Jan-02	Jul-02	Jan-03	Jul-03	Jan-04
13									
14		Bond Cash Flows	-	3.0000	3.0000	3.0000	3.0000	3.0000	103.0000
15		PV Factor	-	0.9615	0.9246	0.8890	0.8548	0.8219	0.7903
16		PV Cash Flow	-	2.8846	2.7737	2.6670	2.5644	2.4658	81.4024
17									
18		Sum of Cash Flows		118.0000					
19		Price (NPV) at 8.0%		94.7579					
20									

The price is 94.7579. Note that the principal of 100 is repayable with the last coupon and the interest payments occur at the end of each period.

The example also contains a sensitivity table to demonstrate how the bond price responds to changes in yield (see Figure 14.2). As the yield increases, so the price of the bond falls.

Sensitivity.

Fig 14.2

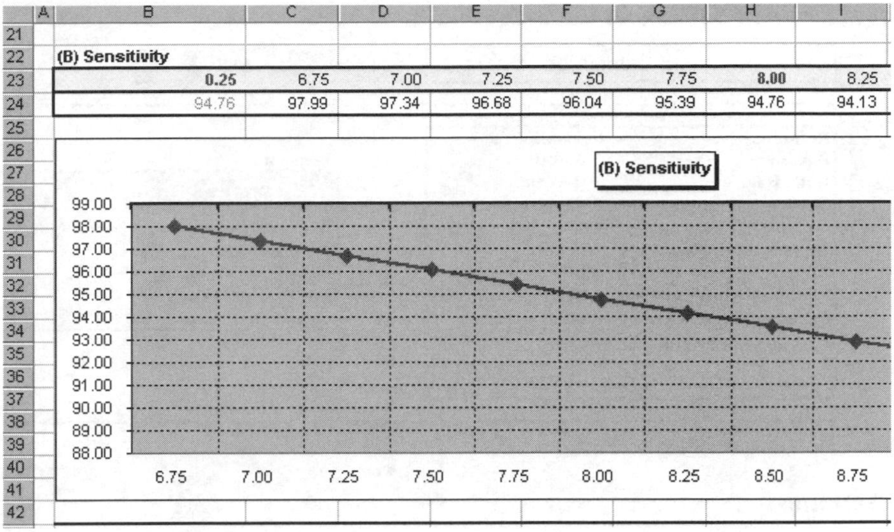

(B) Sensitivity							
0.25	6.75	7.00	7.25	7.50	7.75	8.00	8.25
94.76	97.99	97.34	96.68	96.04	95.39	94.76	94.13

2. YIELD MEASURES

Yield to maturity

If you know the yield of a bond, you can calculate the market price. If you know the price then you can compute the yield. These measures are similar to the net present value and the internal rate of return. There are a number of yield measures and the yield above is usually referred to as:

- yield to maturity (YTM);
- yield;
- redemption yield;
- gross redemption yield (GRY).

The yield is an iterative formula which, like the internal rate of return, assumes that all cash flows can be re-invested at the same rate. This is a failing with internal rates of return; nevertheless, most investors wish to know the implied return on an investment.

The yield measures are in the Model sheet. The example in Figure 14.3 is a four-year bond with a coupon rate of 9% and a settlement date 4.5 years before maturity. All the examples are saved as scenarios using `Tools, Scenarios, New` and can be accessed using the combo box control to the right of the sheet.

The model calculates the clean price of 103.5724 as the present value of the coupons and principal (see Figure 14.4). There have been 180 coupon days based on a 360-day year since the last coupon date. Therefore half of one coupon is accrued and added to form the dirty price.

Fig 14.3 **Bond calculator.**

Bond Calculator | Menu | Update Table | v1.0 1-Jan-2001

Reference	Example 1
Amount:	1,000.0
Issue Date:	1-Jan-00
Settlement:	1-Apr-01
Maturity 4.5 Years:	1-Oct-05
Redemption Value:	100.000
Coupon %:	9.000
Yield to Maturity:	8.000
Price:	0.000
Coupons per Annum:	1: Annual
Basis:	US (NASD) 30/360

Summary

Clean price:	103.5724
Coupon days: 180 dys	4.5000
Dirty price:	108.0724
Yield to maturity:	8.0000
Duration:	3.7559 yrs
Modified duration:	3.4776 yrs
Change in price per 1:	3.6019

Fig 14.4 **Workings.**

(A) Price			
Clean price:		103.5724	Present value of coupons and principal
Coupon days:	180 days		Days in this coupon period
Accrued interest at 9%		4.5000	Simple interest based on number of days in coupon period
Dirty price:		108.0724	Clean price plus accrued interest
Price amount:		108,072	Nominal value multiplied by amount
(B) Yield			
Current yield:		8.6896	Coupon/Price
Adjusted coupon yield:		7.9343	[Coupon + ((Redemption-Clean)/Years to Maturity)] / [Clean]
Yield to maturity:		8.0000	Calculated yield
(C) Duration			
Duration:		3.7559 yrs	Maturity: 4.5667 years
Modified duration:		3.4776 yrs	Macaulay Duration = Duration / [1+(Yield / No of Coupons)]
Change in price per 1%:		3.6019	Duration * Price * [1/1+Int] * 1%
(D) Dates			
Days to next coupon:		180 days	Days remaining in this coupon period
Interest remaining		-4.5000	Interest still to be accrued in period
Ex dividend price		99.0724	Clean price minus interest remaining in period
Next coupon date:		1-Oct-01	
No of remaining coupons:		5	Number until maturity
Total coupon amount paid:		11.2500	Coupon amounts pain since issue date

Current yield

This is a simple measure and is calculated as:

Current yield = Coupon rate / [Clean price / 100]

In this case, it is 9% / [103.57/100] = 8.6896%. The method ignores the time value of money and therefore it cannot be used for comparing different maturity dates and coupon periods.

Simple yield to maturity

The simple yield to maturity again does not consider the time value of money:

[Coupon + ((Redemption – Clean) / Years to Maturity)] / [Clean / 100]

The scenario, Example 3, shows a six-year bond paying annual 10% coupons and priced at 95.00. The yield results are shown in Figure 14.5.

Fig 14.5

Yield calculations.

	B	C	D	E	F
17					
18	**(A) Price**				
19	Clean price:		95.0000		Present value of coupons and principal
20	Coupon days:	0 days			Days in this coupon period
21	Accrued interest at 10%		0.0000		Simple interest based on number of days in coupon period
22	Dirty price:		95.0000		Clean price plus accrued interest
23	Price amount:		95,000		Nominal value multiplied by amount
24	**(B) Yield**				
25	Current yield:		10.5263		Coupon/Price
26	Adjusted coupon yield:		11.4037		[Coupon + ((Redemption-Clean)/Years to Maturity)] / [Clean]
27	Yield to maturity:		11.1883		Calculated yield

3. DURATION

The maturity of a bond is not a suitable indicator for a bond since the cash flows occur during the period to and at maturity. A bond with a longer maturity may be more risky since an investor is exposed to changes in yield rates for a longer period. Duration attempts to provide a weighted measure of maturity in the formula:

$$Duration = \frac{\sum PVofCashflow * PeriodNo}{Price}$$

The cashflow sheet shows the calculation of duration using the function DURATION and by building up the cash flows. The results in cell D56 and H55 are the same (see Figure 14.6). The formula in cell H55 is:

```
=DURATION(C12,EDATE(C12,C5*(12/C8)),C6/100,C9/100,C8,0)
DURATION(Settlement,Maturity,Coupon Yield,Frequency,Basis)
```

Basis is the days/years convention. The cell formula uses EDATE to find the maturity date since this is not an input variable. This function allows you to advance by a multiple of months.

Fig 14.6

Duration.

	A	B	C	D	E	F	G	H	I
44									
45		(C) Duration							
46									
47		Period	0	1	2	3	4	5	6
48									
49		PV Cash Flow	-	2.88	2.77	2.67	2.56	2.47	81.40
50		Cash Flow * Period	-	2.8846	5.5473	8.0010	10.2577	12.3289	488.4144
51									
52									
53		Sum of Weights		527.4339					
54		Price		94.7579		Excel Function			
55						Calculated Duration		2.783 yrs	
56		Duration = Sum / Price		2.783 yrs					
57									
58									
59		(D) Change in Interest Rates							
60									
61		Duration		2.783 yrs					
62		Price		94.7579					
63		Periodic Interest Rate		4.0000					
64									
65		Change per 1%		2.5357		Formula = D * P * [1 / (1 + r)] * r			
66									
67									

If the bond carries no coupon as in a zero coupon bond, then the duration will always be its maturity. Duration can be applied to any groups of cash flows and is useful when linked to the concept of immunization. If yields fall then the following occurs:

- earnings on reinvesting coupons will fall;
- price of the bond rises if held to maturity.

At some point between the date and maturity, the loss of interest returns and the capital gain from a higher bond price balance or cancel each other out. If an investor devises an immunized portfolio:

- the present value of assets equals the present value of liabilities;
- the duration of assets is equal to the duration of liabilities.

There is a further formula on the sheet which calculates the price movement based on a 1% yield change. The coupon rate is the periodic rate rather than the annual rate. This will of course be the same for annual bonds:

Formula = –Duration * Price * [1 / (1 + periodic coupon rate)] * 0.01

This formula is an approximation since the actual changes for larger figures are not a straight line but a curve. The formula equates to Slope * Change in Yield.

You can calculate the slope using the function SLOPE as in cell G61:

```
=-SLOPE(C24:M24,C23:M23)
```

There is a further variant of duration called the modified duration (also called volatility) on the Model sheet in cell D30. Using Example 1, the answer is 3.4776 years against duration of 3.7559 years. This uses the Excel function MDURATION, or you could calculate it with this formula:

Modified Duration = Duration / [1 + (Yield / No. of Coupons)]

The modified duration can also be used for calculating the price change per 1% of yield:

–Dirty Price * Change in Yield * Modified Duration

Using Example 1 on the Model sheet, the model uses a standard format to display a data table and chart (see Figure 14.7). There is a control to look up the values in cells B48 to B54 and the model uses an INDEX function in cells B56 to I56 to look up the selected values. The chart then uses this array as the series.

Fig 14.7

Sensitivity chart.

	A	B	C	D	E	F	G	H	I
41									
42		Sensitivity Table: Yield Across Settlement Date Down							
43									
44		**Interval Acros**	0.5		**Select a line to chart**		1-Apr-01		4
45		**Interval Down**	1 days						
46									
47		**103.5724**	**6.50**	**7.00**	**7.50**	**8.00**	**8.50**	**9.00**	**9.50**
48		1-Jan-01	109.89	107.80	105.75	103.76	101.82	99.93	98.08
49		1-Feb-01	109.73	107.67	105.66	103.70	101.78	99.91	98.09
50		1-Mar-01	109.57	107.54	105.56	103.63	101.75	99.91	98.11
51		**1-Apr-01**	109.42	107.42	105.47	103.57	101.72	99.90	98.13
52		1-May-01	109.27	107.31	105.39	103.52	101.69	99.91	98.16
53		1-Jun-01	109.12	107.19	105.31	103.47	101.67	99.91	98.20
54		1-Jul-01	108.98	107.08	105.23	103.42	101.65	99.93	98.24
55									
56		Date: 1-04-2001	109.42	107.42	105.47	103.57	101.72	99.90	98.13
57		Change per 0.5%	2.00	1.95	1.90	1.86	1.81	1.77	
58									

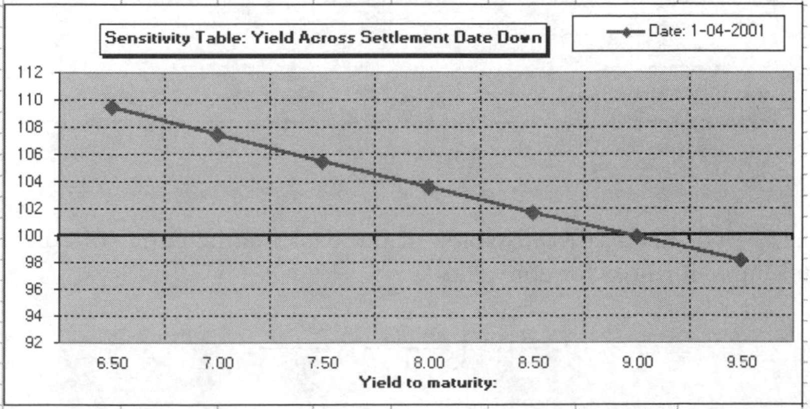

As noted above, the formula for changing the bond price due to yield is an approximation and you can see this by looking at the differences between the periods in row 57. The data table produces the correct results taking into account the convexity of the bond. This is the curvature of the present value profile.

Consider Example 5 shown in Figure 14.8 of a four-year bond paying a coupon of 10% on a yield to maturity of 8%. The model calculates the price as 106.6243, the duration as 3.5042 years and the change in price resulting from an increase in the yield of 1% as –3.4596.

Fig 14.8

Example 5.

	B	C	D	F	G	I
4						
5	Reference		Example 5			
6	Amount:		1,000.0		Summary	
7	Issue Date:		1-Jan-00		Clean price	106.6243
8	Settlement:		1-Jan-01		Coupon days 0 dys	0.0000
9	Maturity 4 Years:		1-Jan-05		Dirty price	106.6243
10	Redemption Value:		100.000		Yield to maturity	8.0000
11	Coupon %:		10.000		Duration	3.5042 yrs
12	Yield to Maturity:		8.000		Modified duration	3.2446 yrs
13	Price:		0.000		Change in price per 1%	(3.4596)
14	Coupons per Annum:		1: Annual			
15	Basis:		US (NASD) 30/360			
16						
17						
18	(A) Price					
19	Clean price		106.6243	Present value of coupons and principal		
20	Coupon days	0 days		Days in this coupon period		
21	Accrued interest at 10%		0.0000	Simple interest based on number of days in coupon period		
22	Dirty price		106.6243	Clean price plus accrued interest		
23	Price amount		106,624	Nominal value multiplied by amount		
24	(B) Yield					
25	Current yield		9.3787	Coupon/Price		
26	Adjusted coupon yield		7.8256	[Coupon + ((Redemption-Clean)/Years to Maturity)] / [Clean]		
27	Yield to maturity		8.0000	Calculated yield		
28	(C) Duration					
29	Duration		3.5042 yrs	Maturity: 4.00 years		
30	Modified duration		3.2446 yrs	Duration / [1+(Yield / No of Coupons)] = Slope of series		
31	Change in price per 1%		(3.4596)	Duration * Price * [1/1+Int] * 1%		
32	(D) Dates					
33	Days to next coupon		360 days	Days remaining in this coupon period		
34	Interest remaining		-10.0000	Interest still to be accrued in period		
35	Ex dividend price		96.6243	Clean price minus interest remaining in period		
36	Next coupon date		1-Jan-02			
37	No of remaining coupons		4	Number until maturity		
38	Total coupon amount paid		10.0000	Coupon amounts pain since issue date		
39						

In the workings, there is some of the basic mathematics of convexity. The simple formula for convexity is:

$$C = 10^8 \left[\frac{\Delta P_{d+1}}{P_d} + \frac{\Delta P_{d-1}}{P_d} \right]$$

This involves calculating the price change for plus and minus 100 basis points as per the data table (see Figure 14.9). Convexity is calculated as:

```
Cell P37 =((N35/D19)+(P35/D19))*10^8
```

The formula for a change in price is then:

$$\Delta Price = -ModifiedDuration * \Delta Yield + \frac{Convexity}{2} * \Delta Yield^2$$

This formula is in cell P38 as:

```
=-D30*C44+(P37/2)*(C44/100)^2
```

The errors between the data table, which is the most accurate, against the simpler approximate answers are given in cells P51 to P53. With greater differences, the simpler formula of [Duration * Price * [1 / 1 + Int] * Change] becomes more inaccurate.

Fig 14.9

Convexity.

	L	M	N	O	P
31					
32		**Convexity Workings**			
33			**7.990**	**8.000**	**8.010**
34		106.6243	106.6589	106.6243	106.5897
35		Change	0.0346		(0.0346)
36					
37		(1) Convexity			14.3309
38		Change in price per 1%			(3.2439)
39		Revised price using convexity			103.3803
40		Variance to simple formula			0.2156
41					
42		(2) Simple Formula			
43		Change in price per 1%			(3.4596)
44		Revised price using simple formula			103.1647
45					
46		(3) Data Table			
47		Data table change per 1%			(3.3846)
48		Data table Price			103.2397
49					
50		(4) Variances			
51		Data table to convexity			(0.1406)
52		Data table to simple formula			0.0750
53		Convexity to simple formula			0.2156

4. PORTFOLIO RESULTS

The Bonds application contains another calculator called Bond together with its table of bonds in the Database sheet. This is an alternative to scenarios since you enter data on a data form. This could be accessed manually using `Data, Form`. A simple macro is assigned to the buttons on both sheets and the working code is:

```
Sheets("Database").Select
Range("b3").Select
ActiveSheet.ShowDataForm
```

Data is automatically entered on the sheet in a range called Database (see Figure 14.10).

Fig 14.10 **Enter bond data.**

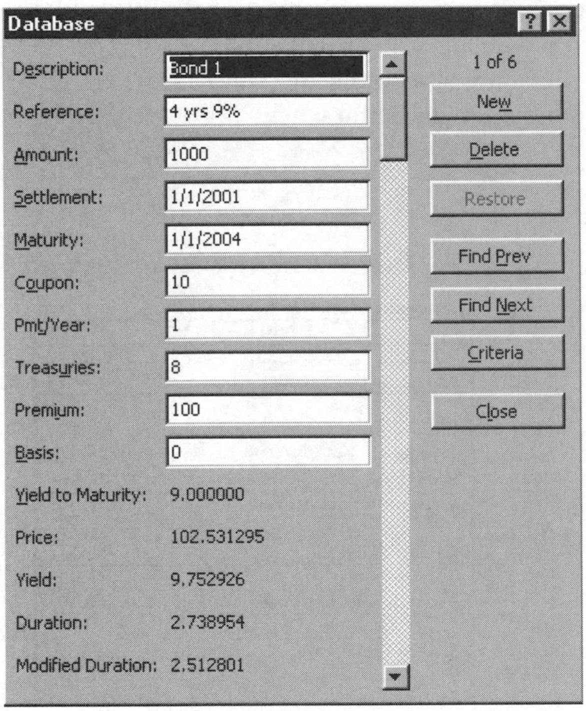

You can then view bonds on the Bond sheet by using the combo box to select individual items. Figure 14.11 shows an example of a three-year bond with a coupon of 10% based on a yield of 9%.

The price, yield, duration and modified duration are derived using functions on the Database sheet. All the data is looked up using the OFFSET function linked to cell E7. You simply go down the page by the number of lines or index returned by the combo box control. This same method could be adapted to other lists of data to save creating multiple scenarios.

Fig 14.11

Bond calculator.

Row	B	D	F	G
5	Select a bond from the database to display below:			
6			Enter Data	
7	Bond 1	1		
10	**Description:**	Bond 1	**Explanation of Basis**	
11	**Reference:**	4 yrs 9%	0	US (NASD) 30/360
12	**Amount:**	1000.0	1	Actual/actual
13	**Settlement:**	1-Jan-01	2	Actual/360
14	**Maturity 3 Years:**	1-Jan-04	3	Actual/365
15	**Coupon %:**	10.000	4	European 30/360
16	**Coupons per Annum:**	1		
17	**Frequency:**	Annual		
18	**Treasuries %:**	8.000		
19	**Premium (Basis Points):**	100		
20	**Yield to Maturity %:**	9.000		
21	**Basis:**	0		
24	**Calculated Price:**	102.5313		
25	**Duration:**	2.7390 yrs		
26	**Mod Duration**	2.5128 yrs		
27	**Change in Price per 1%**	2.5764	**Duration * Price * [1/1+Int] * 1%**	
28	**Next Coupon Date**	1-Jan-02		
29	**Coupon Days**	0		
30	**No of Remaining Coupons**	3		
32	**Portfolio Value**	463,646		
33	**Duration**	4.4913 yrs		
34	**Modified Duration**	4.1704 yrs		

The model also keeps a running check on the portfolio in rows 32 to 34. The portfolio value is calculated using the SUMPRODUCT function. This multiplies out the prices by the amounts to form the total portfolio value. The duration and modified duration are the weighted amounts using the formulas. For example, duration:

```
=SUMPRODUCT(Database!D$6:D$100,Database!M$6:M$100,
Database!O$6:O$100)/D32
```

This is:

$$Duration = \frac{\sum IndividualDuration * IndividualValue}{TotalPortfolioValue}$$

Modified duration follows the same principles:

$$ModifiedDuration = \frac{\sum IndividualModifiedDuration * IndividualValue}{TotalPortfolioValue}$$

The duration gives the sensitivity of the portfolio to changes in yield. This includes the assumption that all the yields move in parallel; however, this is a simple risk measure. Matching modified durations of assets and liabilities will of course reduce risk.

5. SUMMARY

This chapter has presented a model of bond mathematics using the methodology and layout set out in earlier chapters. The model performs bond pricing and includes several yield measures and duration, and predicts changes in prices based on altered yield. Finally there is a portfolio model which uses an accompanying database to store individual bonds and derives portfolio results.

15

Investment analysis

Companies invest capital in a range of projects, which hopefully will result in positive cash flows and thereby add value to the company to pay repay all the providers of capital. This includes both shareholders and debt providers as discussed in Chapter 13 on the cost of capital. It follows from the cost of capital logic that a company should invest in projects that provide a return above the cost of capital and reject projects that fail this test. Such decisions are linked to strategy, since a company may be replacing old equipment, investing in new areas or replying to competition.

Financial modelling assists this process since it is possible to create a cash flow model to encompass all the rules and cash flows. As discussed, modelling helps to identify the variables, discover new variables and understand better how the variables behave. A stylized process could be as shown in Figure 15.1.

This chapter discusses a model up to stage 5, while Chapter 16 adds risk techniques. The objective is to add to the models introduced in earlier chapters such as Investment_Model or PPP and this chapter uses a file called Project_Model.

1. INVESTMENT MODEL REVISITED

While there is a whole range of qualitative factors in capital budgeting decisions, the Excel model concentrates on producing quantitative answers to management tests about the investment. Management must decide on an investment in return for the future cash flows and therefore the model needs to present the best estimate of the future. Investments need to possess a good chance of success and fit with management strategy for the business as a whole.

Fig 15.1 **Project.**

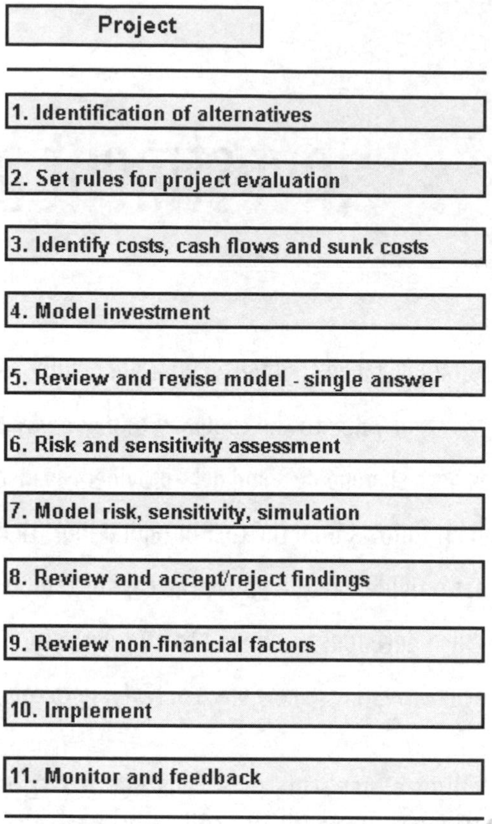

The investment can be viewed as an extensive time line diagram where cash out is deemed negative and cash in is positive. In the simple example shown in Figure 15.2, an investment of 100,000 is followed by positive amounts of 15,000 per annum and a final residual cash flow of 10,000.

Fig 15.2 **Time line.**

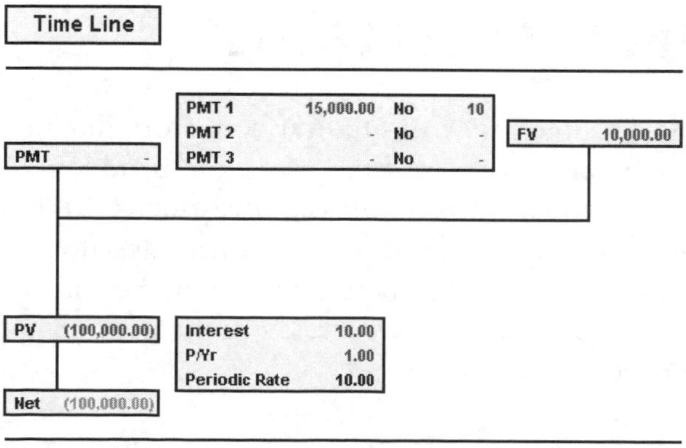

The model has the inputs shown in Figure 15.3. The decision is to invest 1,000,000 in a project to sell product at 50 per unit with price reductions over time. The cost price is 40 per unit with cost improvements over the five-year project life. Sales have to be funded and working capital is set at 10% of sales. The pre-tax cost of funds is 10% and the marginal tax rate 30%. The model has to include the tax depreciation on the equipment and the control links to four options. These options are UK writing down allowances at a 25% declining balance and US tax depreciation for the three-, five- and seven-year classes (depreciation methods are discussed in Chapter 18 in more detail).

Fig 15.3

Inputs.

Scenario Name:	Base Case
Prepared by:	Project Management
Product Code:	MJD-987
Manager:	Matthew Miles
Start Date:	1-Jun-01
Initial Investment:	1,000,000.00
Initial Sales Price per Unit:	50.00
Annual Price Change:	(5.00%)
Initial Cost per Unit:	40.00
Annual Cost Improvement:	10.00%
Project Life:	5.00 yrs
Residual Value:	0.00
Working Capital as % of Sales:	10.00%
Cost of Funds:	10.00%
Tax Rate:	30.00%
Tax Payment Delay:	1 yrs
Tax Method:	UK Writing Down Allowances
Finance Lease or Buy:	Buy Equipment

There are a number of methods that can be used to evaluate the investment and the model seeks to pick out the attractiveness of the project. The methods are:

- payback period and discounted payback – how long it takes to get 1,000,000 back;
- accounting return – the average accounting profit to the average investment (return on invested capital);
- net present value – discounted cash flow;
- internal rate of return;
- benefit to cost ratio – present value of benefits divided by the initial investment;
- management tests – cash flow etc.

Below the inputs, the model generates a manufacturing account, income statement, balance sheet and cash flow (see Figure 15.4). The cash flows that must be included are:

- incremental – the cash flows must be extra and dependent on the investment rather than existing cash flows;
- when the company is paying tax then the after-tax cash flows should be evaluated against an after-tax discount rate. In the example above, the cost of funds is 10% and the tax rate 30%.

Fig 15.4

Income statement and balance sheet.

Row	B	D	E 0 Jun-01	F 1 Jun-02	G 2 Jun-03	H 3 Jun-04	I 4 Jun-05
28	Sales Volume			**50,000**	**50,000**	**50,000**	**50,000**
29	Price per Unit			50.00	47.50	45.13	42.87
31	Sales Revenue			2,500,000	2,375,000	2,256,250	2,143,438
33	Annual Cost per Unit			40.00	36.00	32.40	29.16
34	Manufacturing Cost			(2,000,000)	(1,800,000)	(1,620,000)	(1,458,000)
37	**Profit and Loss Account**						
38	Sales Revenue			2,500,000	2,375,000	2,256,250	2,143,438
39	Cost of Sales			(2,000,000)	(1,800,000)	(1,620,000)	(1,458,000)
40	Contribution			500,000	575,000	636,250	685,438
41	Selling and Administration Costs			**(125,000)**	**(125,000)**	**(125,000)**	**(125,000)**
42	Recovery of Development Costs			(200,000)	(200,000)	(200,000)	(200,000)
43	**Net Operating Profit/(Loss)**		-	175,000	250,000	311,250	360,438
45	Interest Payable	-		-	-	-	-
47	Profit before Tax		-	175,000	250,000	311,250	360,438
49	Tax		75,000	(56,250)	(92,813)	(121,734)	(144,401)
51	**Profit after Tax**		**75,000**	**118,750**	**157,188**	**189,516**	**216,037**
54	**Balance Sheet**						
55	Fixed Asset		1,000,000	1,000,000	1,000,000	1,000,000	1,000,000
56	Depreciation		-	(200,000)	(400,000)	(600,000)	(800,000)
57	Net Fixed Assets		1,000,000	800,000	600,000	400,000	200,000
59	Cash		(1,000,000)	(800,000)	(393,750)	36,563	486,547
61	Total Assets		-	-	206,250	436,563	686,547
63	Working Capital - (Liability)/Asset			(250,000)	(237,500)	(225,625)	(214,344)
65	Tax		(75,000)	56,250	92,813	121,734	144,401
66	Timing/Deferred Tax		-	-	-	-	-
68	Loans		-	-	-	-	-
70	Shareholders Funds		75,000	193,750	350,938	540,453	756,490
72	Total Liabilities		-	-	206,250	436,563	686,547

Excluded costs include the following:

- Sunk costs that the company has already incurred. For example, an existing building may already have been lying idle and this could be viewed as an opportunity cost or zero since it is already empty and not being used.
- Non-cash costs such as depreciation of fixed assets and amortization of goodwill. These are accounting entries and not physical cash flows.
- Financing costs are usually included in the discount rate unless the cash flows considered are those available to equity holders and compared to a cost of equity. This is to avoid double counting of the funding effect.
- Costs which are not certain. The model errs on the side of caution and away from 'ungrounded optimism'.

The sales volume and overhead costs are inputs and therefore marked in blue. All other lines are based on the inputs area. The balance sheet checks itself and cash is used to make the accounts balance.

The accounting statements above are then translated into a cash flow by taking the operating profit and adding back depreciation and changes in working capital to produce net operating cash flow (see Figure 15.5). The cash flow follows the same general format as in Chapter 9 to create a cash flow before financing in row 90. The cumulative cash in row 92 is then compared with the balance sheet cash position to ensure that the cash flow also balances.

Fig 15.5

Cash flow.

	0 Jun-01	1 Jun-02	2 Jun-03	3 Jun-04	4 Jun-05
Cash Flow					
Operating Profit	-	175,000	250,000	311,250	360,438
Non-Cash Costs	-	200,000	200,000	200,000	200,000
EBITDA	-	375,000	450,000	511,250	560,438
Change in Working Capital	-	(250,000)	12,500	11,875	11,281
Net Operating Cash Flow	-	125,000	462,500	523,125	571,719
CAPEX	(1,000,000)	-	-	-	-
Interest		-	-	-	-
Tax		75,000	(56,250)	(92,813)	(121,734)
Cash Flow before Financing	(1,000,000)	200,000	406,250	430,313	449,984
Cumulative Cash	(1,000,000)	(800,000)	(393,750)	36,563	486,547
Cash Flow as % of Profit		114.3%	162.5%	138.3%	124.8%
Balance Sheet Cash	(1,000,000)	(800,000)	(393,750)	36,563	486,547
CheckSum	-	-	-	-	-

2. PAYBACK PERIOD

With the grid of cash flows in place, the model then calculates the results for each of the methods. Net present value is theoretically the optimum method since it includes the time value of money where a dollar today is worth more than a dollar tomorrow. Also the method depends only on the forecast cash flows in the model and alternative net present values from different projects can be ranked in terms of attractiveness. Corporations, however, still extensively use payback since it is straightforward to understand and tells you simply how long you have to wait to get your initial investment back.

The model calculates this in two ways:

- Using a MATCH function to look for the period closest to zero, where the '1' is the final constant in the function inputs. This finds the value over three years and the cumulative cash flow in row 92 duly crosses zero between years 2 and 3.

  ```
  =MATCH(0,$E$92:$K$92,1)
  ```

  1 = largest value that is less than or equal to the lookup value.
  0 = first value that is exactly equal to the lookup value.
  –1 = smallest value that is greater than or equal to the lookup value.

- The second method is more complex and seeks to return the exact number of years and months. This is built up in the workings in rows 247 to 251 (see Figure 15.6).

Fig 15.6 **Payback.**

	D	E	F	G	H	I	J
99							
100		0	1	2	3	4	5
101		Jun-01	Jun-02	Jun-03	Jun-04	Jun-05	Jun-06
245							
246	**Payback**						
247	Cash Flow	(1,000,000)	(800,000)	(393,750)	36,563	486,547	951,929
248	Year	-	-	-	430,313	-	-
249	Month	-	-	-	35,859	-	-
250	Match	-	-	-	(393,750)	-	-
251	Months	-	-	-	11	-	-
252							
253	**Discounted Payback**						
254	Cash Flow	(1,000,000)	(813,084)	(458,250)	(106,986)	236,304	568,115
255	Year	-	-	-	-	343,291	-
256	Month	-	-	-	-	28,608	-
257	Match	-	-	-	-	(106,986)	-
258	Months	-	-	-	-	4	-

Row 247 repeats the cash flows and row 248 works out the year where the cash flow goes positive and calculates the total cash flow from negative to positive in the year. Here 430,313 is made up of 393,750 plus 36,563. The formula in cell H248 is:

```
=IF(G247<0,IF(H247>0,IF(SUM($D$248:G248)<>0,0,H247-
G247),0),0)
```

Row 249 divides the cash flow by 12 months and this is then divided into the negative balance of 393,750. The result is 11 months so the payback is two years and eleven months and this is worked out in cell E106:

```
=MATCH(0,$E$92:$K$92,1)-1&" years and
"&TEXT(SUM($E$251:$K$251),"0")&" months"
```

The payback method ignores any cash flows after payback is reached and therefore the discounted payback is also calculated. Based on the after-tax discounted cash flows, the workings in row 254 repeat the same exercise based on the revised cash flows. Now the payback is somewhat longer at over three years.

Despite all the disadvantages, payback serves as a useful yardstick. For example, in times of uncertainty, cash flows in the future are more risky and it may be better to accept projects with lower returns, but which produce strong cash flows in the early periods.

3. ACCOUNTING RETURN

The accounting return is a non-time value of money approach, which simply finds the average profit and divides it into the capital outlay. This is equivalent to looking at the return on invested capital (ROIC). The formula in cell E108 is:

```
=AVERAGE(F43:K43)/(ABS(IF(E90=0,CapitalValue,E90))/2)
```

The IF statement serves only to ensure that the formula picks up the initial investment in the form of the first cash flow or capital value from inputs. This method is based only on the accounting method and the return could be altered, for example, by changing the depreciation method. Similarly, initial equipment valuations could alter the overall returns.

4. NET PRESENT VALUE

Net present value is the method put forward by most management finance textbooks as offering a framework for effective decision making. By taking into account the time value of money and all the incremental cash flows, the periodic cash flows can be discounted at a suitable cost of capital. The net present value is positive if the project earns a return above the cost of capital or negative if the project fails to produce a sufficient return. Projects can then be ranked over similar periods in order of attractiveness.

The model discounts the individual cash flows in row 103 at a net of tax discount rate and the net present value is 595,905 (see Figure 15.7). When you use the NPV function, you discount the outstanding cash flows and add the cash flow at period 0, otherwise you are assuming the investment and the cash flows start one period beyond the present.

Fig 15.7 **NPV.**

	A	B	C	D	E	F	G	H
99								
100					0	1	2	3
101					Jun-01	Jun-02	Jun-03	Jun-04
102		**Results**						
103		Present Value of Cash Flow at 7.0%			(1,000,000)	186,916	354,834	351,263
104		Cumulative Present Value			(1,000,000)	(813,084)	(458,250)	(106,986)
105								
106		**Payback Period**			**2 years and 11 months**			
107		**Discounted Payback**			**3 years and 4 months**			
108		**Accounting Rate of Return**			**49.86%**			
109								
110		**Present Value of Cash Flow at 7.0%**			**1,595,905**			
111		**Less Initial Investment**			**(1,000,000)**			
112		**Net Present Value at 7.0%**			**595,905**			
113		**Internal Rate of Return**			**24.49%**			
114		**Benefit : Cost Ratio**			**159.59%**			
115								

There are some problems with discounted cash flows and care is needed not to produce misleading answers:

- *Equity and entity*. The cash flows do not include the cost of debt and the cost of capital needs to be a weighted cost of capital. If the cost of finance is taken into account, then the cash flows applicable to shareholders need to be assessed including the net of the initial investment provided by shareholders. The cost of equity capital is not subject to a reduction due to tax.
- *Inflation*. Inflation is not included and the cash flows are assumed not to include inflation. If inflation is included in the cash flows then the discount rate should be altered using the Fisher formula, which is:

  Nominal rate = $(1 + r)(1 + I) - 1$
  r = Discount rate
  I = Inflation rate

  This is shown in the workings using a 3% inflation rate (see Figure 15.8). The net present value drops to 490,251 and a data table illustrates other combinations. The rule is that you have to compare like with like and be aware of the possible errors.

Fisher formula.

Fig 15.8

	A	B	C	D	E	F	G
259							
260		Inflation Adjustment Workings: Fisher Formula = (1+r)(1+I) – 1					
261		Inflation		3.00%			
262		Inflation Adjusted Rate		13.30%			
263		After Tax Rate		9.31%			
264		NPV		490,251			
265		Variance		(105,654)			
266							
267		Interval		1%			
268			0.00%	1.00%	2.00%	3.00%	4.00%
269		490,251	595,905	559,480	524,279	490,251	457,347
270							
271							

- *Taxation*. The model assumes that the company will pay tax for the whole of the period and will make sufficient profits to shelter the full cost of the assets acquired for the project. This model is set up for UK and US tax and the answer varies slightly depending on the method chosen. The UK reducing balance method produces a long tail of depreciation and, for simplicity, this model uses any utilized depreciation in the last period.
- *Tax delay*. The model uses a simple cost of funds and does not take into account the delay between the end of the accounting period and the tax payment and credit date. The discount rate is 10% * (1 – 30% tax) factored up for the tax delay of one period or 12 months:

$$Int = Int_{pre\text{-}tax} - \frac{Int_{pre\text{-}tax} * TaxRate}{(1 + Int_{after\text{-}tax})^n}$$

where:

Int = user's after-tax borrowing rate adjusted for the tax delay
$Int_{pre\text{-}tax}$ = user's pre-tax interest rate entered on the Inputs schedule
n = average tax delay expressed in year. This is an entry on the Inputs schedule. The tax delay is 12 months.

The calculated rate is 7.2% (see Figure 15.9) and this leads to a slight difference in the net present value.

- *Real options*. This model assumes that 'it is now or never' and ignores the concept of active management. There may be the option to abandon or to invest more depending on how the situation progresses. This is termed an option, since management has the right but not the obligation to undertake a future activity. Classic net present value methodology may reject projects that research or limited investment could transform into success. The next chapter includes some modelling on this subject.

Fig 15.9

Adjusted discount rate for tax delay.

	A	B	C	D	E
270					
271		Delay Adjusted Discount Rate			
272		Delay Adjusted Discount Rate			7.1963%
273		Variance			0.1963%
274		Present Value of Cash Flow at 7.2%			1,586,501
275		Present Value of Cash Flow at 7.0%			1,595,905
276		Variance			(9,404)
277					
278					

- *Risk*. Many companies use a simple hurdle or 'risk adjusted' rate to assess projects. While it is logical to add a margin for risk, this will tend to penalize longer-term projects more excessively. If all the managers know that the hurdle rate is 20%, then only projects of a certain nature will be sent up the line for approval. This could lead to imperfect decision making.

In this example, inflation is excluded and all cash flows are nominal rather than real flows. Inflation is presently low in Western Europe and the US, however, one should compare like with like.

5. INTERNAL RATE OF RETURN

The internal rate of return is related to the net present value and is the rate at which the net present value is zero. Thus, it is the inherent rate in the project. If the rate is above the net of tax cost of funds then the net present value must also be greater than zero. This is calculated using the IRR function.

There is the chance that a project could yield multiple internal rates of return since there will be another solution every time the cash flows cross zero. The function in Excel tries to overcome this problem as you insert a guess or starting point for the iterations. This is cell E113 where the guess is 0.1 or 10%:

```
=IF(ISERROR(IRR(E90:K90,0.1)),0,IRR(E90:K90,0.1))
```

The model could use more complex functions for NPV and IRR. These are in the Analysis Toolpak and are called XNPV and XIRR. These allow you to insert cash flows and dates and derive day-to-day answers when dealing with uneven periods. The results are as shown in Table 15.1.

Table 15.1

More complex calculations for NPV and IRR

	Toolpak	Calculated	Variance
NPV	595,710	595,905	(195)
IRR	24.48%	24.49%	–0.01%

6. BENEFIT COST RATIO

This is another way of looking at net present value. When funds are short, it is useful to look at the benefits gained for every dollar invested. This is simply the present value of future cash flows divided by the initial investment. In the example, 1,595,905 / 1,000,000 = 159.59%.

This method is sometimes known as the profitability index and it seeks to identify the most efficient projects in terms of cash flows.

7. MANAGEMENT TESTS – CASH FLOW ETC.

The model provides management information in a summary at the top of the schedule. This is to provide immediate feedback as you change the variables and also act as a management summary (see Figure 15.10).

Management tests.

Fig 15.10

Management Tests of Project Acceptability: Buy Equipment			
Payback < 3 years	3 yrs	3.00 yrs	Yes
Minimum IRR 20.00%	20%	24.49%	Yes
Positive Operating Profit > 0	0		Yes
Operating Cash Flow 120%	120%		Yes
Net Present Value > 0	0	595,905	Yes
Modified IRR at 12.0%	12%	16.37%	
Payback Period		2 years and 11 months	
Discounted Payback		3 years and 4 months	
Accounting Rate of Return		49.86%	
Benefit : Cost Ratio		159.59%	

The tests that have to be passed are clearly displayed together with the results. The code checks for a positive operating profit and cash flow greater than 120% of profit in each period and displays either 'Yes' or 'No' depending on the results.

The code is set out in workings to the right of the main schedule starting on row 43. The top line of the workings displays the cell reference for the operating profit if it falls below the test. The second line displays '1' if the line above is not equal to zero. Finally the MATCH function at cell N48 looks for '1' along row 44:

```
=IF(SUM(N44:S44)=0,0,MATCH(1,N44:S44,0))
```

This information is then transferred to cell K10:

```
=IF(SUM(N43:S43)<>0,"No - check period "&N48,"Yes")
```

The procedure is then repeated for the cumulative cash flow in row 94. This approach makes the workings clearer to understand and saves the need for complex cell formulas based on nested IF statements. It also tells management where to look if the project fails to meet one of the tests.

The summary also contains a modified internal rate of return based on a deposit rate of 12% using the formula:

```
=MIRR(E90:K90,CostofFunds*(1-D20),I14*(1-D20))
```

8. SCENARIOS

The example discussed so far is a scenario called ‘Base Case’. There are two other saved scenarios called ‘Optimistic’ and ‘Pessimistic’ to illustrate how the net present value flexes with changes in key variables (see Figure 15.11).

Fig 15.11

Scenarios.

	A B C	E	F	G
1				
2	Scenario Summary			
3		Base Case	Pessimistic	Optimistic
5	Changing Cells:			
6	Scenario	1	2	3
7	Payback < 3 years	3 yrs	3 yrs	3 yrs
8	Minimum IRR 20.00%	20%	20%	20%
9	Positive Operating Profit > 0	0	0	0
10	Operating Cash Flow 120%	120%	120%	120%
11	Net Present Value > 0	0	0	0
12	Modified IRR at 12.0%	12%	12%	12%
13	Scenario Name:	Base Case	Pessimistic	Optimistic
14	Prepared by:	Project Management	Project Management	Project Management
15	Product Code:	MJD-987	MJD-987	MJD-987
16	Manager:	Matthew Miles	Matthew Miles	Matthew Miles
17	Start Date:	1-Jun-01	1-Jun-01	1-Jun-01
18	Initial Investment:	1,000,000.00	1,000,000.00	1,000,000.00
19	Initial Sales Price per Unit:	50.00	50.00	50.00
20	Annual Price Change:	(5.00%)	(10.00%)	-
21	Initial Cost per Unit:	40.00	40.00	40.00
22	Annual Cost Improvement:	10.00%	5.00%	15.00%
23	Project Life:	5.00 yrs	5.00 yrs	5.00 yrs
24	Residual Value:	0.00	0.00	0.00
25	Working Capital as % of Sale:	10.00%	10.00%	10.00%
26	Cost of Funds:	10.00%	10.00%	10.00%
27	Tax Rate:	30.00%	30.00%	30.00%
28	Tax Payment Delay:	1 yrs	1 yrs	1 yrs
29	Sales Volume 1	50,000	50,000	50,000
30	Sales Volume 2	50,000	50,000	50,000
31	Admin 1	(125,000)	(125,000)	(125,000)
32	Admin 2	(125,000)	(125,000)	(125,000)
33	Lease or Buy	1	1	1
34	Tax Depreciation Type	1	1	1
35	Result Cells:			
36	Payback	3.00 yrs	7.00 yrs	3.00 yrs
37	Payback_Result	Yes	No	Yes
38	IRR	24.49%	-12.98%	46.57%
39	IRR_Result	Yes	No	Yes
40	Positive_Operating_Profit	Yes	No - check period 3	Yes
41	Positive_Operating_Cash_Fl	Yes	No - check period 3	Yes
42	NPV	595,905	(467,528)	1,674,778
43	NPV Rule	Yes	No	Yes
44	MIRR	16.37%	-2.36%	25.68%
45	Payback	2 years and 11 months	6 years and 0 months	2 years and 3 months
46	Accounting Return	33.23%	10.69%	56.12%
47	Benefit : Cost Ratio	159.59%	53.25%	267.48%

The present value now ranges from minus 467,000 to plus 1,674,000. The shaded area on the revised cases shows the variables used. It is a good idea to work from a base case as previously discussed and to form an audit trail of the combinations considered for inclusion. This way, you have a record of all your workings.

9. SENSITIVITY ANALYSIS AND CHARTS

The initial model produces a single answer and sensitivity analysis tries to answer 'what-if' questions by adding multiple answers. There are usually one or two variables which are important and this model picks out first the sale price per unit against the discount rate and secondly the starting sale price per unit against initial cost price per unit (see Figure 15.12).

Fig 15.12

Sensitivity (A).

(A) Sensitivity: Initial Sales Price per Unit: Across : Cost of Funds: Down

Data Table Intervals

Initial Sales Price per Unit:	1.00
Cost of Funds:	1.00%

595,905	47.00	48.00	49.00	**50.00**	51.00	52.00
8.00%	252,411	390,091	527,771	665,452	803,132	940,813
9.00%	223,900	359,309	494,719	630,128	765,537	900,947
10.00%	196,306	329,506	462,705	595,905	729,105	862,304
11.00%	169,592	300,641	431,690	562,740	693,789	824,838
12.00%	143,723	272,679	401,634	530,590	659,546	788,502

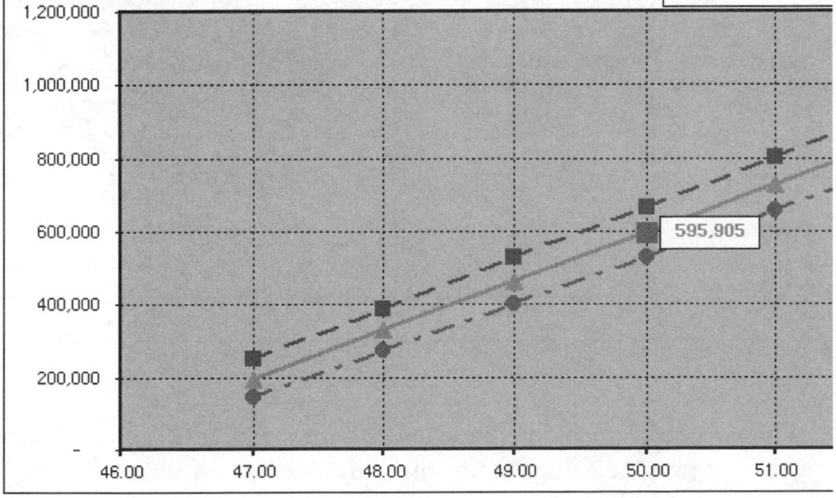

The table follows the same pattern discussed earlier with inputs for the intervals and a scattergraph for the outside lines together with the middle series. The chart type uses a scattergraph and this provides the possibility of displaying the answer as a single point. The data table uses conditional formatting to pick out the answer.

The two input values for the table are linked to a macro assigned to the button at the top together with the combo boxes. The macro merely copies the cells in Inputs and paste specials the values into the tables. This is to ensure that the result stays in the centre of the graph and the user need not re-input the tables when the values are changed in the Inputs area.

The same pattern is repeated for the second data table (see Figure 15.13).

Fig 15.13 **Sensitivity (B).**

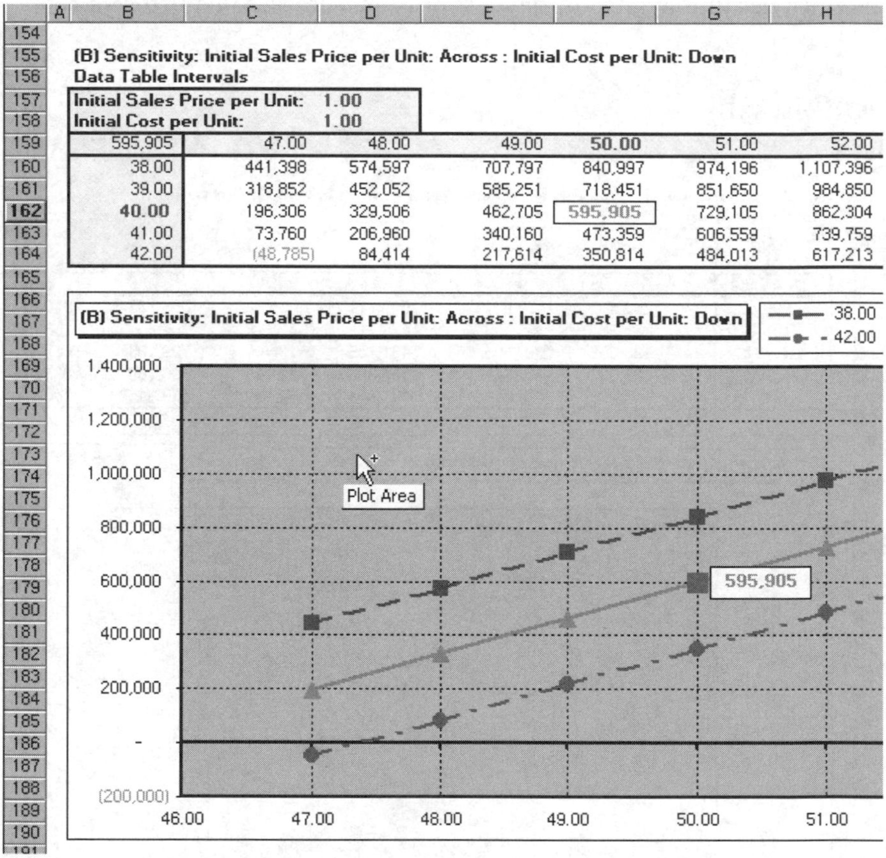

(B) Sensitivity: Initial Sales Price per Unit: Across : Initial Cost per Unit: Down

Data Table Intervals

Initial Sales Price per Unit:	1.00
Initial Cost per Unit:	1.00

595,905	47.00	48.00	49.00	50.00	51.00	52.00
38.00	441,398	574,597	707,797	840,997	974,196	1,107,396
39.00	318,852	452,052	585,251	718,451	851,650	984,850
40.00	196,306	329,506	462,705	595,905	729,105	862,304
41.00	73,760	206,960	340,160	473,359	606,559	739,759
42.00	(48,785)	84,414	217,614	350,814	484,013	617,213

The two tables provide management with a great deal of information on the net present value at differing sales, costs and discount rates. This analysis could of course be extended to provide information on other variables; however, these three variables are likely to be the most important for initial investigation. As an alternative, Figure 15.14 shows the results for the 'Pessimistic' scenario, which definitely fails to meet the tests. The only differences to the Base Case are an annual price reduction of 10% and a cost improvement of only 5%.

Fig 15.14

Pessimistic summary.

	G	H	I	J	K	L
5						
6	Management Tests of Project Acceptability: Buy Equipment					
7						
8	Payback < 3 years		3 yrs	7.00 yrs	No	
9	Minimum IRR 20.00%		20%	-12.98%	No	
10	Positive Operating Profit > 0		0		No - check period 3	
11	Operating Cash Flow 120%		120%		No - check period 3	
12	Net Present Value > 0		0	(467,528)	No	
13						
14	Modified IRR at 12.0%		12%	-2.36%		
15	Payback Period			6 years and 0 months		
16	Discounted Payback			6 years and 0 months		
17	Accounting Rate of Return			-14.53%		
18	Benefit : Cost Ratio			53.25%		

Fig 15.15

Pessimistic data table.

	A	B	C	D	E	F	G	H
116								
117		(A) Sensitivity: Initial Sales Price per Unit: Across : Cost of Funds: Down						
118		Data Table Intervals						
119		Initial Sales Price per Unit:	1.00					
120		Cost of Funds:	1.00%					
121		(467,528)	47.00	48.00	49.00	**50.00**	51.00	52.00
122		8.00%	(824,676)	(699,333)	(573,991)	(448,648)	(323,306)	(197,963)
123		9.00%	(828,328)	(704,967)	(581,606)	(458,245)	(334,884)	(211,523)
124		**10.00%**	(831,823)	(710,392)	(588,960)	**(467,528)**	(346,097)	(224,665)
125		11.00%	(835,171)	(715,618)	(596,065)	(476,511)	(356,958)	(237,405)
126		12.00%	(838,378)	(720,655)	(602,931)	(485,208)	(367,485)	(249,762)

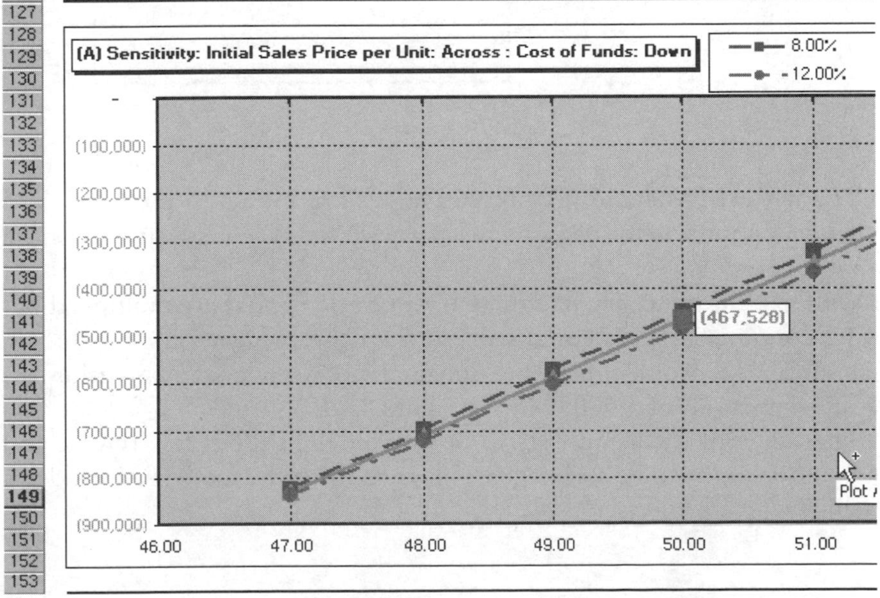

The table in Figure 15.15 gives some idea that the project fails the tests and the negative numbers all over the table show that this is not just a marginal failure on the NPV test.

10. CAPITAL RATIONING

The next problem is to look at capital rationing, where an organization may have only limited capital and wishes to solve the problem of where best to invest its funds. The model Project_Allocation uses Solver to find the optimum combination of projects which maximize the net present value. With 12 competing projects, there are a large number of possible combinations and therefore an optimization approach is needed to solve the problem. Indeed, there are 2 ^ N combinations, which here equate to 4,096.

The inputs for the allocation model are shown in Figure 15.16.

Fig 15.16 **Allocation inputs.**

	A	B	C	D	E	F
5						
6		Number	Project Name	Cost	NPV	Include
7						
8		1	A11	100,000.00	25,000.00	Y
9		2	B11	200,000.00	100,000.00	Y
10		3	C11	400,000.00	100,000.00	Y
11		4	D11	600,000.00	150,000.00	N
12		5	E11	50,000.00	10,000.00	Y
13		6	F11	725,000.00	250,000.00	Y
14		7	G11	1,200,000.00	250,000.00	N
15		8	H11	1,750,000.00	300,000.00	N
16		9	I11	350,000.00	25,000.00	N
17		10	J11	450,000.00	100,000.00	N
18		11	K11	650,000.00	250,000.00	Y
19		12	L11	850,000.00	200,000.00	Y

The project costs and net present values are inputs to the table. The 'Include' column is formatted so that 1 = 'Y' and 0 = 'N' using custom number formats.

On the right-hand side, the present value and capital are multiplied out using column F. If F is equal to zero then the project is not included. Therefore, the problem is to maximize cell I21 while staying within the capital constraint of 3,000,000 (see Figure 15.17).

The range of inclusions has to be greater than 0 but less than 1 and each inclusion must be an integer. This is to force the model to include or exclude whole projects.

Fig 15.17

Solver inputs.

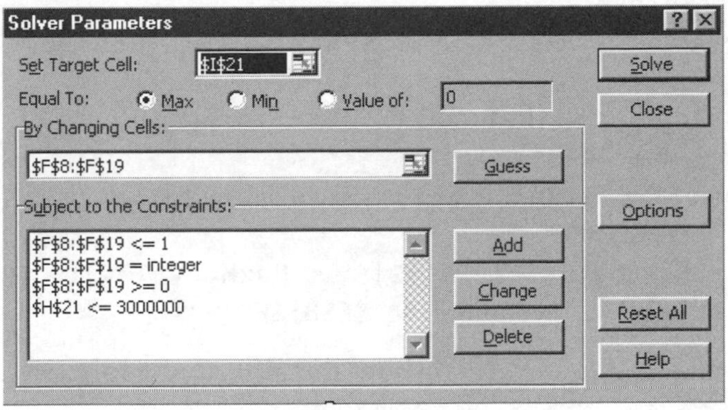

Fig 15.18

Allocated projects.

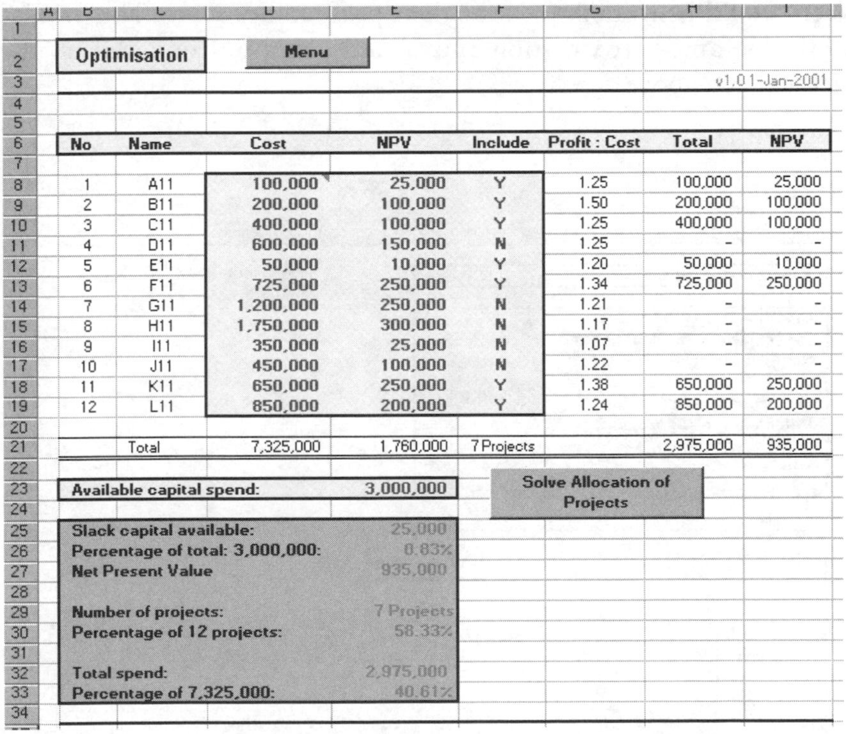

Optimisation | Menu

v1.0 1-Jan-2001

No	Name	Cost	NPV	Include	Profit : Cost	Total	NPV
1	A11	100,000	25,000	Y	1.25	100,000	25,000
2	B11	200,000	100,000	Y	1.50	200,000	100,000
3	C11	400,000	100,000	Y	1.25	400,000	100,000
4	D11	600,000	150,000	N	1.25	-	-
5	E11	50,000	10,000	Y	1.20	50,000	10,000
6	F11	725,000	250,000	Y	1.34	725,000	250,000
7	G11	1,200,000	250,000	N	1.21	-	-
8	H11	1,750,000	300,000	N	1.17	-	-
9	I11	350,000	25,000	N	1.07	-	-
10	J11	450,000	100,000	N	1.22	-	-
11	K11	650,000	250,000	Y	1.38	650,000	250,000
12	L11	850,000	200,000	Y	1.24	850,000	200,000
	Total	7,325,000	1,760,000	7 Projects		2,975,000	935,000

Available capital spend:	3,000,000
Slack capital available:	25,000
Percentage of total: 3,000,000:	0.83%
Net Present Value	935,000
Number of projects:	7 Projects
Percentage of 12 projects:	58.33%
Total spend:	2,975,000
Percentage of 7,325,000:	40.61%

Solve Allocation of Projects

The model accepts 58% of the projects with 25,000 capital spare with a net present value of 935,000 (see Figure 15.18). This routine is also programmed and assigned to the button. This sets up the Solver routine and adds the constraints. Solver is registered as a reference using `Tools, Options` in the Visual Basic editor since Solver will not run in code unless it is registered with the application file. An extract of the code is:

```
SolverAdd CellRef:="$F$8:$F$19", Relation:=4, Formula
Text:="integer"
SolverAdd CellRef:="$F$8:$F$19", Relation:=3, Formula
Text:="0"
SolverAdd   CellRef:="$H$21",   Relation:=1,   Formula
Text:=Range("e23")
SolverAdd CellRef:="$F$8:$F$19", Relation:=1, Formula
Text:="1.000001"
SolverOk   SetCell:="$I$21",   MaxMinVal:=1,   ValueOf:
=Range("e23"), ByChange:= "$F$8:$F$19"
```

There is also a small chart to show the allocated projects (see Figure 15.19).

You will note that the model picks those projects with the highest profitability (ratio of present value to cost) and a quick way of looking at the projects would be to rank them by their profitability score. This would, however, be an approximation and would suboptimize based on the model outlined above.

Fig 15.19 **Solver chart.**

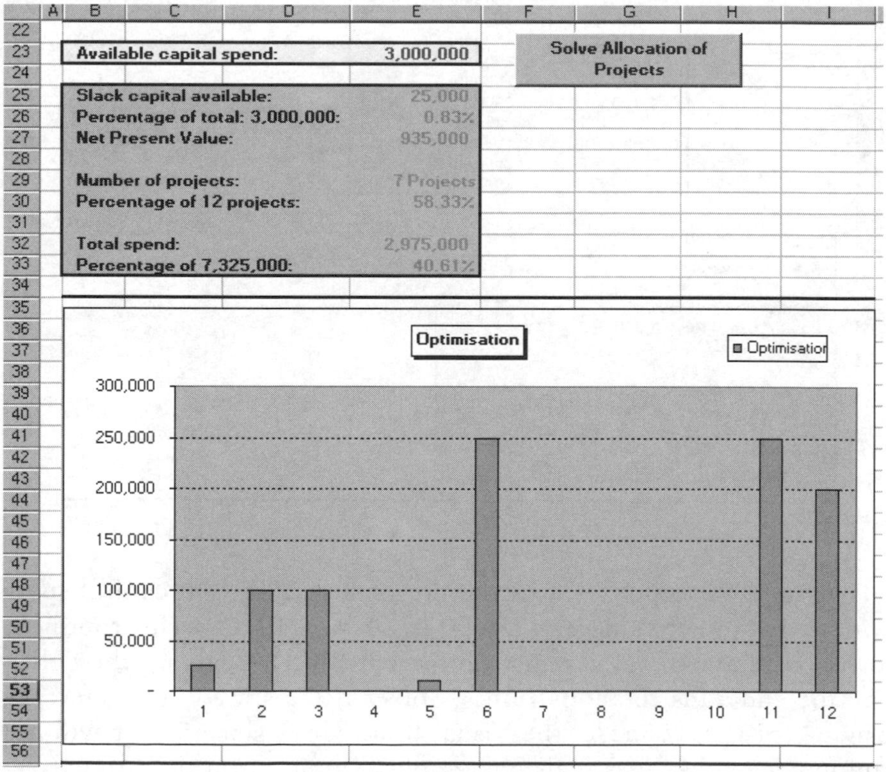

11. SUMMARY

This chapter has extended the net present value analysis outlined in earlier chapters on model design. The project model details the accounting reports and provides worked solutions using:

- payback and discounted payback;
- return on invested capital;
- net present value;
- internal rate of return and modified internal rate of return;
- profitability index;
- management tests;
- scenarios;
- sensitivity tables;
- capital allocation and maximizing net present values.

This analysis does not include assessments of risk. The next chapter, however, uses the same model and discusses methods of including risk in the modelling.

16

Risk analysis

The previous chapter discussed the project investment model (Project_Model) and calculated the return measures such as payback and net present value. This chapter discusses the other schedules in the file Project_Model concerned with risk. There is of course no return without risk and there is a tendency in modelling to believe that the cash flows from investment models are somehow 'real'. The inputs for the model may or may not occur and at best are a considered estimate of what might happen two or three years into a project time span.

Since finance theory teaches that rational people are 'risk adverse' then the next stage of the exercise should be to include in the model techniques for estimating the risk or uncertainty. The model should be tested to see how likely the organization is to achieve the desired net present value. The upsides may not be a problem, but management needs to assess the possibility of lower than anticipated returns. Again, following theory, if the project earns a lower rate than the cost of capital, then the shareholder value in the company diminishes.

1. RISK ASSESSMENT PROCESS AND ANALYSIS

Two types of risk can be identified:

- *project risk* – which is the variability of the project return;
- *corporate risk* – since management need to invest in a mixture of projects, which have varying degrees of risk and potential return.

Risk could also be split into two categories:

- *risk* – which can be described and quantified using some of the techniques in this chapter;
- *uncertainty* – which can be defined as random events.

Sources of risk and uncertainty could include one or more of the following:

- commercial and administration;
- competitive responses leading to reduced demand;
- market shifts especially with new technology;
- financial – liquidity, profitability and financial structure;
- knowledge and information dissemination;
- legal issues;
- currency issues both on the supply and sales sides;
- partners, suppliers and subcontractors;
- political events in home and overseas markets;
- economic cycles and the effect on demand and prices;
- quality issues leading to reduced sales;
- resource availability leading to lower production;
- technical ability of company;
- innovation, copyright and the availability of new technologies;
- management competence and drive.

Project risk is related to corporate risk since the latter will change if management invests in risky projects. The matrix in Figure 16.1 is the classic Ansoff matrix which summarizes growth vector requirements. It is outside the scope of this book to review all the strategic elements in investment analysis. However, diversification at the bottom right-hand corner would appear more risky than market penetration. In this context, it means new products and new markets.

The Probability sheet in the file Project_Model demonstrates expected outcomes using data from the three scenarios. The input line allows you to insert the probability of each of the scenarios and the control to select a line from the data (see Figure 16.2). Probability theory tells us that the expected value is the weighted average of the possible outcomes and the right-hand side of the table uses the SUMPRODUCT function to compute the values. This is the reference in cell G16:

```
=SUMPRODUCT(D16:F16,D$5:F$5)
```

Fig 16.1

Ansoff matrix.

Ansoff Matrix

Product	Present	New
Mission		
Present	Market Penetration	Product Development
New	Market Development	Diversification

Ansoff I (1965), Corporate Strategy

(*Source*: Ansoff, 1965.)

Fig 16.2

Probability.

	B	D	E	F	G
5	Probability:	0.50	0.30	0.20	
7	Select:	NPV		2	
9	NPV	595,905.05	(467,528.29)	1,674,778.36	492,649.71
10	Result	297,952.53	(140,258.49)	334,955.67	
12	Weighted NPV		492,649.71		Units:$0
13	Standard Deviation		874,600.60		
14	Coefficient of Variation		1.78		

Scenario	Base Case	Pessimistic	Optimistic	Weighted NPV
Payback	3.00 yrs	7.00 yrs	3.00 yrs	4.20 yrs
NPV	595,905	(467,528)	1,674,778	492,650
IRR	24.5%	(13.0%)	46.6%	17.7%
MIRR	16.4%	(2.4%)	25.7%	12.6%
Accounting Return	33.2%	10.7%	56.1%	31.0%
Benefit : Cost Ratio	159.6%	53.2%	267.5%	149.3%

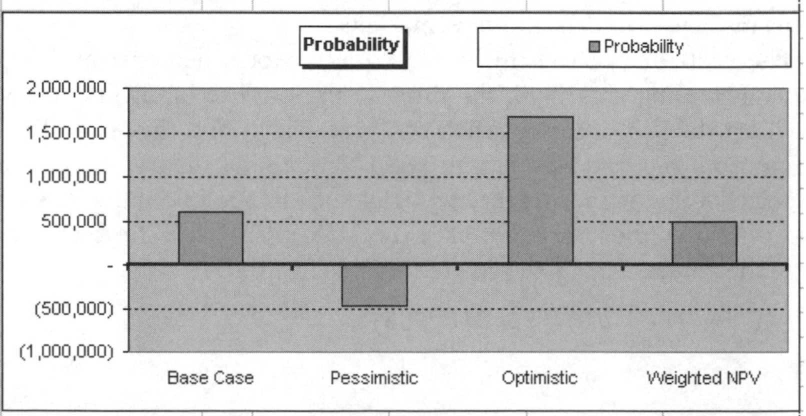

The graph is a column chart, which plots the series to show each of the initial outcomes and the weighted outcome:

```
=SERIES(Probability!$B$2,Probability!$D$14:$G$14,
Probability!$D$9:$G$9,1)
```

The modelling process should include these stages:

- risk identification as inputs and variables;
- quantification of risk using the techniques below;
- management testing of acceptability;
- application of methods for reducing risk;
- risk evaluation, review and incorporation into the modelling and decision process.

Diversification of projects should reduce risk as demonstrated in the stock models, which calculated an optimum risk and return. Here, the model should calculate the amount by which the result is expected to vary from the single point answer. The techniques on further sheets in the file Project_Model are:

- risk adjusted rate – increasing premium to cover risk;
- standard deviation – absolute risk;
- coefficient of variation – relative risk;
- certainty equivalents – evaluating only the certain cash flows;
- real options – using the options approach to investment appraisal;
- simulation (Monte Carlo simulation).

2. RISK ADJUSTED RATE

The Model sheet uses an input cost of funds and then discounts the after-tax cash flows at a net of tax rate. The rate is assumed as the corporation's cost of capital, which is the opportunity cost of capital for an average project. The usual approximation is the weighted average cost of capital (WACC). This supposes that the risk in the project is the same as corporate risk, which may or may not be correct.

In theory, the discount rate should include the unsystematic risk, which is the element of risk that cannot be diversified and reduced. The discount rates are reviewed in the Risk_Adjusted sheet, where increasing the discount rate lowers the net present value and hence the attractiveness of the project.

Many companies use a hurdle rate for projects or a divisional beta. Divisions that produce strong cash flow may be considered less risky than those divisions dependent on new products or technology. The problem is deciding how high the rate should be or the risk relative to the average for the division or the corporation. The techniques of data tables and scenario analysis used in the last chapter assist with showing how variables 'behave', but do not underpin the theoretical discount rate.

There is a practical point. If managers know that the hurdle rate is 20%, there is a tendency to skew the modelling to ensure that a project meets the criteria and may result in over-optimism. Moreover, a discount rate should reflect the difference in risk to an average project and uncertain projects should be required to meet more rigorous acceptance criteria. The net result should be a rate that includes the project cost of capital and its relative risk. Since capital budgeting requires a mix of quantitative and qualitative analysis this can never be a precise science. The process of modelling should, however, assist in identifying risks in and between competing projects.

This example uses a risk premium factor of 5%, which reduces the net present value from 595,905 to 439,855 (see Figure 16.3).

Fig 16.3

Risk adjusted rate.

	A	B	C	D	E
4					
5		Risk Factor			5%
6					
7		Tax Rate			30.00%
8		Cost of Funds			10.00%
9		Net of Tax Rate			7.00%
10					
11		Adjusted Rate			15.00%
12		Adjusted Net of Tax Rate			10.50%
13					
14		NPV at 7.0%			595,905
15		Revised NPV at 10.50%			439,855
16					

A data table and chart completes the range of outcomes based on progressive factors. Figure 16.4 shows a simple data table using conditional formatting to pick out the answer. The risk premium of 5% removes 26% of the net present value.

As an alternative, Table 16.1 could select discount rates based on project type, which fits in with the strategy, business school models which use different risk premiums for different risk profiles.

Table 16.1

Investment	Premium
Replacement and repair	0%
Cost reduction	2%
Expansion	5%
New product / new market	10%

Risk table.

Fig 16.4

Revised Net Present Values							
Risk Factor		**1.00%**					
	2.0%	3.0%	4.0%	**5.0%**	6.0%	7.0%	8.0%
439,855	530,590	499,418	469,185	**439,855**	411,395	383,772	356,953
Variance	(65,315)	(96,487)	(126,720)	(156,050)	(184,510)	(212,134)	(238,952)
Percentage	(11.0%)	(16.2%)	(21.3%)	(26.2%)	(31.0%)	(35.6%)	(40.1%)

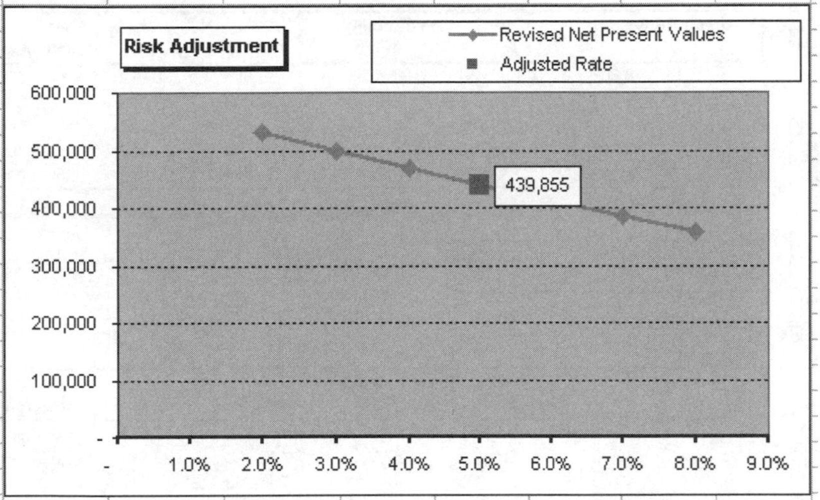

3. VARIATION AND STANDARD DEVIATION

Another technique is to calculate the standard deviation. This is the statistical measure of variance around a probability distribution. The expected value is the probability weighted average; however, variability may be more usefully expressed as the standard deviation. If you are comparing two or more projects, the variability may show up the more risky projects. The formula is:

$$\sigma = \sqrt{\sum_{i=1}^{n} (A_i - \bar{A})^2 P_i}$$

A_i = value of an expected outcome
$\bar{A}$ = expected value as the weighted average of the outcomes
n = number of possible outcomes
p_i = probability of a possible outcome.

The sheet called Deviation uses the above formulas for the cost of funds and cost price per unit and looks up the data for the discount rate in the Model sheet (see Figure 16.5).

Fig 16.5

Standard deviation.

Probability	10%
	20%
	40%
	20%
	10%
Sale Price	50.00

Management Summary

	Standard Deviation	Coefficient of Variation
A	36,934	0.06
B	134,242	0.23

Units:$0

(A) Cost of Funds

Discount Rate	NPV A	Probability p	A*p	(A-Aa)	p*(A-Aa)^2
8.00%	665,452	10%	66,545	68,912	474,888,130
9.00%	630,128	20%	126,026	33,588	225,634,771
10.00%	595,905	40%	238,362	(635)	161,144
11.00%	562,740	20%	112,548	(33,800)	228,490,805
12.00%	530,590	10%	53,059	(65,949)	434,933,098
Expected (Aa)			596,540		1,364,107,948

Standard Deviation:	36,933.83	Standard Deviation = Absolute Risk
Sdev/Aa:	0.06	Coefficent of Variation = Relative Risk

(B) Initial Cost Price per Unit

Cost Price	NPV A	Probability p	A*p	(A-Aa)	p*(A-Aa)^2
38.00	840,997	10%	84,100	245,091	6,006,982,464
39.00	718,451	20%	143,690	122,546	3,003,491,232
40.00	595,905	40%	238,362	-	-
41.00	473,359	20%	94,672	(122,546)	3,003,491,232
42.00	350,814	10%	35,081	(245,091)	6,006,982,464
Expected (Aa) =			595,905		18,020,947,391

Standard Deviation:	134,242.12	Standard Deviation = Absolute Risk
Sdev/Aa:	0.23	Coefficent of Variation = Relative Risk

The control allows you to choose a sale price per unit and the index number is translated back into a cost price in the workings at the bottom. There is a LOOKUP function in column C to look for the sale price in the first data table in the Model sheet and then to read off the value in each of the rows. This example is in cell C16, which finds the value 665,452 in cell F122 in the Model sheet:

```
=LOOKUP($C$44,Model!$C$121:$I$121,Model!C122:I122)
```

The probabilities are inputs and the calculations are across the page:

- expected value is the weighted average of the outcomes;
- variance is the net present value for the row minus the expected value;
- variances are then squared and multiplied by the probability;
- standard deviation is the square root of the sum of column G.

The larger the standard deviation, the less likely that the result will be close to the mean. The sheet Project_SDev compares two projects with the same range of net present values (see Figure 16.6). The net present values and probabilities are inputs. The standard deviation is higher for Project B, which exhibits more dispersion. This is also shown on the graph, as a result of which most managers would prefer Project A which bunches more closely around the mean.

Fig 16.6

Two projects.

Project A — Units: $0

NPV	Probability p	A*p	(A–Aa)	p*(A–Aa)^2
100,000	10%	10,000	(200,000)	4,000,000,000
200,000	20%	40,000	(100,000)	2,000,000,000
300,000	40%	120,000	-	-
400,000	20%	80,000	100,000	2,000,000,000
500,000	10%	50,000	200,000	4,000,000,000
Expected (Aa)		300,000		12,000,000,000

Standard Deviation:	**109,544.51**	Standard Deviation = Absolute Risk
Sdev/Aa:	**0.37**	Coefficent of Variation = Relative Risk

Project B

	Probability p	A*p	(A–Aa)	p*(A–Aa)^2
	15%	15,000	(200,000)	6,000,000,000
	20%	40,000	(100,000)	2,000,000,000
	30%	90,000	-	-
	20%	80,000	100,000	2,000,000,000
	15%	75,000	200,000	6,000,000,000
Expected (Aa)		300,000		16,000,000,000

Standard Deviation:	**126,491.11**	Standard Deviation = Absolute Risk
Sdev/Aa:	**0.42**	Coefficent of Variation = Relative Risk

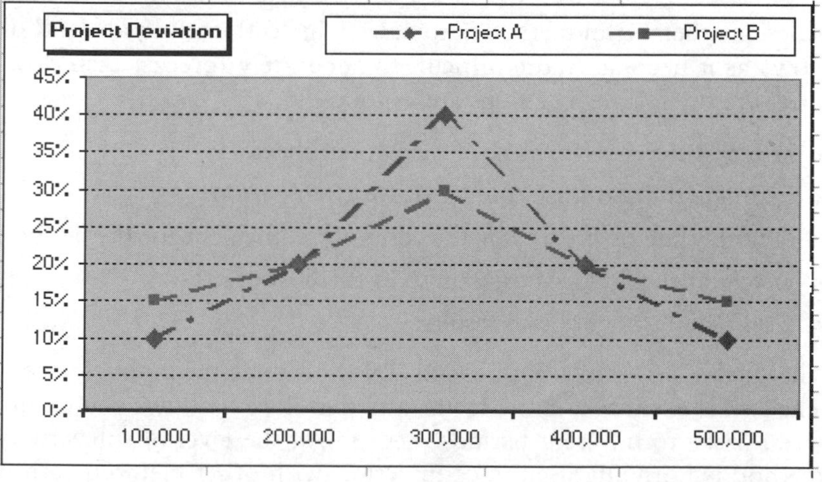

4. COEFFICIENT OF VARIATION

Standard deviation portrays the absolute risk and is useful provided that two projects are for the same value. The coefficient of variation is the relative risk and the formula is:

$$Coefficient = \frac{\sigma}{\bar{A}}$$

This is simply the standard deviation divided by the expected value. With standard deviation, larger numbers cause higher values even if the variances are unchanged. The coefficient of variation provides a value which can be utilized in projects with differing capital values.

The above example shows how the coefficient increases with an increase in dispersion caused by the change in probabilities. The coefficient of variation could be used in the formulation of risk premiums since a high coefficient means greater risk. For example, Table 16.2 uses a cost of funds of 10%. A coefficient of 0.25 to 0.50 is assumed an 'average' risk and therefore no premium is applied.

Table 16.2 **Formulation of risk premiums**

Coefficient of variation	Premium	Risk adjusted discount rate
≤ 0.25	− 2%	8%
> 0.25 and ≤ 0.50	0	10%
> 0.50 and ≤ 0.75	+ 2%	12%
> 0.75	+ 5%	15%

5. CERTAINTY EQUIVALENTS

A less mathematical method is to assess the 'certainty equivalent' of cash flows as it becomes more difficult to accurately forecast cash flows further into the future. The steps are as follows:

- Forecast the cash flows as in the Model sheet.
- Estimate the certainty equivalent for each period.
- Multiply the cash flows by the certainty equivalent for the period.
- Discount the factored cash flows at the cost of capital.
- Compare to the original results.

The method is simple but depends on the subjective inputs for certainty. The risk is enshrined in the factor and therefore it allows you to allot different risks to different periods. Because of the level of subjectivity, this method is normally used in conjunction with other methods rather than as a stand-alone tool.

The method is documented on the Certainty sheet in the Project_Model. The inputs are the certainty coefficients. The project cash flows are looked up from the Model sheet and multiplied by the factors. The result is a net present value of 420,022 or a reduction of 29%. The management summary shows the differences between the original and revised figures (see Figure 16.7).

Certainty equivalent.

Fig 16.7

	A	B	C	D	E	F	G	H	I	J
4										
5		Certainty Equivalent Coefficient			100%	95%	95%	80%	80%	80%
6										
7		Results		NPV	IRR					Units:$0
8		Original Result		595,905	24.5%					
9										
10		Certainty Equivalent		420,022	20.2%					
11										
12		Variance (C-O)		(175,883)	(4.3%)					
13		Percent		(29.5%)	(17.4%)					
14										
15				0	1	2	3	4	5	6
16				Jun-01	Jun-02	Jun-03	Jun-04	Jun-05	Jun-06	Jun-07
17										
18		Project Cash Flows		(1,000,000)	200,000	406,250	430,313	449,984	465,382	41,705
19										
20		Certainty Equivalent Coefficient			100%	95%	95%	80%	80%	80%
21		**Net Cash Flows**		**(1,000,000)**	**200,000**	**385,938**	**408,797**	**359,988**	**372,306**	**33,364**
22										
23		Variance			-	(20,313)	(21,516)	(89,997)	(93,076)	(8,341)
24		Percentage			-	(5.0%)	(5.0%)	(20.0%)	(20.0%)	(20.0%)
25										
26		NPV @ 7.0%			420,022					
27		IRR %			20.23%					
28										

Comparison of cash flows.

Fig 16.8

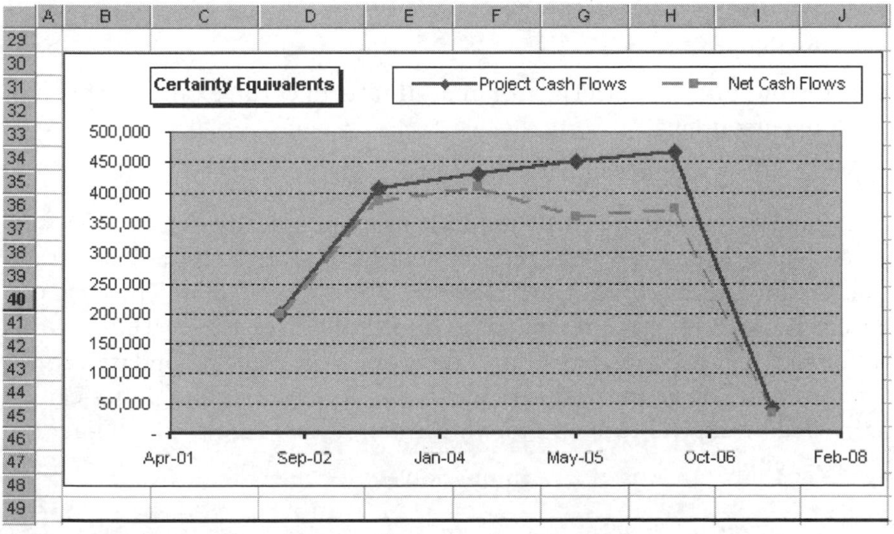

A cash flow chart illustrates the reduced certain cash flows in the later periods (see Figure 16.8). As with payback, this method would tend to favour projects with shorter lives.

6. REAL OPTIONS

The 'classic' net present value model suffers from weaknesses in dealing with certain types of project appraisal. It assumes:

- investments are 'all or nothing' and that once committed nothing can be changed;
- no choice of timing or implementation;
- no active management of possibilities or problems which affect the cash flows;
- no competitor action or changes in the macro or industry environment.

Many companies operate in increasingly volatile environments where it is necessary to set up pilot projects and then decide at a later stage to commit further resources or abandon projects. The changing level of risk can be assessed at each stage and new scenarios calculated. This flexibility is known as real options since a corporation with an opportunity to invest is holding the equivalent of a financial call option. It has the right but not the obligation to proceed. It follows therefore that an irreversible investment uses up the option since the company gives up the opportunity to wait for more information. The theory states that a company should therefore seek to use its options optimally.

A number of alternatives could be available during the life of a project:

- Abandon if the cash flows do not meet management expectations.
- Reduce the scale of operations.
- Grow the project.
- Alter the mix of materials or manufacturing, for example through more outsourcing.
- Make follow-on investments in related areas.

The standard net present rule could lead companies to reject proposals based on the expected value, certainty equivalents or a risk adjusted rate. The Options sheet contains an example on two scenarios. The first is a Base Case with the net present value of 595,905 (see Figure 16.9). If this is not selected, use the control and then press the button 'Update Project Options'. The objective in this model is to show how probabilities can be narrowed by expenditure on more information that results in a higher net present value.

Fig 16.9

Options base case.

	A	B	C	D	E	F	G	H
5		**Scenario Name:**	Base Case				**Management Summary**	
6		**Oppportunity Benefit / (Cost -**						**Amount**
7							**Result NPV**	595,910
8			**Low**	**Medium**	**High**		**Original NPV**	595,905
9		**Initial Capital Cost (CAPX):**	33.3%	33.3%	33.3%		**Variance**	5
10		**Sales Price per Unit:**	33.3%	33.3%	33.3%			
11		**Saved Scenario:**	Base Case					
12		**Most Likely CAPEX Scenari**	CAPEX: prob. 33% : 1,000,000					
13								
14		**(1) Present Value of Future Cash Flows**						
15		**Key Variables**	**Probability**		**Low**	**Medium**	**High**	
16		PV before CAPX	Probability		33%	33%	33%	
17			CAPEX		900,000	1,000,000	1,100,000	
18								
19		Sale price per unit	49.00	33%	1,542,047	1,462,705	1,383,363	
20			50.00	33%	1,675,247	1,595,905	1,516,563	
21			51.00	33%	1,808,447	1,729,105	1,649,763	
22								
23		**Weighted Net Present Value**	**50.00**		**1,675,252**	**1,595,910**	**1,516,568**	
24								
25		**Weighted Net Present Value**		**595,910**				
26		**Variance: 0.0%**		**5**				
27								
28		**(2) Present Values less Initial Capital Cost (CAPX)**						
29		**Key Variables**	**Probability**		**Low**	**Medium**	**High**	
30		Present value variances to CAPEX above			642,047	462,705	283,363	
31		Net present value			775,247	595,905	416,563	
32					908,447	729,105	549,763	
33								
34		Probabilities: Variance * prob CAPEX * prob Sales			71,331	51,406	31,491	
35					86,121	66,198	46,289	
36					100,940	81,012	61,104	
37								
38		**(3) Present Values for selected Capital Cost (CAPX)**						
39		Selected CAPEX Net present value * Sales price probability			1,462,705	33%	487,564	
40		(Column 2)			1,595,905	33%	531,915	
41					1,729,105	33%	576,432	
42								
43		**Project present value based on CAPEX: prob. 33% : 1,000,000**					1,595,910	
44		**Initial capital value**					(1,000,000)	
45		**Oppportunity benefit / (cost) of delay or more information**					-	
46		**Net present value and percent of original capital**					**595,910**	**59.6%**

There is a data table as shown in Figure 16.10 in the workings on the Model sheet and there is a low, medium and high value for the sale price per unit and the capital value. The interval is controlled by cells E280 and E281 on the model sheet. This generates a grid of nine net present values for each of the combinations.

Table 1 on the Options schedule displays the present value of cash flows before subtraction of the initial capital value. Thus the middle answer is 1,595,905, which without the 1,000,000 capital value produces the net present value of 505,905.

Table 2 is the result in Table 1 less the capital value for that column. For example, 642,047 in the left-hand corner in cell E30 is 1,542,047 minus 900,000. The second part of the table multiplies out the variances by the probabilities as a check.

Fig 16.10 **Data table from the Model sheet.**

	A	B	C	D	E	F
278						
279		**Project Options Workings**				
280		**Initial Capital Investment Across:**			**100,000**	
281		**Year One Sales Down:**			**1**	
282		CAPX Across	595,905	900,000	**1,000,000**	1,100,000
283		Year One Units	49.00	542,047	462,705	383,363
284			**50.00**	675,247	595,905	516,563
285			51.00	808,447	729,105	649,763
286						

Table 3 uses an INDEX function to find the column of figures as in the example from cell E39 below, where cell N10 is the index number for the capital value:

```
=INDEX($E$19:$G$21,1,$N$10)
```

The values are multiplied by the probabilities for respective sale prices per unit and added. The capital value is then subtracted from the result and compared against the original net present value. The value of the option could be in the cost of gaining new information or conducting a fuller market analysis, which could change the probabilities and therefore the result.

Select the second scenario, Information. The macro to update the values is assigned to the combo control or the button and it should run automatically. This inserts a cost into cell C6, changes the probable capital value to 900,000 and updates the probabilities. This results in the schedule shown in Figure 16.11.

Spending 20,000 narrows the probabilities and results in a higher net present value. This is 212,622 higher than the original as in cell G49 and this is the value of the option. This example could be made more complex if there were also changes to the timing and competitive action. The model already assumes a reduction in selling price and cost improvements during the life of the project.

A scenario summary has been produced using `Tools, Scenarios, Summary` to show the results (see Figure 16.12).

In a volatile market, the ability to manage risk and change increases in importance. The traditional net present value approach may not always constitute the optimum solution. The ability to amend and take interim decisions may be increasingly important together with the role played by active management. Since commitment to projects reduces flexibility and 'destroys' options, the approach outlined above shows the benefit of incorporating a risk approach. In modelling, you could consider:

- staggering expenditure as a series of decision points with the ability to increase or reduce to avoid 'all or nothing' break points;
- researching other acquisition methods, for example operating leases with early termination clauses;
- considering alternatives for the plant to increase value in the event of exercising an abandonment option.

Fig 16.11

Information scenario.

	A	B	C	D	E	F	G	H
5		Scenario Name:	R&D/Information				Management Summary	
6		Oppportunity Benefit / (Cost (20,000)						Amount
7							Result NPV	808,527
8			Low	Medium	High		Original NP	595,905
9		Initial Capital Cost (CAPX):	70.0%	20.0%	10.0%		Variance	212,622
10		Sales Price per Unit:	20.0%	20.0%	60.0%			
11		Saved Scenario:	Information : Option (20,000)					
12		Most Likely CAPEX Scenari	CAPEX: prob. 70% : 900,000					
13								
14		(1) Present Value of Future Cash Flows						
15		Key Variables	Probability		Low	Medium	High	
16		PV before CAPX	Probability		70%	20%	10%	
17			CAPEX		900,000	1,000,000	1,100,000	
18								
19		Sale price per unit	49.00	20%	1,542,047	1,462,705	1,383,363	
20			50.00	20%	1,675,247	1,595,905	1,516,563	
21			51.00	60%	1,808,447	1,729,105	1,649,763	
22								
23		Weighted Net Present Value	50.40		1,728,527	1,649,185	1,569,843	
24								
25		Weighted Net Present Value		649,185				
26		Variance: 8.9%		53,280				
27								
28		(2) Present Values less Initial Capital Cost (CAPX)						
29		Key Variables	Probability		Low	Medium	High	
30		Present value variances to CAPEX above			642,047	462,705	283,363	
31		Net present value			775,247	595,905	416,563	
32					908,447	729,105	549,763	
33								
34		Probabilities: Variance * prob CAPEX * prob Sales			89,887	18,508	5,667	
35					108,535	23,836	8,331	
36					381,548	87,493	32,986	
37								
38		(3) Present Values for selected Capital Cost (CAPX)						
39		Selected CAPEX Net present value * Sales price probability			1,542,047	20%	308,409	
40		(Column 1)			1,675,247	20%	335,049	
41					1,808,447	60%	1,085,068	
42								
43		Project present value based on CAPEX: prob. 70% : 900,000					1,728,527	
44		Initial capital value					(900,000)	
45		Oppportunity benefit / (cost) of delay or more information					(20,000)	
46		Net present value and percent of original capital					808,527	89.8%
47								
48		Original project net present value					595,905	66.2%
49		Variance and percentage variance					212,622	35.7%

Fig 16.12 **Scenario summary.**

		Current Values:	Base Case	&D/Information
Scenario Summary				
Changing Cells:				
	Scenario	2	1	2
	Capital Value	1	2	1
	Scenario Name:	R&D/Information	Base Case	R&D/Information
	Oppportunity Benefit / (Cost):	(20,000)	-	(20,000)
	Capital Probability Low	70.0%	33.3%	70.0%
	Capital Probability Medium	20.0%	33.3%	20.0%
	Sale Price Probability Low	20.0%	33.3%	20.0%
	Sale Price Probability Medium	20.0%	33.3%	20.0%
Result Cells:				
	Revised NPV	808,527	595,910	808,527
	Revised IRR	89.8%	59.6%	89.8%
	Original NPV	595,905	595,905	595,905
	Original IRR	59.6%	59.6%	59.6%
	NPV Variance	212,622	5	212,622
	IRR Variance	35.7%	0.0%	35.7%

Notes: Current Values column represents values of changing cells at time Scenario Summary Report was created. Changing cells for each scenario are highlighted in gray.

7. SIMULATION

Scenario analysis allows you to keep different views of the world on the same sheet. You can load, for example, base case, optimistic and pessimistic. While this offers advantages over a single answer, there are times when there are significant elements of risk to be captured in a model. In a standard model, you define the inputs such as sale price per unit or cost of funds and calculate the results.

In a simulation model, the analyst specifies the probability distribution of each uncertain variable. Most variables such as the tax rate are unlikely to change. However, there are variables which are likely to be more important than others. The question to be answered now is not, 'What is the net present value?' but 'How likely is the company to achieve this level of net present value?' In this example, these sensitive variables could be:

- sale price per unit;
- number of units;
- cost price per unit;
- cost of funds.

These variables drive the profit and loss account and therefore cash flow. The steps in a simulation are as follows:

- Select the variables for variation together with a distribution. This example adopts the sales price and cost prices per unit using a normal distribution.
- The inputs are therefore the mean together with the degree of variability either side of the mean.
- Run the model through a large number of runs so that the model can pick variables at random within the distributions and log all combinations. This is equivalent to rolling a dice where this model runs through 1,000 loops.
- Plot a scattergraph of the results.
- Count the number of results within defined ranges.
- Plot a histogram of the results.

Fig 16.13

Simulation inputs.

	A	B	C	D
4				
5		Scenario Name:		Base Case
6		Prepared by:		Project Management
7		Product Code:		MJD-987
8		Manager:		Matthew Miles
9		Start Date:		01-Jun-01
10		Initial Investment:		1,000,000.00
11		Initial Sales Price per Unit:		50.00
12		Annual Price Change:		(5.00%)
13		Initial Cost per Unit:		40.00
14		Annual Cost Improvement:		10.00%
15		Project Life:		5.00 yrs
16		Residual Value:		0.00
17		Working Capital as % of Sales:		10.00%
18		Cost of Funds:		10.00%
19		Simulation Sales Price per Unit:		50.00
20		Deviation:		4.00
21		Cost Price per Unit		40.00
22		Price per Unit Variation:		4.00

The example uses the existing sale and cost prices of 50.00 and 40.00 with variability of 4.00 (see Figure 16.13). Since these variables are now distributions, the answer will also be a range distribution. The button 'Run Simulation' is assigned to a macro called Simulation, which performs the following:

- declares variables and a two-dimensional array variable called NPV to hold 1,000 values by seven across;
- zeroes the existing results;

- sets calculation to semi-automatic so that the data tables do not slow down the application;
- sets up the high and low values for the two variables;
- sets the mid point for the data table at cell b70;
- enters a 1,000 value loop;
- randomizes the selected variables (sale and cost price per unit) within a normal distribution;
- recalculates the model and stores the results for NPV, IRR and the management tests;
- exits the loop after 1,000 loops;
- populates the table at J5;
- recalculates the management summary and charts.

This is the text of the macro:

```
Sub Simulation()

Dim NPV(1000, 7)
Dim CostPrice, HighRate, LowRate, StdRate, RandomFactor,
Count
Dim Price, HighPrice, LowPrice, StdPrice, InputCostPrice,
InputPrice

Range("Simulation_Results") = ""
Randomize
Application.Calculation = xlSemiautomatic

InputCostPrice = Range("Model!d14")
InputPrice = Range("Model!d12")
Range("simulation!b70") = (Int(Range("Model!j12") /
10000)) * 10000 ' set centre of frequency table
Price = Range("Simulation!d19")
CostPrice = Range("simulation!d21")
HighRate = CostPrice + Range("Simulation!d22")
LowRate = CostPrice - Range("Simulation!d22")
HighPrice = Price + Range("Simulation!d20")
LowPrice = Price - Range("Simulation!d20")
StdRate = (HighRate - LowRate) / 4
StdPrice = (HighPrice - LowPrice) / 4

For Count = 1 To 1000    'START OF LOOP
  RandomFactor = Rnd
  Range("Model!d12") = Application.NormInv(RandomFactor,
  Price, StdRate)
```

```
    RandomFactor = Rnd
    Range("Model!d14") = Application.NormInv(RandomFactor,
    CostPrice, StdPrice)

    NPV(Count, 0) = Range("Model!d14")
    NPV(Count, 1) = RandomFactor
    NPV(Count, 2) = Range("Model!j12")
    NPV(Count, 3) = Range("Model!d12")
    NPV(Count, 4) = Range("Model!k9")
    NPV(Count, 5) = Range("Model!k10")
    NPV(Count, 6) = Range("Model!k11")
    NPV(Count, 7) = Range("Model!k12")
    Range("Simulation!f6") = Count

Next Count          'END OF LOOP

Application.Calculation = xlAutomatic
Range("Simulation_Results") = NPV
Range("Model!d12") = Range("simulation!d19")
Range("Model!d14") = Range("simulation!d21")

End Sub
```

You can press the 'Run Simulation' button and the model will recalculate 1,000 times. You can watch the progress on the counter as it increases to 1,000. On completion, the model will update the results table on the right with a fresh set of data. The model saves the net present value and the other management information for each simulation.

The scatter plot is updated and this revises the frequency table and histogram. The spread of the data in the shape of the histogram will demonstrate visually how closely the data is packed. Another test could be to check how many results are less than a pre-defined value such as zero. This could confirm how likely the project is not to pass the key test of a positive net present value.

The sheet, Simulation, follows the area format with the elements described above down the page and the record of results on the right-hand side. There is a management summary at the top with statistical output.

Figure 16.14 shows the retained results. Each loop saves the net present value, input values and the results of the management tests.

A scattergraph is presented as shown in Figure 16.15 based on the net present values. This is simply using the series below where column J is the cost price and column L the net present values. There is also a trend line in red using the command `Chart`, `Add Trendline` to show the tendency. The equation and the R-Squared values are also inserted using trend line options.

```
=SERIES(Simulation!$L$3,Simulation!$J$5:$J$1004,
Simulation!$L$5:$L$1004,1)
```

Fig 16.14 **Loop results.**

	J	K	L	M	N	O
2	**Simulation Results**					
3	**Cost Price**	**Factor**	**NPV**	**Sale Price**	**Payback < 3 year:**	**Minimum IRR 20.00:**
4						
5	39.99	0.4973	707,906.57	50.83	Yes	Yes
6	42.43	0.8882	74,048.39	48.32	No	No - check period 1
7	39.88	0.4767	297,750.32	47.65	No	Yes
8	42.66	0.9081	227,690.29	49.68	No	Yes
9	40.03	0.5057	289,022.37	47.72	No	Yes
10	41.83	0.8203	337,356.25	49.75	No	Yes
11	40.37	0.5737	764,591.54	51.61	Yes	Yes
12	37.96	0.1537	731,301.32	49.14	Yes	Yes
13	36.98	0.0656	595,489.51	47.22	Yes	Yes
14	45.47	0.9969	650,816.08	55.44	Yes	Yes
15	39.50	0.4022	519,263.73	48.97	Yes	Yes
16	41.43	0.7633	231,244.86	48.58	No	Yes
17	42.97	0.9313	431,794.15	51.50	No	Yes
18	38.37	0.2075	420,884.56	47.19	No	Yes
19	37.02	0.0680	1,178,777.13	51.63	Yes	Yes
20	40.99	0.6903	361,265.75	49.15	No	Yes
21	40.97	0.6854	743,286.93	52.00	Yes	Yes
22	41.02	0.6947	438,033.72	49.75	No	Yes
23	41.38	0.7553	(71,588.09)	46.26	No	No - check period 1
24	40.46	0.5915	587,144.14	50.36	Yes	Yes
25	38.58	0.2386	1,007,395.99	51.78	Yes	Yes
26	40.80	0.6545	808,362.12	52.33	Yes	Yes
27	38.50	0.2262	1,171,834.50	52.94	Yes	Yes
28	39.10	0.3267	440,102.11	48.00	No	Yes
29	39.12	0.3295	779,888.12	50.57	Yes	Yes
30	41.26	0.7357	540,073.65	50.74	Yes	Yes

Fig 16.15 **Scattergraph.**

	A	B	C	D	E	F
23						
24		**Net Present Value at 50.00 varying by 4.00 and a Unit Price of 40.00 varying by 4.00**				
25						
26		**Payback < 3 years**	3 yrs		3.00 yrs	Yes
27		**Minimum IRR 20.00%**	20%		24.49%	Yes
28		**Positive Operating Profit > 0**	0			Yes
29		**Operating Cash Flow 120%**	120%			Yes
30		**Net Present Value > 0**	0		595,905	Yes
31						

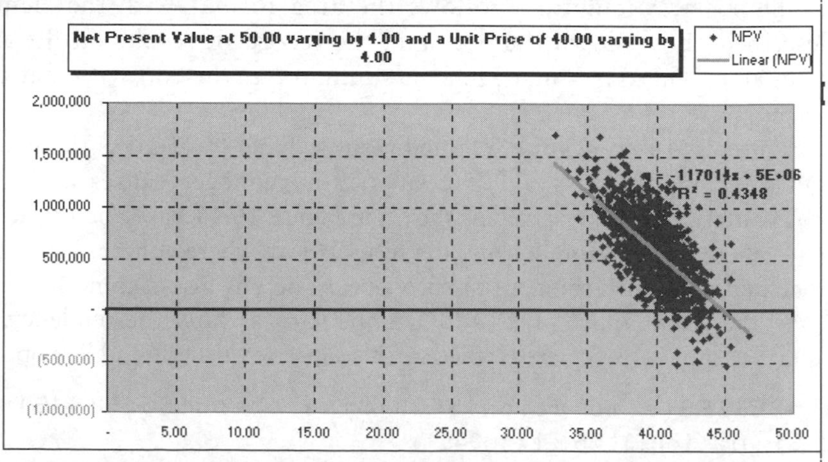

Below the chart, there is a frequency table to count the number of results between defined values (see Figure 16.16). The number of results uses FREQUENCY, which is an array command and entered using CTRL, SHIFT and ENTER. This places the array brackets around all the cells in the range. An example of the final entry in cell C65 is:

```
{=FREQUENCY(L:L,$B$65:$B$75)}
```

Histogram.

Fig 16.16

Simulation Frequency Results with an Interval of 200,000

Interval	200,000.00

Amount	No of Results	Percentage
(410,000)	3	0.3%
(210,000)	8	0.8%
(10,000)	25	2.5%
190,000	90	9.0%
390,000	158	15.8%
590,000	219	21.9%
790,000	223	22.3%
990,000	131	13.1%
1,190,000	97	9.7%
1,390,000	35	3.5%
1,590,000	9	0.9%
	998	100.0%

	Cost Price	Sale Price
Minimum:	32.67	43.0523
Maximum:	46.77	56.1296
Mean:	39.90	49.8930

Minimum Probability:	0.0001
Maximum Probability:	0.9996

Less than zero NPV % of trials	3.6%

Arithmetic Mean	593,358
Median	587,284
Skew	0.048
Kurtosis	0.022

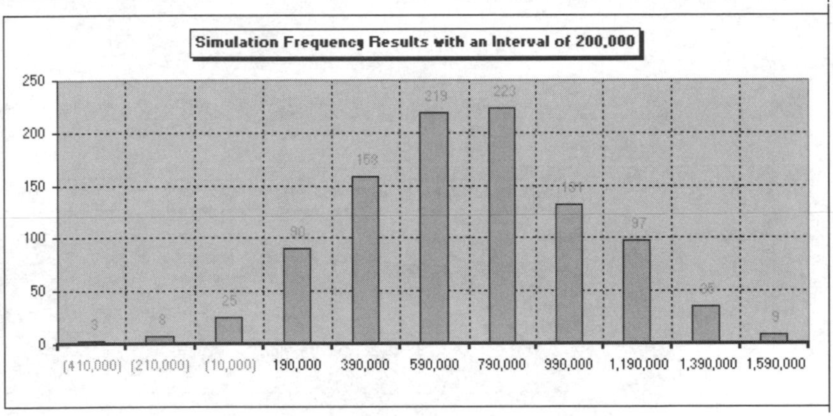

Since numbers are difficult to understand in a table, the histogram plots the number of results in each range and illustrates the variability of results. This table clusters around the existing result of circa 600,000, and less than 4% of the results are less than zero. These are all the possible outcomes from 1,000 simulation tests.

The Management Summary at the top provides the statistical data and makes use of Excel functions such as QUART, SKEW, KURT and STDEVP (see Figure 16.17).

Fig 16.17 **Management summary.**

Simulation
1,000

Management Summary

Quartiles	Value	No of Results
0	(534,884)	1
1	354,052	249
2	587,284	250
3	817,023	250
4	1,701,810	250
Total Results		1,000
Range		2,236,694
Mean		593,358
Median		587,284
Skew		0.048
Kurtosis		0.022
Standard Deviation		349,900
Coefficient of Variation		0.59

At the bottom, there is also a summary chart of the quartile ranges (see Figure 16.18). This provides the limits for each 25% of the data together with the minimum and maximum values.

Fig 16.18 **Quartiles.**

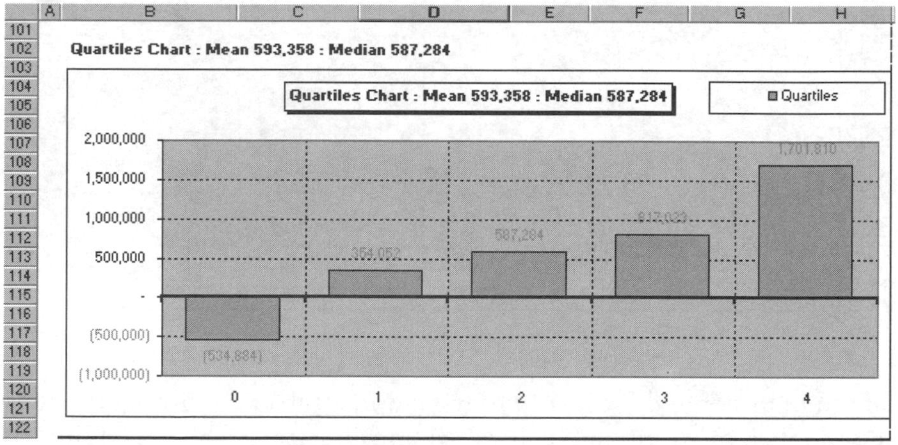

To illustrate the approach with a second example, the second scenario on the sheet called 'Pessimistic' changes the sale price from 50 to 45 and leaves all the other data the same. Load this scenario using `Tools`, `Scenarios` or change the sale price manually. This simulation produces marked differently results with an average net present value below zero (see Figure 16.19).

Fig 16.19

Pessimistic scenario.

Scenario Name:	Base Case
Prepared by:	Project Management
Product Code:	MJD-987
Manager:	Matthew Miles
Start Date:	01-Jun-01
Initial Investment:	1,000,000.00
Initial Sales Price per Unit:	45.00
Annual Price Change:	(5.00%)
Initial Cost per Unit:	40.00
Annual Cost Improvement:	10.00%
Project Life:	5.00 yrs
Residual Value:	0.00
Working Capital as % of Sales:	10.00%
Cost of Funds:	10.00%
Simulation Sales Price per Unit:	45.00
Deviation:	4.00
Cost Price per Unit	40.00
Price per Unit Variation:	4.00

Simulation
1,000

Management Summary

Quartiles	Value	No of Results
0	(1,275,751)	1
1	(327,533)	249
2	(84,224)	250
3	161,570	250
4	1,071,892	250
Total Results		1,000
Range		2,347,643
Mean		(79,897)
Median		(84,224)
Skew		0.017
Kurtosis		0.007
Standard Deviation		368,015
Coefficient of Variation		(4.61)

Net Present Value at 45.00 varying by 4.00 and a Unit Price of 40.00 varying by 4.00

Payback < 3 years	3 yrs	5.00 yrs	No
Minimum IRR 20.00%	20%	4.95%	No
Positive Operating Profit > 0	0		No - check period 1
Operating Cash Flow 120%	120%		Yes
Net Present Value > 0	0	(70,093)	No

Fig 16.20

Pessimistic histogram.

Simulation Frequency Results with an Interval of 200,000

Interval	200,000.00

Amount	No of Results	Percentage
(410,000)	183	18.3%
(210,000)	187	18.7%
(10,000)	205	20.5%
190,000	198	19.8%
390,000	112	11.2%
590,000	77	7.7%
790,000	29	2.9%
990,000	7	0.7%
1,190,000	2	0.2%
1,390,000	-	-
1,590,000	-	-
	1,000	100.0%

	Cost Price	Sale Price
Minimum:	32.36	39.3210
Maximum:	47.93	52.4506
Mean:	40.18	45.0933

Minimum Probability:	0.0001
Maximum Probability:	1.0000
Less than zero NPV % of trials:	57.5%
Arithmetic Mean	(79,897)
Median	(84,224)
Skew	0.017
Kurtosis	0.007

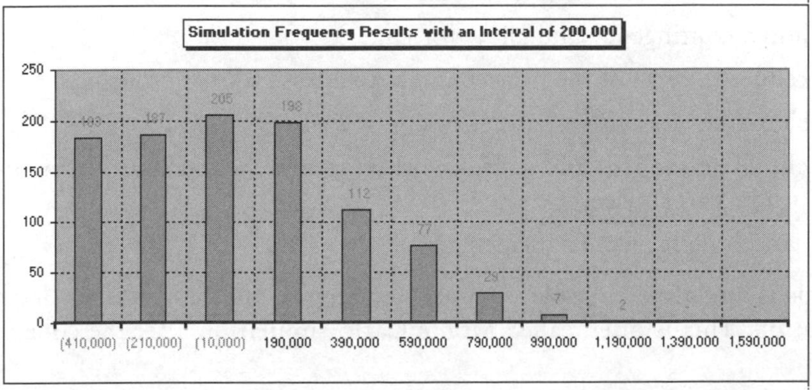

The shape of the histogram shows the changed risk profile skewed to the right (see Figure 16.20). Nearly 60% of the results are less than zero. Standard deviation has also increased to 368,000.

A summary of both simulations is on the Simulation_Results sheet together with a calculation of variance and percentage variance (see Figure 16.21).

Fig 16.21

Simulation results.

Simulation Results

Menu

v1.0 1-Jan-2001

Quartiles	Base Case	Pessimistic	Variance	%
0	(534,884)	(1,275,751)	(740,867)	139%
1	354,006	(327,948)	(681,954)	(193%)
2	587,223	(84,571)	(671,795)	(114%)
3	816,232	160,697	(655,535)	(80%)
4	1,701,810	1,071,892	(629,918)	(37%)
Range	2,236,694	2,347,643	110,949	5%
Mean	593,358	(79,897)	(673,255)	(113%)
Median	587,284	(84,224)	(671,508)	(114%)
Skew	0.048	0.017	(0.030)	(63%)
Kurtosis	0.022	0.007	(0.014)	(65%)
Standard Deviation	349,900	368,015	18,115	5%
Coefficient of Variation	0.59	(4.61)	(5.20)	(881%)

The simulation modelling clearly shows the increase in risk if the sale price per unit is lowered and all other inputs remain the same. The response could be:

- increase prices since the original estimates were correct;
- do nothing (cost outweighs benefit);
- collect more data to better understand risk and perhaps increase the probability of an acceptable outcome;
- add a contingency and allow for risk;
- reduce the size of the project and take a less risky approach;
- share the risk with a partner or contractor;
- eliminate the risk and consider other approaches such as buying in the product or service;
- cancel the project or financing.

This is a relatively simple example to demonstrate the workings of a simulation. This is often called Monte Carlo simulation after the code word used by von Neumann on the Second World War Manhattan Project to develop an atomic bomb.

More complex models can be constructed using add-ons to Excel such as @RISK® and Crystal Ball®. These provide a great deal of flexibility in terms of the number of distributions and the ability to manipulate the model and produce different types of management report. For example, there is the ability to correlate different variables to ensure that each scenario is possible. Another advantage is that you develop the model in Excel and use it within the Monte Carlo add-on without changing the underlying Excel model.

The contact address for @RISK is:

Palisade Corporation, 31 Decker Road, Newfield, NY 14867, USA
Tel 800-432-7475 or 607-277-8000; Fax 607-277-8001
sales@palisade.com, www.palisade.com

Simulation methods still rely on some subjectivity. For each variable, you need the probability distribution and the correlation among distributions. Risk modelling using Monte Carlo simulation does call for caution in both the outputs and the communication of the results. Most management want to know if the project passes or fails and not that 20% of the trials fail. Nevertheless, simulation techniques are increasingly being used through the acceptance of known products such as @RISK in areas such as project finance and pensions.

8. SUMMARY

Risk and uncertainty are realities and models which do not take account of potential variance may be failing to model systems correctly. Risk could be defined as variability in the system, while uncertainty arises from outside the system beyond the control of management. This chapter has introduced modelling techniques to assist with the following:

- including sources of risk as inputs;
- calculating potential variability through standard deviation, coefficient of variation and certainty equivalents;
- calculating the options value through the real options approach;
- running Monte Carlo simulations.

While some of these techniques rely on some subjectivity, the modelling is a framework for more informed decision making and these methods are more advanced than calculating a payback or a single-point net present value with no further investigation. The Project_Model application uses the techniques and demonstrates the value of incorporating one or more of the above methods in order to increase understanding and demonstrate the limited level of risk in the Base Case scenario.

17

Depreciation

Excel contains a number of functions for calculating depreciation for tax or accounting purposes and the model Depreciation summarizes the different methods. The model uses functions and first principles for these methods:

- straight line accounting;
- sum of digits (also called the Rule of 78);
- declining balance (as used for UK tax);
- modified accelerated cost recovery system (MACRS) used in the US for tax depreciation.

Depreciation is a notional or book-keeping entry, which attempts to match the writing off of an asset with its useful life. This is a charge against profits rather than a physical cash flow since a depreciation method can change reported profits but not the underlying net operating cash flow. An increase in depreciation life will increase profits and a reduction will reduce profits.

Some countries such as the UK and the US use differing methods for accounting and for tax assessment. The reported profits may use straight line depreciation, but the tax authorities add back depreciation and replace it with another method such as declining balance.

The Excel functions for depreciation are listed in Table 17.1.

Table 17.1 **Excel functions for depreciation**

Function	Usage
SLN	Straight line
SYD	Sum of digits
DB	Declining balance
DDB	Double declining balance
VDB	Declining balance allowing a switch to straight line at an optimum point

The model sheet in the file Depreciation contains an inputs box and allows you to select a method to compare against an amortization curve (see Figure 17.1). Amortization is the division of a regular payment into interest and principal based on a constant rate. The main inputs for depreciation comprise the date, capital value, residual value and depreciation period. The interest rate is used to calculate a rental for the amortization table. The factor and bottom two inputs are used in the declining balance methods and the workings for the controls are at the bottom of the sheet.

Depreciation inputs.

Fig 17.1

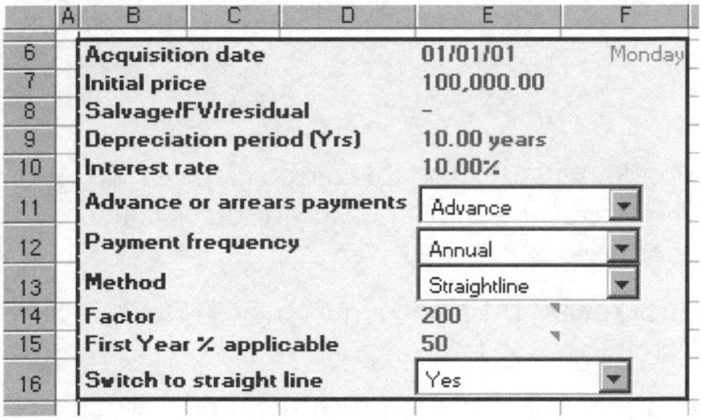

Some of the cells are named to make the formulas easier to understand:

dblFV	=Model!$E$8
dblPV	=Model!$E$7
dblYearOne	=Model!$E$15
dblYears	=Model!$E$9
intDCompounding	=Model!$C$94
intFactor	=Model!$E$14
IntRate	=Model!$E$10
strStraightLine	=Model!$C$108

The Model sheet looks up data from the Deprn_Data sheet and there are stand-alone sheets to demonstrate the functions, UK methods and US MACRS method.

1. STRAIGHT LINE

Straight line is the simplest method where the amount to be written off is divided by the number of periods. In the example shown in Figure 17.2, the life is ten years and therefore the annual figure is 10,000.

Fig 17.2 **Straight line.**

	(A) Depreciation			
Date	Period	Straightline Deprn	% Capital	Written Down Value
1-Jan-01	1	10,000.00	10.0%	90,000.00
1-Jan-02	2	10,000.00	10.0%	80,000.00
1-Jan-03	3	10,000.00	10.0%	70,000.00
1-Jan-04	4	10,000.00	10.0%	60,000.00
1-Jan-05	5	10,000.00	10.0%	50,000.00
1-Jan-06	6	10,000.00	10.0%	40,000.00
1-Jan-07	7	10,000.00	10.0%	30,000.00
1-Jan-08	8	10,000.00	10.0%	20,000.00
1-Jan-09	9	10,000.00	10.0%	10,000.00
1-Jan-10	10	10,000.00	10.0%	-
1-Jan-11	11	-	-	-
1-Jan-12	12	-	-	-

The function SL will calculate this result as in cell C6 on the Functions sheet. The IF statement ensures that no result is calculated beyond the total number of periods.

```
=IF(B6<=dblYears*intDCompounding,SLN(dblPV,dblFV,dblYears
*intDCompounding),0)
```

If there were a salvage of 10,000, then the model would spread 90,000 over the ten periods and it would set depreciation at 9,000 per period. This simple formula is used for accounting depreciation and it assumes that the asset is consumed at a constant rate. This may be different to the write-down in market values, for example with a computer system, which could be expected to lose value rapidly in the early periods.

2. SUM OF DIGITS

The sum of digits method is sometimes called the Rule of 78 since 12 + 11 + 10 … + 1 = 78. This produces an approximation to a constant rate formula instead of calculating an amortization table. The formula is:

Total factor = $[n * (n + 1)] / 2$ where n is equal to the number of periods

This example would be (10 * 11) / 2 = 55.

The first period is then calculated as (10 / 55) * 100,000 = 18,181.81. The second period is 9 / 55 and so on. You can either calculate it manually or use the function SYD (see Figure 17.3). If you copy down beyond the life, the function will error and so again you have to insert an IF statement to suppress calculation. This is cell E6 on the Functions sheet together with the input box:

```
=IF(B6<=dblYears*intDCompounding,SYD(dblPV,dblFV,dblYears*
intDCompounding,B6),0)
```

Fig 17.3

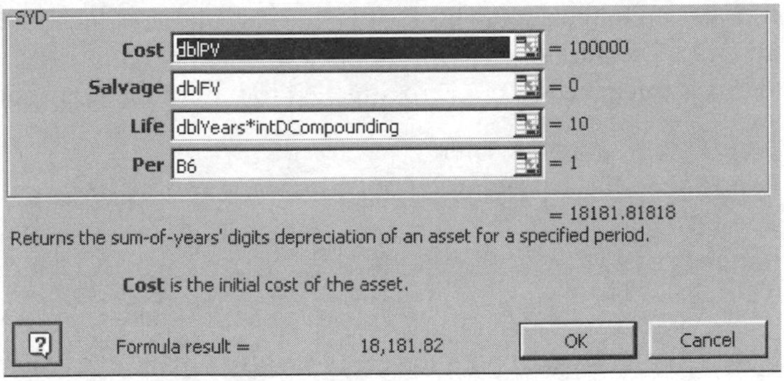

Select Sum of Digits on the Model sheet and the control select the next set of data by offsetting across the page using the values in D99 on the Model sheet:

```
=IF(D98=1,1,IF(D98=2,3,IF(D98=3,5,9)))
```

As can be seen in Figure 17.4, this method derives more depreciation in the early periods and more accurately the likely market value of the goods. It is, however, more complex than the straight line method and therefore less likely to be used in accounting. Sum of Digits is used for splitting interest on loans, hire purchase or lease purchase contracts in order to book more interest in early periods.

Sum of digits schedule.

Fig 17.4

	A	B	C	D	E	F	G
19				(A) Depreciation			
20		Date	Period	Sum of Digits Deprn	% Capital	Written Down Value	% Capital
21		1-Jan-01	1	18,181.82	18.2%	81,818.18	81.8%
22		1-Jan-02	2	16,363.64	16.4%	65,454.55	65.5%
23		1-Jan-03	3	14,545.45	14.5%	50,909.09	50.9%
24		1-Jan-04	4	12,727.27	12.7%	38,181.82	38.2%
25		1-Jan-05	5	10,909.09	10.9%	27,272.73	27.3%
26		1-Jan-06	6	9,090.91	9.1%	18,181.82	18.2%
27		1-Jan-07	7	7,272.73	7.3%	10,909.09	10.9%
28		1-Jan-08	8	5,454.55	5.5%	5,454.55	5.5%
29		1-Jan-09	9	3,636.36	3.6%	1,818.18	1.8%
30		1-Jan-10	10	1,818.18	1.8%	- 0.00	-
31		1-Jan-11	11	-	-	- 0.00	-
32		1-Jan-12	12	-	-	- 0.00	-

3. DECLINING BALANCE

The declining method is used in UK tax depreciation in the form of writing-down allowances. The standard rate is 25% where the charge is 25%

of the previous capital balance. This means that the charge is high in the early periods and then becomes smaller and smaller. The model requires a factor for input and this is calculated by a macro attached to the combo box control.

```
If Range("d98") <> 4 Then
    Range("e14") = (Range("e9") / 4) * 100 'UK
    Else
    Range("e14") = 200 'US MACRS
End If
```

This ensures that the correct charge is applied whatever the period chosen. The formula for calculating a particular period is:

```
(PV*(F/100))/(Periods))*(1-((F/100)/(Periods)))^(No-1)
```

PV	= capital value
F	= depreciation factor calculated as (Years / 4) * 100
Periods	= total number of periods calculated as the number of years multiplied by the number of periods in year
No	= period number.

The function DDB provides a result over ten years and the calculation then adds the remaining 'tail' in the next period. The first period is 25% of the initial capital 100,000 and the second period is 25% of the written-down value, 75,000. In period 11, the remaining 5,631 is accelerated and taken in one period (see Figure 17.5).

Fig 17.5 **Declining balance method.**

	A	B	G	H	I	J	K
4							
5			DDB	Capital	VDB	%	Capital
6		1	25,000.00	75,000.00	20,000.00	20.0%	80,000.00
7		2	18,750.00	56,250.00	16,000.00	16.0%	64,000.00
8		3	14,062.50	42,187.50	12,800.00	12.8%	51,200.00
9		4	10,546.88	31,640.63	10,240.00	10.2%	40,960.00
10		5	7,910.16	23,730.47	8,192.00	8.2%	32,768.00
11		6	5,932.62	17,797.85	6,553.60	6.6%	26,214.40
12		7	4,449.46	13,348.39	6,553.60	6.6%	19,660.80
13		8	3,337.10	10,011.29	6,553.60	6.6%	13,107.20
14		9	2,502.82	7,508.47	6,553.60	6.6%	6,553.60
15		10	1,877.12	5,631.35	6,553.60	6.6%	0.00
16		11	5,631.35	-	-	-	-
17		12	-	-	-	-	-

The formula in Functions cell G6 (see Figure 17.6) is:

```
=IF(B6<=dblYears*intDCompounding,DDB(dblPV,dblFV,dblYears
*intDCompounding,B6,intFactor/100),0) + IF(B6=dblYears*
intDCompounding+1,H5,0)
```

Function DDB.

Fig 17.6

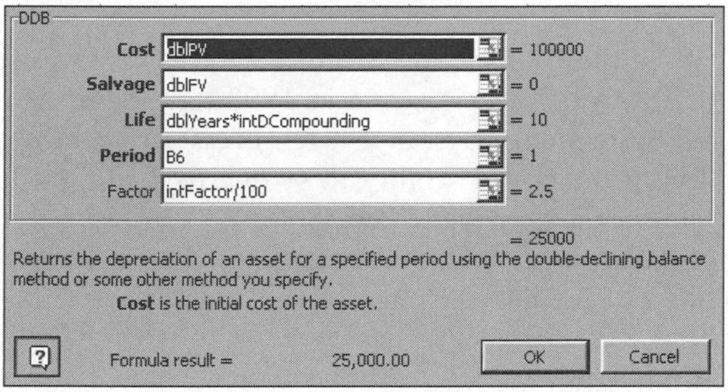

The schedule in Deprn_Data allows the tail of capital outstanding to continue getting smaller and smaller (see Figure 17.7). This would occur with UK tax with an asset in the general pool where 25% is applied to the outstanding capital value each year.

Declining balance.

Fig 17.7

	A	B	G	H
4				
5			DDB	Capital
6		1	25,000.00	75,000.00
7		2	18,750.00	56,250.00
8		3	14,062.50	42,187.50
9		4	10,546.88	31,640.63
10		5	7,910.16	23,730.47
11		6	5,932.62	17,797.85
12		7	4,449.46	13,348.39
13		8	3,337.10	10,011.29
14		9	2,502.82	7,508.47
15		10	1,877.12	5,631.35
16		11	1,407.84	4,223.51
17		12	1,055.88	3,167.64
18		13	791.91	2,375.73
19		14	593.93	1,781.79
20		15	445.45	1,336.35
21		16	334.09	1,002.26
22		17	250.56	751.69
23		18	187.92	563.77
24		19	140.94	422.83
25		20	105.71	317.12
26		21	79.28	237.84
27		22	59.46	178.38
28		23	44.60	133.79
29		24	33.45	100.34
30		25	25.08	75.25
31		26	18.81	56.44
32		27	14.11	42.33
33		28	10.58	31.75
34		29	7.94	23.81
35		30	5.95	17.86
36		31	4.46	13.39
37		32	3.35	10.05
38		33	2.51	7.53
39		34	1.88	5.65

4. US MACRS

For tax purposes the US uses the Modified Accelerated Cost Recovery System (MACRS), which was enacted in 1993 to replace the Accelerated Cost Recovery System dating from 1981. This is a type of declining balance method with the crucial ability to switch to a straight line method when beneficial for the taxpayer to do so.

The cost of the asset is expensed over a defined period called the recovery or class life. The life depends on the type of asset (see Table 17.2).

Table 17.2 **MACRS class life**

MACRS Class	Property
3 years	Certain special manufacturing tools
5 years	Cars, light trucks, computers and certain special manufacturing equipment
7 years	Most industrial equipment, office equipment and fixtures
10 years	Longer-life industrial equipment
27.5 years	Residential rental real property
39 years	Non-residential real property including commercial and industrial buildings

The method uses a 200% declining balance method. The example in the application has a ten-year life, therefore the first period is 200 / 10 = 20% or 20,000. There is a further rule in that the first year is halved to stop people claiming a full year's depreciation for an asset that may have been acquired on the last day of the tax year. The actual charge is therefore 10,000.

In year 2 the brought forward capital is 90,000. This is multiplied by 2 and divided by 10, which equals 18,000. The schedule shown in Figure 17.8 emerges.

Fig 17.8 **MACRS schedule.**

	A	B	I	J	K	L	M
4							
5			MACRS	SL	Adopt	%	Capital
6		1	10,000.00	10,000.00	10,000.00	10.00%	90,000.00
7		2	18,000.00	9,473.68	18,000.00	18.00%	72,000.00
8		3	14,400.00	8,470.59	14,400.00	14.40%	57,600.00
9		4	11,520.00	7,680.00	11,520.00	11.52%	46,080.00
10		5	9,216.00	7,089.23	9,216.00	9.22%	36,864.00
11		6	7,372.80	6,702.55	7,372.80	7.37%	29,491.20
12		7	5,898.24	6,553.60	6,553.60	6.55%	22,937.60
13		8	4,587.52	6,553.60	6,553.60	6.55%	16,384.00
14		9	3,276.80	6,553.60	6,553.60	6.55%	9,830.40
15		10	1,966.08	6,553.60	6,553.60	6.55%	3,276.80
16		11	655.36	3,276.80	3,276.80	3.28%	-
17		12	-	-	-	0.00%	-
18		13	-	-	-	0.00%	-

Column I calculates the value using the above formula. This is the computation in cell I6 on the Deprn_Data sheet:

```
(((PV*(200/100)/Periods)*(1-((200/100)/Periods))^(No-1))
*IF(No=1,FYC/100,1)
```

PV = capital value
F = the 200% MACRS factor
Periods = total periods calculated as the number of years multiplied by the number of periods in year
No = period number
FYC = first-year convention, where the first year is multiplied by 50%.

Since the first-year convention factor is assumed to be 50%, there are 9.5 years outstanding at the end of year 1. The second column calculates the straight line depreciation for the capital outstanding over the number of periods. Column K contains an IF statement, which adopts the straight line charge if this is greater than the MACRS calculation. Column M subtracts the depreciation from the previous capital as the carried forward capital outstanding. The net result is that the asset is fully depreciated in 11 accounting periods.

Excel does contain a function called VDB, which follows this methodology (see Figure 17.9); however, there is no switch for the first-year convention. This is cell I6 on the Functions sheet:

```
VDB(dblPV,dblFV,dblYears*intDCompounding,B5,B6,2,FALSE)
```

Function VDB.

Fig 17.9

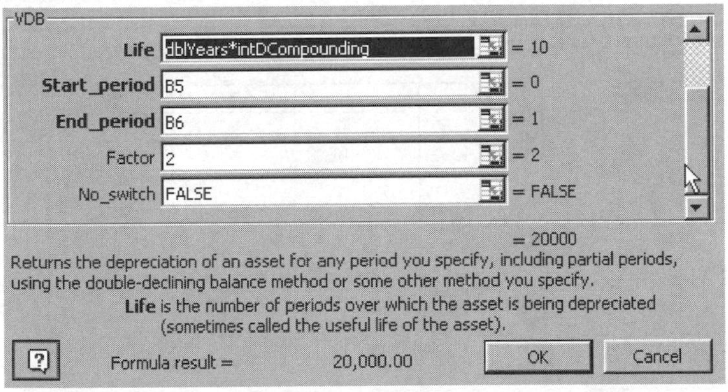

The entries are more complex since you have to specify the start and end of the period together with the factor (here 2 for 200%) and whether a switch to straight line is not required. FALSE means that the function will switch to straight line depreciation at the optimum point. Figure 17.10 shows the MACRS summary schedule.

Fig 17.10

MACRS summary.

(A) Depreciation					
Date	Period	US MACRS Deprn	% Capital	Written Down Value	% Capital
1-Jan-01	1	10,000.00	10.0%	90,000.00	90.0%
1-Jan-02	2	18,000.00	18.0%	72,000.00	72.0%
1-Jan-03	3	14,400.00	14.4%	57,600.00	57.6%
1-Jan-04	4	11,520.00	11.5%	46,080.00	46.1%
1-Jan-05	5	9,216.00	9.2%	36,864.00	36.9%
1-Jan-06	6	7,372.80	7.4%	29,491.20	29.5%
1-Jan-07	7	6,553.60	6.6%	22,937.60	22.9%
1-Jan-08	8	6,553.60	6.6%	16,384.00	16.4%
1-Jan-09	9	6,553.60	6.6%	9,830.40	9.8%
1-Jan-10	10	6,553.60	6.6%	3,276.80	3.3%
1-Jan-11	11	3,276.80	3.3%	-	-
1-Jan-12	12	-	-	-	-

The bottom of the Deprn_Data sheet contains a full MACRS table with the classes 3 to 10 years (see Figure 17.11). The formulas are calculated in the cell as nested IF statements. This is complicated to understand and it is better to break down such calculations as on the other schedules.

Fig 17.11

MACRS table.

MACRS Depreciation Table				
Years:	3	5	7	10
1	33.33%	20.00%	14.29%	10.00%
2	44.44%	32.00%	24.49%	18.00%
3	14.81%	19.20%	17.49%	14.40%
4	7.41%	11.52%	12.49%	11.52%
5	-	11.52%	8.92%	9.22%
6	-	5.76%	8.92%	7.37%
7	-	-	8.92%	6.55%
8	-	-	4.46%	6.55%
9	-	-	-	6.55%
10	-	-	-	6.55%
11	-	-	-	3.28%
12	-	-	-	-
	100.00%	100.00%	100.00%	100.00%

5. AMORTIZATION

The model also provides an amortization schedule on the main Model sheet. This is simply a calculation for the interest element in a regular payment. The model calculates a rental over ten years at the interest rate of 10% nominal (see Figure 17.12).

Fig 17.12

PMT function.

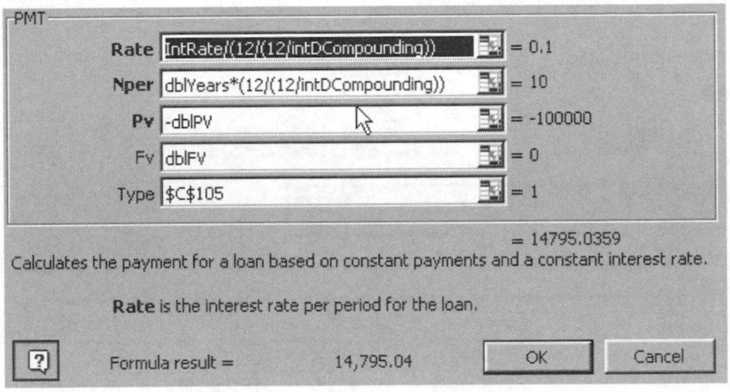

The first rental is in advance and payable on inception and therefore the whole rental is applied to the initial principal of 100,000. The carried forward capital is therefore 100,000 – 14,795.04 = 85,204.96. In the next period, the amortized interest is 85,204.96 multiplied by 10% or 8,520.50. The capital reduction is therefore the rental less the interest, which is 6,274.54. In future periods, the interest declines and the capital repayment increases. The final cumulative capital must equal the initial capital value on inception and likewise the cumulative interest must equal the total charges. Figure 17.13 shows the full amortization schedule.

Fig 17.13

Amortization schedule.

	B	C	H	I	J	K	L
19			(B) Amortisation				
20	Date	Period	Rental at 10.0%	Amortised Interest	Principal	Remaining Balance	Variance
21	1-Jan-01	1	14,795.04		14,795.04	85,204.96	4,795.04
22	1-Jan-02	2	14,795.04	8,520.50	6,274.54	78,930.42	1,069.58
23	1-Jan-03	3	14,795.04	7,893.04	6,901.99	72,028.43	(2,028.43)
24	1-Jan-04	4	14,795.04	7,202.84	7,592.19	64,436.24	(4,436.24)
25	1-Jan-05	5	14,795.04	6,443.62	8,351.41	56,084.83	(6,084.83)
26	1-Jan-06	6	14,795.04	5,608.48	9,186.55	46,898.27	(6,898.27)
27	1-Jan-07	7	14,795.04	4,689.83	10,105.21	36,793.06	(6,793.06)
28	1-Jan-08	8	14,795.04	3,679.31	11,115.73	25,677.33	(5,677.33)
29	1-Jan-09	9	14,795.04	2,567.73	12,227.30	13,450.03	(3,450.03)
30	1-Jan-10	10	14,795.04	1,345.00	13,450.03	(0.00)	0.00
31	1-Jan-11	11	-	-	-	(0.00)	0.00
32	1-Jan-12	12	-	-	-	(0.00)	0.00

The variance is the difference between straight line charges and amortization principal. In the example, the total payable over ten years is 147,950.36 and the charges are 47,950.36.

6. COMPARISON

The Comparison schedule summarizes the results for the four methods (see Figure 17.14).

Fig 17.14 **Comparison.**

	SL	SYD	DDB	MACRS
1	10,000.00	18,181.82	25,000.00	10,000.00
2	10,000.00	16,363.64	18,750.00	18,000.00
3	10,000.00	14,545.45	14,062.50	14,400.00
4	10,000.00	12,727.27	10,546.88	11,520.00
5	10,000.00	10,909.09	7,910.16	9,216.00
6	10,000.00	9,090.91	5,932.62	7,372.80
7	10,000.00	7,272.73	4,449.46	6,553.60
8	10,000.00	5,454.55	3,337.10	6,553.60
9	10,000.00	3,636.36	2,502.82	6,553.60
10	10,000.00	1,818.18	1,877.12	6,553.60
11	-	-	1,407.84	3,276.80
12	-	-	1,055.88	-
13	-	-	791.91	-
14	-	-	593.93	-
15	-	-	445.45	-
16	-	-	334.09	-
17	-	-	250.56	-
18	-	-	187.92	-
19	-	-	140.94	-
20	-	-	105.71	-
Total:	100,000.00	100,000.00	99,682.88	100,000.00

Comparison — v1.0 1-Jan-2001

There is a line graph of the periodic depreciation derived from the different methods at the bottom of the schedule (see Figure 17.15). There is a cross-over point at period 5 where the declining balance methods begin to show lower values than the results from straight line depreciation. The declining balance and MACRS methods accelerate the depreciation for tax purposes in order to give a 'tax break' for investment. The MACRS series shows the characteristic rise due to the first-year convention followed by a declining balance and then acceleration on switching to straight line depreciation.

At the bottom of the Model sheet, there is a comparison of capital outstanding using each of the four methods (see Figure 17.16). Only the amortization curve is above the straight line series. The others are all below reflecting the increased depreciation in the early periods.

Periodic depreciation.

Fig 17.15

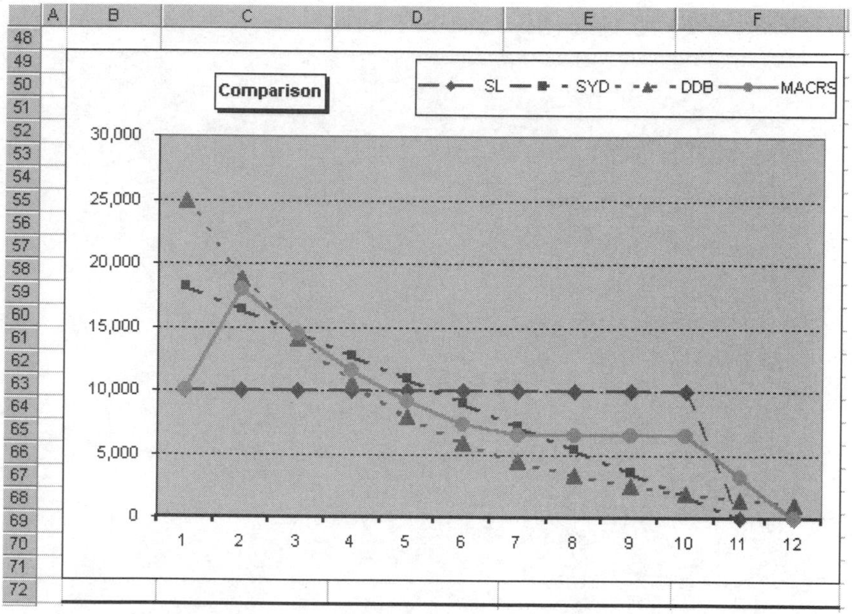

Capital outstanding.

Fig 17.16

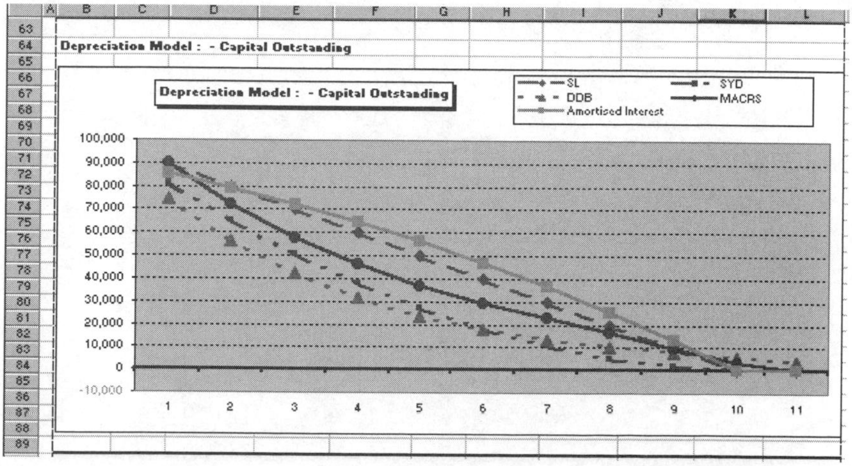

7. SUMMARY

This chapter has discussed a model for computing different depreciation methods and amortization. The methods are:

- straight line;
- sum of digits;
- declining balance;
- MACRS double declining method.

18

Leasing

A lease is an agreement whereby a leasing company or lessor purchases an asset for renting to a lessee, client or user. This is essentially a loan arrangement except that the lessor is the owner of the asset and this is usually the only security, whereas a loan may be secured on the other assets of the company. The file called Leasing, used in this chapter, includes templates for examining the benefits of leasing including the cost of leasing and its accounting classification.

Leasing varies between different countries due to:

- taxation arrangements as to who claims the tax depreciation on the asset;
- expiry arrangements where there could be options for purchase, run-on rentals and only return options;
- accounting and balance sheet treatment since some leases do not appear as borrowings in client accounts and thereby affect gearing (leverage) and interest cover ratios.

The benefits of leasing for the clients can be summarized as:

- retains cash in the business for other more valuable purposes;
- spreads the cost of the asset over its expected life and matches with the revenue an asset generates;
- provides an extra source of finance in addition to banking facilities;
- provides flexibility, especially if the lease contains break or upgrade options, for example on computer systems;
- provides convenience especially, with sales-aid arrangements at the point of sale;
- has potentially a lower cost when compared with purchasing or bank loans;
- may provide advantageous balance sheet treatment, especially if the borrowings are not noted in the financial accounts.

When modern leasing began in the US in the 1950s, all leases were considered short-term rentals and therefore not included as borrowings. This position changed in 1976 with the introduction of the US financial accounting standard called FASB 13, which classified leases as:

- finance or capital leases that effectively transfer the economic ownership to the user;
- operating leases where the owner remains on risk for the value of the residual or salvage value of the asset on expiry of the lease. These leases call for the lessor to include some form of residual that is not underwritten by the user.

The classification guidelines have been followed in the UK and most other European countries. However, there is no one standard due to the differences in accounting approaches and standards. This chapter uses mainly US terminology since many international companies adhere to US GAAP for reporting purposes.

The US standard defines four main rules, which if any are breached classifies the lease as a finance lease and is therefore to be accounted for on a balance sheet broadly as a loan. Thus if you fail on one you fail on them all. If the rules are not broken, then the user need only expense the rentals and add a note to the accounts regarding the future obligation to pay the rental amounts. The rules are:

- no bargain purchase option defined as an amount less than the market value;
- no automatic title transfer on expiry or during the term of the lease;
- rental period less than 75% of the asset's economic life in the hands of multiple users;
- present value of the rentals is less than 90% of the fair market value of the asset.

It follows that most users would prefer operating leases (off balance sheet) funding due to its simplistic accounting and potential lower periodic cost. Therefore, this chapter focuses on models for ascertaining the cost of funding, the financial benefits of leasing, lease accounting and checking the settlement against the market value of the asset. The main 'rule' is the present value of rentals and structuring an off balance sheet lease. It is beyond the scope of this book to provide a full in-depth analysis of leasing and you should refer to Day (2000), a comprehensive leasing manual by the same author.

This chapter introduces the model called Leasing for client evaluation of the following:

- rental calculations and the basics of the time value of money;
- lease versus purchase analysis to ascertain if leasing is advantageous over purchasing;

- classification into finance and operating leases and targeting different types of leases;
- lease accounting method;
- settlements and exposure analysis.

1. RENTAL CALCULATIONS

The Calculator in the Leasing application is set up in the same way as a hand-held financial or business calculator and utilizes functions, controls, buttons and macros to direct the user (see Figure 18.1).

Calculator.

Fig 18.1

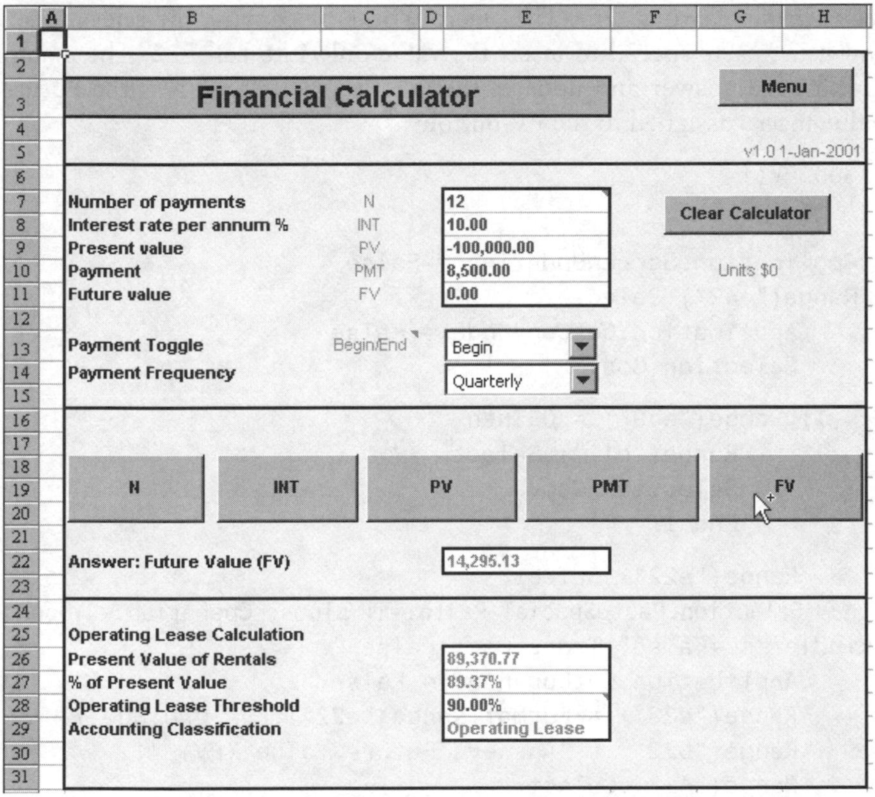

The idea is to calculate the missing variable of the five components. In the example above, there are 12 quarterly payments of 8,500 payable at the beginning of every quarter based on a capital value of 100,000 and a nominal interest rate of 10%. The missing variable is the future or residual value to make the equation below agree:

$$0 = PV + (1 + iS)\,PMT\left[\frac{1-(1+i)^{-n}}{i}\right] + FV\,(1+i)^{-n}$$

n	= number of periods
i	= periodic interest rate
PV	= present value or capital value
PMT	= periodic payment
FV	= future or residual value
S	= switch for payments at the beginning of the period (1) or at the end (0).

The design of this calculator starts with the interface and all the workings for the calculator are at the bottom. The cells E45 to E49 only calculate if the variable above is zero. The macro works by copying the relevant cell and using paste special to insert the value only into cell E22. The macro formats the answer and updates the label to the left. This is the Future Value macro assigned to the FV button:

```
Sub FV()
'

Application.ScreenUpdating = False
Range("e49").Select
    Application.CutCopyMode = False
    Selection.Copy

  If Range("e49") = 0 Then
        Range("e11").Select
        Selection.Copy
        End If

    Range("e22").Select
    Selection.PasteSpecial Paste:=xlValues, Operation:=xlNone,
SkipBlanks:=False, Transpose:=False
    Application.CutCopyMode = False
    Range("e22") = Format(Range("e22"), "#,##0.000")
    Range("b22") = "Answer: Future Value (FV) "
    Range("A1").Select
    Application.ScreenUpdating = True

End Sub
```

In this example, a final payment of 14,395 is needed if the rate is 10% and the rental is 8,500. If this final payment were the responsibility of the lessor, then the interest rate to the user would fall. To calculate this we only need to zero the interest rate and press INT to find the answer of 1.45%.

The Calculator makes use of the Excel functions in Table 18.1 to calculate the variables. Each of the functions needs the other variables and the payment switch between advance and arrears payments. The RATE function in Figure 18.2 requires NPER, PMT, PV, FV and the payment type. It is a convention that payments in are positive and payments out are negative. Therefore the model uses the ABS or absolute function to ensure that the present value is negative and the payment is negative.

Table 18.1

Excel functions

Function	Action
NPER	Number of periods required
RATE	Periodic interest rate – needs to be multiplied if more than one payment in year
PV	Present value of the payments and future value
PMT	Payment
FV	Future value or terminal payment

Fig 18.2

RATE function.

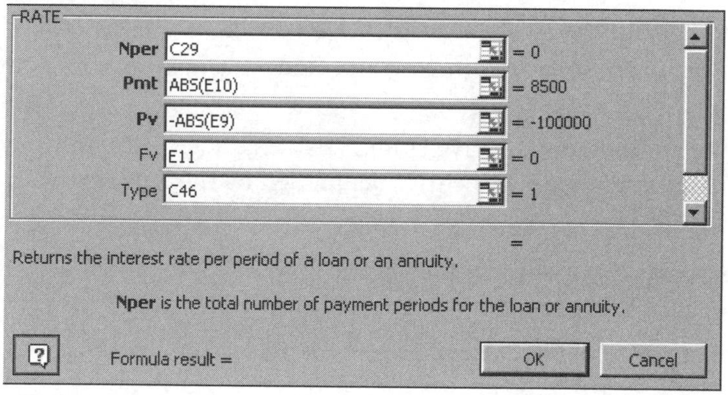

At the bottom, there is a lease classification section which present values the rental assuming that the final rental is not paid by the lessee. The present value is compared to the input variable 90% of the capital value. If the value were below, the lease would be an operating lease under this test.

2. LEASE VERSUS PURCHASE

Lease versus purchase is in reality another version of an investment model except that you are analysing two courses of action. You can either lease the equipment or acquire it through purchase or a loan arrangement. The steps are as follows:

- Forecast the incremental rental cash flows (not accounting entries) including other payments.
- Ignore payments that are the same for both, for example maintenance.
- Plot the tax relief on the rentals.
- Add back the tax depreciation for purchasing that you forgo due to leasing. In the US and UK, the legal owner rather than the economic owner claims the tax depreciation.
- Add up the cash flows for each period to derive the net cash flow.
- Discount at a suitable rate to find the net present value of leasing. If this is above the capital value, then leasing is less attractive than purchasing.

The usual assumptions for this type of analysis are as follows:

- The organization has come to a positive decision about acquiring the asset.
- The organization can use leasing or borrowing to finance the asset.
- The organization has to borrow and does not possess sufficient liquid funds.
- Leasing and borrowing have similar risk characteristics and there is no difference in the type of security demanded by the lenders.
- Inflation is disregarded.
- Uncertainty about corporation tax is ignored. The model assumes that the organization can claim tax relief at the earliest possible opportunity.
- There are no economies of scale to be gained from leasing.

The model needs to calculate the net present value of the rentals payable and other cash flows at the client's cost of funds. This could be completely different from the interest rate offered by the lessor. The lessor could benefit from a lower cost of funds or be able to pass on tax benefits in the pricing. The client may be a small company with a higher cost of funds.

The depreciation and the finance portion of the rentals on a finance lease are allowable against tax and therefore the model provides for interest relief based on the organization's marginal corporation tax rate.

The year end and tax delay together are important since the model needs to calculate the rentals in each tax year and when the tax is payable or reclaimable. The amount and the timing of cash flows are important.

First-year allowances at 40% are currently available to small businesses in the UK. One hundred per cent write-off in the first year is possible on certain areas of scientific research. Twenty-five per cent of the balance is available in subsequent years and in the first year to larger businesses. The UK uses a 25% declining balance method. This is of course higher than for lessors of finance leases who are restricted to 25% and time restricted on the amount of allowances in the first year.

The tax rate for small businesses is currently 20% to 30%. The funding cost is the rate for an overdraft, term loan or hurdle rate. Alternatively, where a lessee has liquid funds, you could use an opportunity cost of capital. The model uses this rate in discounted cash flow calculations and therefore the alternative rate is important.

The entries to the Model sheet are the capital value, number of rentals, final rental (if applicable), the frequency and whether in advance or arrears (see Figure 18.3). The acquisition in the example is in quarter 2 half way through the tax year. The cost of funds is 8%. The tax delay average is two quarters and the tax rate 30%.

Fig 18.3

Model inputs.

	A	B	C	D
2		**Leasing - Lease v. Purchase**		
4				
6		Client	Systematic	
7		Reference	(1) Fin Lease	
8		Start Date	01-Jan-01	
9		Capital Value	100,000.00	
10		Quarterly Rental	9,250.00	
11		Number of Rentals	12	
12		Final Rental	0.00	
13		Rental Frequency	Quarterly	
14		Advance or Arrears	Advance	
15		Period in Tax Year	2	
16		Client Cost of Funds	8.00%	
17		Tax Delay	2	
18		Tax Rate	30.00%	
19		Tax Depreciation	MACRS 5 yrs	
20				

When clients pay corporation tax you need to consider all the cash flows. First, rentals are a cost to the business and the consequent depreciation and finance charges are allowable against tax. Second, the client waives the right to claim capital allowances on the asset and therefore the loss of tax cashflow has to be factored into the equation.

The discount rate is the pre-tax rate factored first for the tax rate. In this example:

Pre-tax rate 8.00% multiplied by (1 – tax rate)
8.00% * 0.70 = 5.60%

Most companies in the UK currently account for tax nine months after the year-end although this is changing over the next few years as the UK adopts payment in four equal instalments. This timing difference has to be included in the calculation of the after-tax discount rate. The formula is:

$$Int = Int_{pre\text{-}tax} - \frac{Int_{pre\text{-}tax} * DisplacementFactor * TaxRate}{(1 + Int_{after\text{-}tax})^n}$$

where:

Int = user's after-tax borrowing rate
$Int_{pre\text{-}tax}$ = user's pre-tax interest rate entered on the Inputs schedule
n = average tax delay expressed in year – the tax delay here is averaged as two quarters or six months.

As regards the displacement factor, there is usually the assumption that leasing displaces an equivalent amount of borrowing capacity (i.e. the factor equals 1). You can relax this assumption by entering a percentage factor as, for example, 0.8 for 80%. Theoretically leasing should displace virtually an equal amount of debt; however, in practice, leasing does increase debt capacity by providing additional lines of credit. This follows the paper by Myers, Dill and Bautista (1976).

The lowering of debt displacement has the effect of increasing the discount rate. In this example:

$$Int = 0.08 - \frac{0.08*1.0*0.30}{(1 + 0.056)^{0.50}}$$

Post-tax interest rate equals 5.6645%.

Assumptions:

1. Factored* is calculated as follows:
   r* = int – [(int * (debt displacement * corporate tax)) / (1 + (int * (1 – corporate tax)) ^ tax delay]
   Debt to leasing displacement ratio: 1.00
   Formula: 8% – ((8% * (1 * 30%)) / (1 + (8% * (1 – 30%))) ^ (0.5))
   r* 5.66% as above against a net of tax rate of 5.6%.
2. Assumes organization pays mainstream corporation tax.
3. Assumes a tax delay equal to two periods.

The model obtains the written-down allowances from multiplying the capital by the allowance percentage and then by the tax rate as per the table below. There is a table at the bottom with the percentages for the UK and US. In the final year, the model accelerates the remaining UK allowances to ensure that all tax depreciation is utilized within the set number of periods.

Figure 18.4 shows the cash flows for the finance or capital lease below the charts on the schedule. Since this is the 'detail' it is placed below the charts and reporting. The rentals are in column D and the formulas use IF statements to ensure that the correct number of rentals are posted. The workings for columns E and G are on the right-hand side.

Fig 18.4

Finance lease cash flows.

	C	D	E	F	G	H	I
65							
66	**Period**	**Rental**	**Tax Relief**	**Capital**	**Tax Deprn**	**MACRS 5 yrs**	**Net Cash Flow**
67							
68	1	(9,250.00)	-	-	-	-	(9,250.00)
69	2	(9,250.00)	-	-	-	-	(9,250.00)
70	3	(9,250.00)	-	-	-	-	(9,250.00)
71	4	(9,250.00)	-	-	-	-	(9,250.00)
72	5	(9,250.00)	5,550.00	20.0%	(20,000.00)	(6,000.00)	(9,700.00)
73	6	(9,250.00)	-	-	-	-	(9,250.00)
74	7	(9,250.00)	-	-	-	-	(9,250.00)
75	8	(9,250.00)	-	-	-	-	(9,250.00)
76	9	(9,250.00)	11,100.00	32.0%	(32,000.00)	(9,600.00)	(7,750.00)
77	10	(9,250.00)	-	-	-	-	(9,250.00)
78	11	(9,250.00)	-	-	-	-	(9,250.00)
79	12	(9,250.00)	-	-	-	-	(9,250.00)
80	13	-	11,100.00	19.2%	(19,200.00)	(5,760.00)	5,340.00
81	14	-	-	-	-	-	-
82	15	-	-	-	-	-	-
83	16	-	-	-	-	-	-
84	17	-	5,550.00	11.5%	(11,520.00)	(3,456.00)	2,094.00
85	18	-	-	-	-	-	-
86	19	-	-	-	-	-	-
87	20	-	-	-	-	-	-
88	21	-	-	11.5%	(11,520.00)	(3,456.00)	(3,456.00)
89	22	-	-	-	-	-	-
90	23	-	-	-	-	-	-
91	24	-	-	-	-	-	-
92	25	-	-	5.8%	(5,760.00)	(1,728.00)	(1,728.00)
93	26	-	-	-	-	-	-
94	27	-	-	-	-	-	-
95	28	-	-	-	-	-	-
96							
97		(111,000.00)	33,300.00		(100,000.00)	(30,000.00)	(107,700.00)

The model needs to be able to count periods and decide when new accounting years start. It then needs to be able to count the tax delay to place the tax relief on the rentals and the lost tax depreciation in the correct periods (see Figure 18.5).

Fig 18.5

Tax computations.

	K	L	M	N	O	P	Q	R
65								
66	Tax Counter	Tax Year	Rentals	Offset Tax	Offset Tax	Tax %	Tax	IRR
67								
68	2	-	-					90,750.00
69	3	-	-					(9,250.00)
70	4	1	(18,500.00)	-	-	-	-	(9,250.00)
71	1	-	-	-	-	-	-	(9,250.00)
72	2	-	-	5,550.00	1	20.0%	(20,000.00)	(9,700.00)
73	3	-	-	-	-	-	-	(9,250.00)
74	4	2	(37,000.00)	-	-	-	-	(9,250.00)
75	1	-	-	-	-	-	-	(9,250.00)
76	2	-	-	11,100.00	2	32.0%	(32,000.00)	(7,750.00)
77	3	-	-	-	-	-	-	(9,250.00)
78	4	3	(37,000.00)	-	-	-	-	(9,250.00)
79	1	-	-	-	-	-	-	(9,250.00)
80	2	-	-	11,100.00	3	19.2%	(19,200.00)	5,340.00
81	3	-	-	-	-	-	-	-
82	4	4	(18,500.00)	-	-	-	-	-
83	1	-	-	-	-	-	-	-
84	2	-	-	5,550.00	4	11.5%	(11,520.00)	2,094.00
85	3	-	-	-	-	-	-	-
86	4	5	-	-	-	-	-	-
87	1	-	-	-	-	-	-	-
88	2	-	-	-	5	11.5%	(11,520.00)	(3,456.00)
89	3	-	-	-	-	-	-	-
90	4	6	-	-	-	-	-	-
91	1	-	-	-	-	-	-	-
92	2	-	-	-	6	5.8%	(5,760.00)	(1,728.00)
93	3	-	-	-	-	-	-	-
94	4	7	-	-	-	-	-	-
95	1	-	-	-	-	-	-	-
96								
97			(111,000.00)	33,300.00		100.0%	(100,000.00)	

Column K starts with the input period in the tax year and increments one on each row. If the number is above the possible number of periods in the year (for example five with quarterly rentals), it reverts to one. This is cell K67:

```
=IF(K68+1>(12/Interval),1,K68+1)
```

Column L works out the final period in the tax year and then works out the tax year number. This is required since the tax depreciation percentages are different in each year. This is cell L70 for the first tax year:

```
=ROUNDUP((IF(K70=(12/Interval),C70/(12/Interval),0)),0)
```

Column M has to add the rentals for the last periods and it uses an OFFSET function to count back from a starting point by the number of periods in a year (12 / Interval). This formula derives the total rentals upon which tax relief can be calculated:

```
=IF(K70=(12/Interval),SUM(OFFSET(D69,-(12/Interval)+1,0)
:D69),0)
```

Column N calculates the tax relief two periods later using the input delay factor. This is cell N72:

```
=-IF(K72<TaxDelay,0,OFFSET(M72,-TaxDelay,0)*TaxRate)
```

Columns O, P and Q work back to the tax year number and use this value in a look-up command in the table. The control selects a set of depreciation values from the table and inserts them into cells J104 to J111. The LOOKUP command searches for the tax year number in cells C105 to C111 and the result vector is in column J. This is the formula in cell P72:

```
=IF(072<>0,LOOKUP(072,$C$105:$C$111,$J$105:$J$111),0)
```

The tax depreciation percentage is multiplied by the capital value in column Q and then by the tax rate in column H. The result is the following cash flows:

- rentals;
- relief on rentals;
- tax depreciation.

The management report is at the top of the schedule to show the user the answer, consisting of the net present value and the expected gains or losses from leasing (see Figure 18.6).

Management summary.

Fig 18.6

	A	B	C	D	E	F	G	H
6		Client	Systematic		Management Summary			
7		Reference	(1) Fin Lease		Net Present Value at 5.60%			99,689.68
8		Start Date	01-Jan-01		Factored NPV at 5.66%			99,603.70
9		Capital Value	100,000.00		Leasing Gain			0.40%
10		Quarterly Rental	9,250.00		Lease or Buy?			Lease
11		Number of Rentals	12					
12		Final Rental	0.00		Client Classification			
13		Rental Frequency	Quarterly		Inherent Interest Rate			7.83%
14		Advance or Arrears	Advance		Pre-tax PV test at 8.00%			99,778.34
15		Period in Tax Year	2					
16		Client Cost of Funds	8.00%		Accounting Classification			
17		Tax Delay	2		Decision Percentage			90.00%
18		Tax Rate	30.00%		Lease Classification			Capital
19		Tax Depreciation	MACRS 5 yrs		Lessor Rate			7.83%
20								

The NPV function is used to discount the outstanding cash flows at the periodic discount rate (see Figure 18.7). This is cell H8 that uses the periodic discount rate from the workings at row 133:

```
=-NPV(E133,I$69:I$95)-I$68
```

Fig 18.7

Discount rate workings.

	A	B	C	D	E	F	G	H
127								
128		**Comparison:**						
129		**Debt Displacement Factor**			1			
130		**Results**					**XNPV/XIRR Functions**	
131			**Gross**	**Net tax**	**Factored***			
132		Discount rate	8.0000%	5.6000%	5.6645%		XNPV	99,772.30
133		Periodic Rate	2.0000%	1.4000%	1.4161%		IRR	5.37%
134		Net present value					XIRR	5.49%
135		Pretax interest rate	97,821.91					
136		Spread rates		99,689.68	99,603.70			
137		Finance lease	5.37%					
138								

The leasing gain is calculated together with a decision in cell H10:

```
=IF(H8>CapitalValue,"Buy","Lease")
```

The interest rate is calculated on the basis that the client does not pay the final rental and this residual is the responsibility of the lessor. The calculation is:

```
=RATE(RentalPeriods,PeriodicRental, – ABS(CapitalValue)
,0,AdvArr) * (12/Interval)
```

The model present values the rentals at the client's cost of funds and this is slightly less than 100,000 since the inherent rate is 7.83% and the client's cost of funds was input at 8%. The next decision is the type of lease by the present value test. The decision percentage is an input cell in H17, but this approximately 90% for both the UK and the US. Since the present value is greater than 90%, the model classifies the lease as a finance lease.

In order to confirm the results, there is a sensitivity table and charts to demonstrate the gains or losses (see Figure 18.8).

The answer is highlighted through conditional formatting and the central value is updated using the macro to copy down the cost of funds value. As the discount rate goes down, then leasing becomes less attractive. The second chart illustrates the potential gains from the data table (see Figure 18.9):

```
=SERIES(Model!$B$25,Model!$C$25:$I$25,Model!$C$27:$I$27,1)
```

There is a second example saved as a scenario in the model. This is an operating lease at the equivalent of a zero interest rate (see Figure 18.10).

The user only pays a proportion of the capital cost over the rental period and the lessor must sell or re-lease the equipment in order to recover the full investment in the asset. The net present value shows a substantial benefit for leasing since the model assumes that the user would recover no salvage on the eventual disposal of the equipment (see Figure 18.11). This is probably true of certain computer equipment but may not be true of other assets.

Sensitivity chart.

Fig 18.8

	A	B	C	D	E	F	G
21							
22		Sensitivity to Discount Rate: Pre-Tax Rate 8.0% equals PV 99,690					
23							
24		Interval	1.00%				
25		Pre-tax Rates	5.00%	6.00%	7.00%	8.00%	9.00%
26		99603.69567	102,528.16	101,538.95	100,564.21	99,603.70	98,657.17
27		Leasing Gain / (Loss)	(2,528.16)	(1,538.95)	(564.21)	396.30	1,342.83
28		Percentage	(2.5%)	(1.5%)	(0.6%)	0.4%	1.3%

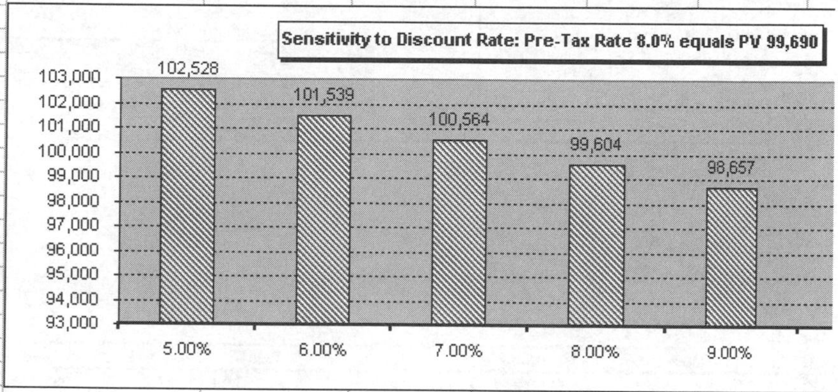

Leasing gains.

Fig 18.9

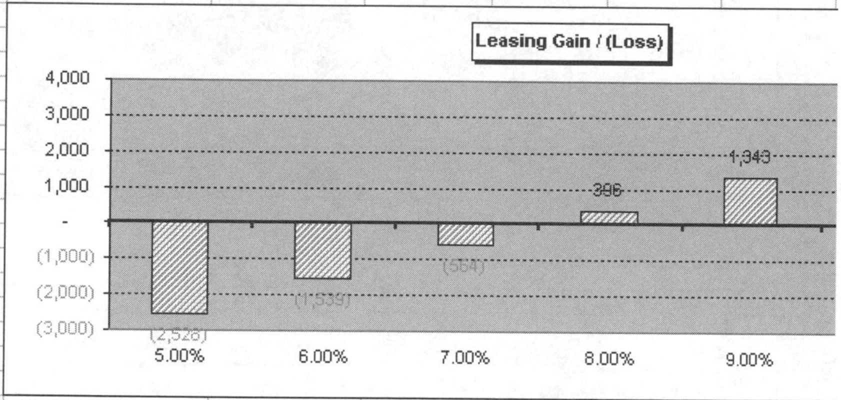

Fig 18.10

Operating lease inputs.

Row	B	C	E–G	H
6	Client	Systematic	Management Summary	
7	Reference	(2) Op Lease	Net Present Value at 5.60%	92,360.79
8	Start Date	01-Jan-01	Factored NPV at 5.66%	92,278.98
9	Capital Value	100,000.00	Leasing Gain	7.72%
10	Quarterly Rental	8,333.00	Lease or Buy?	Lease
11	Number of Rentals	12		
12	Final Rental	0.00	Client Classification	
13	Rental Frequency	Quarterly	Inherent Interest Rate	0.00%
14	Advance or Arrears	Advance	Pre-tax PV test at 8.00%	89,886.80
15	Period in Tax Year	2		
16	Client Cost of Funds	8.00%	Accounting Classification	
17	Tax Delay	2	Decision Percentage	90.00%
18	Tax Rate	30.00%	Lease Classification	Operating
19	Tax Depreciation	MACRS 5 yrs	Lessor Rate	0.00%
20				

Fig 18.11

Sensitivity charts.

Row	B	C	D	E	F	G
24	Interval	1.00%				
25	Pre-tax Rates	5.00%	6.00%	7.00%	8.00%	9.00%
26	92278.97897	95,063.40	94,121.12	93,193.06	92,278.98	91,378.63
27	Leasing Gain / (Loss)	4,936.60	5,878.88	6,806.94	7,721.02	8,621.37
28	Percentage	4.9%	5.9%	6.8%	7.7%	8.6%

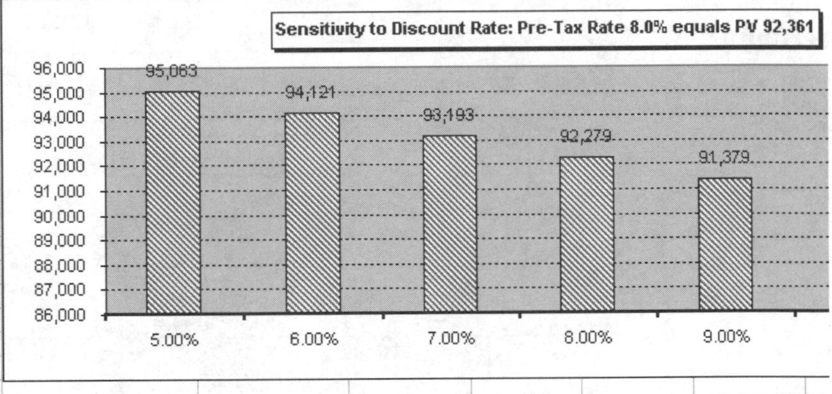

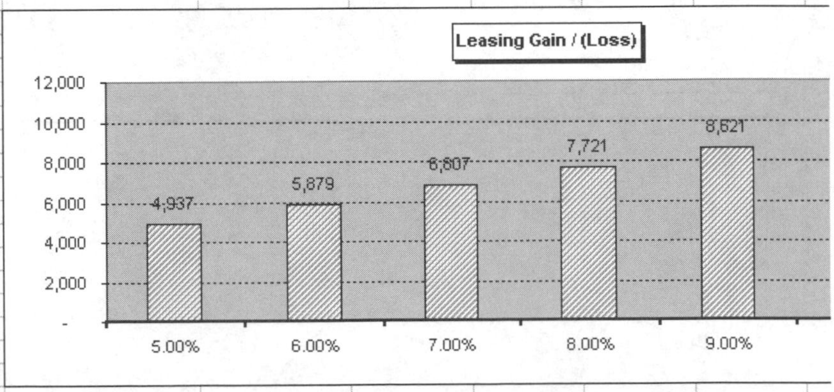

3. CLASSIFICATION

The model includes two sheets for classification and generating rentals. This problem requires Excel to work back from the leasing classification to a residual value to make the deal work. The model uses the same functions and controls as used in the Calculator sheet (see Figure 18.12).

Classification.

Fig 18.12

	A	B	C
4			
5		No of Rentals (N)	12
6		Interest Rate (I)	10.000%
7		Frequency	Quarterly
8		Present Value (PV)	100,000.00
9		Future Value (FV)	16,508.24
10		Begin/End	Advance
11			
12		Payment (PMT)	8,343.49
13			
14		Client Interest Rate	8.000%
15		Fair Market Value (FMV)	100,000.00
16		Basis	90.000%
17		Threshold	90,000.00
18			
19		Present Value (PV)	89,999.96
20		% Fair Market Value	90.00%
21		Accounting Classification	Operating Lease
22			
23		Data Table of Rentals	
24			
25		Interval	1.000%
26		Data Table	89,999.96
27		5.000%	93,595.63
28		6.000%	92,371.76
29		7.000%	91,173.42
30		8.000%	89,999.96
31		9.000%	88,850.75
32		10.000%	87,725.20
33		11.000%	86,622.69

The GoalSeek targets cell C19 to the threshold of 90,000 by changing the residual value in cell C9 to the solution of 16,508.24. The rental also reduces to 8,343.49.

```
Range("c19").Goalseek Goal:=Range("c17"), ChangingCell:
=Range("c9")
```

This calculation is necessary since the lessor and lessee interest rates are different and the residual value is ignored by the lessees for clarification purposes. Thus, both parties calculate the classification using their own inputs.

A second sheet called Rental_Table uses the same methodology to generate data tables of rentals (see Figure 18.13). This allows the user to see many other combinations of rentals without having to change the two key variables of interest rate and residual value.

Fig 18.13 **Rental data table.**

No of Rentals (N)	12
Interest Rate (I)	10.00%
Present Value (PV)	100,000.00
Future Value (FV)	16.51%
Frequency	Quarterly
Begin/End	Advance
Payment (PMT)	8,343.49

Interest Interval	0.25%
FV Interval	1.00%

Rate Table: Interest Rate Across

	9.00%	9.25%	9.50%	9.75%	10.00%	10.25%	10.50%
8,343.49	8,203.52	8,238.48	8,273.47	8,308.47	8,343.49	8,378.53	8,413.58

Rate Table: Future Value (PV) Across : Interest Rate Down

8,343.49	12.51%	13.51%	14.51%	15.51%	16.51%	17.51%	18.51%
8.75%	8,457.36	8,385.16	8,312.96	8,240.77	8,168.57	8,096.37	8,024.17
9.00%	8,491.12	8,419.22	8,347.32	8,275.42	8,203.52	8,131.62	8,059.72
9.25%	8,524.90	8,453.29	8,381.69	8,310.09	8,238.48	8,166.88	8,095.28
9.50%	8,558.70	8,487.39	8,416.08	8,344.78	8,273.47	8,202.16	8,130.85
9.75%	8,592.52	8,521.51	8,450.50	8,379.48	8,308.47	8,237.46	8,166.45
10.00%	8,626.37	8,555.65	8,484.93	8,414.21	8,343.49	8,272.77	8,202.05
10.25%	8,660.23	8,589.81	8,519.38	8,448.95	8,378.53	8,308.10	8,237.67
10.50%	8,694.12	8,623.99	8,553.85	8,483.72	8,413.58	8,343.45	8,273.31
10.75%	8,728.04	8,658.19	8,588.35	8,518.50	8,448.66	8,378.81	8,308.97
11.00%	8,761.97	8,692.41	8,622.86	8,553.30	8,483.75	8,414.19	8,344.63
11.25%	8,795.92	8,726.66	8,657.39	8,588.12	8,518.85	8,449.58	8,380.32

4. ACCOUNTING

The UK accounting for leases was originally set out in SSAP 21, *Accounting for Leases and Hire Purchase Contracts*, which was published in 1984. This established for the first time the rules for capitalizing leases and followed in broad terms the principles set by the US standard FASB 13 in 1976. In addition, it broke new ground by introducing the concept of 'substance over form'. The later standard FRS 5, *Reporting the Substance of Transactions*, adds to SSAP 21 and is discussed on page 271.

Usually SSAP 21 requires users to capitalize lease transactions according to their substance rather than legal ownership. Where a lease transfers 'substantially all the risks and rewards of ownership' to the user, the user capitalizes the asset and treats the transaction as if the equipment had been acquired through a borrowing or loan facility. This definition is in SSAP 21, paragraph 15. This ended the previous state of affairs whereby a user could have effective economic ownership without reporting the borrowings on its balance sheet.

For the purposes of SSAP 21, an operating lease is simply a lease other than a finance lease. This does not transfer 'substantially all the risks and rewards of ownership' and therefore does not need to be capitalized. This means in practice that the lessor maintains a substantial interest in the equipment. The rental agreement does not write off the equipment and therefore the lessor must deal in the equipment in order to realize 100% of the capital plus charges. The retention of risk is an important concept in determining the position of the parties.

SSAP 21 provides guidance on the transfer of risks and rewards in the simple 90% test:

> It should be presumed that such a transfer of risks and rewards occurs if at the inception of the lease the present value of the minimum lease payments, including any initial payment, amounts to substantially all (normally 90 per cent or more) of the fair value of the leased asset.

The real position may be obvious; however, lessors may structure leases to appear as operating leases in the users' books and still capitalize them themselves. Each party can have a different view on the need for capitalization. As lease products have become more complex problems have arisen regarding capitalization. For example, the inclusion of complex options, side agreements, conditional provisions and third-party or user guarantees make it difficult to reach a decision using these simple tests.

FRS 5 states that where the standard overlaps with another standard, then the one with the more specific provisions should be followed. Since SSAP 21 refers specifically to leasing, this standard is often followed. Where the lease is part of an overall arrangement, then the effect of the whole transaction would need to be considered in the light of FRS 5. The particular provision in FRS 5 that applies is that the substance of the transaction should be considered and not just its legal form. The overall effect of FRS 5 is to ensure that SSAP 21 is applied in spirit and not just through the application of the mechanical 90% test.

There are still problems with the application of SSAP 21 and FRS 5, namely:

- *Lease term* – the minimum period includes the period of the contractual obligation (primary period) plus further periods where the user has to continue to lease the asset. Problems can arise with the definition of the primary period, cancellation and break options, exchange and upgrade options and options to extend the lease.
- *Break clauses* – clauses for a 'walk' option are often not clear; however, inclusion of the break clauses reduces the minimum payments' present value below 90%.
- *Upgrade clauses* – some computer lessors use 'technology refresh' clauses where the downside is effectively rolled into the next lease. These are discussed in Chapter 10.
- *Renewal options* – sometimes renewals require unusually long notice periods such that the user can only with great difficulty lease the equipment for the actual minimum period entered on the lease schedule.
- *Rental variations* – return provisions sometimes attract extra rentals to compensate the lessor in part for equipment returns.
- *Residual guarantees* – some leases call for a minimum below 'market value'. It is not clear if this rental should be included as a final payment.
- *Interest rates* – in most cases, users can calculate the inherent rate in the lease. Where the user does not know the exact residual value used by the lessor, then he may use the incremental borrowing rate.

Accounting entries

The finance lease example is 12 quarterly rentals of 9,250 and these results feed through to the Accounting sheet from the lease versus purchase example on the Model sheet.

Using SSAP 21, an asset and liability should be entered on the balance sheet at the present value of the lease payments. This is usually the capital value. The finance charge for each period is allocated to each period using the amortization as set out in Chapter 17 on Depreciation. This splits up the interest based on the capital outstanding and the capital repayment is the balance of the rental. This is another reason why you need to know the inherent rate in the lease.

The Accounting sheet uses a profit and less account and balance sheet side by side. Figure 18.14 shows the cash flow on the second page. The inherent rate is 7.83% and the profit and loss entries are calculated as the depreciation plus the actuarial finance charge:

Depreciation per annum (100,000 / 12 periods)	8,333
Obligation at 1.96% (100,000 – 9,250 = 90,750 * 1.96%	1,779
Total	10,109

Accounting income statement.

Fig 18.14

	(A) Profit and loss					
Period no	Obligation at start of period	Rents paid	Obligation during period	Depreciation	Actuarial finance charge	Total charges
1	100,000.00	(9,250.00)	90,750.00	8,333.33	1,776.01	10,109.34
2	92,526.01	(9,250.00)	83,276.01	8,333.33	1,629.74	9,963.07
3	84,905.75	(9,250.00)	75,655.75	8,333.33	1,480.61	9,813.94
4	77,136.36	(9,250.00)	67,886.36	8,333.33	1,328.56	9,661.89
5	69,214.92	(9,250.00)	59,964.92	8,333.33	1,173.53	9,506.87
6	61,138.45	(9,250.00)	51,888.45	8,333.33	1,015.47	9,348.81
7	52,903.92	(9,250.00)	43,653.92	8,333.33	854.32	9,187.66
8	44,508.25	(9,250.00)	35,258.25	8,333.33	690.02	9,023.35
9	35,948.26	(9,250.00)	26,698.26	8,333.33	522.49	8,855.83
10	27,220.76	(9,250.00)	17,970.76	8,333.33	351.69	8,685.03
11	18,322.45	(9,250.00)	9,072.45	8,333.33	177.55	8,510.88
12	9,250.00	(9,250.00)	(0.00)	8,333.33	(0.00)	8,333.33
13	(0.00)	-	(0.00)	-	(0.00)	(0.00)
14	(0.00)	-	(0.00)	-	(0.00)	(0.00)

In the next year the interest is [90,750 – 9,250] * 1.96% = 1,629. The balance sheet is composed of the asset less depreciation and as liabilities the capital outstanding (see Figure 18.15).

Balance sheet.

Fig 18.15

(B) Balance sheet		Units $0
Net book asset value	Liabilities	Timing diff.
91,666.67	92,526.01	(859.34)
83,333.33	84,905.75	(1,572.41)
75,000.00	77,136.36	(2,136.36)
66,666.67	69,214.92	(2,548.25)
58,333.33	61,138.45	(2,805.12)
50,000.00	52,903.92	(2,903.92)
41,666.67	44,508.25	(2,841.58)
33,333.33	35,948.26	(2,614.93)
25,000.00	27,220.76	(2,220.76)
16,666.67	18,322.45	(1,655.78)
8,333.33	9,250.00	(916.67)
-	(0.00)	0.00
-	(0.00)	0.00

The difference between the total profit and loss charge of 10,109 in year 1 and the rental of 9,250 gives rise to a small timing difference of

850. This disappears by the end of the lease when all the charges of 11,000 have been allocated.

The chart of the columns on the table shows the declining interest charge and the static depreciation together with the total charge crossing the rental series (see Figure 18.16).

Fig 18.16 **Accounting entries chart.**

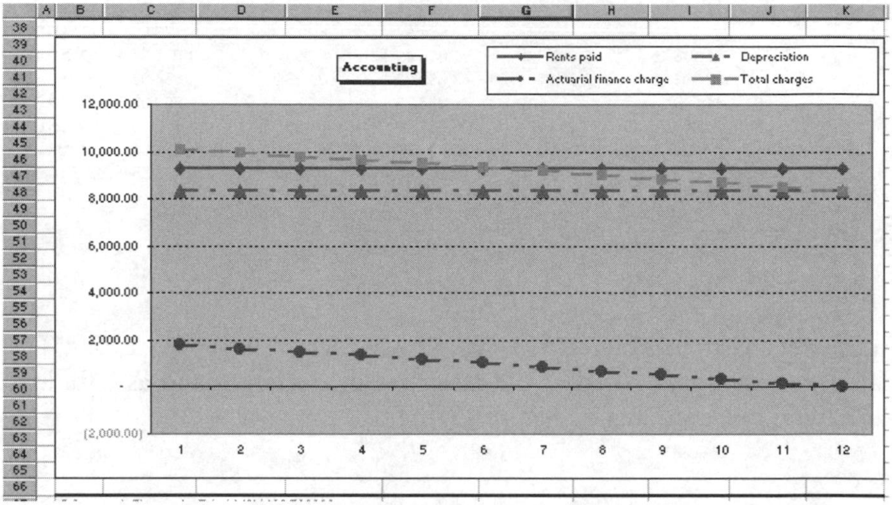

Operating leases are accounted for differently. The rentals are recorded as an expense in the user's profit and loss account. The asset is not recorded as an asset and no liability is shown on the balance sheet. There is, however, a requirement to note operating lease commitments as a note to the accounts. The future commitments have to be split between payments committed in the next year and payments between two and five years after the balance sheet date. If the lease is classified as an operating lease, then the entries are simplified as the rental expense only. This is the reference in cell E8 using the Function LEFT to find the first character:

```
IF(LEFT(Classification,1)="O",0,SUM(C8:D8))
```

5. SETTLEMENTS

Some lease contracts contain a voluntary termination clause, which provides for the exact provisions in the event that the client wishes to terminate during the initial rental period. Alternatively the default clause will detail what is payable in case of a default termination during the period. Since equipment rarely declines in value at the same rate as the lease capital outstanding, the model seeks to plot the settlement, the market value and the difference between the two. This is the sheet called Settlements in the Leasing model.

Essentially, the totals outstanding are payable, usually less a discount for early payment. Against the settlement, there may be a credit for the value of the equipment depending on the type of lease contract. Table 18.2 is a summary of typical expiry options for the two types of leases.

Table 18.2

Typical expiry options

Option	Settlement discount	Equipment	Participation in sale proceeds
Finance lease	Normally	Agency sale	Yes – majority of proceeds
Operating lease	No	No	No

There is usually a provision for users to return equipment to an address nominated by the lessor. This is an extra cost for the user, which they do not usually consider when taking out the contract. There could be a further burden, for example in the case of a car, where the condition has to be strictly in accordance with the contract. If the lessor has placed a residual value on the asset, he requires it to be in good condition to maximize the sale price. The lessor will charge for any damage and losses.

Therefore, check the lease contract for these points:

- Who has ownership of the equipment on termination?
- What is the early termination discount rate?
- Are the sale proceeds set against the termination sum?
- Who sells the equipment? If the lessor sells it, what are the safeguards to ensure that he attains the maximum price?
- What costs can the lessor deduct if he is responsible for the sale?

The Settlements sheet looks up the information in the Model schedule and allows you to choose a discount rate to be applied to the rental stream (see Figure 18.17). Most agreements use a relatively low discount rate, which is between 0 and 5%. The settlement is the net present value of the outstanding payments to be compared against the market value.

The model uses a control with the entries in the right-hand table to generate the discount rate and the periodic percentage reductions are inputs on the schedule. The settlement NPV uses the periodic interest rate as in cell F14:

```
=IF(E14=0,0,NPV($D$7/(12/Model!$C$119),D15:$D$33))
```

Fig 18.17

Settlements.

	A	B	C	D	E	F	G	H	I	J
5										
6		Select Settlement Rate		Settlement rate 5%				Settlement rate 5%		5.00%
7		Discount Rate Used		5.00%				Other rate 3%		3.00%
8		FASB 13 Classificatio		Capital				Inherent rate 7.83%		7.83%
9		Maximum Exposure		(13,151)						1
10		Period Number		6						
11		Average (Exposure)/C		(4,485)	Equates to (4.5%) of PV					Units $0
12										
13		No	Date	Rental Payments	Outstanding Rents	Settlement at 5%	% Value Deduction	Equipment Value	(Exposure) or Cover	Percent of Settlement
14		1	Jan-01	(9,250)	101,750	(94,515)	10.00%	90,000	(4,515)	4.8%
15		2	Apr-01	(9,250)	92,500	(86,446)	10.00%	80,000	(6,446)	7.5%
16		3	Jul-01	(9,250)	83,250	(78,277)	10.00%	70,000	(8,277)	10.6%
17		4	Oct-01	(9,250)	74,000	(70,005)	10.00%	60,000	(10,005)	14.3%
18		5	Jan-02	(9,250)	64,750	(61,630)	10.00%	50,000	(11,630)	18.9%
19		6	Apr-02	(9,250)	55,500	(53,151)	10.00%	40,000	(13,151)	24.7%
20		7	Jul-02	(9,250)	46,250	(44,565)	5.00%	35,000	(9,565)	21.5%
21		8	Oct-02	(9,250)	37,000	(35,872)	5.00%	30,000	(5,872)	16.4%
22		9	Jan-03	(9,250)	27,750	(27,070)	5.00%	25,000	(2,070)	7.6%
23		10	Apr-03	(9,250)	18,500	(18,159)	5.00%	20,000	1,841	(10.1%)
24		11	Jul-03	(9,250)	9,250	(9,136)	5.00%	15,000	5,864	(64.2%)
25		12	Oct-03	(9,250)	-	-	5.00%	10,000	10,000	-
26		13	Jan-04	-	-	-	5.00%	5,000	-	-
27		14	Apr-04	-	-	-	5.00%	-	-	-
28		15	Jul-04	-	-	-	-	-	-	-
29		16	Oct-04	-	-	-	-	-	-	-
30		17	Jan-05	-	-	-	-	-	-	-
31		18	Apr-05	-	-	-	-	-	-	-
32		19	Jul-05	-	-	-	-	-	-	-
33		20	Oct-05	-	-	-	-	-	-	-
34		21	Jan-06	-	-	-	-	-	-	-
35		22	Apr-06	-	-	-	-	-	-	-
36		23	Jul-06	-	-	-	-	-	-	-
37		24	Oct-06	-	-	-	-	-	-	-
38		25	Jan-07	-	-	-	-	-	-	-
39		26	Apr-07	-	-	-	-	-	-	-
40		27	Jul-07	-	-	-	-	-	-	-
41		28	Oct-07	-	-	-	-	-	-	-
42										
43		Total		(111,000)			100.00%			

The net equipment value is calculated in column H and compared against the settlement in column I. To illustrate the results, the chart at the bottom of the schedule highlights the asset cover or exposure.

The usual formula for a finance lease is shown in Table 18.3 using the figures for period 4 with eight rentals outstanding.

Table 18.3

Formula for a finance lease

Item	Amount
Rentals outstanding – 8 * 9,250	74,000
5% per annum discount	–3,995
Sale value of equipment	–60,000
Total payable	10,005

The graph in Figure 18.18 shows clearly the period when the sale proceeds do not cover the potential settlement. The area graph below the line denotes the exposure or the shortfall between the settlement and the equipment value. When the exposure is above the line, then the client makes a 'profit' on settlement.

Fig 18.18

Settlement chart.

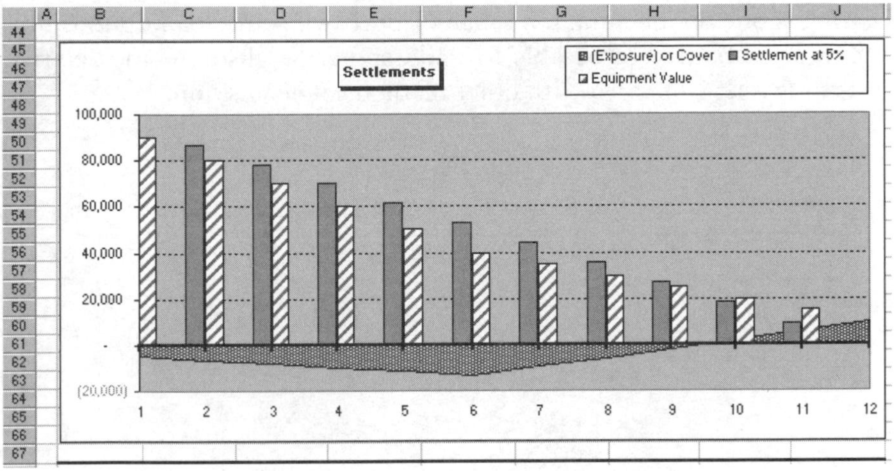

In keeping with other applications, the summary at the top provides the information on the maximum exposure and its period number. This uses the MAX Function and then looks for its index number down the list of values.

This is the reference in cell D9: `=MIN(I14:I41)`. The value is then matched and the function in D10 returns the position on the list: `=MATCH(D9,I14:I41,0)`. The MATCH types are:

- 1 Largest value that is less than or equal to lookup value. Array must be placed in ascending order.
- 0 First value that is exactly equal to lookup value. Array can be in any order.
- –1 Smallest value that is greater than or equal to lookup value. Array must be placed in descending order.

6. SUMMARY

The Leasing application includes tools for reviewing leases:

- interest rates to check the cost of borrowing;
- client evaluation (lease versus purchase) for comparing the net present value of leasing against borrowing;

- lease classification and data tables to decide between operating and finance leases;
- accounting entries;
- settlements, market value and exposure computations.

Leasing is one option among a range of borrowing and loan options and potential users need to be able to understand the absolute and relative costs of leasing compared with other methods of acquisition.

Company valuation

Earlier chapters have included models on analysing and forecasting company performance, the cost of capital and investment analysis. This chapter looks specifically at valuing companies and builds on some of the techniques in these chapters. The purpose here is to review different techniques around a model called Valuation which builds up to a comparison report of the different methods.

Valuing companies is not an exact science and different individuals will have an array of ideas about the value of assets or growth prospects. Companies are worth whatever investors are prepared to pay. Building a model provides a framework for consideration and assists with the analysis. Models built for the purpose will arrive at different valuations for different purposes. Here are some examples of different purposes:

- annual report where the accounting value is reported to stakeholders;
- takeover and acquisition where the value normally includes a premium for control;
- divestment by a public company;
- merger with another concern in the same sector;
- management buyout from a larger company where there could be an element of deferred consideration;
- trade sale to a third party;
- bankruptcy and liquidation where the business is not considered a 'going concern'.

Modern businesses also vary in their fixed assets. Knowledge-based companies usually possess very little in the way of fixed assets and their value is in the people, brands or their proprietary rights to software or other copyright. Shares in a public company, which are tradable on a stock exchange, are also worth more than shares in a private company or a public company traded on an exchange where the share has few market makers.

A number of factors could be considered to increase the value of the company:

- Companies can also be considered the sum of cash flows from different projects just as with the investment models in Chapters 15 and 16. The growth prospects could be expected to produce further earnings.
- The capital structure and its cost of capital could be changed to boost earnings.
- Synergies or other advantages may be available to some acquirers.

Building a model provides the framework for examining the valuations in detail and the opportunity for 'what-if' or risk analysis. The model used in this chapter is Valuation and the different valuation methods contained in the file are:

- accounting value – the shareholders' funds;
- adjusted accounting value – accounting value with adjustments for undervalued or overvalued assets;
- dividends – the value of the dividends over time;
- market pricing – stock market methods using share prices and earnings per share;
- free cash flow – the discounted value of future cash flows.

1. ACCOUNTS

The first sheet in the file Valuation sets out some basic data on the company in the form of a balance sheet, earnings and market information (see Figures 19.1 and 19.2). This mode includes only the last balance sheet; however, you could perform some of the same calculations on the accounts analysis model, Financial_Analysis.

This company's accounts show a net worth or shareholders' funds (equity) of 188,000 and little in the way of borrowings. In a more complex model, it would be beneficial to have a number of years in a columnar format together with ratio analysis to ascertain the financial performance of the company over time.

The model separates the methods by sheets and uses graphics wherever possible to illustrate the results. All the inputs are colour-coded and there are comments to explain the calculations.

Fig 19.1

Net assets.

	A	B	C	D	E	F	G	H
4								
5		**(A) Balance Sheet Inputs**						
6		Accounts Date			30-Jun-01			
7								
8		**Tangible Assets**						
9		Freehold land and buildings			10,000			Units $000
10								
11		Long leashold property			30,000			
12		Plant and equipment			30,000			
13		Fixtures and fittings			5,000			
14						75,000		
15		**Intangible Assets**						
16		Licences			3,000			
17		Investment			35,000			
18						38,000		
19		**Total Fixed Assets**					113,000	
20								
21		**Current assets**						
22		Licence prepayments			48,000			
23		Work in progress			25,000			
24		Debtors			90,000			
25		Short term deposits			45,000			
26		Cash at hand and at bank			10,000			
27						218,000		
28								
29		**Current Liabilities**				125,000		
30								
31		**Creditors due after more than one year**				18,000		
32								
33		**Net Assets**					188,000	

Fig 19.2

Shareholders' funds (net worth).

	A	B	C	D	E	F	G	H
34								
35		**Shareholders' funds**						
36		Share capital			25,000			
37		Share premium			5,000			
38		Profit and loss account			158,000			
39								
40		**Net Worth**					188,000	
41								
42		CheckSum					-	
43								
44		**(B) Income and Market Inputs**						
45		Nominal share value			0.25			
46		Current share price			6.000			
47		Operating Profit			45,000			
48		Earnings after tax			30,000			
49		EBITDA			40,000			
50		Number of shares			100,000			
51		Earnings per share			0.300			
52		Market value of shares			600,000			
53		Enterprise value			582,000			
54		EV/EBITDA			14.550			
55								

In section B, there is the market and earnings information used in the model. Since all the options need this information, the inputs have been kept together and there is also some initial calculation of earnings per share and the enterprise value. The enterprise value is the addition of the market values of debt and equity.

The market value is simply the price per share multiplied by the number of shares. The number of shares is derived from the share capital divided by the nominal value per share. The total market value and the price per share are the benchmarks against which to compare the calculated values for the company.

2. ADJUSTED ACCOUNTING VALUE

Annual accounts pose important problems for valuation purposes and may not provide a fair market value for these reasons:

- differing accounting standards, conventions and standards in different countries and continents;
- differing approaches where certain countries such as Germany allow a more conservative approach to recognizing profits;
- creative accounting and changing accounting methods;
- leasing and other off balance sheet financing instruments;
- inventory accounting methods and write-offs;
- depreciation methods and periods;
- goodwill and merger accounting;
- intangibles such as brands, patents, software or research and development capitalization.

The accounting net worth depends on the above factors and one method is to adjust the accounting values for perceived extra value. For example, property may not have been revalued to take account of increases and therefore the statement of historic value hides the increased worth. The Adjusted_Value sheet provides a template for adjusting values and examining the variances (see Figure 19.3).

The schedule calculates the revised value and value per share and the notes area at the bottom provides a space for recording workings. Criticisms of this method include:

- The method is based on the replacement cost of assets and this divulges no information about the organization's future earning power.
- The method ignores the value of information, non-financial capital and the ability of management to grow the company.

Fig 19.3

Adjusted value.

	A	B	C	D	E	F	G
4							
5		**(A) Valuation: Book Value**			**188,000**		
6							
7		**(B) Adjusted Value**		**Accts Value**	**Value**		**Variance**
8							
9		Market Value		30,000	**35,000**		5,000
10		Replacement Plant		30,000	**27,000**		(3,000)
11		Replacement F&F		5,000	**5,000**		-
12							
13		Licences		3,000	**5,000**		2,000
14		Investment		35,000	**40,000**		5,000
15							
16		Current assets		218,000			-
17		Current Liabilities		125,000			-
18		Adjustments			**(1,000)**		(1,000)
19							
20		Creditors due after more than one year		18,000			-
21		Adjustments			-		-
22							
23		Other Adjustments			-		-
24					-		-
25							
26		**Total adjusted value at Jun-2001**			**196,000**		**8,000**
27		**Value per share**			**1.96**		
28							
29		**Notes**					
30							
31		1. Market value of property					
32		2. Plant adjusted to disposal value					
33							
34							
35							
36							

3. DIVIDENDS

Companies can also be viewed as a stream of dividends and this method values these payments using the Gordon growth model. The formula is:

$$P_1 = \frac{D_1}{E(R_1) - g}$$

D_1 = dividend for next period, i.e. $D_0 * (1 + g)$

$E(R_1)$ = desired return

g = implied growth = cost of equity – dividend yield / (1 + dividend yield)

The model calculates the growth (g) by using the RATE function between the starting dividend of 10.00 and the finishing dividend of 12.50 (see Figure 19.4). The expected growth is the shareholder's expectations over the following periods.

These models are very sensitive to changes in the growth rate and there is a data table together with a button for updating. This copies the input growth variable down into the data table. The chart displays the answer as a single point series and a series of the data table (see Figure 19.5).

Fig 19.4

Dividend model.

	A	B	C	D	E	F	G	H	I
4									
5				Jun-01	Jun-02	Jun-03	Jun-04	Jun-05	Jun-06
6									
7		Historic Dividend		10.00	10.50	11.00	11.50	12.00	12.50
8									
9		Expected Growth %		11.00					Units $000
10									
11		Growth %		4.56		=RATE(5,0,-D7,I7,0)*100			
12									
13		Growth value per share		2.031		=(I7/100)*(1+D11/100)/(D9-(D11/100))			
14									
15		Dividend valuation Growth value * No of shares				203,083			
16		Value per share				2.03			
17									

Fig 19.5

Sensitivity chart.

	A	B	C	D	E	F	G	H	I
18									
19		Sensitivity Table to Growth Rate							
20		Interval Across	1.00					Slope	(38,204)
21			8.00	9.00	10.00	11.00	12.00	13.00	14.00
22		203,083	380,394	294,643	240,441	203,083	175,772	154,936	138,517

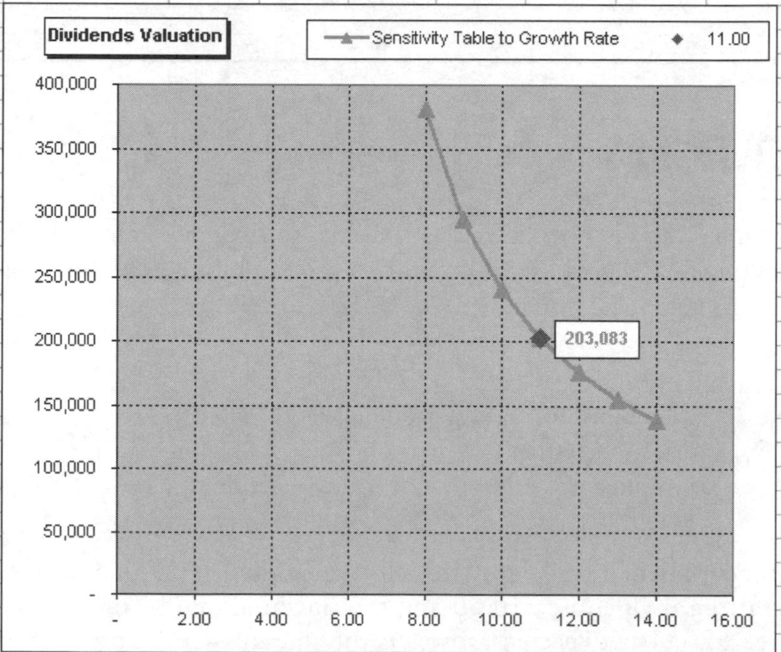

Dividend methods suffer from three important failings:

- Policy on dividends can change, especially on takeover.
- The area of signalling theory states that management often signals its intentions using dividends and prospects. Often a company will retain dividends at a particular level in order to bolster a share price especially if prospects are declining.
- There is no examination of future prospects in terms of earnings or growth.

4. STOCK MARKET

Stock market methods using share prices, earnings per share and price/earnings per share (P/E) ratios overcome some of the disadvantages of accounting or dividend-based methods. They are:

- understood by the market and the analysts and available in the *Financial Times* each day;
- simplistic and easy to calculate on a basic calculator without the need for the time value of money or discounted cash flow calculations.

The model is on a sheet called Market, which uses the share information from the bottom of the Accounts sheet to compute a valuation and P/E ratio (see Figure 19.6).

Market method.

Fig 19.6

	A	B	C	D	E	F	G	H	I
4									
5		**Current market value**							
6		**Current market value**	**Share price * No share**		**600,000**				Units $000
7		**Value per share**			**6.00**				
8									
9		**Current P/E**	**Share price / EPS**		**20.00**				
10									
11		Earnings after tax				30,000			
12		Number of shares	Share capital / Nominal value			100,000			
13		Earnings per share (EPS)	Earnings / No of shares			0.300			
14									
15		Current share price				6.000			
16		P/E Ratio	Share price / Earnings per share			20.000			
17									
18		**Projected Market Value**							
19			**P/E**	**Valuation**	**Per Share**		**Variance to Market**		
20		**Low P/E**	25.00	**750,000**	**7.50**		**150,000**	**25.0%**	
21									
22		**High P/E**	30.00	**900,000**	**9.00**		**300,000**	**50.0%**	
23									

You get the same result if you multiply the share price by the number of shares or, alternatively, if you multiply earnings by the P/E ratio. This model uses a high and low P/E to derive two valuation figures. There is also a data table and chart to demonstrate the variation with progressive P/E ratios (see Figure 19.7).

Fig 19.7 **P/E chart.**

	B	C	D	E	F	G	H	I
25	Sensitivity Table to P/E							
26	Interval Across	2.50						
27		22.50	25.00	27.50	30.00	32.50	35.00	37.50
28	900,000	675,000	750,000	825,000	900,000	975,000	1,050,000	1,125,000

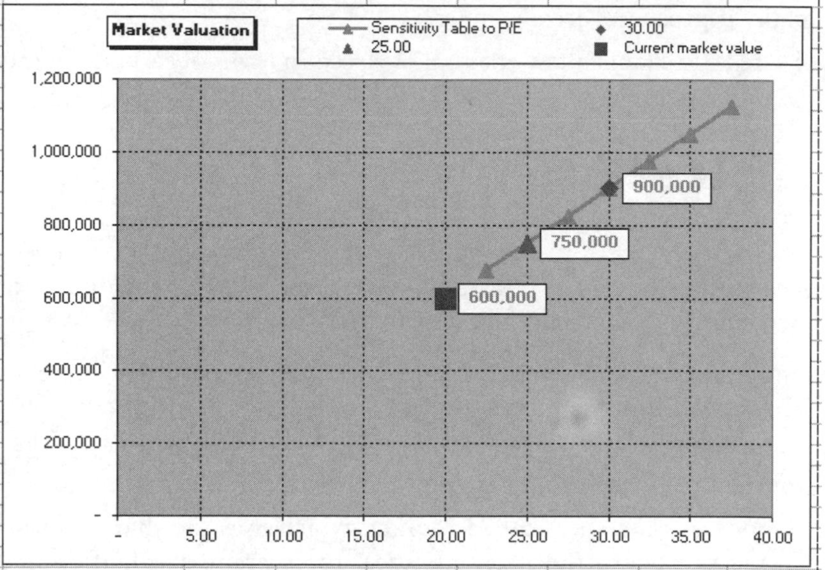

This method also suffers from weaknesses such as the following:

- A high P/E denotes a share with growth prospects, but this is also dependent on market sentiment for the sector and the market.
- The method is not based on time value money concepts or *real* future prospects.
- Companies invest now for returns in future periods and this is not included in the method. One criticism of UK and US stock markets is usually their 'short-termism'.
- A company may issue shares at any time and optimism may overvalue shares and stock market sectors.

5. FREE CASH FLOWS

Free cash flow methods examine closely the company and its potential prospects by computing a net present value of future cash flows. This forces management to focus on real cash flows and prospects rather than accounting information and links with modern theories of enhancing and maximizing shareholder value. The essential idea is that management should be concerned with value management.

This approach is well suited to modelling since you can generate scenarios and 'what-if' analyses to understand better the behaviour and linkages between factors.

The value of the corporation is argued to be the discounted value of its future prospects since cash is the only meaningful measure of investment return that is valid. This solves all the problems of accounting models and creative accounting. Furthermore, the method can be applied to publicly traded and private companies.

Method

The sheet in the Valuation model called Free-Cash_Flows is a template for all the stages of the calculation. The process would normally start with an analysis of the company and its prospects as outlined in the Financial_Analysis model and include over a suitable time horizon:

- examination of the macro environment for the organization;
- analysis of the industry, products and markets;
- forecast of the important drivers such as sales, cost of goods sold, administration expenses, debt and working requirements, etc.

This model uses a shortened route to generate a cash flow and the steps on the template are as follows:

- Forecast operating cash flows and prepare related financial statements.
- Determine a suitable discount rate (cost of capital using a weighted average cost of capital formula).
- Determine a suitable residual value (continuing value using an EV/EBITDA multiple or Gordon growth model).
- Calculate the present value of the two items above at the weighted average cost of capital.
- Add cash and cash equivalents and subtract debt.
- Resulting figure is the equity value.
- Interpret and test results of calculations and assumptions using sensitivity analysis.

The model compares the results to other methods with tables and charts. You could compare the future projections to the historic data using trend lines in order to critically review all assumptions and inputs. Changes can then be made or the complexity of the model increased to include other variables.

Inputs and free cash flow

The inputs are simplified and are retained in a linear relationship to sales. Sales growth is constant in each period and of course you could make the model more complex with more control over each period. There are also inputs for the Capital Asset Pricing Model, cost of debt and the Weighted Average Cost of Capital (WACC) (see Figure 19.8). At the bottom, there is a control to allow a choice on how the terminal value is calculated together with inputs:

- EV/EBITDA multiple;
- perpetuity growth rate.

Fig 19.8

Free cash flow inputs.

	A	B	C	D	E
4					
5		**Sales growth**	15.00%		
6		**Depreciation/NBV of Fixed Assets**	10.00%		
7		**Fixed Assets % of Sales**	20.00%		
8		**Depreciation % of Fixed Assets**	12.00%		
9		**Working Capital % of Sales**	5.00%		
10		**Tax rate**	30.00%		
11		**Cost of Debt**	10.00%		
12		**Risk Free Rate**	5.00%		
13		**Risk Premium**	6.00%		
14		**Share Beta**	1.20		
15		**Forecast Debt/Equity Ratio**	15.00%	Historic ratio 9.6%	
16		**(A) EV/EBITDA multiple**	15.0	Historic ratio 14.6	
17		**(B) Growth Model rate**	1.00%		
18		**Select Terminal Value Method**	(A) EV/EBITDA multiple at 15		
19					
20		**(A) Forecast**			
21			**Jun-01**	**Jun-02**	**Jun-03**
22			0	1	2
23					
24		Forecast operating profit		51,750	59,513
25		Add back depreciation		5,442	6,217
26		**EBITDA**		**57,192**	**65,730**
27					
28		Change in net operating assets		(2,588)	(2,976)
29					
30		**Net Operating Cash Flow**		**54,605**	**62,754**
31					
32		Tax payments		(15,525)	(17,854)
33		Less expenditure on PP&E		(10,350)	(11,903)
34					
35		Other/Adjustments		–	–
36		**Free cash flow**	–	**28,730**	**32,998**
37					

Other data is looked up from the Accounts sheet at the beginning. The result is a free cash flow for each period as the cash available to the enterprise. The calculation is:

Net operating profit
+ Depreciation, amortization and other non-cash items
= Earnings before interest, tax, depreciation and amortization (EBITDA)
– Changes in working capital
= Net operating cash flow
– Capital expenditure (CAPX)
– Tax paid
= Free cash flow available to pay debtholders and shareholders as the owners of the enterprise value.

The reason for using the cash flows available to debt and equity is that the debt/equity ratio can then be amended to analyse the effect of different capital structures. If you derived the equity cash flows directly, you could only review one leverage structure at a time.

Cost of capital

The cost of capital needs to reflect systematic risk and therefore the weighted average cost of capital is calculated (see Figure 19.9). Equity is calculated using the Capital Asset Pricing Model:

$$E(R_1) = R_f + \beta_i[E(R_m) - R_f]$$

$E(R_i)$ = expected return on share i
R_f = risk-free rate
$E(R_m)$ = expected return on the market
β_i = beta of share i.

The beta input is based on a historic debt/equity ratio and therefore the beta is ungeared in cell C41 and then regeared in cell C42. The formulas for unleveraging are:

$$Beta_u = \frac{Beta_l}{1 + (1 - Tax)\left(\frac{Debt}{Equity}\right)}$$

$$Beta_l = \left[1 + (1 - Tax)\left(\frac{Debt}{Equity}\right)\right](Beta_u)$$

The formulas is cells C41 and C42 are:

```
=Share_Beta/(1+(1-Tax_rate)*C39)
=(1+(1-Tax_rate)*Forecast_Debt_Equity_Ratio)*C41
```

The formula for the cost of capital in cell C47 is:

```
=C45*Forecast_Debt_Equity_Ratio+C43*(1-Forecast_Debt
_Equity_Ratio)
```

Fig 19.9

Cost of capital and terminal value.

	A	B	C
37			
38		**(B) Weighted Average Cost of Capital**	
39		Exisitng Debt/Equity Ratio	9.57%
40		Existing WACC	11.70%
41		Unleveraged beta (β)	1.125
42		Releveraged beta based on D/E of 15.0%	1.243
43		Cost of equity using CAPM	12.46%
44			
45		Cost of debt at 10.0% after 30.0% tax	7.00%
46			
47		**WACC**	**11.64%**
48			
49		**(C) Terminal Value**	
50		(A) EV/EBITDA multiple at 15	1,497,817
51		(B) Growth Model rate at 1.0%	475,418
52		Selected	1
53		Terminal Value	1,497,817
54			
55		**Discounted Terminal Value**	**863,777**
56			
57		**(D) PV of Cash Flows at 11.64%**	**136,359**
58			
59		**(E) Enterprise Value (EV)**	
60		**PV + Terminal Value (C+D)**	**1,000,136**
61			
62		**(F) Equity Value**	
63		Enterprise value	1,000,136
64		Debt (Balance sheet)	(18,000)
65		Cash and Deposits	55,000
66		Other adjustments	-
67			
68		**Equity Value**	**1,037,136**
69			

Terminal value

The enterprise must have a value at the end of the forecasting period, which could introduce a range of values from break-up to a going concern. Great care needs to be taken in the method and inputs since the terminal value usually forms more than 50% of the overall computed enterprise value. The choices are in the combo box (see Figure 19.10).

Terminal value choices.

Fig 19.10

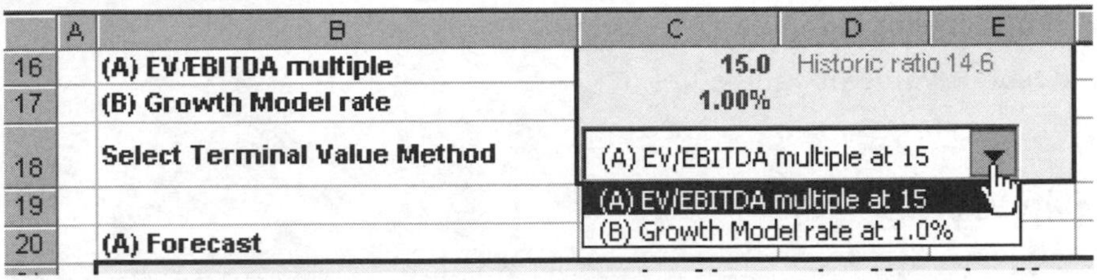

Terminal value in this example is calculated using an EV/EBITA multiple variable from the inputs section. This is simply multiplied by the final EBITA in row 26 as in cell C50:

```
=H26*EV_EBITDA_multiple
```

The Gordon growth model is used to calculate a value in perpetuity. Since this model is sensitive, it is usual to use a nil or low growth figure. This example uses 1% in cell C51 and the revised WACC in cell C47:

```
=(H36*(1+Growth_Model_rate))/(C47-Growth_Model_rate)
```

Present value

The terminal value is discounted back over the five-year period using a PV function as it is a single cash flow in cell C55:

```
=PV(C47,H22,0,-C53,0)
```

The present value of the free cash flows is calculated using the XNPV, which includes inputs for the cash flows and the dates. This is one of the advanced functions in the add-in, Analysis Toolpak.

The present values are added to form the enterprise value which is the sum of the market value of debt and the market value of equity. Adjustments are then made to subtract the debt and add cash and cash equivalents. The result is the equity value as in cell C68 (see Figure 19.11). This process could be summarized as:

- Calculate valuation free cash flows for defined time horizon.
- A = Discount at cost of capital.
- Calculate terminal cash flow by perpetuity model, e.g. [Final Cash Flow * (1 + Growth)] / (Cost of Capital – Growth).
- B = Terminal cash flow discounted at cost of capital.
- Add A + B = Enterprise value.

- Add cash, deposits and marketable securities.
- Subtract debt and minority interests.
- Result = Value of equity.

Fig 19.11 **Equity value.**

	A	B	C	D	E	F
48						
49		**(C) Terminal Value**				
50		(A) EV/EBITDA multiple at 15	1,497,817			
51		(B) Growth Model rate at 1.0%	475,418			
52		Selected	1			
53		Terminal Value	1,497,817			
54						
55		**Discounted Terminal Value**	**863,777**		=PV(C51,H25,0,-C58,0)	
56				**Note:**		
57		**(D) PV of Cash Flows at 11.64%**	**1[illegible]359**	This uses XNPV and therefore the Analysis Toolpak must be installed otherwise you will get an error here		
58						
59		**(E) Enterprise Value (EV)**				
60		**PV + Terminal Value (C+D)**	**1,000,136**			
61						
62		**(F) Equity Value**				
63		Enterprise value	1,000,136		**Number of shares**	
64		Debt (Balance sheet)	(18,000)		**Implied share price (A**	
65		Cash and Deposits	55,000		**Current share price (E**	
66		Other adjustments	-		**Variance (A-B)**	
67					**Market to Book**	
68		**Equity Value**	**1,037,136**			
69						

The above result implies a share price of 10.37 against a current share price of 6.00 with a variance of 4.73. This suggests a premium to the current share price and a large multiple against the accounting net worth of 188,000. The free cash flow method suggests a market to book of 55% and 319% against the current share price. These figures are on the comparison sheet.

This chapter has not included any detail on the analysis required of the company, sector and prospects. However, the next question would be to examine closely the answer and test the result against changes in variables. You need to consider the following:

- Test the result to ensure that all the important drivers been included and are within the correct and achievable bands.
- Is the result in line with market or other expectations of value?
- How does the free cash flow result compare against other methods such as earnings, accounting and dividends.
- There is always uncertainty and risk in the forecast. This needs to be considered in the model and could be factored into the calculations. For example, final cash flows are more uncertain than more recent cash flows.

Sensitivity

The model contains saved scenarios and there is a sensitivity table to demonstrate a range of results (see Figure 19.12). The axes are the sales growth across and the weighted average cost of capital down.

Sensitivity table.

Fig 19.12

	A	B	C	D	E	F	G	H	I
70									
71		(G) Sensitivity Assessment							Units $000
72									
73		Sales Growth Interval Across	2.00%						
74		WACC Interval Down	1.00%				Slope per 1%		39,244
75		1,037,136	9.0%	11.0%	13.0%	15.0%	17.0%	19.0%	21.0%
76		8.6%	932,712	1,008,028	1,088,738	1,175,132	1,267,511	1,366,186	1,471,479
77		9.6%	894,860	966,876	1,044,047	1,126,649	1,214,970	1,309,307	1,409,967
78		10.6%	858,983	927,874	1,001,691	1,080,702	1,165,179	1,255,407	1,351,681
79		11.6%	824,962	890,890	961,530	1,037,136	1,117,971	1,204,306	1,296,422
80		12.6%	792,683	855,802	923,430	995,809	1,073,190	1,155,834	1,244,008
81		13.6%	762,044	822,498	887,268	956,585	1,030,691	1,109,833	1,194,268
82		14.6%	732,945	790,871	852,928	919,340	990,337	1,066,155	1,147,042

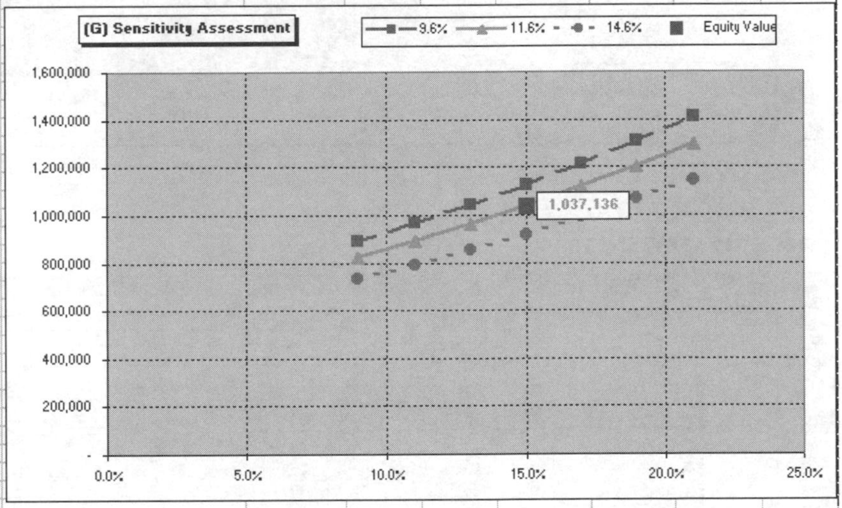

Comparison

The comparison summarizes the results from each of the methods with both actual and per share values (see Figure 19.13). The market to book is also calculated as the price per share divided by the accounting value per share of 1.88.

Another way of viewing the values is on a per share basis and reviewing the variances against current market value as a benchmark (see Figure 19.14).

Fig 19.13

Comparison chart.

	Equity Valuation	Per Share	Variance	%	Market to Book
Accounts Net Worth	188,000	1.88	(4.12)	(68.7%)	100.0%
Adjusted Accounting Value	196,000	1.96	(4.04)	(67.3%)	104.3%
P/E Valuation at a P/E of 30.0	900,000	9.00	3.00	50.0%	478.7%
Dividend Growth Model	203,083	2.03	(3.97)	(66.2%)	108.0%
Free Cash Flow Valuation	1,037,136	10.37	4.37	72.9%	551.7%
Current Market Value	600,000	6.00	-	-	319.1%

Units $000

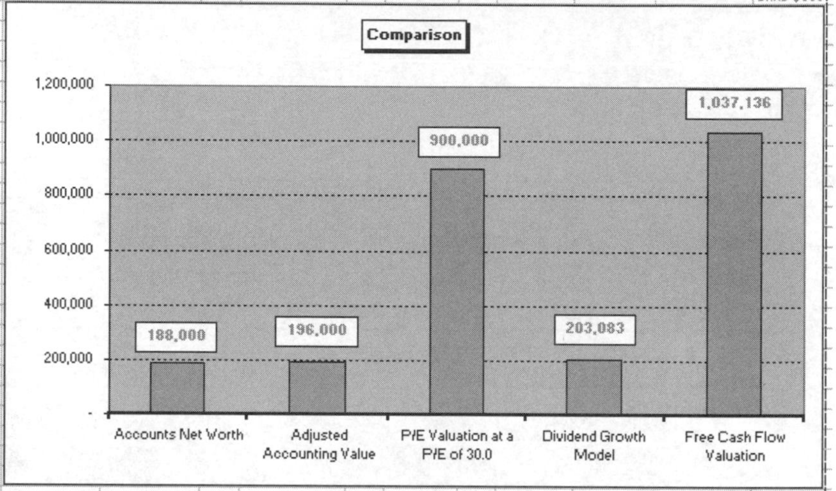

Fig 19.14

Share price comparison.

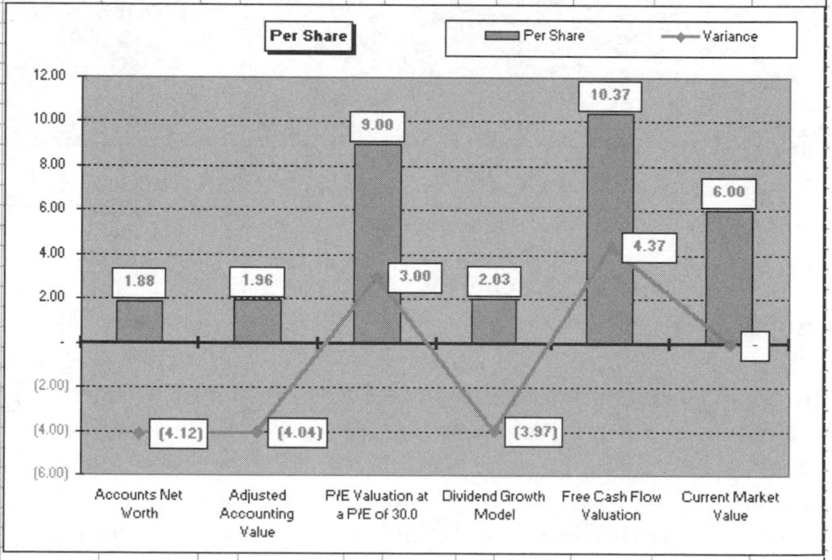

6. SUMMARY

The Valuation model uses a modular approach and includes several methods of valuing companies, concentrating on the free cash flow method. This method encompasses forecasting, growth prospects and the results that a corporation could achieve over a defined time horizon. Using the shareholder value approach, finance concentrates on market values and modelling provides a workable framework for examining all the variables and testing the assumptions. Valuations can then be reviewed by purpose whether it is for a trade sale or a takeover.

20

Optimization

Solver has been used in this book to search for answers to problems by solving the inputs needed to produce a particular answer. This chapter introduces a number of examples of optimization and targeting. Excel uses the logic of the model to work backwards and perform 'reverse what-if'. You could of course enter different inputs to a cell and converge yourself on a solution, but Excel is usually faster!

This chapter discusses three models using Solver for optimization. The files are:

- Optimization_LP
- Optimization_Margin
- Optimization_Pensions.

1. ELEMENTS OF OPTIMIZATION MODELS

Many business problems are concerned with allocating resources or finding the 'best' solutions among many possible combinations. First some examples:

- You need to have a minimum level of staffing in a store, but nobody can work more than 40 hours in any given week or more than five consecutive days. The problem is to solve the minimum number of staff needed. Such problems can be resolved with the add-in Solver using advanced mathematics.
- You need to solve the percentage contributions and growth rates on a personal pension to ensure a sufficient final fund to purchase an annuity for retirement. The constraints are the growth rates and the percentages to be allocated to different funds.

- You are manufacturing a number of products, which achieve different margins and need different material and labour inputs. Given that the inputs are a scarce resource in terms of stock or available hours, how many of each product should you produce to achieve the maximum margins?

Each of these problems has many solutions and these are characterized by results which may be at or near the optimum. The techniques in Excel allow you to build models to test numbers of possible scenarios and adjust models to find solutions based on constraints.

The basic version of Solver is shipped with Excel and upgrades are available:

Frontline Systems Inc.
PO Box 4288,
Incline Village, NV 89450, USA
Tel 775-831-0300
Fax 775-831-0314
E-mail info@frontsys.com
Web www.frontsys.com

The basic parameters of optimization models are:

- inputs – as with all models in this book the inputs are clearly marked and are best saved using the Scenario Manager;
- decision variables – the variables which Solver will change in order to produce the desired result in the target cell;
- objective function (target cell) – the quantity you want to maximize, minimize or set at a particular value;
- constraints – the rules that you have to follow. For example, you cannot use more than 100 of Input A since there are no more in stock. Alternatively, you cannot bill more hours since you only have ten staff. There is a left side, a relation (≤, = or ≥) and a right-hand side value, for example $A$1 > 24.

The template in Figure 20.1 details the three sections. Here three products require different inputs and produce varied margins. The constraint is that the total used must be less than or equal to the constraints in column I. The model therefore maximizes the objective function while remaining within the constraints.

Some constraints such as people can only be whole numbers and this specifies that the solution value for A1 must be an integer or whole number such as –1, 0 or 1 to within a small tolerance. These are called integer constraints. The presence of even one such integer constraint in a Solver model makes the problem an integer programming problem, which may be much more difficult to solve than the equivalent problem without the integer constraint.

Fig 20.1 **Template.**

	A	B	C	D	E	F	G	H	I
4									
5		**(A) Decision Variables**							
6		**Decision Variable Names**	**Prod 1**	**Prod 2**	**Prod 3**				
7		**Decision Variables**	122.5	62.5	2.5				
8									
9		**(B) Objective Function (Target Cell)**							
10		**Product Values**	20	25	30				
11									
12		**Objective Function**	4087.5						
13									
14		**(C) Constraints**							
15		**Constraint names**					**LHS**	**Operator**	**RHS**
16		Input 1	1	4	1		375	<=	500
17		Input 2	0	4	0		250	<=	250
18		Input 3	2	0	2		250	<=	250
19		Input 4	0	1	2		67.5	<=	125
20		Input 5	0	1	1		65	<=	65

There are two types of solution, feasible and optimal solutions. A solution (values for the decision variables) for which all of the constraints in the Solver model are satisfied is called a feasible solution. The Solver proceeds by first finding a feasible solution, and then seeking to improve upon it, changing the decision variables to move from one feasible solution to another feasible solution until the objective function has reached its maximum or minimum. This is called an optimal solution.

Optimization planning problems fall into different linear and non-linear categories. The latter allow any continuous relationship between the variables whereas linear problems can be expressed mathematically as:

$$\text{MaxMin } Z = C_1X_1 + C_2X_2 + \ldots C_nX_n$$

where

Z = Result cell
X = Different decision with 1 to n possibilities
C = Profit or cost associated with the decision

The constraints are usually unequal, for example,

$$A_{11}X_1 + A_{12}X_2 + \ldots A_{1n}X_n \leq B_1$$

$$A_{21}X_1 + A_{22}X_2 + \ldots A_{2n}X_n \leq B_2$$

The stages in planning these models are as follows:

- Plan the model as areas on a sheet with the inputs together at the top. You need to be clear about the nature of the problem you are trying to solve.
- Write down the objectives – you want a particular result in a cell as a minimum, maximum or desired value – objective function or target cell.

- Decide on the cells that will change – decision variables.
- Plan the constraints and the values as minimum, integer or other values. These are the rules that the model must abide by when searching for an acceptable solution. It is usually a good idea to progressively layer on constraints rather than constraining the model too much. If Solver cannot find a feasible solution, it will post an error message.

When you run the model, Solver will produce management reports on the answer, sensitivity and limits to provide you with an audit trail. It is always useful to save your work as separate scenarios so that you have a record for the future.

2. LINEAR PROGRAMMING

The model shown in Figure 20.2 solves the maximum contribution by varying the product mix of five products, which each carry different contribution margins. This is in the file, Optimization_LP.

The manual inputs to Solver (see Table 20.1) are shown in Figure 20.3.

Fig 20.2

Linear programming model.

	A	B	C	D	E	F	G	H	I
6		(A) Linear Model							
7		Input A	500.0		Results				
8		Input B	250.0		Maximum Contribution		35,833.33		
9		Input C	750.0						
10		Units	Hours						
11									
12		Products	1	2	3	4	5		Sum
13		Contribution	250.0	500.0	750.0	1,000.0	1,250.0		3,750.0
14		Input A Hours	10.0	10.0	15.0	15.0	15.0		65.0
15		Input B Hours	-	10.0	5.0	-	15.0		30.0
16		Input C Hours	10.0	-	10.0	25.0	25.0		70.0
17									
18		Calculated Productic	-	5.0	-	16.7	13.3		35
19									
20		Production Plan							
21			1	2	3	4	5	Total	Slack
22		Contribution	-	2,500	-	16,667	16,667	35,833	
23		Input A Hours	-	50	-	250	200	500	-
24		Input B Hours	-	50	-	-	200	250	-
25		Input C Hours	-	-	-	417	333	750	-

Table 20.1

Model section	Reference
Decision variables	The level of production in cells C18 to G18.
Objective function (target cell)	H22 – multiplies the production in row 18 by the margins in row 13.
Constraints	The maximum number of hours are inputs in cells C7 to C9. The totals in cells H23 to H25 must be less than or equal to the maximum.

Fig 20.3 **Solver.**

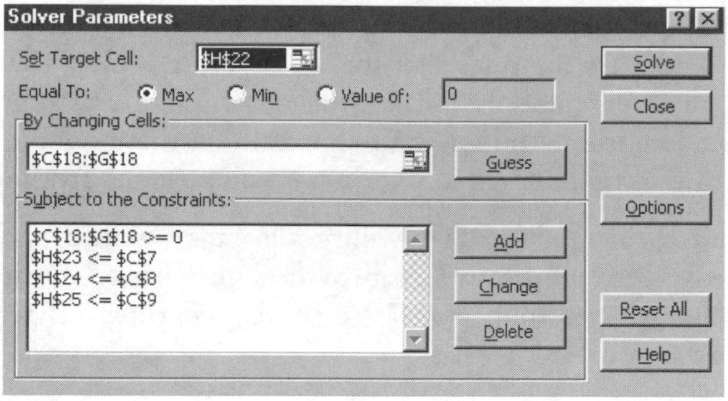

Solver finds an answer of 35,833 and this is saved as a scenario called Base Case. There is no slack and all the hours are allocated. The reports are saved on a separate sheet:

- Answer – shows the objective function (target cell), decision variables (adjustable cells) and the constraints. Binding constraints have zero slack and are used in full.
- Sensitivity – shows how sensitive the solution is to small changes in the formula in the target cell or the constraints. The reduced gradient is the amount by which a cost input must be reduced for the associated decision variable to find a solution. The Lagrange multiplier or shadow price shows the effect of changing the value by one. Non-binding constraints have a zero shadow price.
- Limits – lists the target cell and the adjustable cells with their respective values, lower and upper limits, and target values. The lower limit is the smallest value that the adjustable cell can take while holding all other adjustable cells fixed and still satisfying the constraints. The upper limit is the greatest value.

The code for Solver is assigned to the Solver button and this resets the model and adds the parameters before invoking Solver.

```
SolverReset
SolverOptions precision:=0.001
SolverOk SetCell:="$H$22", MaxMinVal:=1, ValueOf:="0",
ByChange:="$C$18:$G$18"

SolverAdd CellRef:="$C$18:$G$18", Relation:=3, FormulaText
:="0"
SolverAdd CellRef:="$H$23", Relation:=1, FormulaText:="$C$7"
SolverAdd CellRef:="$H$24", Relation:=1, FormulaText:="$C$8"
SolverAdd CellRef:="$H$25", Relation:=1, FormulaText:="$C$9"

SolverSolve userFinish:=True
```

The code at the bottom of the model sheet uses a Dual Model approach which values each resource, and the objective is to maximize contribution while minimizing resources. Since there are three products, the equation is:

Value each resource and minimize $500x + 250y + 750z$

The problem is to ensure that contributions for each unit of production are met from the resources available. In the example, there are three inputs and five possible products with different contributions (see Figure 20.4).

Fig 20.4

Dual model.

	A	B	C	D	E	F	G	H	I	J
26										
27		(B) Dual Model								
28										
29		Value each resource and minimise 500x + 250y + 750z								
30										
31		Input A Hours (x)	33.33	Binding		Results				
32		Input B Hours (y)	16.67	Binding		Maximum Contribut		35,833		
33		Input C Hours (z)	20.00	Binding						
34										
35		Input A Hours	333	333	500	500	500		2,167	
36		Input B Hours	-	167	83	-	250		500	
37		Input C Hours	200	-	200	500	500		1,400	
38										
39		Total	533	500	783	1,000	1,250		4,067	
40										
41		Imputed Cover / (Cos	(283)	-	(33)	-	-			
42										
43		Make: Yes or No	No	Yes	No	Yes	Yes			
44										
45		Input A Hours * x	-	10	-	15	15		500	
46		Input B Hours * y	-	10	-	-	15		250	
47		Input C Hours * z	-	-	-	25	25		750	1,500
48										
49		Dual Model Productic	-	5.00	-	16.67	13.33		35.00	
50										
51		Total	-	100	-	667	733		1,500	
52										
53		Notes								
54		Linear model: value resources to give a minimum overall valuation to the factory compatible with optimum production.								
55										
56		Need values for each resource (500x + 250y + 750z) and obtain production pattern. Contribution must be 'covered' by a valu								
57										
58		No production if there is a negative imputed cover								
59										

The first section multiplies out the amounts in rows 14 to 16 by the decision variables in cells C31 to C33 (see Table 20.2). The calculation in row 41 checks if they are 'covered' and row 43 rejects the products if there are not feasible within the constraints. The next section in rows 45 to 47 includes the required inputs per product if the production is feasible. The production pattern is then solved by two Solver macros B and C (see Tables 20.2 and 20.3).

Table 20.2 Solver macro B

Model section	Reference – Solver_OptionB
Decision variables	C31 to C33 – the value of each of the inputs A, B and C.
Objective function (target cell)	I32 – this is product of the hours and the value of each hour.
Constraints	The hours in row 39 have to be greater than or equal to the input contributions to force the model to be greater than zero.

```
SolverReset
SolverAdd CellRef:="$C$39", Relation:=3, FormulaText
:="$C$13"
SolverAdd CellRef:="$D$39", Relation:=3, FormulaText
:="$D$13"
SolverAdd CellRef:="$E$39", Relation:=3, FormulaText
:="$E$13"
SolverAdd CellRef:="$F$39", Relation:=3, FormulaText
:="$F$13"
SolverAdd CellRef:="$G$39", Relation:=3, FormulaText
:="$G$13"
SolverAdd CellRef:="$C$31:$C$33", Relation:=3, FormulaText
:="0"

SolverOk SetCell:="$i$32", MaxMinVal:=2, ValueOf:="0",
ByChange:="$C$31:$C$33"
SolverSolve userFinish:=True
```

Table 20.3 Solver macro C

Model section	Reference – Solver_OptionC
Decision variables	C49 to G49 – the dual value production.
Objective function (target cell)	J47 – the total number of calculated hours.
Constraints	Cells I45 to I47 greater than or equal to C7 to C9 as the total number of hours for the input.

```
SolverReset
  SolverAdd CellRef:="$C$49:$G$49", Relation:=3, FormulaText
  :="0"
  SolverAdd CellRef:="$I$45", Relation:=3, FormulaText
  :="$C$7"
```

```
  SolverAdd CellRef:="$I$46", Relation:=3, FormulaText
  :="$C$8"
  SolverAdd CellRef:="$I$47", Relation:=3, FormulaText
  :="$C$9"

  If Range("c31") > 0 Then TargetValue = TargetValue +
  Range ("c7")
  If Range("c32") > 0 Then TargetValue = TargetValue +
  Range ("c8")
  If Range("c33") > 0 Then TargetValue = TargetValue +
  Range ("c9")

  SolverOk SetCell:="$j$47", MaxMinVal:=3, ValueOf:
=TargetValue, ByChange:= "$C$49:$G$49"
  SolverSolve userFinish:=True
```

The macros are linked and assigned to the button so that the routines A, B and C run automatically. The net result is two methods of solving the production mix problem.

3. MARGIN MAXIMIZATION

A second file called Optimize_Margin demonstrates a different solution. Here, there are two products with varying margins with three inputs. The model parts are given in Table 20.4 and Figure 20.5.

Table 20.4

Model section	Reference – Solver_Option
Decision variables	C6 and D6 are the quantities of each product.
Objective function (target cell)	Maximize the margin in cell C15 (named Total_Profit).
Constraints	There are amounts in stock in cells E10 to E12 and these must remain above zero. The decision variables must be integers.

Fig 20.5

Maximize profit inputs.

	A	B	C	D	E	F	G	H
4								
5			Product A	Product B	Inventory	Used	Possible Inventory	
6		Production Quantity:	75	125				
7		Margin Per Unit:	500	1,000				
8								
9		Materials Requirements:						
10		Input 1:	5	1	500	500	TRUE	-
11		Input 2:	8	2	1,125	850	TRUE	275
12		Input 3:	-	4	500	500	TRUE	-
13								
14								
15		(A) Solver Total Margin	162,500					
16								

The model is resolved by a simple Solver routine assigned to the button to maximize the margin by changing the quantities (see Figure 20.6). The quantities have to be greater than zero and be integers. With integer programming problems, Solver will not produce sensitivity or limits reports.

Fig 20.6 **Solver.**

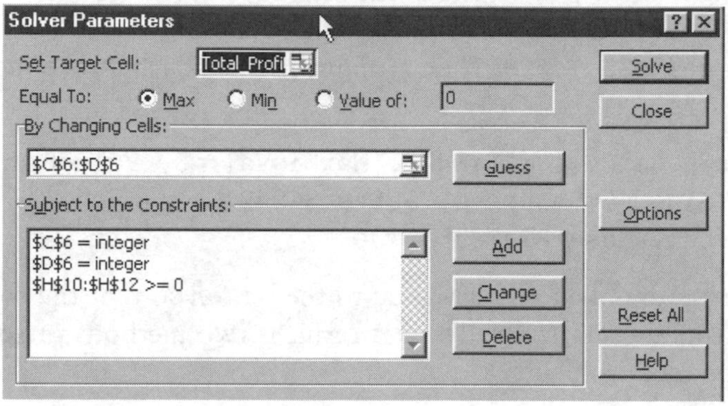

The macro code is:

```
SolverReset
SolverAdd CellRef:=Range("h10:h12"), Relation:=3,
FormulaText:="0"
SolverAdd CellRef:="$C$6", Relation:=4, FormulaText
:="integer"
SolverAdd CellRef:="$D$6", Relation:=4, FormulaText
:="integer"

SolverOk SetCell:="$C$15", MaxMinVal:=1, ValueOf:="0",
ByChange:="$C$6:$D$6"
SolverSolve
```

There is also another solution using a data table to generate combinations of Product A and Product B (see Figure 20.7). Cells G10 to G12 produce the answer TRUE or FALSE using the code:

```
Cell G10: =E10>=F10
```

Using these answers, the formula in the top left of the data table will only display and answer if cells G10 to G12 are TRUE in that the production is possible within the constraints. To save space on the data table the results are divided by 1,000.

```
Cell J9: =IF(AND(G10:G12),Total_Profit/1000,"")
```

Fig 20.7

Data table.

	J	K	L	M	N	O	P	Q	R	S	T	U	V	W	X	Y	Z
5	(B) Data Table Solution																
6	Product A Interval Across					5											
7	Product B Interval Down					5											
8	Data Table: Product A= Across Product B= Down																
9	163	0	5	10	15	20	25	30	35	40	45	50	55	60	65	70	75
10	0	0	3	5	8	10	13	15	18	20	23	25	28	30	33	35	38
11	5	5	8	10	13	15	18	20	23	25	28	30	33	35	38	40	43
12	10	10	13	15	18	20	23	25	28	30	33	35	38	40	43	45	48
13	15	15	18	20	23	25	28	30	33	35	38	40	43	45	48	50	53
14	20	20	23	25	28	30	33	35	38	40	43	45	48	50	53	55	58
15	25	25	28	30	33	35	38	40	43	45	48	50	53	55	58	60	63
16	30	30	33	35	38	40	43	45	48	50	53	55	58	60	63	65	68
17	35	35	38	40	43	45	48	50	53	55	58	60	63	65	68	70	73
18	40	40	43	45	48	50	53	55	58	60	63	65	68	70	73	75	78
19	45	45	48	50	53	55	58	60	63	65	68	70	73	75	78	80	83
20	50	50	53	55	58	60	63	65	68	70	73	75	78	80	83	85	88
21	55	55	58	60	63	65	68	70	73	75	78	80	83	85	88	90	93
22	60	60	63	65	68	70	73	75	78	80	83	85	88	90	93	95	98
23	65	65	68	70	73	75	78	80	83	85	88	90	93	95	98	100	103
24	70	70	73	75	78	80	83	85	88	90	93	95	98	100	103	105	108
25	75	75	78	80	83	85	88	90	93	95	98	100	103	105	108	110	113
26	80	80	83	85	88	90	93	95	98	100	103	105	108	110	113	115	118
27	85	85	88	90	93	95	98	100	103	105	108	110	113	115	118	120	123
28	90	90	93	95	98	100	103	105	108	110	113	115	118	120	123	125	128
29	95	95	98	100	103	105	108	110	113	115	118	120	123	125	128	130	133
30	100	100	103	105	108	110	113	115	118	120	123	125	128	130	133	135	138
31	105	105	108	110	113	115	118	120	123	125	128	130	133	135	138	140	143
32	110	110	113	115	118	120	123	125	128	130	133	135	138	140	143	145	148
33	115	115	118	120	123	125	128	130	133	135	138	140	143	145	148	150	153
34	120	120	123	125	128	130	133	135	138	140	143	145	148	150	153	155	158
35	125	125	128	130	133	135	138	140	143	145	148	150	153	155	158	160	163
36	130																
37	135																
38	140																
39	145																
40	150																
41		-	-	-	-	-	-	-	-	-	-	-	-	-	-	-	26
42																	

Where production is not possible, such as 75 of A and 130 of B in cell Z36, nothing is displayed. This method displays the potential frontier with a grid of possible production.

The next stage is to extract the answer from the table. Cell D18 extracts the maximum value in the table:

```
=MAX(K10:AI40)
```

Next, this value is matched along the row to find B and down the column to find A. This uses a `MATCH` function, for example cell Z41:

```
=IF(ISERROR(MATCH($D$18,Z10:Z40,0)),0,MATCH($D$18,Z10
:Z40,0))
```

To ensure no error messages, the IF statement and `ISERROR` function suppress errors to zero. This formula finds the maximum value of 163. Cell AJ41 adds the row and subtracts one to produce the result 25.

```
=SUM(K41:AI41)-1
```

Since the interval for A is entered in cell O6 as 5, the answer for quantity B must be 25 * 5, which equals 125. The same procedure is repeated for quantity A and the result is 75. The total contribution is multiplied out to form a check on the answer in cell

```
=IF(C24<>Total_Profit,"ERROR: Contributions do not match","")
```

The quantities of A and B are summarized in cells C21 and D21. Figure 20.8 shows the results in chart form.

Fig 20.8 **Production chart.**

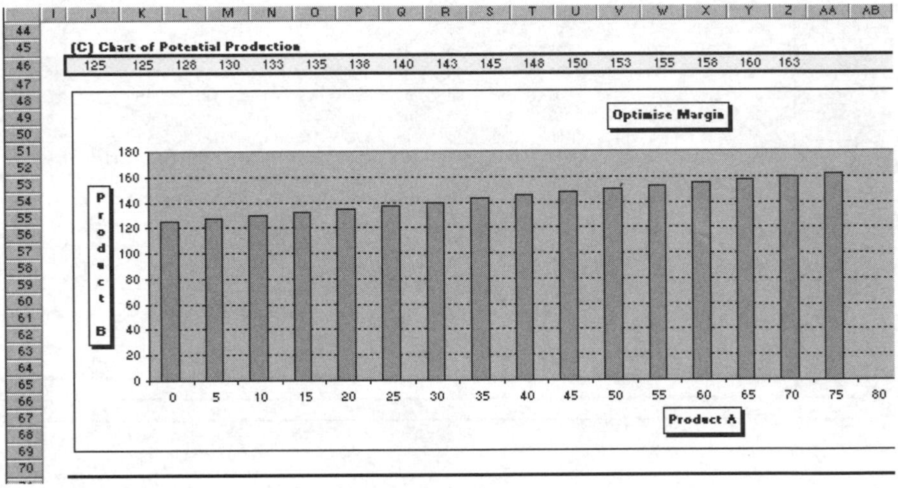

4. PENSIONS

This model is called Optimization_Pension and this demonstrates building a pension fund and purchasing an annuity. This is an alternative optimization model, which does not use linear programming techniques. Instead, there are several ways of growing pension funds and this model targets certain of the variables. This is kept simple without inflation or fees to illustrate the compounding effect and the two major problems with "Money Purchase" personal pensions:

- growth rates during the working period;
- annuity rates at the point of purchase.

The inputs to the model are shown in Figure 20.9.

Fig 20.9

Pensions inputs.

Reference:		Base Case	
Age:		35.0 years	
Retirement Age:		60.0 years	
Current or Starting Income:		50,000	
Contribution Percentage:		17.500%	
Portfolio Segment A:	50.0%	7.000%	
B:	20.0%	6.000%	
C:	10.0%	6.000%	
D:	20.0%	9.000%	
Annuity Rate:	100%	5.000%	
Inflation:		0.000%	
Starting Date:		1-Jan-00	

Results	
Starting Contribution	8,750.00
Portfolio Size	600,583.58
Annual Annuity after 25.0 yr:	30,029.18
Current Salary %	60.058%
Merged Growth Rate	7.100%
Maximum Salary Contributic	17.500%
Percentage Spare	0.000%

Target Annuity by Contribution Percentage

Target Annual Anuity: 30,000

Select Percentage Income or Growth Rate:

Goalseek: Contribution Percentage | Goalseek

Date	Period	Contribution	Adjustment	Total	A	B
1-Jan-00	1	8,750.00	-	8,750.00	4,375.00	1,750.00
1-Jan-01	2	8,750.00	-	8,750.00	4,375.00	1,750.00
1-Jan-02	3	8,750.00	-	8,750.00	4,375.00	1,750.00
1-Jan-03	4	8,750.00	-	8,750.00	4,375.00	1,750.00
1-Jan-04	5	8,750.00	-	8,750.00	4,375.00	1,750.00
1-Jan-05	6	8,750.00	-	8,750.00	4,375.00	1,750.00
1-Jan-06	7	8,750.00	-	8,750.00	4,375.00	1,750.00
1-Jan-07	8	8,750.00	-	8,750.00	4,375.00	1,750.00
1-Jan-08	9	8,750.00	-	8,750.00	4,375.00	1,750.00
1-Jan-09	10	8,750.00	-	8,750.00	4,375.00	1,750.00

The current and retirement ages establish the number of periods and the contribution is a percentage of salary. There is a working table on the right to note the maximum percentages for each age band. The pension is divided into segments with different returns and the management summary on the right displays a merged return rate. The annuity rate is the eventual rate for the pension. The objective is to target an annual annuity by growing the fund in the interim.

In the schedule the contribution is divided between the funds and then future valued with the brought forward fund acting as the present value. The formula in cell K29 is the sum of the future values for columns G to J where the contributions are divided into monthly amounts by dividing by 12.

```
=FV($D$11/12,12,-$G$29/12,0,0)+FV($D$12/12,12,-
H29/12,0,0)+FV($D$13/12,12,-I29/12,0,0)+FV($D$14/12,12,-
J29/12,0,0)
```

The model also allows for one-off contributions or adjustments in any of the years and these are added to the fund. The pull down box, button and assigned macros allow a number of options to achieve the desired annuity:

- contribution percentage – altering the figure up to the maximum allowable in the workings table;

- growth percentage for each fund;
- starting income required;
- retirement age needed to grow a sufficient fund;
- portfolio percentages change the percentages allocated to each portfolio segment.

An IF statement controls which macro runs when you press the button.

```
If Range("d151") = 1 Then
  Application.Run "Goalseek"
ElseIf Range("d151") = 2 Then
  Application.Run "SolverGrowth"
ElseIf Range("d151") = 3 Then
  Application.Run "GoalseekIncome"
ElseIf Range("D151") = 4 Then
  Application.Run "SolverRetirementAge"
  Else
  Application.Run "SolverPortfolio"
End If
```

In each of the macros, the objective is to set cell H9 to the target D21 by changing the variable cells subject to constraints such as the contribution percentage remaining below the government age maximum or remaining above zero. This is the contribution percentage macro:

```
SolverReset
  SolverOptions precision:=0.001
  SolverOk SetCell:=Range("$H$9"), MaxMinVal:=3, ValueOf
:=Range("$d$21"), ByChange:=Range("$D$10")
  SolverAdd CellRef:=Range("$D$10"), Relation:=1,
FormulaText:=Range("$H$14")
  SolverAdd CellRef:=Range("$D$10"), Relation:=3,
  FormulaText:="0"
  SolverOk SetCell:=Range("$H$9"), MaxMinVal:=3,
  ValueOf:=Range("$d$21"), ByChange:=Range("$D$10")
  SolverSolve userFinish:=True
```

The initial case is saved as a scenario called Base Case and there are five further scenarios, one for each of the options in the combo box. There is also a scenario summary as a separate report (see Figure 20.10).

The sensitivity table and fund charts at the bottom show the increases in annuity by increasing the annuity rate or the overall growth rate (see

Fig 20.10

Scenario summary.

Scenario Summary	Current Values:	Base Case	Contribution %	Growth %	Starting Income
Changing Cells:					
Scenario	1	1	2	3	4
Reference:	Base Case	Base Case	Contribution %	Growth %	Starting Income
Age:	35.0 years	35.0 years	35.0 years	35.0 years	35.0 years
Retirement Age:	60.0 years	60.0 years	60.0 years	60.0 years	60.0 years
Current or Starting Income:	50,000	50,000	50,000	50,000	48,951
Contribution Percentage:	17.500%	17.500%	14.569%	17.500%	17.500%
A %	50.0%	50.0%	50.0%	50.0%	50.0%
A Return	7.000%	7.000%	7.000%	10.369%	7.000%
B %	20.0%	20.0%	20.0%	20.0%	20.0%
B Return	6.000%	6.000%	6.000%	4.140%	6.000%
C %	10.0%	10.0%	10.0%	10.0%	10.0%
C Return	6.000%	6.000%	6.000%	2.069%	6.000%
D Return	9.000%	9.000%	9.000%	4.140%	9.000%
Annuity	5.000%	5.000%	5.000%	5.000%	5.000%
Inflation	0.000%	0.000%	0.000%	0.000%	0.000%
Start Date	1-Jan-00	1-Jan-00	1-Jan-00	1-Jan-00	1-Jan-00
Target Annuity	30,000	30,000	30,000	30,000	30,000
Data Table Across	7.0%	7.0%	7.0%	10.4%	7.0%
Data Table Down	5.0%	5.0%	5.0%	5.0%	5.0%
0	17.50%	17.50%	17.50%	17.50%	17.50%
36	20.00%	20.00%	20.00%	20.00%	20.00%
45	25.00%	25.00%	25.00%	25.00%	25.00%
51	30.00%	30.00%	30.00%	30.00%	30.00%
56	35.00%	35.00%	35.00%	35.00%	35.00%
61	40.00%	40.00%	40.00%	40.00%	40.00%
Result Cells:					
Starting Contribution	8,750.00	8,750.00	7,284.58	8,750.00	8,741.50
Portfolio Size	600,583.58	600,583.58	499,999.98	600,000.00	600,000.00
Annual Annuity after 25.0 yrs	30,029.18	30,029.18	25,000.00	30,000.00	30,000.00
Current Salary %	60.058%	60.058%	50.000%	60.000%	60.058%
Merged Growth Rate	7.100%	7.100%	7.100%	7.048%	7.100%

Notes: Current Values column represents values of changing cells at time Scenario Summary Report was created. Changing cells for each scenario are highlighted in gray.

Figure 20.11). This type of model is sensitive to changes in growth, which is due to compounding effects over a number of years.

Figure 20.11 shows a scatterchart with interconnecting lines. The result is plotted as a single point to show where it fits within the results. The fund size shows the compounding of the fund towards the final value of 600,000 needed to purchase the annuity at 6% (see Figure 20.12).

Fig 20.11

Sensitivity chart.

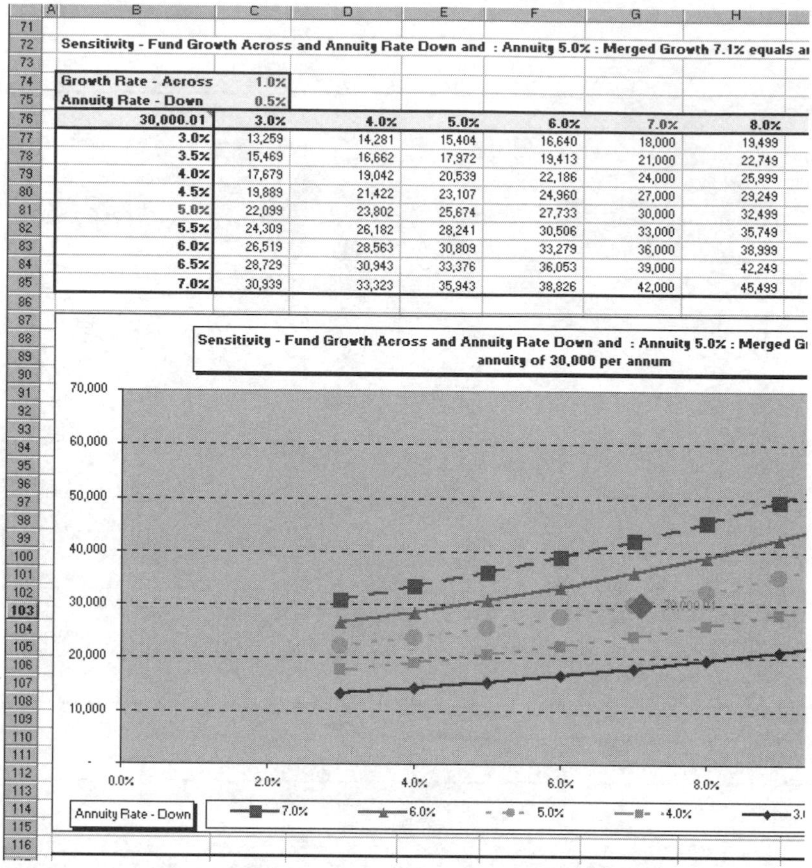

Sensitivity - Fund Growth Across and Annuity Rate Down and : Annuity 5.0% : Merged Growth 7.1% equals a

Growth Rate - Across	1.0%					
Annuity Rate - Down	0.5%					
30,000.01	**3.0%**	**4.0%**	**5.0%**	**6.0%**	**7.0%**	**8.0%**
3.0%	13,259	14,281	15,404	16,640	18,000	19,499
3.5%	15,469	16,662	17,972	19,413	21,000	22,749
4.0%	17,679	19,042	20,539	22,186	24,000	25,999
4.5%	19,889	21,422	23,107	24,960	27,000	29,249
5.0%	22,099	23,802	25,674	27,733	30,000	32,499
5.5%	24,309	26,182	28,241	30,506	33,000	35,749
6.0%	26,519	28,563	30,809	33,279	36,000	38,999
6.5%	28,729	30,943	33,376	36,053	39,000	42,249
7.0%	30,939	33,323	35,943	38,826	42,000	45,499

Fig 20.12

Fund size.

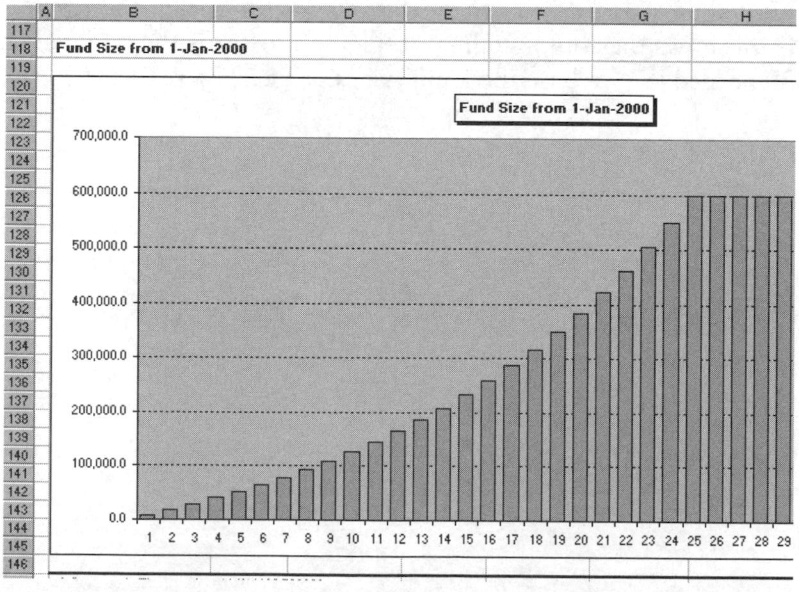

5. SUMMARY

Optimization and targeting are common problems where there are scarce resources and a method is needed to balance the conflicting demands. This chapter has introduced three models using Solver to perform the calculations and target results. The difficulty is often to define the problem and therefore it is often useful to write down the three essential inputs and structure the model accordingly:

- decision variables, which change to produce a target result;
- objective function or target cell;
- constraints – the rules that you have to follow.

21

Decision trees

Chapter 16 added risk techniques to a project model to examine the possible variance or confidence in the answer. Most business alternatives involve an element of risk or uncertainty and one aspect of modelling is to try to quantify risk so that more reasoned judgements can be made. Similarly many decisions involve alternatives and decision trees quantify the gain or cost of following different alternatives by applying probability mathematics as in the file for this chapter, Decisions.

For example, you could be faced with acquiring differently priced and specified computer systems for a particular task but you are not sure of market conditions and which size of installation you will need. You have carried out market research and have estimates for the likely market conditions. The surveys have a given accuracy and so you need to put a monetary value on each option. This is called the expected monetary value.

1. BAYES' THEOREM

Decision trees are based on a fundamental principal of logic known as Bayes' theorem. This principle was discovered in 1761 by the Englishman Thomas Bayes, and brought into its modern form shortly thereafter by the French mathematician Pierre Simon de Laplace.

The theorem is the fundamental mathematical law governing the process of logical inference and determining the degree of confidence in various possible alternatives based on the information available. This is the process of predictive reasoning to arrive at a logically defensible prediction where one uses Bayes' theorem.

Decision trees are used to select the best course of action in situations where you face uncertainty and as stated above many business decisions fall into this category. A decision maker faces an unknown that seems to make it impossible to choose the right option. Although the decision maker does not know what the outcome of the unknown will be, he or she generally has some knowledge about what the possible outcomes are and how likely each is to occur. This information can be used to select the option that is most likely to yield favourable results. Modelling provides the framework to consider the quantitative factors and perhaps assist with assessing the non-monetary factors.

Bayes' theorem states:

P (A|B) * P(B) = P(B|A) * P(A).

This means that the probability of A over B multiplied by the probability of B must be equal to the probability of B over A multiplied by the probability of A. This can be proved in this example:

Probability of A = 0.4 – Value 200
Probability of B = 0.6 – Value 100

The formula is therefore: 0.4 * 0.6 = 0.6 * 0.4

In a business decision, you can place monetary values against the alternatives, and the expected value would be: (0.4 * 200) + (0.6 * 100) = 140. The decision tree works through a problem by using the probabilities and the cost or benefit of an outcome to derive the expected monetary value.

2. TERMINOLOGY

There is some distinct terminology associated with these models.

Probability

Uncertain events have multiple outcomes. A suitable example is rolling a dice or spinning a roulette wheel. In the case of the dice, the probability of returning a value between one and six is from zero to one. As you roll the dice, you could count the instances of particular numbers and build up a histogram of the occurrences of each number. In the short term, a particular number could occur more times, but with more throws of the dice, the occurrences for each number will become more even.

The sum of all probabilities is one and the probability that an even number will not occur is one minus the probability that it will occur. If the outcomes are mutually exclusive, then the probability that either will happen is the sum of the probabilities. If the two events are independent, then the probability that they will both happen is the product of their probabilities.

Expected monetary value

If you could determine precisely what would happen as a result of choosing each option in a decision, making business decisions would be easy. You could simply calculate the value of each competing option and select the one with the highest value. In the real world, decisions are not quite this simple; however, the process of decision making still requires choosing the most valuable option. The most valuable is still in this case the option that has the highest expected monetary value (EMV).

Suppose you are given the option to play a simple game with a coin. You flip the coin and if it comes up tails, you win $50. If it comes up heads, you win nothing. The problem is to determine the value of the game to you.

Each time you flip the coin you have a 50% chance of winning $50 and a 50% chance of winning nothing. If you were to play the game many times, on average you would win $25 for every time you played. Therefore, $25 is the EMV for this game.

These outcomes can be represented by branches and nodes such as in Figure 21.1. This diagram shows that there is an uncertain event with two possible outcomes: win, which has a value of $50, and lose, which has a value of $0. Furthermore, there is a 50% chance of each outcome. Finally, the EMV of this event is $25. This simple diagram describes the two possible states. There is another state where you choose not to play and the EMV here must be $0.

Fig 21.1 **Decision node.**

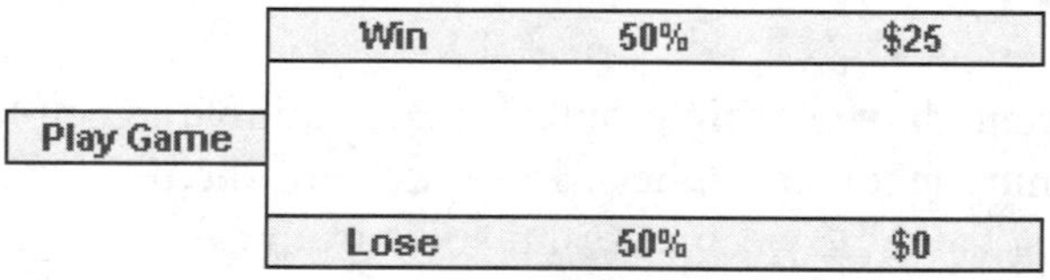

There are three nodes in this tree (play game, win and lose). Play game is the root node while win and lose are the end, or outcome, nodes. The value shown under each node is the expected value of reaching that point in the tree. Before playing the game, you are at the play game node and the combined value of all events following this node is $25. Similarly, if you win, you move to the win node with a value of $50.

The EMV is calculated by multiplying each outcome value by its probability and adding all of the results together:

EMV = $50 * 0.50 + $0 * 0.50 = $25

Utility

Implicit in the decision tree above is that $50,000 is 50,000 times as valuable as $1. Given that individuals usually have limited resources, you would spend the first dollar on the item that provides the greatest value for money. The next dollar would be spent on the next most valuable and so on. The result is that every dollar has slightly less value than the previous dollar.

Organizations often face the same decreasing value of money and it usually has available a limited number of projects in which to invest. The projects with the highest returns get the first dollars. The second best projects get the next dollars. Also, a company's cost of capital (the interest rate paid for money) shows this same non-linear relationship. A company will raise money from the least expensive sources first.

To compensate for this effect, we need to replace monetary outcome values with another measure, which is often called utility. This is a measure of the usefulness of an outcome such as the $50 in the last example.

Information

It is often possible to improve probabilities by purchasing additional information or conducting research. Decision trees allow you to include the real-world fact of imperfect information and learn from previous events. This is similar to the options approach in Chapter 16 where information has a value and can assist in changing the probabilities. For example, the likelihood of high demand is 60% with a probability of 0.4; however, research at a cost of $20,000 could narrow the odds to a probability of 0.6 with accuracy of 90%.

3. DECISION TREE MODEL

The model for this chapter is called Decisions and there are two scenarios. This section discusses the first scenario where the purchase of computer systems is being examined.

The inputs to this model set out the costs and probabilities (see Figure 21.2). An organization is considering installing three different computer systems and their scenario analysis based on differing market conditions has produced net present values. For example, the large system net present value is 150 under high demand and –20 with poor market conditions. The initial probability of high market conditions is 0.4.

Fig 21.2

Computer decision tree inputs.

	A	B	C	D	E
6		Reference		Example 1 -	Computer
7		Probability		High	Low
8		Large System	$000	150.00	(20.00)
9		Medium		100.00	20.00
10		Small		50.00	20.00
11		Probability - High		0.40	
12		Probability - Low			0.60
13		Cost of Market Research		(5.00)	
14		Favourable	High	0.90	
15		Unfavourable	High	0.10	
16		Unfavourable	Low		0.80
17		Favourable	Low		0.20

Market research carried out at a cost of 5,000 yields more information. There are two outcomes from the research, favourable and unfavourable, and the possible states are therefore:

1. Favourable information | high demand = 0.90
2. Unfavourable information | high demand = 0.10
3. Favourable information | low demand = 0.20
4. Unfavourable information | low demand = 0.80

The inputs are in blue and calculated cells in red. The probabilities have to add up to one, and therefore the second stage is calculated to avoid errors. The model has to calculate two types of probability:

- indicative branch such as the probability of favourable or unfavourable market conditions;
- state probabilities such as the probability of high demand and favourable market conditions.

The calculations are shown in Figure 21.3.

Branch calculations.

Fig 21.3

	A	B	C	D	E	F	G	H
19		**Indicative Branch Probabilities**						
20		**First Probabilities**						
21		Probability(Favourable)		Prob_F	=Prob_FH * Prob_H +Prob_FL * Prob_L			0.48
22		Probability(Unfavourable)		Prob_U	=Prob_UH * Prob_H +Prob_UL * Prob_L			0.52
23		**Second Probabilities**						
24		Favourable | High		Prob_FH	=Prob_FH * Prob_H / Prob_F			0.75
25		Favourable | Low		Prob_FL	=Prob_FL * Prob_L / Prob_F			0.25
26		Unfavourable | High		Prob_UH	=Prob_UH * Prob_H / Prob_U			0.08
27		Unfavourable | Low		Prob_UL	=Prob_UL * Prob_L / Prob_U			0.92

These probabilities can then be placed in the decision tree and the possible states for each of the three systems multiplied out (see Figure 21.4). To make the model more understandable, some cells have been named and the labels update themselves following the blue label names in the inputs section. The names are:

```
Prob_F  =Model!$H$21
Prob_FH =Model!$D$14
Prob_FL =Model!$E$17
Prob_H  =Model!$D$11
Prob_L  =Model!$E$12
Prob_U  =Model!$H$22
Prob_UH =Model!$D$15
Prob_UL =Model!$E$16
```

This is the formula in cell E21 using the function LEFT to find the leftmost character of the label:

```
="=Prob_"&LEFT($B$14,1)&LEFT($D$7,1)&" *Prob_"&LEFT($D$7,1)&
"+Prob_"&LEFT($B$14,1)&LEFT($E$7,1)&" * Prob_"&LEFT($E$7,1)
```

There are three possible outcomes:

- No action and the worst case, which is the minimum of the systems. In this case –20 for the large system under adverse market conditions.
- First probability by multiplying out the expected value calculated as the weighted average of the three systems and the positive (0.4) and adverse market conditions (0.6).
- Second probability with the expenditure of $5,000 on additional information with the extra states for favourable and unfavourable reports. There are two blocks for positive and negative reports and the values are transferred to the probability of favourable and unfavourable reports calculated as 0.48 and 0.52. The value transferred is the maximum of the large, medium and small systems from each branch using the function MAX. This is the formula in cell I53:

```
=IF(H57=0,MAX(H48:H53),IF(H53=0,H49,MAX(H49:H57)))
```

Fig 21.4

Decision tree.

	A	B	C	D	E	F	G	H	I	J	K	L
1												
2				Income	Exp	Net Income	Second Prob	Result	Select Max	First Prob	Result	Select Max
3												
4		(1) Worst Case										(20.00)
5												
6		(2) Probability A - before Cost of Market Research										
7			High	150.00	-	150.00				0.40		
8		Large									48.00	
9			Low	(20.00)	-	(20.00)				0.60		
10												
11			High	100.00	-	100.00				0.40		
12		Medium									52.00	52.00
13			Low	20.00	-	20.00				0.60		
14												
15			High	50.00	-	50.00				0.40		
16		Small									32.00	
17			Low	20.00	-	20.00				0.60		
18												
19		(3) Probability B - after Cost of Market Research										
20		(A) Favourable										
21			High	150.00	(5.00)	145.00	0.75					
22		Large						102.50				
23			Low	(20.00)	(5.00)	(25.00)	0.25					
24												
25			High	100.00	(5.00)	95.00	0.75					
26		Medium						75.00	102.50	0.48	49.20	
27			Low	20.00	(5.00)	15.00	0.25					
28												
29			High	50.00	(5.00)	45.00	0.75					
30		Small						37.50				
31			Low	20.00	(5.00)	15.00	0.25					
32												60.20
33		(B) Unfavourable										
34			High	150.00	(5.00)	145.00	0.08					
35		Large						(11.92)				
36			Low	(20.00)	(5.00)	(25.00)	0.92					
37												
38			High	100.00	(5.00)	95.00	0.08					
39		Medium						21.15	21.15	0.52	11.00	
40			Low	20.00	(5.00)	15.00	0.92					
41												
42			High	50.00	(5.00)	45.00	0.08					
43		Small						17.31				
44			Low	20.00	(5.00)	15.00	0.92					
45												

The results show the improvement with more information from the worst case of –20 (see Figure 21.5). The next stage is to conduct sensitivity analysis on the results.

Fig 21.5

Results.

	F	G	H	I	J	K	L	M
6		Management Summary						
7		(1) Worst Case					(20.00)	
8		(2) Probability A - before Cost of Market Research					52.00	
9		(3) Probability B - after Cost of Market Research					60.20	
10		Variance to Worst Case					80.20	
11		Percentage Variance					401.0%	
12		Cost of Market Research					(5.00)	
13		Variance to First Probability					8.20	
14		Percentage Variance					15.8%	
15								
16		Bayes Theorum = P(A|B) * P(B) = P(B|A) * P(A)						
17								

The first sensitivity table plots the probability of Favourable | High – across against Unfavourable | Low – down (see Figure 21.6). The answer is picked out with conditional formatting and there is a combo box for selecting a particular series. The chart is a scattergraph with joined data points and the two single-point series are the first and second probabilities.

The second sensitivity table details the expected values of the first probability of high and low demand. For information, the other results are single-point series (see Figure 21.7).

Fig 21.6

Two-dimensional sensitivity table.

Favourable | High - Acros: 0.10
Unfavourable | Low - Down

Favourable | High 0.90 60.20
Unfavourable | Low 0.80

Units $000

60.20	0.00	0.10	0.20	0.30	0.40	0.50	0.60	0.70	0.80	0.90
1.00	47.00	49.00	51.00	53.00	55.00	57.00	59.00	61.00	63.00	65.00
0.90	47.00	47.00	48.60	50.60	52.60	54.60	56.60	58.60	60.60	62.60
0.80	47.80	47.00	47.00	48.20	50.20	52.20	54.20	56.20	58.20	60.20
0.70	50.20	48.20	47.00	47.00	47.80	49.80	51.80	53.80	55.80	57.80
0.60	52.60	50.60	48.60	47.00	47.00	47.40	49.40	51.40	53.40	55.40
0.50	55.00	53.00	51.00	49.00	47.00	47.00	47.00	49.00	51.00	53.00
0.40	57.40	55.40	53.40	51.40	49.40	47.40	47.00	47.00	48.60	50.60
0.30	59.80	57.80	55.80	53.80	51.80	49.80	47.80	47.00	47.00	48.20
0.20	62.20	60.20	58.20	56.20	54.20	52.20	50.20	48.20	47.00	47.00
0.10	64.60	62.60	60.60	58.60	56.60	54.60	52.60	50.60	48.60	47.00

Select Chart: Unfavourable | Low Probability 0.90 — 2

0.90	47.00	47.00	48.60	50.60	52.60	54.60	56.60	58.60	60.60	62.60

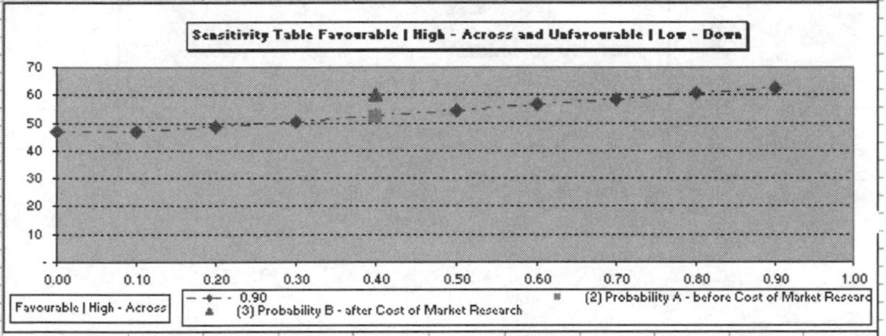

Fig 21.7

Sensitivity table.

Sensitivity Table to Probability - High

	0.00	0.10	0.20	0.30	0.40	0.50	0.60	0.70	0.80	0.90
60.20	15.00	23.00	33.60	46.90	60.20	73.50	86.80	100.10	113.40	128.00

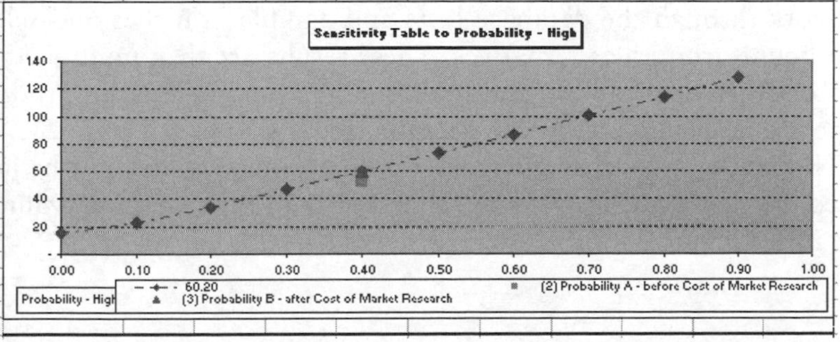

4. INFORMATION EXAMPLE

The second example is saved as scenario two in the Decisions file. The example concerns a company with an information warehouse where there is a 30% chance of the store having major problems. The options are as follows:

- Do nothing and the worst case is minus 450,000.
- Gamble, and if there is a problem the cost is 450,000 and without a problem 300,000.
- Run some tests at a cost of 20,000 where the tests have a 90% probability of accuracy.

The inputs are shown in Figure 21.8.

Fig 21.8 **Information inputs.**

	A	B	C	D	E
6		Reference		Example 2 -	Info
7		Probability		Problem	Clear
8		Database Tests		(400.00)	(400.00)
9		Gamble		(450.00)	(300.00)
10		N/A		-	-
11		Probability - Problem		0.30	
12		Probability - Clear			0.70
13		Cleaning Cost		(20.00)	
14		Reliability	Problem	0.90	
15		Not Reliable	Problem	0.10	
16		Not Reliable	Clear		0.90
17		Reliability	Clear		0.10

There is no third option as in the previous example and therefore the formulas at the nodes disregard a branch if the result is zero. This is the formula at cell I66:

```
=IF(H70=0,MAX(H61:H66),IF(H66=0,H62,MAX(H62:H70)))
```

Probability A multiplies out the options and selects the best case position of minus 345,000. Probability B uses the indicative branch probabilities to work through the database tests and gamble branches and select the maximums from the alternatives. These results are then multiplied by the probabilities of reliability and non-reliability and merged to produce the expected monetary value. The decision tree is shown at Figure 21.9.

The results show that the work on the warehouse may not be justified since the cost with the cleaning is greater than the maximum value without it (see Figure 21.10).

Information decision tree.

Fig 21.9

	A	B	C	D	E	F	G	H	I	J	K	L
47												
48				Income	Exp	Net Income	Second Prob	Result	Select Max	First Prob	Result	Select Max
49												
50		(1) Worst Case										(450.00)
51												
52		(2) Probability A - before Cleaning Cost										
53			Problem	(400.00)	-	(400.00)				0.30		
54		Database Tests									(400.00)	
55			Clear	(400.00)	-	(400.00)				0.70		
56												
57			Problem	(450.00)	-	(450.00)				0.30		
58		Gamble									(345.00)	(345.00)
59			Clear	(300.00)	-	(300.00)				0.70		
60												
61			Problem	-	-	-				0.30		
62		N/A									-	
63			Clear	-	-	-				0.70		
64												
65		(3) Probability B - after Cleaning Cost										
66		(A) Reliability										
67			Problem	(400.00)	(20.00)	(420.00)	0.79					
68		Database Tests						(420.00)				
69			Clear	(400.00)	(20.00)	(420.00)	0.21					
70												
71			Problem	(450.00)	(20.00)	(470.00)	0.79					
72		Gamble						(439.12)	(420.00)	0.34	(142.80)	
73			Clear	(300.00)	(20.00)	(320.00)	0.21					
74												
75			Problem	-	-	-	0.79					
76		N/A						-				
77			Clear	-	-	-	0.21					
78												(358.50)
79		(B) Not Reliable										
80			Problem	(400.00)	(20.00)	(420.00)	0.05					
81		Database Tests						(420.00)				
82			Clear	(400.00)	(20.00)	(420.00)	0.95					
83												
84			Problem	(450.00)	(20.00)	(470.00)	0.05					
85		Gamble						(326.82)	(326.82)	0.66	(215.70)	
86			Clear	(300.00)	(20.00)	(320.00)	0.95					
87												
88			Problem	-	-	-	0.05					
89		N/A						-				
90			Clear	-	-	-	0.95					
91												

Information results.

Fig 21.10

	F	G	H	I	J	K	L	M
6		Management Summary						
7		(1) Worst Case					(450.00)	
8		(2) Probability A - before Cleaning Cost					(345.00)	
9		(3) Probability B - after Cleaning Cost					(358.50)	
10		Variance to Worst Case					91.50	
11		Percentage Variance					20.3%	
12		Cleaning Cost					(20.00)	
13		Variance to First Probability					(13.50)	
14		Percentage Variance					3.9%	

There is also a sensitivity table showing the crossover points when with the cost of information it becomes beneficial to accept probability B (see Figure 21.11). In this instance, it appears that the pivot point is at about zero. The relative position of each option changes as the costs and probabilities are changed.

The results with a 70% possibility of a problem with almost a breakeven position are shown in Figure 21.12.

Fig 21.11

Sensitivity to cost.

Data Table Interv 10.00		Case	1	2	3
		Result	(450.00)	(345.00)	(358.50)
		(50.00)	(450.00)	(345.00)	(388.50)
		(40.00)	(450.00)	(345.00)	(378.50)
		(30.00)	(450.00)	(345.00)	(368.50)
		(20.00)	(450.00)	(345.00)	**(358.50)**
		(10.00)	(450.00)	(345.00)	(348.50)
		-	(450.00)	(345.00)	(338.50)
		10.00	(450.00)	(345.00)	(328.50)

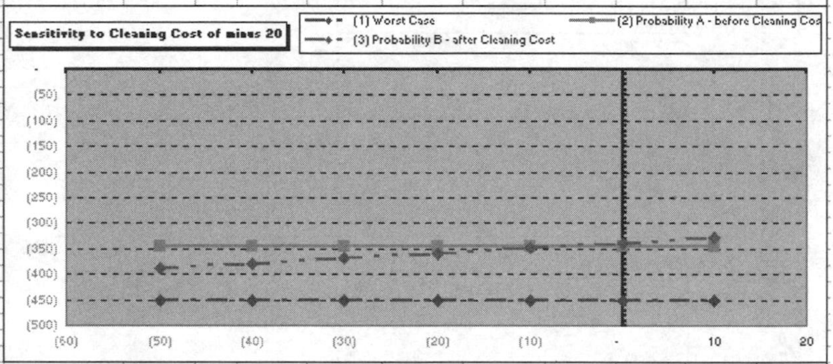

Fig 21.12

Results with 70% probability of a problem.

Management Summary	
(1) Worst Case	(450.00)
(2) Probability A - before Cleaning Cost	(400.00)
(3) Probability B - after Cleaning Cost	(396.50)
Variance to Worst Case	53.50
Percentage Variance	11.9%
Cleaning Cost	(20.00)
Variance to First Probability	3.50
Percentage Variance	-0.9%

5. SUMMARY

Decision trees are useful tools in analysing the costs of distinct alternatives. The model discussed in the chapter contains two examples with the probabilities and branches worked out using Bayes' theorem. The probabilities of different market conditions were estimated and with the cost of new research and an accuracy rate, monetary values were calculated for three different outcomes. In addition, the application includes sensitivity analysis and charts to provide more information on the results.

22

Risk management

Risk management is a wide-ranging subject in business, which encompasses adverse events affecting the organization. While insurance can be used to defer risks such as fire or theft, there are many events for which insurance cannot provide adequate protection. You can split adverse events into two categories:

- risk is where a probability can be ascertained with a degree of certainty from past events;
- uncertainty refers to random events, which in normal circumstances cannot be foreseen.

Most organizations specialize in certain activities and prefer to use risk management products to control adverse future events. For example, an importer may use risk management products for buying forward and thereby fix margins on sales in the domestic market and reduce the volatility of its cash flow. The main business is importing goods and not speculation on future exchange rates. Risk management products are available to control known risks.

This chapter introduces templates for risk management products in a file called Risk_Management for these product areas:

- forward rates
- swaps
- foreign exchange
- futures
- options
- options pricing.

1. FORWARD RATE AGREEMENTS

A forward rate agreement is an off balance sheet instrument to make a settlement in the future. In effect, you agree to pay or receive at a future date the difference between the agreed interest rate and the rate prevailing on the settlement date. This is a bank-based product with no involvement from an exchange or other intermediary. It is calculated based on the notional principal and it allows, for example, an importer to fix a rate for a point in the future.

The variables are:

- start date
- finish maturity date
- contract rate
- market rate
- contract amount.

The formula for calculating the settlement amount is:

$$Settlement\_Amount = \frac{(L - f) * n / Year * Contract\_Amount}{1 + (L * n / Year)}$$

where:

F = forward rate agreement amount
L = interest rate (LIBOR) current at the beginning of the period
N = number of days in the contract period
$Year$ = number of days in year.

In the example shown in Figure 22.1, the company wants to 'lock in' an interest rate of 12.5% for three months' time and requests its bank to write an FRA agreement. On the settlement date, interest rates have fallen to 11.5% and therefore the client makes up the difference on the contract. This is an indication of the cash flows on settlement. Since, the eventual rate is below the contract amount, the client pays the settlement amount. If the rate were above the rate, then the client would receive the difference.

The model is straightforward and includes a data table, conditional formatting and a chart to illustrate the sensitivity (see Figure 22.2). The model is set out in areas, but because of the simplicity, the calculation of settlement is performed in cell G8 by repeating the formula above. The model also decides whether the bank or the client pays the settlement amount.

Fig 22.1

Forward rate agreement.

Settlement Position

		Annual	92 days
Receive (+)	LIBOR under FRA	12.50%	3.15%
	Fixed FRA rate under FRA	-	
	Borrower		
Pay (-)	LIBOR to cash lender	(12.50%)	(3.15%)
	Fixed FRA rate under FRA	(1.00%)	(0.25%)
Net Position		**(1.00%)**	**(0.25%)**

Fig 22.2

FRA model.

Inputs

Start Date	1-Jun-01
Finish Date	1-Sep-01
Contract Rate	12.50%
Market Rate	11.50%
Contract Amount	1,000,000

Management Summary

Days	92 days
Days in current year	365 days
Settlement	(2,449.54)
Payable	Paid by Client
Percentage	(0.24%)
Difference in rates	(1.00%)

Sensitivity to Market Rate

Units $0

Market Rate Interval 1.00%							
	8.50%	9.50%	10.50%	**11.50%**	12.50%	13.50%	14.50%
(2,449.54)	(9,870.72)	(7,384.81)	(4,911.12)	**(2,449.54)**	-	2,437.60	4,863.35
	Client	Client	Client	Client	Bank	Bank	Bank

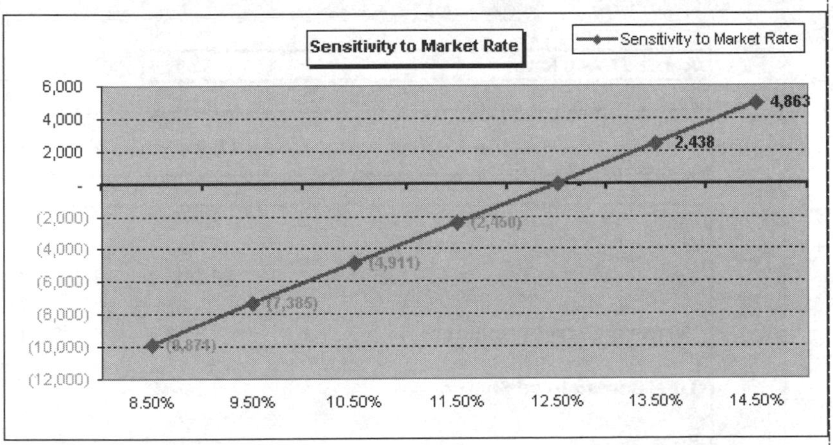

2. SWAPS

A forward rate agreement helps to hedge the cost of borrowing. An alternative could be to fix interest rates using a swap. In essence, a swap is an agreement between two parties to exchange interest rates and can include interest rates and more than one currency. While an FRA allows you to fix specific periods, swaps allow more flexibility over longer periods and can reduce the cost of borrowing for both parties.

As with a forward rate agreement, a swap involves no payment or exchange of principal: only the interest is exchanged. This is netted off rather than transferred gross. The motivation for the swap is a difference in the pricing of interest rates or the desire to fix rates. There are often discrepancies in the pricing of different funding methods or pricing in different geographic markets, which can be shared by setting up a swap arrangement between the parties.

A swap is best illustrated by the scenario Example 1 on the Swap sheet in the file Risk_Management (see Figure 22.3). Company AA can borrow at a fixed rate of 7% or at base plus 2% (7%). Company BB can borrow fixed at 8.75% of variable at base plus 3%. Between the fixed rates, there is a discrepancy of 1.75% and 1% on the variable rate, which could be shared between the parties. Company AA may prefer the floating rate and Company BB the fixed rate. By sharing some of the interest difference, the parties can reduce their cost of borrowing. In the transaction, the bank acts as an intermediary and the contracts are dealt with separately. To understand the cash flows, the model plots the movements between the parties.

Fig 22.3 **Swap inputs.**

	A	B	C	D	E	F
4						
5		Agreed Swap Rate			5.500%	
6						
7					Fixed	Variable
8						
9		AA			7.000%	2.000%
10						
11		BB			8.750%	3.000%
12						
13		Variance on risk premiums			1.750%	1.000%
14						
15		Total Benefit to be Shared			0.750%	
16						
17		Benefit Split			0.250%	0.250%
18						
19		Bank Margin			0.250%	
22						

In this example, there is 0.75% difference between the rates. Figure 22.4 shows the cash flows involved.

Fig 22.4

Cash flows.

	A	B	C	D	E
22					
23		Company: AA			
24		Issues fixed and receives floating			
25					
26		Company AA Pays LIBOR to Bank			-
27		Investors receive Fixed Rate 7.000%			(7.000%)
28		Receives Swap Rate less Margin of 0.25%			5.250%
29		Sum: Total Payable for Floating Rate			(1.750%)
30		Total Gain over Variable at 2.00%			0.250%
31					
32		Company: BB			
33		Issues floating and receives fixed			
34					
35		Bank Pays LIBOR to Company BB			-
36		Investors receive LIBOR + 3.000%			(3.000%)
37		Company BB pays Bank Swap Rate			(5.500%)
38		Sum: Total Payable for Fixed Rate			(8.500%)
39		Total Gain over Fixed at 8.75%			0.250%
40					
41		Total Variance A + B			0.500%
42		Total Bank Gain 0.750% - 0.500%			0.250%

Company AA and Company BB both receive a gain of 0.25% over their variable or fixed amounts. Company AA pays base plus the bank's margin of 0.25% and receives base plus 2%. This is a 1.75% margin to be paid over base. The net position is a 0.25% gain.

Company BB pays the bank the fixed rate of 8.5% which is 0.25% less than the fixed rate of 8.75%. The gain of 0.75% is therefore in this example split evenly between the two companies and the bank. Both borrowers have reduced their net cost of borrowing and the intermediary has also earned a margin.

A further table in the model sets out the flows to each party (see Figure 22.5)

The benefits to each party depend on the differential and overall interest rates and the tables in Figure 22.6 demonstrate the sensitivity to fixed and variable rates for each party. The benefits for AA reduce as fixed rates increase, but increase for BB which wants fixed rates. For BB, the benefits are the same down each column of the data table since fixed rates are required.

Fig 22.5 Tabular cash flows.

Cash Flows (Cash In = Positive, Cash Out = Negative)

	AA	Dealer	BB
Investor receives fixed rate of 7.000%	(7.000%)		
Dealer receives LIBOR + 3.000%			(3.000%)
Bank pays AA swap rate - margin	5.250%	(5.250%)	
BB pays swap rate including margin		5.500%	(5.500%)
AA notionally pays LIBOR	-	-	
Bank notionally pays BB LIBOR		-	-
Total	(1.750%)	0.250%	(8.500%)
Cost without swap (fixed and floating)	2.000%		8.750%
Cost with swap	1.750%	0.250%	(8.500%)
Total Gain to each Party	0.250%	0.250%	0.250%

Fig 22.6 Sensitivity table.

Sensitivity Table AA: Fixed Across and Variable Rate Down

LIBOR - Across	0.250%
AA - Down	0.250%

Units $0

0.25%	6.25%	6.50%	6.75%	7.00%	7.25%	7.50%	7.75%
4.75%	(0.5000%)	(0.5000%)	(0.5000%)	(0.5000%)	(0.5000%)	(0.5000%)	(0.5000%)
5.00%	(0.2500%)	(0.2500%)	(0.2500%)	(0.2500%)	(0.2500%)	(0.2500%)	(0.2500%)
5.25%	-	-	-	-	-	-	-
5.50%	**0.2500%**	**0.2500%**	**0.2500%**	**0.2500%**	**0.2500%**	**0.2500%**	**0.2500%**
5.75%	0.5000%	0.5000%	0.5000%	0.5000%	0.5000%	0.5000%	0.5000%
6.00%	0.7500%	0.7500%	0.7500%	0.7500%	0.7500%	0.7500%	0.7500%
6.25%	1.0000%	1.0000%	1.0000%	1.0000%	1.0000%	1.0000%	1.0000%

Sensitivity Table BB: Fixed Across Variable Rate Down

0.25%	8.00%	8.25%	8.50%	8.75%	9.00%	9.25%	9.50%
4.75%	**0.2500%**	0.5000%	0.7500%	1.0000%	1.2500%	1.5000%	1.7500%
5.00%	-	**0.2500%**	0.5000%	0.7500%	1.0000%	1.2500%	1.5000%
5.25%	(0.2500%)	-	**0.2500%**	0.5000%	0.7500%	1.0000%	1.2500%
5.50%	(0.5000%)	(0.2500%)	-	**0.2500%**	0.5000%	0.7500%	1.0000%
5.75%	(0.7500%)	(0.5000%)	(0.2500%)	-	**0.2500%**	0.5000%	0.7500%
6.00%	(1.0000%)	(0.7500%)	(0.5000%)	(0.2500%)	-	**0.2500%**	0.5000%
6.25%	(1.2500%)	(1.0000%)	(0.7500%)	(0.5000%)	(0.2500%)	-	**0.2500%**

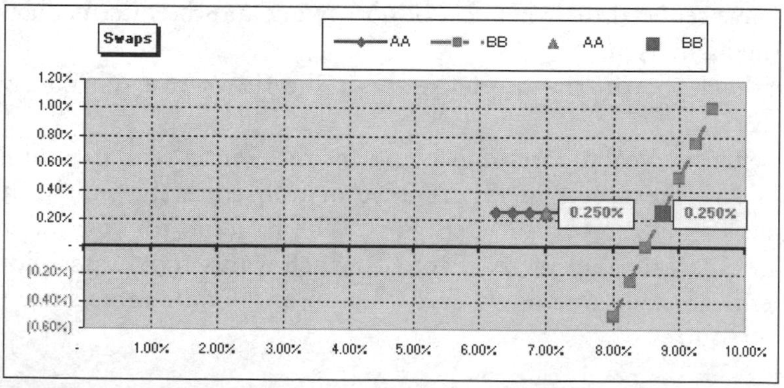

3. FOREIGN EXCHANGE

The application includes a schedule for calculating forward exchange rates. Forward outrights are the purchase or sale of currency for settlement on a fixed date in the future. The future outright rate is a reflection of the spot rate and the interest rates in the two currencies. It holds that there should be interest rate parity since you could:

- buy foreign currency now and place funds on deposit for three months;
- put domestic currency on deposit for three months and then buy foreign currency;
- buy foreign currency forward at the quoted rate.

The theory states that if interest rate parity does not hold, there would be an arbitrage opportunity to move funds into one currency or the other. The formulas for calculating forward rate directly and the difference between the current spot and the forward rate are:

$$Forward\_Outright = \frac{\left(1 + Variable\_Rate^{*}\left(\frac{Days}{Year}\right)\right)}{\left(1 + Base\_Rate^{*}\left(\frac{Days}{Year}\right)\right)}$$

$$Forward\_Margin = \left(\frac{Days^{*}\ Spot^{*}\ (Variable\_Rate - Base\_Rate)}{Year + (Days^{*}\ Base\_Rate)}\right)$$

where:

Base rate	= domestic rate
Variable rate	= foreign rate.

The schedule called FOREX contains these formulas together with a sensitivity table (see Figure 22.7). In the example, the inputs are:

Base currency rate (USD)	3%
Variable currency rate (EUR)	5%
Spot rate (EUR/USD)	1.21
Days	31
Notional days in year	360

The base currency interest rate is higher than the foreign rate and therefore one would expect the forward outright to rise. The outright in cell I7 is:

```
=Spot*((1+Var_Int*(Days/Days_in_Year))/(1+Base_Int*(Days
/Days_in_Year)))
```

The forward margin in cell I8 is:

```
=(Days*Spot*(Var_Int-Base_Int))/(Days_in_Year+
(Days*Base_Int))
```

Fig 22.7 **FOREX.**

Inputs	
Start Date	1-Jun-01
Finish Date	2-Jul-01
Spot Rate	1.2100
Base Currency Rate	3.00%
Variable Currency Rate	5.00%
Contract Amount	1,000,000
Days in Year	360

Management Summary	
Days	31.00
Forward Outright	1.2121
Forward Margin	0.0021
Amount	1,212,079
Percentage Gain/(Loss)	0.17%
Difference in rates	2.00%

Sensitivity Table : 3.00% Across and 5.00% Down

Units $0

Base Currency Rate - Across	1.000%
Variable Currency Rate - Down	0.250%

Slope per 1% change (0.0010)

1.2121	-	1.00%	2.00%	3.00%	4.00%	5.00%	6.00%
4.25%	1.2144	1.2134	1.2123	1.2113	1.2103	1.2092	1.2082
4.50%	1.2147	1.2136	1.2126	1.2116	1.2105	1.2095	1.2084
4.75%	1.2149	1.2139	1.2129	1.2118	1.2108	1.2097	1.2087
5.00%	1.2152	1.2142	1.2131	1.2121	1.2110	1.2100	1.2090
5.25%	1.2155	1.2144	1.2134	1.2123	1.2113	1.2103	1.2092
5.50%	1.2157	1.2147	1.2136	1.2126	1.2116	1.2105	1.2095
5.75%	1.2160	1.2149	1.2139	1.2129	1.2118	1.2108	1.2097

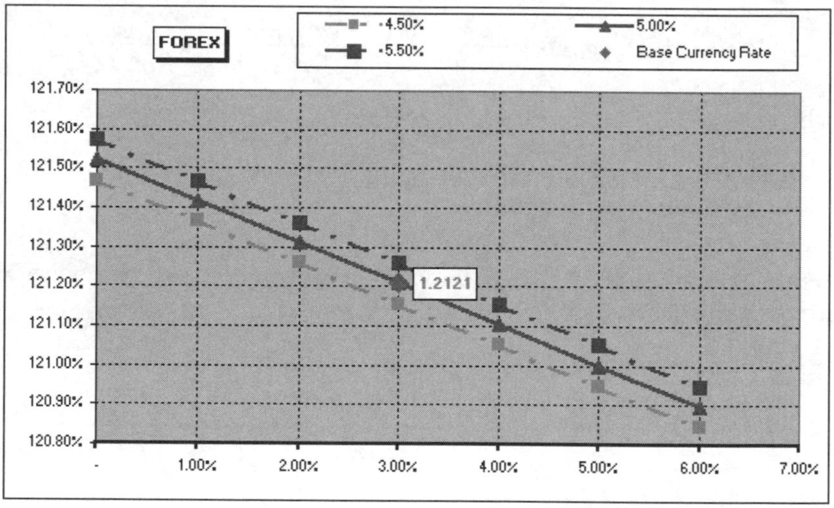

4. FUTURES

Futures allow risk to be managed by fixing future prices for commodities and instruments. Futures differ from forward agreements in two important ways:

- the contracts are standardized in amount and settlement dates;
- settlement is guaranteed by an exchange such as SIMEX in Singapore or CBOT in Chicago.

The contracts are traded on the markets and both parties are protected by the exchange keeping track of the price changes on the contract. The product is not an option and the parties have an obligation to perform and deliver the product on time. Therefore such products are often used for covering base or non-seasonal cash flows, while options are used for contingent or non-seasonal requirements. Since both parties deposit an initial margin, then the variations can be passed on to the two parties. If a party does not pay the balance to bring the account back into credit, then the exchange closes the contract. This is known as marking to market.

The schedule called Futures shows a simple example by using controls to pick data from a table and calculate the profit or loss against the spot rate on the maturity date of the contract (see Figure 22.8). The controls use the workings on the right and the information flows logically down the schedule.

Buying the future at 750 yields a loss since the spot rate in June is 724. Since you have to buy five units, the total loss is 130. Commodities A and F will yield a profit since the spot rate at maturity is greater than the futures rate.

Fig 22.8

Futures.

	A	B	C	D	E	F	G	H
4								
5		Buy = Obligation to buy on expiry						Units $0
6		Sell = Obligation to sell commodity at a fixed price on expiry						
7		Prices are quoted per tonne						
8								
9		**Commodity**	**Contract Size**	**Jan Spot**	**June Future**		**Spot June**	**Spot-Future**
10								
11		A	10	620.00	680.00		790.00	110.00
12		B	5	785.00	750.00		724.00	(26.00)
13		C	50	115.00	125.00		110.00	(15.00)
14		D	100	69.00	75.00		75.00	-
15		E	100	70.00	80.00		70.00	(10.00)
16		F	20	40.00	90.00		102.00	12.00
17								
18								
19		**Select Commodity:**	B					
20								
21		**Quantity:**	5.00					
22								
23		**Buy or Sell:**	Buy					
24								
25		**June Future**	750.00					
26		**Spot June**	724.00					
27								
28		**Profit/(Loss)**	(26.00)					
29								
30		**Total Profit/(Loss)**	(130.00)					
31								
32								

5. OPTIONS

Options are similar to futures in that they allow risk to be traded through exchanges. While options trading existed in the nineteenth century, the key date for modern options trading is 1973 when the Chicago Board of Options Exchange (CBOE) was set up as the first registered exchange for the trading of options. Options use precise definitions:

- *Call*: a call option is a contract giving its owner the right (but not the obligation) to buy at a fixed price at any time on or before a given date.
- *Put*: a put option is a contract giving its owner the right (but not the obligation) to sell at a fixed price at any time on or before a given date.

American options use the above definitions whereas European options can only be exercised on the expiry date. Since you can allow an option to lapse if it is worthless, options are often used for contingent or uncertain cash flows to cover risk. Just as with insurance, the costs increase the closer you come to the forward rates and therefore there is a trade-off between cover and expenses.

The sheet called Option_Payoff demonstrates the workings of an option. The scenario called Example 1 contains the example shown in Figure 22.9. The call option is the right to buy some shares at 5.00 over a period ending in June. The underlying price at the time of writing the contacts is 5.00 and the price of the option is 0.78. This fixes the maximum loss at 0.78 since this is a right and not an obligation to buy. Likewise, the maximum loss on the put options is limited to 0.38. The courses of action are:

- *price rises*: sell the option in the market or exercise the option on expiry;
- *price falls*: allow the option to lapse as it is worthless.

The inputs section checks the pricing of the call and put options since the pricing should equate to call/put parity through this formula:

Spot + Put = Call + Present value of exercise price

The present value is calculated in the model using the basic formula 1 / (1 + Interest rate) using the periodic interest rate entered in the above section. Plotting the payoffs for a call and a put are clearer in Excel and the schedule contains tables and charts (see Figure 22.10).

If the share price were below the strike price of 5.00 plus the cost of the option of 0.78, the table shows losses and the option would not be exercised. The maximum loss is fixed at 0.78. Above 5.78, the profits increase since the price remains at 5.78.

Fig 22.9

Options inputs.

Commodity	Contract Size	Exercise or Strike Price	Total	June Call	June Put	Current Price
Shares	1,000	5.00	5,000.00	0.78	0.38	5.25
Interest Rate for Period	3.00%					

Call (Buy) or Put (Sell):	Call
Cost with Option	5,780.00
Maximum Loss	(780.00)

Put-call Parity Formula	S + P = C + Present Value of Exercise Price	S = Share Price
S + P	5.63	P = Put
C	0.78	C = Call
PV	4.85	
C + PV	5.63	
Error	(0.00)	
Error on Parity	None: S + P = C + Present Value of Exercise Price	

Fig 22.10

Call option table and payoff diagrams.

Interval for Graph and Table	0.20	Cost with option	Adopt	Cost without Option	Profit / (Loss)
Expiry Security Price	4.00	4,780.00	4,780.00	4,000.00	(780.00)
	4.20	4,980.00	4,980.00	4,200.00	(780.00)
	4.40	5,180.00	5,180.00	4,400.00	(780.00)
	4.60	5,380.00	5,380.00	4,600.00	(780.00)
	4.80	5,580.00	5,580.00	4,800.00	(780.00)
	5.00	5,780.00	5,780.00	5,000.00	(780.00)
	5.20	5,980.00	5,780.00	5,200.00	(580.00)
	5.40	6,180.00	5,780.00	5,400.00	(380.00)
	5.60	6,380.00	5,780.00	5,600.00	(180.00)
	5.80	6,580.00	5,780.00	5,800.00	20.00
	6.00	6,780.00	5,780.00	6,000.00	220.00
	6.20	6,980.00	5,780.00	6,200.00	420.00
	6.40	7,180.00	5,780.00	6,400.00	620.00
	6.60	7,380.00	5,780.00	6,600.00	820.00
	6.80	7,580.00	5,780.00	6,800.00	1,020.00
	7.00	7,780.00	5,780.00	7,000.00	1,220.00

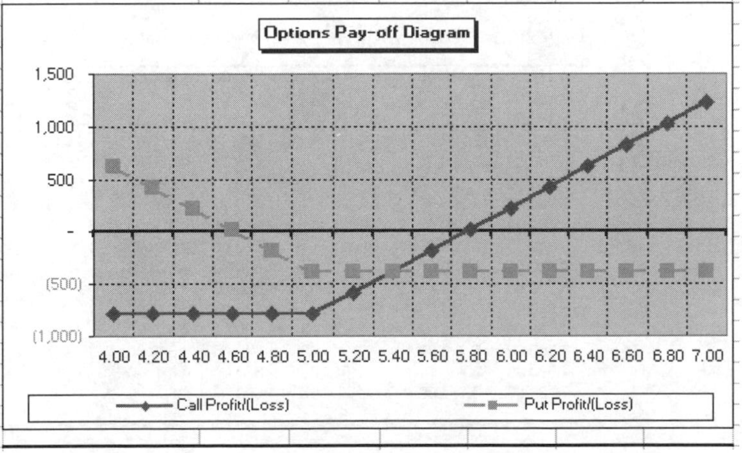

The reverse is true for the put option where the losses increase as the price rises (see Figure 22.11). The breakeven is 5.00 less the price of the option of 0.38.

The chart is driven by the workings area on the right, which calculates both series simultaneously (see Figure 22.12). The code uses simple IF statements to decide whether to adopt the result or not. This means, for example, that the call option will adopt the 5.78 figure.

Fig 22.11 **Put option.**

	A	B	C	D	E	F	G	H
26								
27		**Interval for Graph and Table**	0.20	**Cost with option**	**Adopt**	**Cost without Option**		**Profit / (Loss)**
28		Expiry Security Price	**4.00**	4,620.00	4,620.00	4,000.00		620.00
29			4.20	4,620.00	4,620.00	4,200.00		420.00
30			4.40	4,620.00	4,620.00	4,400.00		220.00
31			4.60	4,620.00	4,620.00	4,600.00		20.00
32			4.80	4,620.00	4,620.00	4,800.00		(180.00)
33			5.00	4,620.00	4,620.00	5,000.00		(380.00)
34			5.20	4,620.00	4,620.00	5,200.00		(380.00)
35			5.40	4,620.00	4,620.00	5,400.00		(380.00)
36			5.60	4,620.00	4,620.00	5,600.00		(380.00)
37			5.80	4,620.00	4,620.00	5,800.00		(380.00)
38			6.00	4,620.00	4,620.00	6,000.00		(380.00)
39			6.20	4,620.00	4,620.00	6,200.00		(380.00)
40			6.40	4,620.00	4,620.00	6,400.00		(380.00)
41			6.60	4,620.00	4,620.00	6,600.00		(380.00)
42			6.80	4,620.00	4,620.00	6,800.00		(380.00)
43			7.00	4,620.00	4,620.00	7,000.00		(380.00)
44								

Fig 22.12 **Workings.**

	L	M	N	O	P	Q	R
20							
21		**Workings**					
22		Call	2				
23		Put					
24							
25							
26		**Workings - Graph**					
27		**Call**	**Adopt**	**Call Profit/(Loss)**	**Put**	**Adopt**	**Put Profit/(Loss)**
28		4,780.00	4,780.00	(780.00)	4,620.00	4,620.00	620.00
29		4,980.00	4,980.00	(780.00)	4,620.00	4,620.00	420.00
30		5,180.00	5,180.00	(780.00)	4,620.00	4,620.00	220.00
31		5,380.00	5,380.00	(780.00)	4,620.00	4,620.00	20.00
32		5,580.00	5,580.00	(780.00)	4,620.00	4,620.00	(180.00)
33		5,780.00	5,780.00	(780.00)	4,620.00	4,620.00	(380.00)
34		5,980.00	5,780.00	(580.00)	4,620.00	4,620.00	(380.00)
35		6,180.00	5,780.00	(380.00)	4,620.00	4,620.00	(380.00)
36		6,380.00	5,780.00	(180.00)	4,620.00	4,620.00	(380.00)
37		6,580.00	5,780.00	20.00	4,620.00	4,620.00	(380.00)
38		6,780.00	5,780.00	220.00	4,620.00	4,620.00	(380.00)
39		6,980.00	5,780.00	420.00	4,620.00	4,620.00	(380.00)
40		7,180.00	5,780.00	620.00	4,620.00	4,620.00	(380.00)
41		7,380.00	5,780.00	820.00	4,620.00	4,620.00	(380.00)
42		7,580.00	5,780.00	1,020.00	4,620.00	4,620.00	(380.00)
43		7,780.00	5,780.00	1,220.00	4,620.00	4,620.00	(380.00)
44							

There are further examples in the application file titled:

- Commodity_Options
- Interest_Options
- Options_Example (with the sheets called Butterfly and Straddle).

Commodity options

Illustrated in Figure 22.13 is a table of prices for call and put options on two commodities. Using controls, it allows you to select a commodity and then an option. The sheet uses OFFSET functions to move down and across the table. For example, this is the code in cell C23. If it is a call, it starts at the top left of the table, moves down based on the strike price (K14) and across one since it is a call (K5).

```
=OFFSET(IF(K9=1,D6,D9),K14,K5)
```

The calculation compares the price against the spot price to derive a profit or loss.

Commodity options.

Fig 22.13

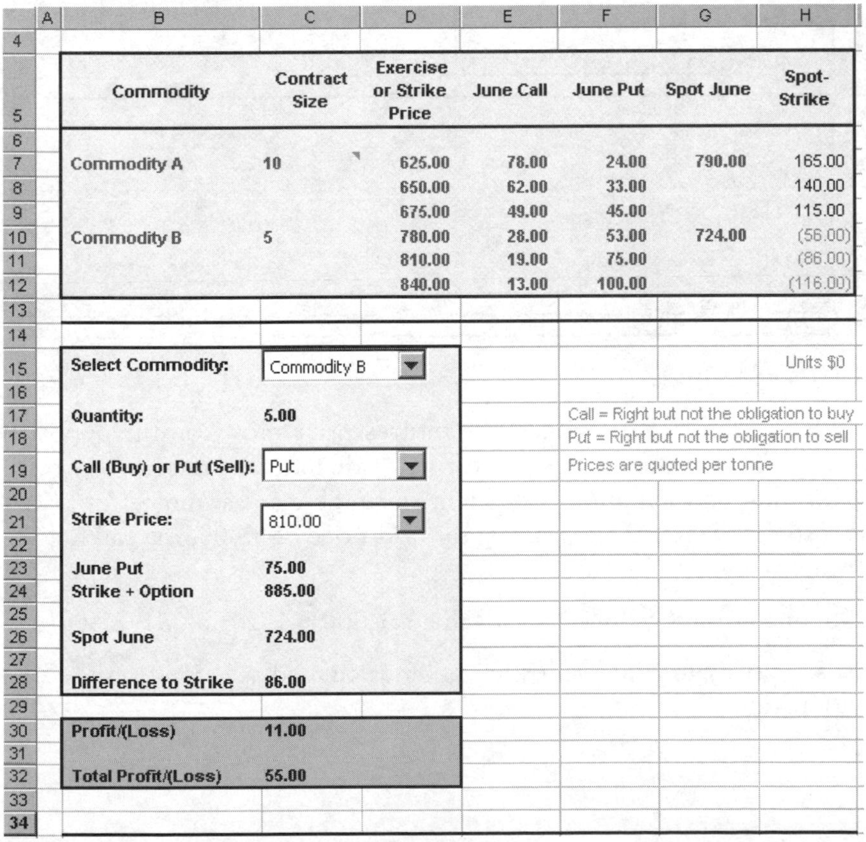

Commodity	Contract Size	Exercise or Strike Price	June Call	June Put	Spot June	Spot-Strike
Commodity A	10	625.00	78.00	24.00	790.00	165.00
		650.00	62.00	33.00		140.00
		675.00	49.00	45.00		115.00
Commodity B	5	780.00	28.00	53.00	724.00	(56.00)
		810.00	19.00	75.00		(86.00)
		840.00	13.00	100.00		(116.00)

Select Commodity:	Commodity B
Quantity:	5.00
Call (Buy) or Put (Sell):	Put
Strike Price:	810.00
June Put	75.00
Strike + Option	885.00
Spot June	724.00
Difference to Strike	86.00
Profit/(Loss)	11.00
Total Profit/(Loss)	55.00

Units $0

Call = Right but not the obligation to buy
Put = Right but not the obligation to sell
Prices are quoted per tonne

Interest options

This example, illustrated in Figure 22.14, contains a schedule of prices together with the call and put premiums. The objective is to calculate the effect of a 1% change in interest rates on the overall gain or loss.

Fig 22.14

Inputs and interest futures.

	B	C	D	E	F	G	H	I
2	Interest Rates			Menu				
3								v1.0 1-Jan-2001
5		Exercise or Strike		Call		Put		
6		9,100.00		360.00		–		
7		9,150.00		245.00		150.00		
8		9,200.00		172.00		204.00		
9		9,250.00		120.00		301.00		
10		9,300.00		76.00		342.00		
12	Current Price	9,215.00						Units $0
14	Contract Amount	1,000						
16	Total Amount	1,000,000			No of Contracts		1000	
18	Frequency	Bi-annual - 6 months			Value of a tick		0.05	
20	Interest Rates Chang	1.00%			100 Ticks			
22	Futures Price Change	(1.00%)			-100 Ticks			
25	(A) Futures Hedge							
27	New Expiry Price	9,115.00			Current Price +/(-) Futures Movement			
29	Profit/(Loss) (A)	(5,000.00)			Futures Movement * No of Contracts * Tick Value			
31	Interest Gain/ (Loss) (B)	5,000.00			Total Amount * Interest Rate * Period			
33	Overall Proft/(Loss)	–		A + B				

As the interest rate changes, the futures price moves in the opposite direction. This is due to the interest loss calculated at the interest rate. The position on the option is different since there are a number of prices and costs (see Figure 22.15). Using the mid-price of 9,200, the call is 172. The gain is:

No. of contracts * Price * Tick value = 1,000 * 172 * 0.05 = 8,600

This is offset by the interest lost of 5,000 calculated as 0.5% over the six-month period.

Options hedge.

Fig 22.15

	A	B	C	D	E	F
35						
36		**(B) Options Hedge**				
37						
38		Implied Interest Rate	7.85%			Formula: 100 - 9215/1000
39						
40		Call (Buy) or Put (Sell):	Call			Call = Right but not the obligation to buy
41						Put = Right but not the obligation to sell commodity
42		Strike Price:	9,200.00			
43						
44		Call	172.00			Look up from above
45						
46		Premium (A)	(8,600.00)			No of Contracts * Price * Tick Value
47						
48		Interest Gain/ (Loss) (B)	5,000.00			Total Amount * Interest Rate * Period
49						
50		Profit on Options (C)	-			
51						
52		**Net Effect**	(3,600.00)		**A + B + C**	
53						

Options example

The Options example sheet together with the schedules called Butterfly and Straddle make up an example of hedging using one or more options to reduce and manage risk. The first sheet contains the main data inputs of the prices together with the call and put premiums (see Figure 22.16).

The control allows you to select a call or a put. This is the code in cell C21, which contains a first IF statement using cell C71 (the result cell from the Call/Put control).

```
=IF($C$71=1,IF($B21>C$18,$B21-C$18-C$19,-C$19),IF($B21<C$18,C$18-$B21-C$19,-C$19))
```

With the call, if the market price is greater than the contract price it calculates a profit, otherwise the loss is the maximum, which is the option price. With a put option, the opposite is true and a margin is available if the market price is below the contract price.

Below the inputs, there is a table showing the results from market prices between 95.00 and 110.00. There are workings for the chart on the right-hand side and column K displays the results from the 'do nothing' alternative. At 103.00, there is no profit or loss; however, below this figure, the losses mount.

The chart plots several of the price lines to illustrate the trade-off on the call option (see Figure 22.17). The losses are limited to the price of the call.

The chart is reversed with a put option where there are gains below the mid price of 103.00 (see Figure 22.18). This method of charting pay-off diagrams makes it easier to understand the profit and losses under different prices.

Fig 22.16

Options example.

	A	B	C	D	E	F	G	H	I
4									
5			(A) Call Options			(B) Put Options			Units $0
6			Strike Price	Premium (points)		Strike Price	Premium (points)		
7									
8		Price less 3	100.00	3.50		100.00	0.60		
9		Price less 2	101.00	2.80		101.00	0.85		
10		Price less 1	102.00	2.15		102.00	1.20		
11		At-the-mone	103.00	1.50		103.00	1.50		
12		Price plus 1	104.00	1.20		104.00	2.20		
13		Price plus 2	105.00	0.85		105.00	2.80		
14		Price plus 3	106.00	0.70		106.00	3.65		
15									
16		Select:	Call						
17		Interval	1.00						
18		Market Price	100.00	101.00	102.00	103.00	104.00	105.00	106.00
19		Call	3.50	2.80	2.15	1.50	1.20	0.85	0.70
20									
21		95.00	(3.50)	(2.80)	(2.15)	(1.50)	(1.20)	(0.85)	(0.70)
22		96.00	(3.50)	(2.80)	(2.15)	(1.50)	(1.20)	(0.85)	(0.70)
23		97.00	(3.50)	(2.80)	(2.15)	(1.50)	(1.20)	(0.85)	(0.70)
24		98.00	(3.50)	(2.80)	(2.15)	(1.50)	(1.20)	(0.85)	(0.70)
25		99.00	(3.50)	(2.80)	(2.15)	(1.50)	(1.20)	(0.85)	(0.70)
26		100.00	(3.50)	(2.80)	(2.15)	(1.50)	(1.20)	(0.85)	(0.70)
27		101.00	(2.50)	(2.80)	(2.15)	(1.50)	(1.20)	(0.85)	(0.70)
28		102.00	(1.50)	(1.80)	(2.15)	(1.50)	(1.20)	(0.85)	(0.70)
29		103.00	(0.50)	(0.80)	(1.15)	(1.50)	(1.20)	(0.85)	(0.70)
30		104.00	0.50	0.20	(0.15)	(0.50)	(1.20)	(0.85)	(0.70)
31		105.00	1.50	1.20	0.85	0.50	(0.20)	(0.85)	(0.70)
32		106.00	2.50	2.20	1.85	1.50	0.80	0.15	(0.70)
33		107.00	3.50	3.20	2.85	2.50	1.80	1.15	0.30
34		108.00	4.50	4.20	3.85	3.50	2.80	2.15	1.30
35		109.00	5.50	5.20	4.85	4.50	3.80	3.15	2.30
36		110.00	6.50	6.20	5.85	5.50	4.80	4.15	3.30
37									

Hedging strategy

The two schedules demonstrate two strategies to use more than one option to reduce overall losses. These are:

- *butterfly* – write two calls at 104.00 and buy a call at 103.00 and one at 105.00;
- *straddle* – buy two calls and buy two puts.

Fig 22.17

Call options chart.

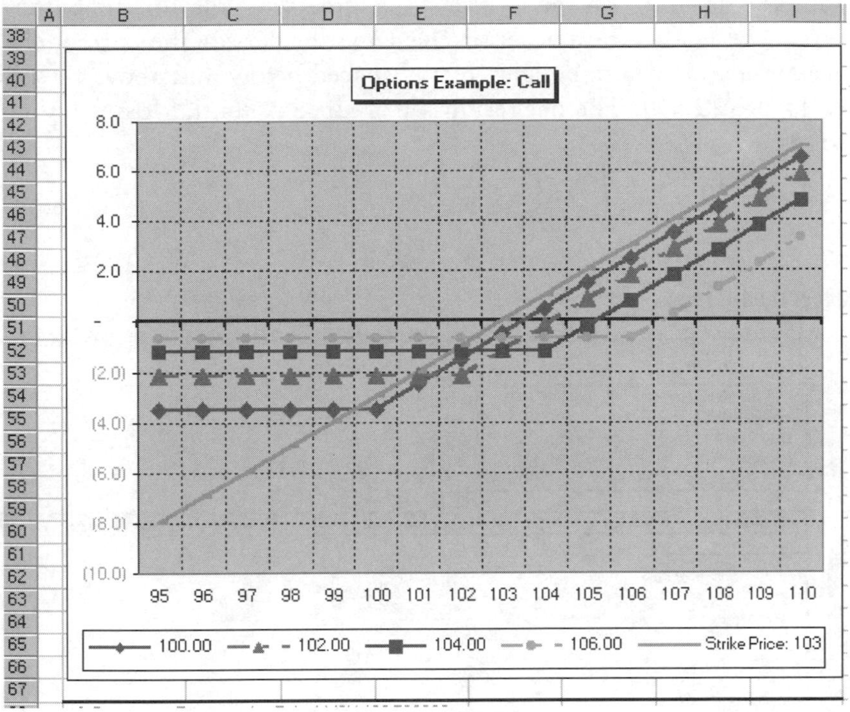

Fig 22.18

Put options chart.

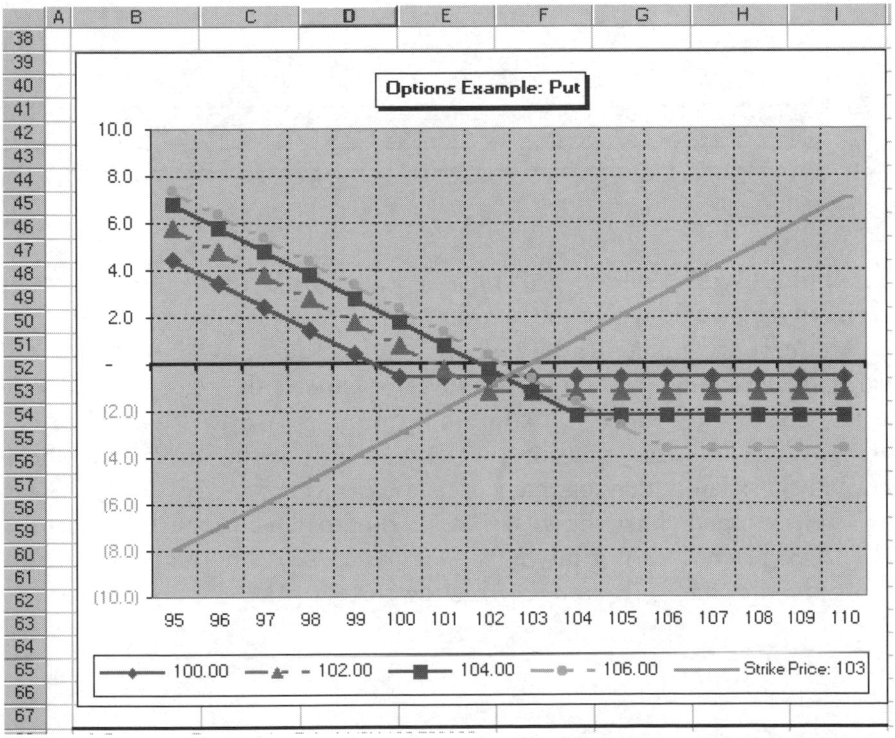

The schedules work through the calculations and the premiums are found by looking up data on the Options_Example schedule for the butterfly strategy, two calls are written on the same share near the current share price and two calls are bought equally spaced below and above the price (see Figure 22.19). The net result is to reduce potential losses on most periods to:

1.20 + 1.20 – 1.50 – 0.85 = 0.05

Fig 22.19

Butterfly options.

	Number	Price	Premium	Units $0
Write Call A	1	104.00	1.20	
Write Call B	1	104.00	1.20	
Buy Call A	1	103.00	1.50	
Buy Call B	1	105.00	0.85	
Interval		1.00		

Market Price	In/Out	Writer	Premium	Net Call	In/Out	Buyer	Premium	Net Put	Overall
95.00	Y	-	2.40	2.40	N	-	(2.35)	(2.35)	0.05
96.00	Y	-	2.40	2.40	N	-	(2.35)	(2.35)	0.05
97.00	Y	-	2.40	2.40	N	-	(2.35)	(2.35)	0.05
98.00	Y	-	2.40	2.40	N	-	(2.35)	(2.35)	0.05
99.00	Y	-	2.40	2.40	N	-	(2.35)	(2.35)	0.05
100.00	Y	-	2.40	2.40	N	-	(2.35)	(2.35)	0.05
101.00	Y	-	2.40	2.40	N	-	(2.35)	(2.35)	0.05
102.00	Y	-	2.40	2.40	N	-	(2.35)	(2.35)	0.05
103.00	Y	-	2.40	2.40	N	-	(2.35)	(2.35)	0.05
104.00	N	-	2.40	2.40	N	1.00	(2.35)	(1.35)	1.05
105.00	N	(2.00)	2.40	0.40	Y	2.00	(2.35)	(0.35)	0.05
106.00	N	(4.00)	2.40	(1.60)	Y	4.00	(2.35)	1.65	0.05
107.00	N	(6.00)	2.40	(3.60)	Y	6.00	(2.35)	3.65	0.05
108.00	N	(8.00)	2.40	(5.60)	Y	8.00	(2.35)	5.65	0.05
109.00	N	(10.00)	2.40	(7.60)	Y	10.00	(2.35)	7.65	0.05
110.00	N	(12.00)	2.40	(9.60)	Y	12.00	(2.35)	9.65	0.05
Average				(0.23)				0.34	0.11
Standard Deviation				3.98				3.95	0.24

The butterfly gives rise to a distinctive graph with a kink in the overall series in the middle where the margin rises to 1.05 (see Figure 22.20).

An alternative is a straddle where a call and put are bought for the same share (see Figure 22.21). The investor expects the price to move one way or the other since the combination gives rise to losses if prices remain the same. Information on the volatility of the underlying share could help to show the possible variance based on historical data.

The combined chart shows the losses due to the cost of the options if the share price does not move (see Figure 22.22). The investor earns a margin if the share price moves from the current price.

Butterfly chart.

Fig 22.20

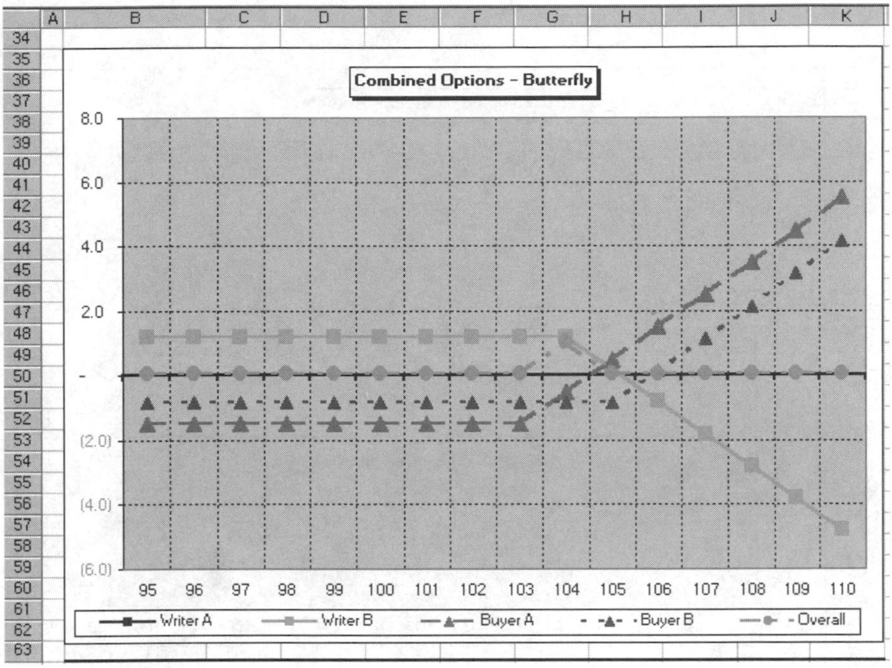

Straddle inputs.

Fig 22.21

	Number	Price	Premium						Units $0
Buy Put A	1	104.00	2.20						
Buy Put B	1	104.00	2.20						
Buy Call A	1	104.00	1.20						
Buy Call B	1	104.00	1.20						
Interval		1.00							
Market Price	**In/Out**	**Put**	**Premium**	**Net Put**	**In/Out**	**Call**	**Premium**	**Net Call**	**Overall**
95.00	Y	18.00	(4.40)	13.60	N	-	(2.40)	(2.40)	11.20
96.00	Y	16.00	(4.40)	11.60	N	-	(2.40)	(2.40)	9.20
97.00	Y	14.00	(4.40)	9.60	N	-	(2.40)	(2.40)	7.20
98.00	Y	12.00	(4.40)	7.60	N	-	(2.40)	(2.40)	5.20
99.00	Y	10.00	(4.40)	5.60	N	-	(2.40)	(2.40)	3.20
100.00	Y	8.00	(4.40)	3.60	N	-	(2.40)	(2.40)	1.20
101.00	Y	6.00	(4.40)	1.60	N	-	(2.40)	(2.40)	(0.80)
102.00	Y	4.00	(4.40)	(0.40)	N	-	(2.40)	(2.40)	(2.80)
103.00	Y	2.00	(4.40)	(2.40)	N	-	(2.40)	(2.40)	(4.80)
104.00	N	-	(4.40)	(4.40)	N	-	(2.40)	(2.40)	(6.80)
105.00	N	-	(4.40)	(4.40)	Y	2.00	(2.40)	(0.40)	(4.80)
106.00	N	-	(4.40)	(4.40)	Y	4.00	(2.40)	1.60	(2.80)
107.00	N	-	(4.40)	(4.40)	Y	6.00	(2.40)	3.60	(0.80)
108.00	N	-	(4.40)	(4.40)	Y	8.00	(2.40)	5.60	1.20
109.00	N	-	(4.40)	(4.40)	Y	10.00	(2.40)	7.60	3.20
110.00	N	-	(4.40)	(4.40)	Y	12.00	(2.40)	9.60	5.20
Average				**1.23**				**0.23**	**1.45**
Standard Deviation				**6.50**				**4.11**	**5.26**

Fig 22.22 **Straddle chart.**

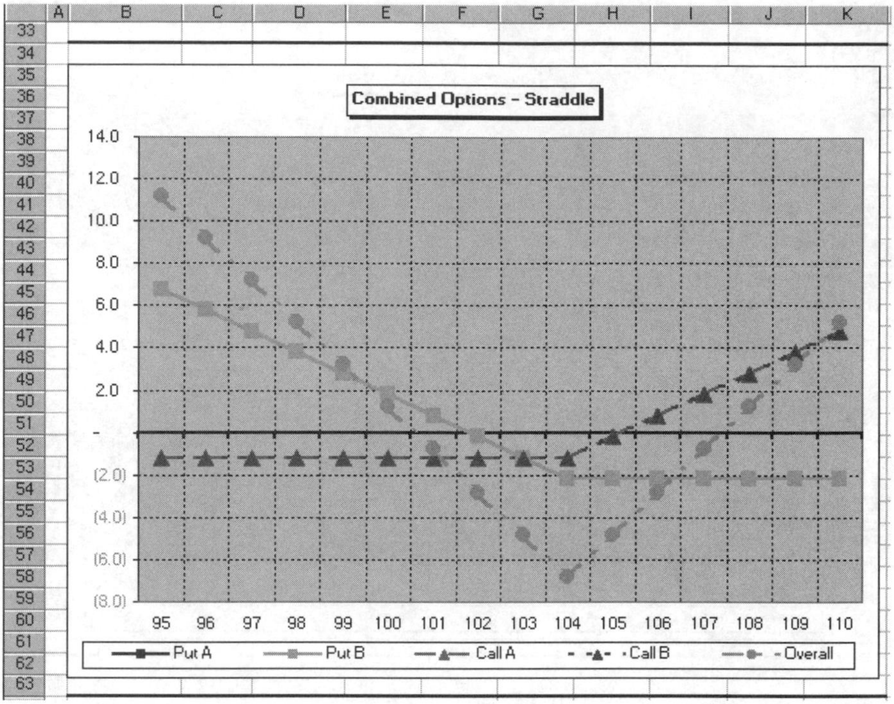

6. BLACK–SCHOLES

The Black–Scholes model for option pricing is on the schedule named Black–Scholes, which uses the approach outlined in their 1973 paper.

Throughout the 1960s the academics developed mathematical models and were convinced that if they could somehow mathematically describe the emotional confidence of the investors they would crack the problem of how to price options. To achieve this end they kept adding more variables, for example for the level of satisfaction, for reasonableness and for aggressiveness. However, the resultant mathematical models failed to price options correctly in the market.

The breakthrough in the Black–Scholes model was to use only observable quantities such as:

- maturity date (T);
- domestic interest rate (Int);
- volatility of the share price as measured by standard deviation (S);
- current stock price (P);
- exercise price (X).

The main assumptions for pricing options using the model are as follows:

- Relative price rises in the future are independent of changes in the current price.
- Interest rates and volatility remain constant during the period. This may not be true since volatility reduces as you near the maturity date.
- The probability distribution of relative price changes is lognormal, which means that there is a smaller probability of significant deviations from the mean.
- There are no transactions costs.

The model in effect prices risk and is based on advanced mathematics. The workings for call and put options are placed at the bottom of the schedule (see Figure 22.23). To make the workings more understandable, the cells have been named as in cells C72 to C76 and this shows how the formula is built up.

Fig 22.23

Black-Scholes workings.

	A	B	C
68		**Definitions and**	
69		Black, F and Schc	
70		May/June, pp 637	
71		Days in current ye	=DATE(YEAR(D5),12,31)-DATE(YEAR(D5)-1,12,31)
72		T	=T
73		r (Int)	=Int
74		S	=S
75		P	=P
76		X	=X
77			
78		**(1) Call Option**	
79		d_1	=(LN(P/X)+(Int+0.5*S^2)*T)/(S*SQRT(T))
80		d_2	=C79-SQRT(T)*S
81		N(d_1)	=NORMSDIST(C79)
82		N(d_2)	=NORMSDIST(C80)
83			
84		Call price	=IF(S<0,0,IF(ISERROR(P*C81-X*EXP(-Int*T)*C82),0,P*C81-X*EXP(-Int*T)*C82))
85			
86		**(2) Put Option**	
87		$-d_1$	=-C79
88		$-d_2$	=-C80
89			
90		N($-d_1$)	=NORMSDIST(C87)
91		N($-d_2$)	=NORMSDIST(C88)
92			
93		Call price	=IF(S<0,0,IF(ISERROR(-(P*C90-X*EXP(-Int*T)*C91)),0,-(P*C90-X*EXP(-Int*T)*C91)))
94			

The schedule includes the variables for this example, which is saved as a scenario called Example 1 (see Figure 22.24). The results from the workings are repeated as a management summary at the top and there are two sensitivity tables, one each for calls and puts. The two axes are the stock price across and the volatility down, and the answers are highlighted by conditional formatting. A macro is linked to the button at the top and this code copies down the share price and volatility to the inputs on each table.

Fig 22.24 **Black–Scholes inputs.**

	A	B	C	D	E	F	G	H	I
4									
5		Start Date		1-Jun-01			Results		
6		Maturity Date		1-Dec-01				Price	% P
7		Days		182 days					
8		Maturity	T	0.499 yrs			Call Price	9.4251	4.28%
9		Interest Rate	Int	8.00%					
10		Volatility	S	12.00%			Put Price	5.6264	2.56%
11		Current Stock Price	P	220.00					
12		Exercise Price	X	225.00					
13									
14		Sensitivity: Call Price							
15		Current Stock Price Across		0.50					Units $0
16		Volatility Down		2.500%					
17								Slope	0.60
18		9.4251	218.50	219.00	219.50	**220.00**	220.50	221.00	221.50
19		4.50%	4.0557	4.3806	4.7186	5.0692	5.4321	5.8065	6.1920
20		7.00%	5.5327	5.8343	6.1448	6.4639	6.7917	7.1277	7.4720
21		9.50%	7.0371	7.3284	7.6262	7.9306	8.2415	8.5588	8.8824
22		**12.00%**	8.5518	8.8376	9.1287	9.4251	9.7266	10.0333	10.3451
23		14.50%	10.0710	10.3539	10.6411	10.9328	11.2287	11.5289	11.8334
24		17.00%	11.5924	11.8737	12.1588	12.4475	12.7400	13.0362	13.3360
25		19.50%	13.1148	13.3954	13.6792	13.9663	14.2566	14.5502	14.8469
26									
27		Sensitivity: Put Price						Slope	(0.40)
28		5.6264	218.50	219.00	219.50	**220.00**	220.50	221.00	221.50
29		4.50%	1.7571	1.5819	1.4199	1.2706	1.1334	1.0078	0.8933
30		7.00%	3.2340	3.0356	2.8461	2.6653	2.4930	2.3291	2.1733
31		9.50%	4.7385	4.5297	4.3275	4.1320	3.9428	3.7601	3.5837
32		**12.00%**	6.2531	6.0389	5.8300	5.6264	5.4279	5.2346	5.0464
33		14.50%	7.7723	7.5552	7.3425	7.1341	6.9300	6.7302	6.5347
34		17.00%	9.2937	9.0750	8.8601	8.6488	8.4413	8.2375	8.0373
35		19.50%	10.8161	10.5967	10.3805	10.1676	9.9579	9.7515	9.5482

The chart at the bottom gives a representation of the two options in the centre of the tables (see Figure 22.25). The selection is linked to a pull-down control and an INDEX function to find the data. This is a scatterchart and the put and call options are plotted as individual series.

There are two important advantages with using the Black–Scholes formula to value the option and this information can be useful in formulating hedging strategies.

- There is no requirement to forecast the price on expiry.
- You can deduct mathematically the price sensitivities since as a call increases:
  - exercise price decreases;
  - time to expiry increases;
  - stock price increases;
  - interest rate increases;
  - volatility increases.

These sensitivities are sometimes known as the 'Greeks' and these formulas are modelled in the workings together with notes on their derivation (see Figure 22.26).

Black-Scholes chart.

Fig 22.25

	A	B	C	D	E	F	G	H	I
37									
38		Select Series	12.00%			4			
39						4.0000			
40		12.00%	8.5518	8.8376	9.1287	9.4251	9.7266	10.0333	10.3451
41		12.00%	6.2531	6.0389	5.8300	5.6264	5.4279	5.2346	5.0464

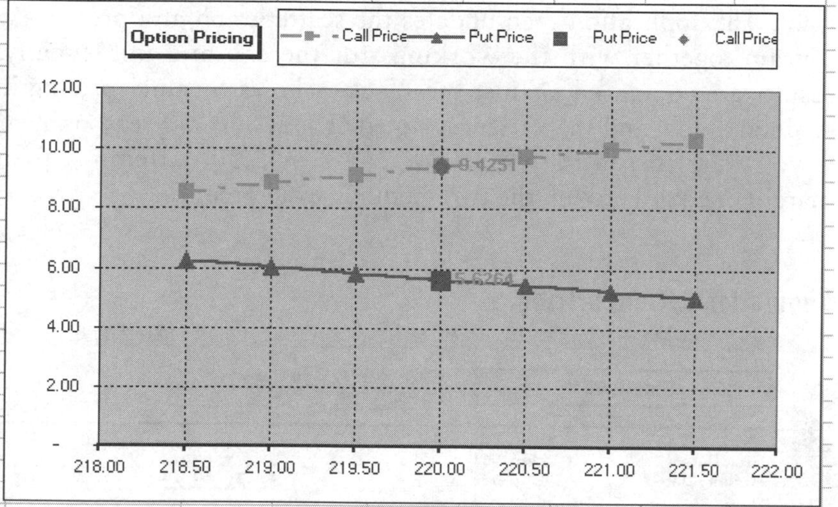

The Greeks.

Fig 22.26

	B	C	D	E–H
103				
104	**(4) Delta**			Change in price when underlying price changes
105	N(d1)		0.5979	
106				
107	**(5) Gamma**			Rate at which delta changes
108	Ln(P/X)		(0.0225)	Gamma highest when option at the money and
109	Adjusted return		0.0363	reduces away from the price
110	Time adjusted volatility		0.0847	
111	d2		0.1632	Writer is always negative gamma
112	N(d2)		0.5648	
113	d1		0.2479	
114	Coefficient		0.3989	
115	(d1^2/2)		0.0307	
116	Exp-(d1^2/2)		0.9697	
117	N'(d1)		0.3869	
118	=N'(d1)/(P*Time_Adj_Volatility)		0.0208	
119				
120	**(6) Theta**			Time decay in an option
121	d1 at 0% Interest		(0.2228)	Minimum when share price equals exercise price
122				
123	Coefficient		0.3989	
124	(d1^2/2)		0.0248	
125	Exp-(d1^2/2)		0.9755	
126	N'(d1)		0.3892	
127	=-P*N'(d1)*S/(2*T^0.5)		(7.2746)	For every 1/100 of a year premium moves by -7.275
128				
129	**(7) Vega**			Sensitivity of an option to a change in volatility
130	=P*T^0.5*N'(d1)		60.4559	Most senstive when at the money
131				

Simulation options pricing

This is an alternative to the Black–Scholes, which although time-consuming will produce a similar result (see Figure 22.27). The Simulation sheet uses the simulation workings from the Project_Model to run 1,000 scenarios. You input a volatility value and variance and the rest of the data is looked up from the Black–Scholes sheet. The volatility is randomized within the variance limits, entered on the Black–Scholes sheet and recalculated. The model recalculates 1,000 times and notes the volatility, call and put results for each scenario. These are then pasted as a table on the right. The application then updates the scattergraph and provides a histogram together with the workings for the call and put. Finally, the results are compared against the Black–Scholes formula pricing in the summary table and the variances noted. The results are reasonably close. If you were to run the model for 2,000 or 3,000 attempts, then the margin of error between the two methods would reduce.

Fig 22.27 **Simulation options pricing.**

Simulation | Menu | Run Simulation | v1.01-Jan-2001

Start Date	1-Jun-01
Maturity Date	1-Dec-01
Days	182 days
Maturity	0.499 yrs
Interest Rate	8.00%
Volatility	20.00%
Current Stock Pric	220.00
Exercise Price	225.00
Volatility	20.00%
Deviation:	4.00%

Simulation
1,000

Prices at a volatility of 20.0% varying by 4.0%

	Black-Scholes	Simulation	Variance
Call Price	14.270	14.183	0.087
% 220.0	6.487%	6.447%	0.040%
Put Price	10.472	10.385	0.087
% 220.0	4.760%	4.720%	0.040%

Quartiles	Call Value	Results	Put Value	Results
0	10.478	1	6.679	1.00
1	13.388	249	9.589	249.00
2	14.164	250	10.365	250.00
3	14.954	250	11.155	250.00
4	17.862	250	14.064	250.00
Total Results		1,000		1,000
Range		7.385		7.385
Mean		14.183		10.385
Median		14.164		10.365
Skew		0.026		0.026
Kurtosis		(0.019)		(0.019)
Standard Deviation		1.210		1.210
Coefficient of Variation		0.085		0.117

The variance between the two is 0.087. The difference will vary each time you re-run the simulation. The results from the table on the right are plotted on the scatterchart and there are two parallel series for the call and the put (see Figure 22.28). The call results show the number and percentage in each of the frequency bins. The simulation macro updates the mid point and you can vary the interval manually.

Simulation results.

Fig 22.28

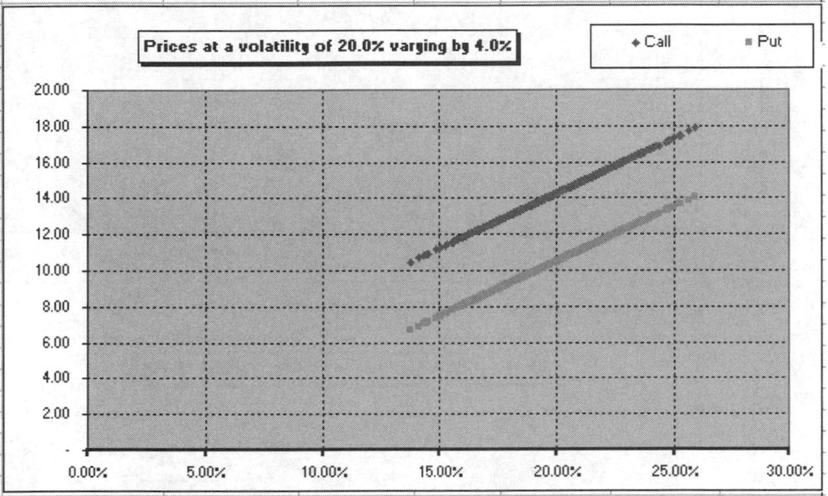

(A) Call: Simulation Frequency Results with an Interval of 0.500

Interval	0.50

Amount	No of Results	Percentage
11.700	19	1.9%
12.200	29	3.0%
12.700	61	6.2%
13.200	98	10.0%
13.700	128	13.1%
14.200	177	18.1%
14.700	162	16.5%
15.200	129	13.2%
15.700	87	8.9%
16.200	57	5.8%
16.700	33	3.4%
	980	100.0%

	Factor	% P
Minimum:	0.0009	4.7627%
Maximum:	0.9984	8.1193%
Mean:	0.4786	6.4469%

Minimum Volatility:	0.1375
Maximum Volatility:	0.2590
Less than zero NPV % of trials:	-
Arithmetic Mean	14.183
Median	14.164
Skew	0.026
Kurtosis	(0.019)
R Squared	1.000
Slope	60.801

The call price is the arithmetic mean in the table on the right. The other statistics of median, skew and kurtosis are also calculated.

The histogram shown in Figure 22.29 provides an illustration of the range of values with the majority of values clustered around the mean. The quartiles chart demonstrates the high and low values and the borders between each 25% band.

Fig 22.29 **Call simulation histogram.**

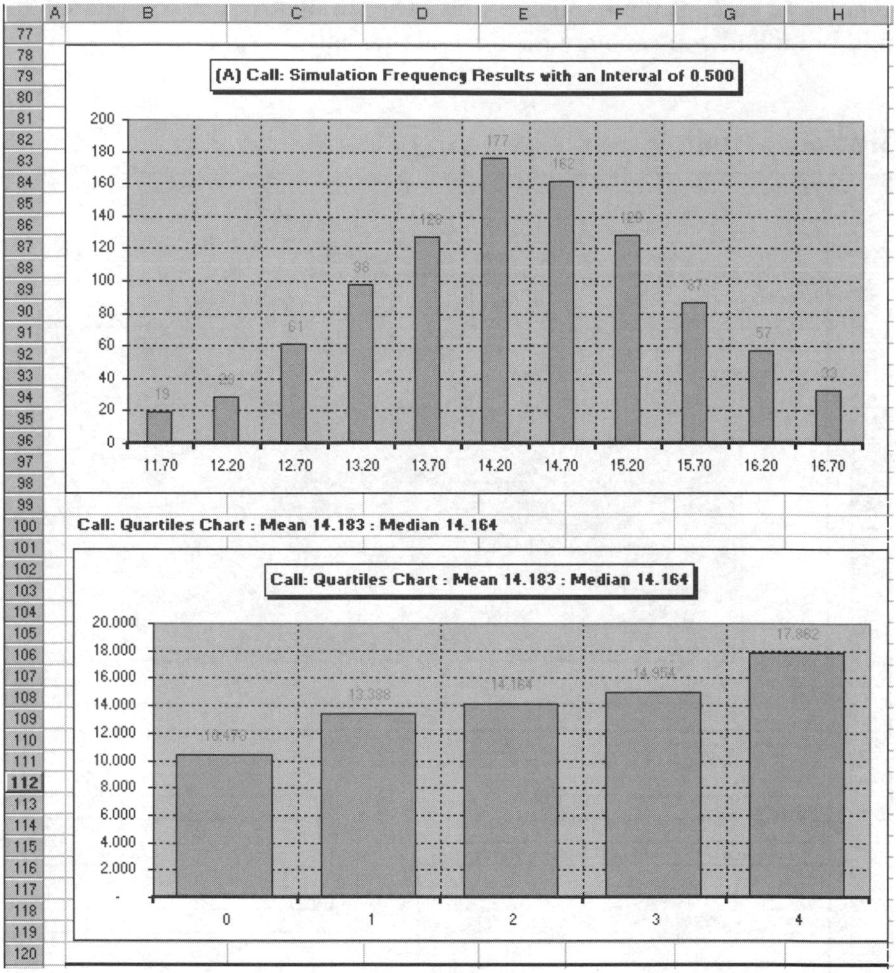

Currency options pricing

The file also contains a variant of the Black–Scholes model developed by Garman and Kohlhagen (1983) for currency options. The layout of the model is the same as the Black–Scholes model and the workings are set out in stages at the bottom. The example uses the inputs shown in Figure 22.30.

Again, the pricing is based on time, volatility, the underlying price and the exercise price. There are now two interest rates for domestic and foreign. Again, there is a button to update the data tables and a chart at the bottom displaying a selected pair of series with single-point answers of the call and put prices (see Figure 22.31).

Fig 22.30

Currency options.

	A	B	C	D	E	F	G	H	I
4									
5		Start Date		1-Jun-01			Results		
6		Maturity Date		16-Aug-01				Price	% P
7		Days		76 days					
8		Maturity	T	0.208 yrs			Call Price	0.0211	1.26%
9		Domestic Int. Rate	Rd	8.00%					
10		Foreign Int. Rate	Rf	15.00%			Put Price	0.0405	2.42%
11		Volatility	S	10.00%					
12		Spot Price	P	1.6770					
13		Exercise Price	X	1.6750					
14									
15		Sensitivity: Call Price							Units $0
16		Volatility Across		0.10					
17		Foreign Int. Rate Down		2.500%					
18								Slope	0.45
19		0.0211	1.3770	1.4770	1.5770	1.6770	1.7770	1.8770	1.9770
20		2.50%	(0.0000)	(0.0000)	(0.0000)	0.0014	0.0777	0.1748	0.2720
21		5.00%	(0.0000)	(0.0000)	0.0000	0.0072	0.0780	0.1748	0.2720
22		7.50%	(0.0000)	0.0000	0.0003	0.0140	0.0801	0.1748	0.2720
23		10.00%	0.0000	0.0000	0.0017	0.0211	0.0840	0.1752	0.2720
24		12.50%	0.0000	0.0002	0.0042	0.0283	0.0891	0.1763	0.2721
25		15.00%	0.0000	0.0008	0.0079	0.0357	0.0949	0.1785	0.2725
26		17.50%	0.0002	0.0020	0.0123	0.0430	0.1012	0.1816	0.2735
27									
28		Sensitivity: Put Price						Slope	(0.53)
29		0.0405	1.3770	1.4770	1.5770	1.6770	1.7770	1.8770	1.9770
30		2.50%	0.3109	0.2137	0.1166	0.0209	0.0000	-	-
31		5.00%	0.3109	0.2137	0.1166	0.0266	0.0003	0.0000	(0.0000)
32		7.50%	0.3109	0.2137	0.1169	0.0334	0.0024	0.0000	0.0000
33		10.00%	0.3109	0.2137	0.1182	0.0405	0.0063	0.0004	0.0000
34		12.50%	0.3109	0.2139	0.1208	0.0478	0.0114	0.0015	0.0001
35		15.00%	0.3109	0.2145	0.1245	0.0551	0.0172	0.0037	0.0005
36		17.50%	0.3110	0.2158	0.1289	0.0625	0.0236	0.0068	0.0015

Fig 22.31

Currency options chart.

	A	B	C	D	E	F	G	H	I
38									
39		Select Series	10.00%			4			
40									
41		10.00%	0.0000	0.0000	0.0017	0.0211	0.0840	0.1752	0.2720
42		10.00%	0.3109	0.2137	0.1182	0.0405	0.0063	0.0004	0.0000

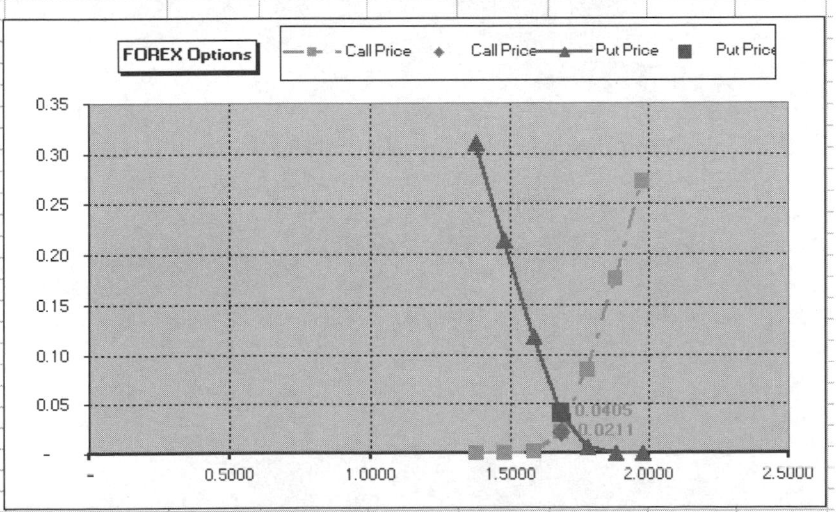

7. SUMMARY

Risk management covers a wide range of banking products and this chapter has sought to set out simple examples of forward rate agreements, foreign exchange forwards, swaps, futures and options. The models are for illustration only to show the layout and basic calculations. The common theme is a desire to manage risk with specialized products.

Modelling checklist

The directory of models includes a model called Modelling_Checklist, which includes three schedules to summarize the modelling process.

1. DESIGN SUMMARY

The process outlined in Figure 23.1 has been used throughout the book for the initial chapters on design and features and the subsequent applications files. In particular, the divisions of areas of activity such as inputs, calculations, workings and reports helps users to understand the model more quickly and aids rapid model development.

Modelling is a development process and you will find that a certain approach will work for you. The approach described in this book is not exclusive; however, it is one that the author has developed over ten years of using Excel financial models.

Keep this summary in your computer and refer to it when you are developing your own models. You can use it as a checklist and add your own steps into the process. The essential point is to have your own method of developing models and to use it every time so that your work acquires a style that can be understood, used and audited by others.

2. FEATURES

The features on the list shown in Figure 23.2 have been used extensively throughout the book to make the basic models more useful and informative. Again, you can add your own features to the list that you use in your sphere of development. Excel models can be made much better with not much more effort and these features do not take long to add to spreadsheet applications. As seen in the book, the inclusion of a combination such as combo boxes, INDEX functions and charts provide dynamic graphs to allow users to analyse several lines on a schedule. It is the combination of features and techniques, which can make your application more powerful.

Fig 23.1

Design summary.

	A	B	C	D	E
4					
5		**No**	**Stage**	**Comments**	**Reply**
6					
7		1	Objectives	What are they? - write them down	Management report
8		2	User needs and interface	Reports	Simple report
9				Audience	
10				Summaries and management reports	
11		3	Key variables and rules	Set down ideas and information flow	Inputs/calculations/reports
12				What are the key inputs?	Initial Template
13		4	Calculations	Key calculations	Net present value and management test
14		5	Write modules and code	How many and what complexity	Menu, model and explanation sheets
15				User interface	Menu sheet
16				Control input to model	Data validation
17		6	Menu structure	Direct user	Provide 'coaching'
18				Simple interface	Colours, formats etc.
19		7	Macros	Automate simple tasks and attach to buttons and controls	Menu macros
20				Concentrate on the ease of user interface	Use of controls where possible
21		8	User assistance	Coaching	Validation, comments
22		9	Management summary	Single sheet or area	Summary
23		10	Risk and multiple answers	Provide for scenarios and multiple answers	Data tables and scenarios
24		11	Testing	Audit toolbar	Check workings of model
25				Test data	
26				EDIT GOTO SPECIAL	
27				Show formulas and constants	
28		12	Protecting and securing	Protect sheets and workbook to prevent changes	Set up printing and securing ready for distribution
29		13	Help	Provide help	Comments
30				Document process and formulae	Names table
31		14	Show to peers - take their advice	Ask others to use and get their comments	
32		15	Control loop	Listen, learn and modify	
33					

Fig 23.2

Features.

	A	B	C	D	E
1					
2		Features			
3				v1.0 1-Jan-2001	
4					
5		No	Item	Included	
6					
7		1	Formats		
8		2	Number formats		
9		3	Lines and borders		
10		4	Colour and patterns		
11		5	Specific colour for inputs and results		
12		6	Data validation		
13		7	Controls - combo boxes and buttons		
14		8	Conditional formatting		
15		9	Use of functions and types of functions		
16		10	Add-ins for more functions		
17		11	Text and updated labels		
18		12	Record a version number, author etc		
19		13	Use names to make formulae easier		
20		14	Paste a names table as part of documentation		
21		15	Comment cells		
22		16	Graphics		
23		17	Dynamic graphs to plot individual lines		
24		18	Data tables		
25		19	Scenarios		
26		20	Goalseek		
27		21	Solver		
28		22	Use of templates		
29					

3. TECHNIQUES

Figure 23.3 provides a list of modelling techniques. Sometimes you may not be sure which techniques will best address a problem. The book includes examples of all the items on the list except for econometric modelling and specialist libraries and add-ins such as @RISK for Monte Carlo simulation. This is a useful checklist to examine when initially planning the sheets and the modelling techniques to be used.

Fig 23.3 **Techniques.**

Modelling Techniques

v1.0 1-Jan-2001

No	Item
1	Simple Input-Calculation-Output Model
2	Scenarios
3	Data Tables
4	Risk - Standard Deviation, Coefficient of Variation, Certainty Equivalents
5	Simulations - Monte Carlo simulation (Crystal Ball, @RISK)
6	Decision Trees
7	Optimisation and Targeting - Goalseek and Solver
8	Forecasting - Time Series Analysis, Trend Lines, Cyclicality, Seasonality, Multiple Regression
9	Econometric Models
10	Specialist Models and Excel Libraries

APPENDIX 1
SOFTWARE INSTALLATION

A CD containing the Excel files and templates accompanies the book. The file names relate to their subjects rather than being named after chapter numbers. This is because some files are used in more than one chapter. The file names are given in each section and there is, in the appendix, a listing of chapter numbers, subjects and applicable files. Follow the instructions below to install the files and create a programme group using the simple SETUP command.

1. SYSTEM REQUIREMENTS

This section summarizes the requirements for using the application:

- IBM-compatible personal computer with an 804086 or higher processor.
- Hard disk with 20Mb of free space.
- Microsoft mouse or other compatible pointing device.
- EGA, VGA or compatible display (VGA or higher is recommended).
- 32 Mb of random access memory. Performance is significantly enhanced with more memory.
- *Windows* 95and *Excel* 97 or later.

2. INSTALLATION

- Insert the CD into your CD-ROM drive.
- Select the Start button in the bottom left of your screen.

- Select Run.
- Write in the space provided: D:\SetUp.exe – then click on OK.
- D is your CD-ROM drive: if this is not correct for your machine then change the letter accordingly.
- The application will now install itself. Follow the instructions on screen to select a destination directory.
- If you are prompted, then restart Windows.

When the installation has finished, open Excel and select Tools – Add-ins (see Figure A.1). You need to make sure that the Analysis Toolpak is selected (see Figure A.2). Ensure also that Solver on this list is also selected.

Fig A.1 **Tools Add-Ins.**

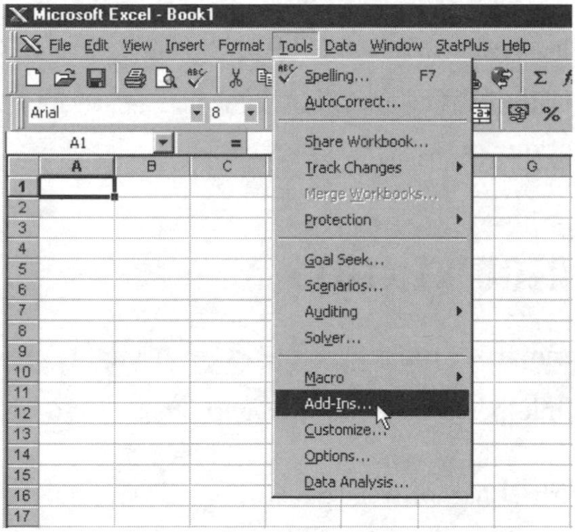

Fig A.2 **Analysis Toolpak.**

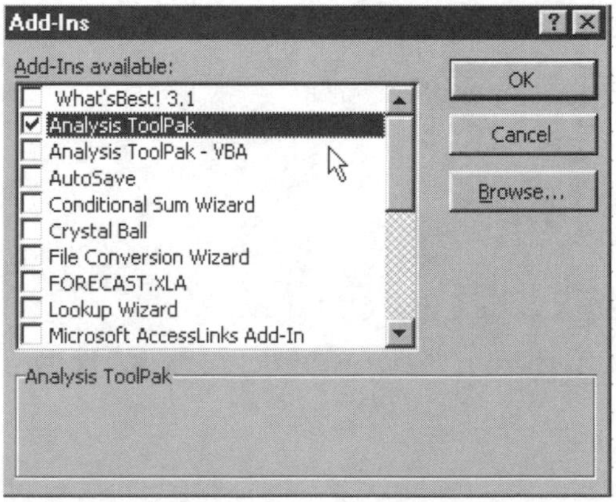

The Toolpak contains extra statistical and financial functions needed by the applications. Click it to select it and press OK. If you do not select it, you will encounter errors on certain files.

3. ACCESSING THE APPLICATION FILES

- You will see that a program group has been created for you. The application will also now appear under Programs on the Start Menu.
- When installed, the program group should include all the files on the accompanying file list (see Figure A.3).
- To access any of the files, simply double-click the icons in the program group.
- You can also open a ReadMe file of installation instructions and a file list.
- Press OK to continue and the selected file will open.
- There is a master file list called Mastering_Financial_Modelling-File_List in the form of an Excel model and a list within the book.

Fig A. 3

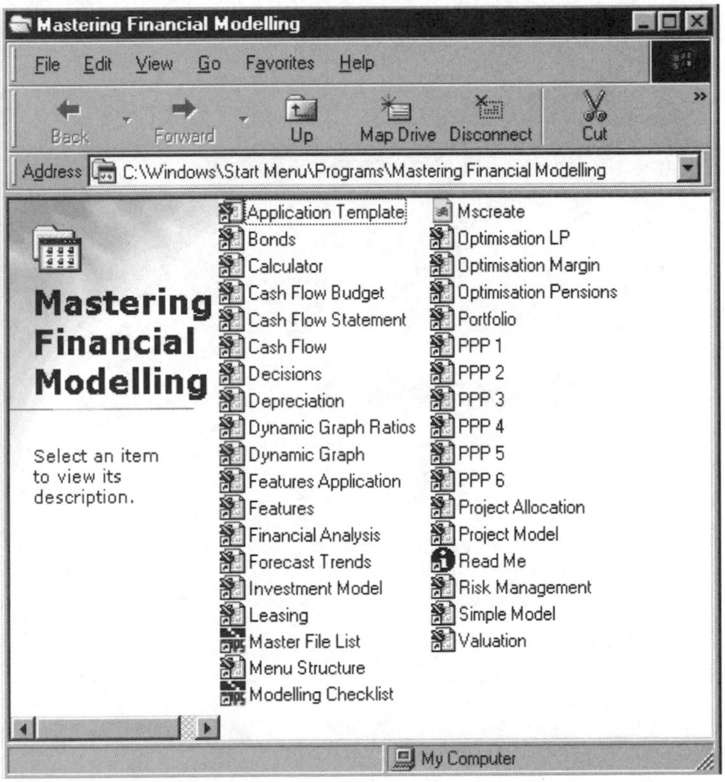

4. SUPPORT

For further information and support contact:

Systematic Finance plc
Orchard House
Green Lane
Guildford
Surrey GU1 2LZ
UK
Tel +44 (0) 1483 532929
Fax +44 (0) 1483 538358
E-mail info@system.co.uk
Web www.system.co.uk or www.financial-models.com

APPENDIX 2
LICENCE

This notice is intended to be a 'no nonsense' agreement between you ('the licensee') and Systematic Finance plc ('Systematic'). The software and associated documentation ('software') are subject to copyright law. They are protected by the laws of England. If you use this software, you are deemed to have accepted the terms and conditions under which this software was supplied.

Files accompanying *Mastering Financial Modelling* are copyright © Systematic Finance plc ('Systematic').

The software has not been audited and no representation, warranty or undertaking (express or implied) is made and no responsibility is taken or accepted by Systematic and its directors, officers, employees, agents or advisers as to the adequacy, accuracy, completeness or reasonableness of the financial models and Systematic excludes liability thereof.

In particular, no responsibility is taken or accepted by Systematic and all liability is excluded by Systematic for the accuracy of the computations comprised therein and the assumptions upon which such computations are based. In addition, the recipient receives and uses the software entirely at its own risk and no responsibility is taken or accepted by Systematic and accordingly all liability is excluded by Systematic for any losses which may result therefrom, whether as a direct or indirect consequence of a computer virus or otherwise.

Copyright © Systematic Finance plc

APPENDIX 3
FILE LIST

Chapter	No	Name	Key features
1	1	Simple_Model	Basic investment model – full of errors
2	1	Calculator	Financial calculator showing interface
3	1	Features	Simple model with features layered on
	2	Dynamic_Graph	Demo of a dynamic graph
	3	Features_Application	Completed application incorporating all the features
4	1	Investment_Model	Layered model to show design and features
5	1	PPP_1	Basic templates
	2	PPP_2	Completed cash flows
	3	PPP_3	Formatting, functions, comments, validation, printing
	4	PPP_4	Combo boxes
	5	PPP_5	Scenarios, data tables, documentation, protecting
	6	PPP_6	Final model
6	1	Financial_Analysis	Credit analysis
	2	Dynamic_Graph_Ratios	
7	1	Cash_Flow_Statement	Calculation of cash flow
	2	Financial_Analysis	
8	1	Forecast_Trend	Forecasts, trends, exponential smoothing, Seasonal decomposition

(continued)

Chapter	No	Name	Key features
8	1	Financial_Analysis	Forecasted statements and analysis
9	1	Financial_Analysis	Forecasted statements and analysis
10	1	Cash_Flow	Basic cash flow budget
	2	Cash_Flow_Budget	Cash flow budget with actual and variance sheets
11	1	Leverage	Leverage and operating leverage
12	1	Portfolio	Portfolio theory
13	1	Portfolio	CAPM, growth model, WACC
14	1	Bonds	Bond pricing, yield, duration, convexity, portfolio results
15	1	Project_Model	NPV model
	2	Project_Allocation	Allocation using Solver
16	1	Project_Model	Risk techniques
17	1	Depreciation	SL, SYD, DB and MACRS methods
18	1	Leasing	Rentals, lease v. purchase, classification, accounting
19	1	Valuation	Accounts, dividends, market and free cash flow valuation
20	1	Optimization_LP	Linear programming
	2	Optimization_Margin	Linear programming plus data table
	3	Optimization_Pensions	Optimizing pension contributions
21	1	Decisions	Bayes' theorem probabilities model
22	1	Risk_Management	Forwards, swaps, FOREX, futures, options
23	1	Modelling_Checklist	Checklists for future use

BIBLIOGRAPHY

The following is a limited list of references and further reading for information purposes.

Ansoff, I. (1985) *Corporate Strategy*, Penguin.

Black, F. and Scholes, M. (1973) 'The pricing of options and corporate liabilities', *Journal of Political Economy*, May/June, pp. 637–54.

Blake, D. (1990) *Financial Market Analysis*. McGraw-Hill.

Brealey, R. A. and Myers, S. (1999) *Principles of Corporate Finance*, 6th edn. McGraw-Hill.

Brigham, E. F., Gapenski, L. C. and Ehrhardt, M. C. (1999) *Financial Management – Theory and Practice*, 9th edn. Dryden Press.

Copeland, T., Koller, T. and Murrin, J. (2000) *Valuation – Measuring and Managing the Value of Companies*, 3rd edn. John Wiley.

Day, A. (1996) *Lease and Finance Evaluation – Applications for Successful Financing Alternatives*. Euromoney.

Day, A. (2000) *The Finance Director's Guide to Purchasing Leasing*. Financial Times Prentice Hall.

Fabozzi, F. (1995) *Investment Management*. Prentice Hall.

Fama, E. F. and French, K. R. (1992) 'The cross-section of expected stock returns', *Journal of Finance*, 47 (2), pp. 427–66.

Garman, M. and Kohlhagen, S. (1983) 'Foreign currency option values', *Journal of International Money and Finance*, 2, pp. 231–7.

Kaplan, R. (1989) *Advanced Management Accounting*. Prentice Hall International.

Markowitz, A. (1952) 'Portfolio selection', *Journal of Finance*, 7 (1), pp. 77–91.

Myers, S. C., Dill, D. A. and Bautista, A. J. (1976) 'Valuation of financial lease contracts', *Journal of Finance*, 31 (3), pp. 799–819.

Rappaport, A. (1998) *Creating Shareholder Value*. Free Press.

Rutterford, J. (1998), *Financial Strategy – Adding Shareholder Value*. John Wiley.

Stern, J. M. and Chew, D. H. (1992) *The Revolution in Corporate Finance*, 2nd edn. Basil Blackwell.

Walsh, C. (1996) *Key Management Ratios*. Prentice Hall.

INDEX

@RISK 241
accessing application files 357
accounting for leases 270–4
accounting return 201, 205
accounting value 280–2
  adjusted 280, 282–3
acid test 111, 112
adjusted accounting value 280, 282–3
aims and objectives 10, 59
allocation model 214–16
American options 332
amortization 243, 251–2
annual reports 101–2
Ansoff matrix 219, 220
areas for improvement 96
asset leverage 109–10, 112
asset turnover 109–10, 112
assets 104–5
assistance, user 65–6, 75–6
audit toolbar 71–2
Auto-Close macro 59
Auto-Open macro 59

balance sheet 101, 104–5
  accounting for leases 272–4
  forecasting 135–8
  investment model 202–3
base case 49–50, 210–11
Bayes' theorem 312–13
benefit cost ratio 201, 209
best case scenario 49–50
beta 173–6
  releveraged 182, 289
Black–Scholes model 342–9
bonds 186–98
borders 23–4
break clauses 272
breakeven analysis 153–62
built-in macros 53–4
butterfly strategy 338–40, 341
buttons 28–33, 89–90

calculations: breaking down into manageable groups 62
call options 332, 333, 337, 338, 339
capital, cost of *see* cost of capital
Capital Asset Pricing Model (CAPM) 169, 173–6
capital rationing 214–16
capital structure 107–8, 111, 112
cash flow 107, 108, 116–21
  bonds 188–9
  certainty equivalents 227–8
  deriving 118–19
  forecasting 138–9
  free 120, 280, 286–94
  investment model 202–3, 209
  monthly cash model 149–50
  net operating cash flow 116, 119
  swaps 327–8
cash flow budgets 146–8
  monthly cash flow 149–50
certainty equivalents 221, 226–8
classical decomposition 128–30

classification of leases 256, 259, 269–70
clean price 187
code, reusable 54
coefficient of determination 174
coefficient of variation 221, 226
colour 24–6
  and patterns 24–5
  specific colour for inputs and results 25–6
combined leverage 161–2
combo boxes 28–33
  for defined entries 90–1
comment cells 41–2, 65, 84
commodity options 335
company valuation 279–95
comparison
  company valuation 293–4
  depreciation methods 252–3
conditional formatting 33–4, 85–6, 167, 168
constraints 297–9
contribution 155
control loop 76
controls 28–33
  see also buttons; combo boxes
convexity 194–5
core ratios 109–10, 112
corporate risk 218–19
correlation 166–7
cost of capital 172–85, 206
  free cash flows 289–90
covariance 165–7
cover ratios 111, 120–1
creditors days 111, 112
currency options pricing 348–9
current ratio 111, 112
current yield 190
cyclicality 128–30

data smoothing 125–8
data tables 46–8
  optimum portfolio 167, 168
  rental 270
  and risk 93–4
data validation 26–8, 65–6, 85
day conventions 187
debt, cost of 179
decision trees 312–22
decision variables 297–9
declining balance method 245–7, 252–3
decomposition, classical 128–30
depreciation 201, 242–54
  lease versus purchase 260–5
design 351
  basics of 10
  example model 78–98
  sample model 58–77
  stages in 9–17, 352
  summary of methodology 79–80
  weaknesses 6–8
  see also features; techniques
determination, coefficient of 174
development 15
dirty price 187
discounted payback 201, 205
displacement factor 262
dividend growth model 176–9
dividends 280, 283–5
documentation 16, 38–40, 75–6, 94–6
drivers, key 132–5
Du Pont (core) ratios 109–10, 112
duration 191–5, 197–8
  modified duration 193, 197–8
dynamic graphs 44–6
  financial analysis 142–4

EDATE function 36–7
Error Alert 26, 27
errors, checking for 70–3
European options 332
example model 78–98
Excel 4, 5
expected monetary value (EMV) 314–15
exponential smoothing 125–8

FASB 13 256
feasible solutions 298
features 18–57, 351, 353
Features_Application model 54, 55–6
file list 361–2
files, accessing 357
finance leases 256, 272–4, 275, 276–7
financial analysis 101–15
  forecasting 131–44
financial leverage 160–1
financial structure 107–8, 111, 112
Fisher formula 206–7
'flash' report 151–2
forecasting 147
  financials 131–44
  models 122–30
foreign exchange 329–30
formatting 20–6, 83, 84
  conditional 33–4, 85–6, 167, 168
formulas
  portfolio analysis 163–7
  use of names to simplify understanding 39–40
  viewing 19–20, 73
forward rate agreements (FRAs) 324–5
free cash flow 120
  company valuation 280, 286–94
Frontline Systems Inc. 297
FRS 5 270, 271–2
function trend 123
functions 83–4
  add-ins for more functions 36–7
  uses and types 35–6
funding gap 111, 112
Future Value (FV) macro 258
futures 330–1

GetSheetNames macro 63–4
Goal*seek* 50–1
Gordon growth model 176–9
graphics 42–4, 151–2
graphs 71
  dynamic 44–6, 142–4
'Greeks', the 344–5
gross gearing 111, 112
gross profit/sales 111, 112
growth 114–15
  Gordon growth model 176–9

hedging 337–42
help 65–6, 75–6
historic forecasts 123
hurdle (risk adjusted) rate 208, 221–3

income statement 101, 102–4
  accounting for leases 272–4
  forecasting 135–8
  investment model 202–3
index function 167–9
individual modules 13–14, 62–3
inflation 206–7
information 315
  real options and 228–32
installation of software 355–8
integer constraints 297
interest options 336–7
interest rates 272
interest relief 260–5
interface with user 10–11, 59–60
internal rate of return (IRR) 201, 208
  modified IRR 210
inventory days 111, 112
investment analysis 199–217
  see also risk analysis
investment model 199–203
  development 58–77

key drivers 132–5
key variables 12, 60–2

labels, updated 37–8
layout 12–13, 20–1
lease versus purchase 260–8

lease term 272
leasing 255–78
leverage 111, 112, 159–62
  combined 161–2
  financial 160–1
  operating 159–60
liabilities 104–5
licence, software 359
linear programming 299–303
lines 23–4
loan cover 111, 120–1

macros 14, 59, 64–5
  built-in 53–4
  simple 89–90
  simulation 233–5
  WACC 180–2
management analysis 142–4, 147, 148
  see also financial analysis
management reporting 15, 66–7
  'flash' report 151–2
  scenarios 49–50
  Solver 52–3
management summaries 15, 66–7, 142
  cash flow budgets 147, 148
  simulation 237–8
management tests 201, 209–10
margin maximization 303–6
marginal WACC 182–4
market pricing method 280, 285–6
marking to market 331
menu structure 14, 63–4, 89
modelling checklist 351–4
Modified Accelerated Cost Recovery System (MACRS) 248–50, 252–3
modified duration 193, 197–8
modified internal rate of return 210
modules, individual 13–14, 62–3
Monte Carlo simulation 221, 232–41
monthly cash model 149–50
moving averages 125, 126
multiple answers 67–70

naïve forecasting 123
names 81–3
  pasting a names table 40, 81, 83
  use to make formulas easier to understand 39–40
needs, user 10–11, 59–60
net gearing 111, 112
net operating cash flow (NOCF) 116, 119
net operating profit/sales 111, 112
net present value (NPV)
  function 35
  investment analysis 201, 204, 205–8
  lease versus purchase 260–8
90% test 271
number formats 21–3

objective function 297–9
objectives 10, 59
Offset function 30–1
operating cycle 107–8, 111, 112
operating leases 256, 274, 275
operating leverage 159–60
optimal solutions 298
optimistic scenario 210–11
optimization 296–311
  elements of optimization models 296–9
optimum portfolio 167–71
options, real (investment appraisal) 207, 221, 228–32
options 332–41
  pricing 342–9

password 55
pattern matching 72–3
patterns 24–5
payback period 44, 201, 204–5
peer group comments 16, 76, 96

pensions 306–9, 310
percent of sales forecasting 132–5
performance analysis 101–15
performance risk *see* profitability
perpetuity model 176–9
pessimistic scenario 210–11, 213
  simulation 238–40
portfolio 163–71
  model for bonds 195–8
  optimum 167–71
PPP models 78–98
preference shares, cost of 179
present value 291–2
price/earnings per share (P/E) ratios 285–6
pricing
  bonds 186–98 passim
  options 342–9
printing 86–7
probability 219–21, 313–14
product mix 157–9
  optimization 299–306
profit before tax/sales 111, 112
profit and loss statement *see* income statement
profitability 107–8, 110–11, 112
profitability index (benefit cost ratio) 201, 209
program sheets 64–5
project investment *see* investment analysis; investment model; risk analysis
project risk 218–19
protection 15–16, 74–5, 94–6
purchase, lease versus 260–8
put options 332, 334, 337, 338, 339

quick ratio 111, 112

R squared 174
ratios 105–12
  forecasting 139–40
  trend analysis 113–14
real options 207, 221, 228–32
renewal options 272
rental calculations 257–9
rental variations 272
return on assets (ROA) 111, 112
return on capital employed (ROCE) 111, 112
return on equity (ROE) 109–10, 112
return on invested capital (ROIC) 111, 112, 201, 205
return on sales 109–12
reusable code 54
risk 93–4
  data tables and 93
  and multiple answers 67–70
  performance analysis 106–8
  portfolio analysis 163–71
  sources of risk 219
risk adjusted rate 208, 221–3
risk analysis 218–41
risk assessment 218–21
risk management 323–50
Rule of 78 244–5
rules 12, 60–2
  constraints 297–9

sample model 58–77
scenarios 49–50, 91–2
  investment analysis 210–11, 213
  real options 228–32
  simulation 238–40
scroll bars 31–3
securing 74–5
seasonality 128–30
sensitivity analysis
  decision trees 318–19, 321–2
  free cash flows 293
  investment analysis 211–14
  risk and multiple answers 67–70
  WACC 180–2
settlements 274–7
share price comparison 293, 294
shareholders' funds 280–2

Simple_Model 6–8
simulation 221, 232–41
simulation options pricing 346–8
smoothing, data 125–8
software
  installation 355–8
  licence 359
solvency 111, 112
Solver 51–3, 126–8, 170–1, 214–16
  optimization 296–311
spinners 31–2
spreadsheets
  history of 4
  poorly designed 6–8
  power of 4–5
SSAP 21 270–2
standard deviation
  portfolio analysis 164–7
  risk analysis 221, 223–5
standardization of accounts 101–2
static report 50
stock market valuation methods 280, 285–6
straddle strategy 338, 340, 341, 342
straight line depreciation 243–4
sum of digits method 244–5
summaries *see* management summaries
sunk costs 203
sustainability 114–15
swaps 326–8
system requirements 355
Systematic Finance plc 358

tables, data *see* data tables
target cell 297–9
targets, breakeven 157
tax delay 207, 208
taxation 207
  lease versus purchase 260–5
techniques 18–57, 353, 354
templates 53–6
terminal value 290–1
testing 15, 70–3, 94–6
text 37–8
time line 200
time series decomposition 128–30
Toolpak 356–7
trade receivables (debtor) days 111, 112
trend analysis 113–14
trend lines 123–5
troubleshooting 70–3

uncertainty 219, 323
updated labels 37–8
upgrade clauses 272
user assistance 65–6, 75–6
user interface 10–11, 59–60
user needs 10–11, 59–60
utility 315

validation, data 26–8, 65–6, 85
valuation of companies 279–95
values only report 50
variables
  decision variables 297–9
  key 12, 60–2
  key drivers 132–5
variance analysis 145–52
variation, coefficient of 221, 226
VDB function 249
version reference 38–9
viewing formulas 19–20, 73
volatility (modified duration) 193, 197–8

weighted average cost of capital (WACC) 179–82
  marginal WACC 182–4
working capital 111, 112
workings box 28–30
worst case scenario 49–50

XNPV function 36–7

year conventions 187
yield measures 189–91
yield to maturity (YTM) 189, 191